Systemic Linguistics

Systemic Linguistics
Theory and Applications

Christopher S. Butler

Batsford Academic and Educational   London

© Christopher S. Butler 1985

First published 1985

All rights reserved. No part of this publication
may be reproduced, in any form or by any means,
without permission from the Publisher

Typeset by Tek-Art Ltd, Kent
and printed and bound in Great Britain by
Biddles Ltd, Guildford and King's Lynn

Published by Batsford Academic and Educational
an Imprint of B. T. Batsford Ltd
4 Fitzhardinge Street, London W1H 0AH

British Library Cataloguing in Publication Data

Butler, Christopher S.
    Systemic linguistics: theory and applications.
    1. Systemic grammar
    I. Title
    410   P149

ISBN 0-7134-3705-7

Contents

Preface

In recent years there has been a considerable reaction against the transformational generative theories which dominated linguistics for two decades. A number of leading linguists have welcomed this counter-reaction, believing that it is a healthy antidote to what many have come to regard as a rather narrow and restrictive approach to language. One important strand of linguistic thought which stands in sharp contrast to Chomskyan linguistics is seen in the work of Michael Halliday, whose theories are now usually known under the title of 'systemic linguistics'. Systemic models are in use in the teaching and research activities of a considerable number of institutions of higher education today.

In view of the increasing interest in systemic linguistics, it is important that work within this framework should be made accessible to linguists whose knowledge is confined to other approaches. Unfortunately, most of the relevant material has remained in the form of articles, often published in rather obscure places, although some have now been brought together into collections such as Kress (1976) and Halliday & Martin (1981). Muir (1972) and Berry (1975, 1977) give book-length accounts, and are valuable sources of information. Both, however, describe a model which dates from the late 1960s and early 1970s, and so have nothing to say about later developments; furthermore, both are introductory in nature, and are aimed at undergraduates, training college students and teachers whose primary interest is in the description of English. Other works, such as those of Sinclair (1972) and Young (1980) are based on Hallidayan models, but are again essentially descriptions of English. Monaghan (1979) provides a more theoretical treatment, but again does not deal adequately with some of the later developments in Halliday's thinking, or with the work of other systemic linguists. Fawcett's (1980) book is concerned largely with the exposition of his own systemic model.

There is, then, a need for a book which gives an overview of the whole field, describing and comparing the various models put forward by Halliday and others working within the systemic tradition. I hope that the present book will go some way towards satisfying this need. It is not, I think, an 'easy' book: it is intended for professional linguists and for those students who already have a good grasp of the fundamental concepts of linguistics, and have been exposed to non-systemic models of language. It would, therefore, be suitable for advanced undergraduates, postgraduates and teachers of linguistics, rather than as an introductory text.

The book first examines the roots of systemic theory in the work of Firth and Malinowski (Chapter 1). It then goes on to discuss the development of these ideas by Halliday, first in his early 'Scale and Category' approach (Chapter 2), then in the later semantically oriented 'systemic functional grammar' (Chapter 3). The place of this grammar within an overall sociolinguistic model is then examined (Chapter 4), and the proposals are subjected to what I hope is constructive criticism (Chapter 5). There is then a chapter on some developments in systemic syntax, as seen in the work of Fawcett and Hudson (Chapter 6). Chapter 7 discusses systemic approaches to other types of linguistic patterning: lexis, phonology and discourse. We then move on to consider descriptions of English and other languages based on systemic models (Chapter 8). Chapter 9 deals with the application of systemic theories to work in stylistics, educational linguistics and artificial intelligence. In Chapter 10 an attempt is made to bring together the various strands from previous chapters, and to highlight the main characteristics of systemic approaches to language, contrasting them with transformational approaches where possible.

While writing the book, I have benefited greatly from discussions with many colleagues and students. My special thanks go to Margaret Berry, who first stimulated my interest in systemic linguistics through her enthusiasm and clear teaching, and was kind enough to spend much valuable time providing me with verbal and written comments on my work. I should also like to thank Mike Stubbs for comments on early drafts of the book, and Andrew Crompton and Tim Gibson for many enjoyable and valuable discussions. Finally, I am grateful to Walter Grauberg, who unselfishly devoted himself to helping me with the mind-numbing task of proof reading. I am, of course, solely responsible for the many inadequacies which, despite the assistance of my friends, remain in the book.

1. The background to Hallidayan linguistics

1.1 Predecessors and principles: an introduction

This book is concerned largely with the work of M.A.K. Halliday and of linguists inspired by his view of language. The reader who is quite unfamiliar with Hallidayan linguistics, but has a fair knowledge of transformational generative and/or other theories, will find here a very different viewpoint on language. Indeed, he may need, at least at first, to suspend certain preconceptions, and to approach language afresh, if he is to appreciate what Hallidayan linguistics has to offer. It is the author's sincere hope that readers who are prepared to do this will feel that the effort has been worthwhile.

The particular characteristics of Halliday's views on language, and of the views of other linguists closely associated (but not always in full agreement) with his work, will emerge as the book proceeds. The reader who stays until the end of the journey will find a discussion of the salient features of this approach in the final chapter. However, on the grounds that even a crude map is a useful guide along the way, a brief account of the background and main concerns of Halliday's work will be given here. A more extensive discussion can be found in the work of Monaghan (1979), reviewed in Butler (1981) and Gregory (1980a).

Halliday's work is the most important modern development of the ideas within the so-called 'London School' of linguistics, whose founding father was J.R. Firth (1890-1960). It is, then, to Firth that we must turn for an initial explanation of Halliday's orientation. Firth was trained as a historian, but had always maintained a lively interest in language, which matured when, in the 1914-18 war, he gained first hand experience of languages spoken in Africa, India and Afghanistan. In 1920, he took up a position as Professor of English at the University of the Punjab in Lahore. Then, in 1928, he moved to the Department of Phonetics at University College London, where he worked under Daniel Jones. During his time at University College, Firth held a number of part-time appointments in linguistics and phonetics, and also returned to India for a brief spell, to study Gujarati and Telugu. In 1938, he accepted a full-time post at the School of Oriental and African Studies (SOAS) in London, where in 1941 he became head of the Department of Phonetics and Linguistics. In 1941, still at SOAS, he was appointed to the first Chair of General Linguistics in Britain.

Firth had a great deal of respect for, and interest in, the work of the long line of English linguists stretching right back to the sixteenth century. In particular, he saw himself as following in the tradition of the great English phoneticians Henry Sweet (1845-1912) and Daniel Jones (1881-1967). Sweet is commonly regarded as the pioneer of modern phonetics, and his *Handbook of Phonetics* (Sweet, 1877) was of great importance in disseminating knowledge of the new science. He was concerned with practical as well as theoretical aspects of phonetics: his attempts to produce a standard system for phonetic transcription were related to issues in spelling reform and the teaching of languages. Jones, too, insisted that phonetics should be rooted in the practical observation and transcription of speech sounds: his *Outline of English Phonetics* (Jones, 1918) and *English Pronouncing Dictionary* (Jones, 1917) have been used by countless language teachers the world over.

Firth, then, inherited from Sweet, Jones and their contemporaries a concern with the description of languages for practical purposes, although he was insistent that linguistics should be considered an autonomous discipline, in that it should have its own terminology and methodology rather than simply borrow these from other fields of academic inquiry. Firth's own experience of Oriental and African languages, and that of his colleagues at SOAS, was important in shaping his contribution to linguistics, and that of his successors in the London School. The work of the SOAS group was not hidebound by the preconceptions which were so common among linguists working solely on Indo-European languages. Furthermore, the languages with which they were dealing were well-established, thriving tongues, with large numbers of speakers, so that any urgency in describing them arose, not from the fear of their extinction, but from the practical concerns of teaching languages such as Japanese, often for restricted purposes, during the Second World War. In this respect, the London School contrasted sharply with the American descriptivists, whose main concern was to describe the North American Indian languages which were on the verge of extinction. As Monaghan (1979, p.20) and Sampson (1980, p.215) have pointed out, this meant that while the American descriptivists felt a need to develop mechanical discovery procedures for the languages they were describing, Firth and his colleagues could afford to indulge in linguistic theory-building.

These differences in background and motivation contributed to the considerable divergence in the views of the London School and of the American descriptivists, among whom Bloomfield was a leading figure. Other factors were connected with the strongly contrasting nature of the influences with which Bloomfield and Firth came into contact in the formative years of their careers. Bloomfield's contact with the ideas of Weiss and others converted him from a mentalist stance in his early years to a behaviourist position in his important book *Language* (Bloomfield, 1933). One significant consequence of this position was the rejection of the study of meaning as being outside the scope of contemporary linguistics. Bloomfield defined the meaning of a linguistic form as 'the situation in which the speaker utters it and the response which it calls forth in the hearer' (Bloomfield, 1933, p.139). Since science did not have at its disposal the means for the rigorous description of everything in the universe, Bloomfield (1933, p.140) concluded that 'the statement of meanings is therefore the weak point in language study, and will remain so until human knowledge advances very far beyond its present state'.

One of the main influences on Firth during the 1930s was his association with Bronislaw Malinowski, who was Professor of Anthropology at the London School of Economics. As we shall see in more detail later, Malinowski's work had convinced him that the language of a community could not be fully understood in isolation from its social contexts of use, and that the meaning of an utterance lay essentially in the use to which it was put. The notion of meaning as function in context (including the social context) was to become central to Firth's view of language. It is thus possible to discern an area of mutual interest for Bloomfield and Firth: both viewed meaning in terms of the situations in which language is produced. Where they differed was in the consequences they drew out from this view: for Bloomfield it meant the rejection of the study of meaning as 'unscientific'; but for Firth it led to a position in which meaning was the cornerstone of linguistic theory.

Firth also expressed opposition to the Saussurean brand of structuralism which dominated European linguistics at the time. The reasons for this will become clear when we discuss Firth's views in more detail: basically, Firth regarded Saussure's approach as too monolithic, himself preferring a model in which the concept of one huge, integrated supersystem for a language was replaced by a large number of individual systems set up for different environments. However, we shall see that Firth's linguistics resembled Saussure's in that it was built around the concepts of syntagmatic and paradigmatic (or, as Saussure would have called it, 'associative') patterning.

In summary, then, Firth's view of language was one in which meaning, viewed as the function of a linguistic item in its context of use, was paramount, and in which one very important type of context was the social context in which an utterance is produced. Linguistic patterning was described in terms of syntagmatic and paradigmatic relations, though the detailed approach differs in important ways from that of Saussurean structuralism.

It was this view of language which Halliday inherited. Born in 1925, Halliday took a first degree in Chinese studies at the University of London, where he came under Firth's influence. He later did graduate work in Peking and Cambridge, and, through his studies on Chinese and on English, began to develop Firth's linguistic model. Just as Firth's sociological orientation, derived from Malinowski, contrasted with Bloomfield's behaviourist, psychological bias, so Halliday's work can be contrasted with Chomsky's along a similar dimension. Halliday's primary interest is in language as a central attribute of 'social man', and his main aim is to account for the ways in which speakers and writers interact with their hearers and readers in social situations. He has little interest in 'what goes on inside people's heads', but views the psychological orientation of much recent linguistics as complementary to his own. This viewpoint has a number of important consequences: for instance, Halliday sees no need for a sharp division between 'competence' and 'performance', or between 'langue' and 'parole', and he is willing to tolerate a much lower degree of idealization of the data than is apparent in many other models of language. An essential aspect of language for Halliday, as for Firth, is its meaningfulness, and this, as we shall see, permeates his linguistic models, leading to rather fluid boundaries between levels of language. Halliday has also inherited Firth's concern with the practical applications of linguistic theory: indeed, his main interest now appears to be the ways in which linguistics can contribute to such applied fields as stylistics, language in education, and artificial intelligence.

Although standing in a clear line of descent from Firth and Malinowski,

Halliday has also recognized the influence, on his own work, of other schools of linguistics. In particular, he has drawn on ideas from Prague School linguistics, from Hjelmslev's glossematics, and from Whorf's views on linguistic relativity. Halliday also claims points of contact with Lamb's stratificational grammar, and with Pike's tagmemics.

Finally, in this brief introduction to the field, it should be noted that not all of the linguists whose work is inspired by Halliday have taken over his theoretical stance completely. In particular, we shall see that Richard Hudson, a colleague of Halliday's during the latter's period at University College, London, has constructed models of language which, though based on Halliday's development of Firth, are rather more like transformational generative models in their aims and the facts they attempt to account for.

1.2 Firth and Malinowski: language as a social phenomenon

Firth believed that meanings were 'intimately interlocked not only with an environment of particular sights and sounds, but deeply embedded in the living process of persons maintaining themselves in society' (Firth in Palmer, 1968, p.13). He therefore proposed to 'study language as part of the social process' (Firth, 1950, p.181 in Firth, 1957a). In this view, Firth was, as we have seen, strongly influenced by his association with Malinowski.

Malinowski's work among the Trobriand Islanders of the South Pacific (see especially Malinowski, 1923, 1935) had caused him to reject an approach to meaning based on the correlation of words and referents, in favour of a semantics which took as its basic unit the sentence, as produced in a particular *context of utterance*. He found that to understand the meaning of what was said, it was necessary to possess some knowledge of the cultural characteristics of Trobriand society, as reflected in the *contexts of situation* in which particular types of utterances were typically produced, and which were themselves regarded as embedded in the *context of culture*. Meaning was seen in terms of the function of utterances, or even of whole texts, in contexts of utterance, or, more generally, in their typical contexts of situation. For Malinowski, then, language was 'regarded as a mode of action, rather than as a countersign of thought' (Malinowski, 1923, p.297). Malinowski's view of meaning as function in context is very similar to that expressed later in the philosopher Wittgenstein's famous dictum that 'the meaning of words lies in their use' (Wittgenstein, 1953, p.80). We shall not explore Malinowski's work in detail here, since our main concern is to show the development of his basic ideas by Firth and later by Halliday. Detailed critical discussion of Malinowski's writings can be found in Langendoen (1968), and summaries of his views are available in, for example, Dinneen (1967, pp.299-302) and Robins (1970, pp.4-5).

In his own appraisal of Malinowski's work, Firth (1957c, p.161 in Palmer, 1968) recognized that Malinowski was not himself primarily interested in elaborating a linguistic theory, and that his 'technical linguistic contribution consists of sporadic comments, immersed and perhaps lost in what is properly called his ethnographic analysis'. Firth's aim was to build Malinowski's concept of context of situation into a specifically linguistic theory. Thus, whereas Malinowski had viewed context of situation in essentially concrete terms, Firth considered it as an abstract schematic construct, 'a group of related categories at a different level from grammatical categories but rather of the same abstract nature' (Firth, 1950, p.182 in Firth, 1957a), which was intended 'for application especially to typical repetitive events in the social process' (Firth, 1957b, p.176 in Palmer, 1968). The categories involved in describing the context of situation are as follows (Firth, 1950, p.182 in Firth, 1957a; 1957d, p.177 in Palmer, 1968):

A. The relevant features of participants: persons, personalities
   (i)   the verbal action of the participants
   (ii) the non-verbal action of the participants
B. The relevant objects
C. The effect of the verbal action.

Such schematic constructs provided a specification of the contexts within which whole utterances or even texts functioned and thereby had meaning. But Firth, the linguist, went much further than Malinowski's anthropological and ethnographic interests had allowed. Context of situation, though of central importance, was just one kind of context in which linguistic units could function. Other contexts were provided by the 'levels' postulated to account for various types of linguistic patterning. Thus grammatical items could be seen as functioning in grammatical contexts, lexical items in lexical contexts, phonological items in phonological contexts, and so on. Furthermore, Firth's view of meaning as function in context led him to regard all these various types of function, at all levels, as aspects of meaning. In Firth's own words (1935, p.19 in Firth, 1957a) 'meaning . . . is to be regarded as a complex of textual relations, and phonetics, grammar, lexicography, and semantics each handles its own components of the complex in its appropriate context'. Meaning is thus dispersed into a number of 'modes'. Firth (1950, p.183 in Firth, 1957a; 1951a, p.192 in Firth, 1957a; also in Palmer, 1968, p.108) likened this to the splitting of white light into its spectral components on passing through a prism. This is clearly a very wide-ranging view of meaning and, as we shall see, has been criticized for its idiosyncracy. Firth even held (1951a, p.192 in Firth, 1957a) that 'it is part of the meaning of an American to sound like one'. Nevertheless, the principle of meaning as function in context, on which Firth's view was based, has remained, though with important refinements, in the development of Firth's ideas by Halliday (see Section 2.2).

Also of importance in later developments (see the account of Halliday's sociosemantic theory in Chapter 4) is Firth's insistence that techniques of linguistic description, based on dispersion into modes, should be applied, not to a language as a whole, but to a 'restricted language', which 'serves a circumscribed field of experience and can be said to have its own grammar and dictionary' (Firth in Palmer, 1968, p.87). As examples of such restricted languages Firth gives the specialist languages of science, sport, narrative, political propaganda, personal reference and address, the writings of a single author, or even a single text. As Palmer (1968, p.8) has observed, 'Firth was a realist and held that it was quite impossible to do everything at once'.

One final point needs to be made about the general orientation of Firth's linguistic theories. Although he was concerned with the setting up of abstract constructs at various levels, Firth insisted that such constructs should always be related back to textual data. Categories set up from an analysis of a limited amount of textual data were to be checked by application to further data of the same kind, this process being referred to by Firth as 'renewal of connection' (see e.g. Firth, 1957d, p.199 in Palmer, 1968).

1.3 System and structure

Within each mode of meaning, or level, Firth saw language as organized along the two axes, syntagmatic and paradigmatic, familiar from structuralist models (though, as we have seen, Firth did not consider himself to be a Saussurean). Elements in syntagmatic association formed *structures* at the level concerned, while events in commutative relation at a particular place in a structure were said to constitute a *system,* in a restricted technical sense of the term. It is, of course, the term 'system', as used in this way, which gives rise to the label 'systemic' normally given to Hallidayan linguistics after about 1966.

In view of its importance in later work, it is instructive to follow Firth's use of the term 'system' from the earliest papers of the 1930s through to the writings of the 1950s. From rather vague and programmatic beginnings, system emerges as a clearly defined organizing principle in the later work. In its earliest uses the term is used very broadly, by analogy with the systems of social and personal behaviour:

Language and personality are built into the body, which is constantly taking part in activities directed to the conservation of the pattern of life. We must expect therefore that linguistic science will also find it necessary to postulate the maintenance of linguistic patterns and systems (including adaptation and change) within which there is order, structure and function. Such systems are maintained by activity, and in activity they are to be studied. It is on these grounds that linguistics must be systemic. (Firth, 1948a, p.143 in Firth, 1957a)

In a slightly later paper, Firth appears to use 'systemic' to mean simply 'described systematically by the spectrum of linguistic techniques':

We must separate from the mush of general goings-on those features of repeated events which appear to be parts of a patterned process, and handle them systematically by stating them by the spectrum of linguistic techniques. The systemic statements of meaning produced by such techniques need not be given existential status. (Firth, 1950, p.187 in Firth, 1957a)

By the following year, however, Firth is making very much more precise statements about systems:

. . . 'linguistic forms' are considered to have 'meanings' at the grammatical and lexical levels, such 'meanings' being determined by interrelations of the forms in the grammatical systems set up for the language. A nominative in a four-case system would in this sense necessarily have a different 'meaning' from a nominative in a two-case or in a fourteen-case system, for example.

A singular in a two-number system has different grammatical meaning from a singular in a three-number system or a four-number system such as in Fijian which formally distinguishes singular, dual, 'little' plural, and 'big' plural. The 'meaning' of the grammatical category *noun* in a grammatical system of, say, three word classes, noun, verb, and particle, is different from the meaning of the category *noun* in a system of five classes in which *adjective* and *pronoun* are formally distinguished from the noun, verb, and particle. (Firth, 1951b, p.227 in Firth, 1957a)

As Palmer (1968, p.7) observes, this view shows a very strong Saussurean orientation: Firth's 'meanings' appear to be identical to Saussure's 'values'. As we shall see, Firth's objection to Saussure's work was concerned, not with the notion of linguistic value, but with the concept of 'une langue une', reflected in Meillet's well-known description of language as 'un système où tout se tient'.

In a paper written in 1957, Firth adds the criteria of exhaustiveness and finiteness to that of mutual determination of values:

Systems of units or terms, set up by the linguist, provide sets of interior relations by means of which their values are mutually determined. In order to have validity, such systems must be exhaustive and closed, so far as the particular state of the language, suitably restricted, is under description. (Firth, 1957c, p.150 in Palmer, 1968)

In contrast with system, the term 'structure' is used quite consistently throughout Firth's work. Structure is 'an inter-relationship of elements within the text or part of the text' (Firth in Palmer, 1968, p.103). The relationship between structure and system is made explicit in the following statement:

. . . *system, systems, terms* and *units* are restricted to a set of paradigmatic relations between commutable units or terms which provide values for the elements of structure. (Firth, 1957d, p.186 in Palmer, 1968)

At the lexical and grammatical levels respectively, the concept of structure is reflected in the more specific phenomena of *collocation* and *colligation*. Collocation, for Firth, refers to the syntagmatic relations into which lexical items habitually enter, and is considered as a part of the meaning of the lexical items concerned. Firth claims, for example, that 'one of the meanings of *night* is its collocability with *dark*, and of *dark*, of course, collocation with *night*' (Firth, 1951a, p.196 in Firth, 1957a). Firth is careful to point out that the collocational approach to meaning is derived solely as an abstraction from formal syntagmatic patterning, and is not concerned in any direct way with the correlation between words and concepts. Although Firth appears to be interested only in habitual co-occurrences of mutually predicting lexical items (such as *dark/night* or *silly/ass*), we shall see in Chapter 7 that the concept of collocation has been extended by later systemic linguists (principally Halliday and Sinclair) to cover co-occurrence of any degree of 'strength'.

The grammatical counterpart of collocation is colligation. Colligations, unlike collocations, are not relations between individual lexical words, but between grammatical categories such as article, noun, and verb. Part of the grammatical meaning of a particular category (e.g. article) is its habitual colligation with other categories (e.g. noun).

The concepts of system and structure extend also to Firth's treatment of phonology. Since this aspect of Firth's work has not had any great impact on subsequent theoretical developments in systemic linguistics, we shall not deal with it in detail here: it should be noted, however, that it is probably for his work on phonology that Firth is best known outside the systemic tradition. Excellent summaries of Firth's approach can be found in Robins (1970, pp.17-22), Sampson (1980, pp.215-23) and (at a rather higher level) Sommerstein (1977, Chapter 3). Basically, Firth's position was that the phonemic approach to phonological description is profoundly unsatisfactory, being unable to provide a satisfying account of many phenomena occurring in the Indian, Oriental and African languages with which Firth and his colleagues at the School of Oriental and African Studies worked. Firth considered that the phoneme was useful only as a basis for transcription, and proposed instead an analysis, set out programmatically in Firth (1948b), in terms of *phonematic units* and *prosodies.*

Prosodies are elements which extend over more than one phonological segment (e.g. over syllables, phonological words, or longer stretches of utterance), or which act to demarcate a particular structure or structural division. Into the first category come not only phenomena such as length, stress and pitch, but also such features as vowel harmony, and the secondary articulations involved in various assimilatory phonotactic processes (lip-rounding, nasalization, and so on). Into the second, demarcative category would come the junctural phenomena involved in, for instance, distinguishing between *I scream* and *ice cream* in English. Prosodic analysis, though not without its problems, provides a natural and satisfying way of handling these suprasegmental phenomena, which proved something of an embarrassment for American-style phonemic analysis.

Phonematic units are what remain when the various prosodies have been abstracted, and are basically segmental units. They are not, however, to be identified with phonemes, since at least some of what would be treated as phonemic in a phoneme-based analysis would be allocated to prosodies in a Firthian treatment.

Returning now to our discussion of system and structure, we may say that the notion of phonematic units is basically a paradigmatic one, whereas that of prosodies is basically syntagmatic. As Robins (1970, p.18) has pointed out, phonematic units are primarily concerned with the contrasts available at particular points in phonological structure, while prosodies are concerned mainly with syntagmatic relations within and between structures. Phonematic units which are in contrast at a particular place in a phonological structure constitute a phonological system operating at that place; prosodic statements, on the other hand, are an aspect of the structural description of utterances.

This brings us to an extremely important principle which distinguishes Firth's views from those of Saussure, and also of some later systemic linguists (see, for example, the discussion of Hudson's work in Chapter 6). Firth was firmly opposed to the 'monosystemic' principle embodied in Meillet's 'un système où tout se tient', preferring a 'polysystemic' approach to language:

> Linguistic analysis must be polysystemic. For any given language there
> is no coherent system (où tout se tient) which can handle and state all
> the facts. (Firth in Palmer, 1968, p.24)

That is, we must set up a large number of systems to account for the
diversity of linguistic phenomena, and not expect to handle everything
within one huge 'supersystem'. More specifically, as implied in our discussion of phonematic units above, systems are to be set up *for particular
places in structures.* Here again is Firth, outlining his views in relation to
the vowel systems of English:

> I am not a phonemicist and do not set up unit segments, each of which
> must be occupied by a phoneme. I do, however, set up vowel systems
> applicable to particular elements of structure. The terms of the vowel
> systems vary according to the element – for instance, in final unstressed
> position, the system has fewer terms than in a stressed position. (Firth
> in Palmer, 1968, p.99)

An element contrasting with certain other elements in one position is not,
then, to be identified with a similar element, with different contrastive
possibilities, operating at a different structural position. Further examples
are provided by Robins:

> In a subordinate clause structure, for example, in which at the verb
> place three tense distinctions are possible, each tense is not to be
> identified with a tense in a system set up for a main clause structure
> in which five tenses commute. Likewise if in syllable initial position
> there is a four term system of nasal consonants m, n, ɲ, and ŋ, and at
> syllable final position a three term system, m, n and ŋ, the consonants
> written m, n, ŋ, in each are not, as phonological elements, the same
> (although it may be convenient to transcribe them alike), because their
> status and function in the phonological contexts of the language,
> their phonological meaning, is necessarily different in the two cases.
> (Robins, 1970, p.11)

The polysystemic approach outlined above is absolutely consistent
with Firth's view of meaning as function in context. The context of a
particular phonological element, or a tense form, includes the other
elements with which it is in paradigmatic relation: if the contrastive
possibilities are different, so is the meaning of the element.

1.4 Criticisms of the Firthian view of language

It would be wrong to claim that Firth's views have secured uncritical
acceptance among a majority of linguists. His approach to language has, in
fact, been largely ignored, especially in the USA, and those comments
which have appeared in the literature have tended to be adversely critical.
Such criticism as there has been centres around Firth's wide-ranging and
admittedly idiosyncratic interpretation of 'meaning' in linguistics, and his
reliance on contextual determination.

A detailed critique of Firth's theory of meaning is to be found in Lyons (1966). Lyons, while recognizing that context of situation must be taken into account in any adequate semantic theory, feels that this notion 'cannot be made to bear all the weight that Firth placed on it' (Lyons, 1966, p.288). He reinterprets Firth's view of meaning as function in context in terms of appropriateness in that context. In these terms, a significant (that is, meaningful, as opposed to nonsensical or meaningless) sentence will be one which is appropriate to the situation in which it is used. Thus Firth (1935, p.24 in Firth, 1957a) finds Sapir's sentence '*The farmer killed the duckling*' nonsensical, because he cannot imagine it ever being employed in any actual context. Lyons (p.292), however, suspects 'that the notion of "significance" is too complex to be handled in this way; that a good deal of significance cannot be accounted for satisfactorily except in terms of the semantic compatibility of the constituent elements of utterances'.

Lyons' criticisms certainly have some substance to them: the examples of social contextual determination of meaning discussed by Firth are well chosen to be favourable to his case. We shall see in Section 5.3 that Halliday, in developing Firth's ideas, concedes that only a small proportion of our everyday language can be described in terms of ranges of options which are predictable from the social context and setting of the language event. However, it seems likely that Lyons' goals as a semanticist are very different from Firth's or indeed Halliday's: Lyons, while theoretically recognizing the importance of contextual variation, has tended to avoid the issue in his own accounts of 'structural semantics' (see, for example, Lyons, 1963, 1968, 1977); for Firth and Halliday, on the other hand, it is a primary aim of the theory to account for the relationships between language and situation.

Lyons also claims (p.293) that Firth's theory of meaning makes no provision for handling the relation of reference. In a footnote, Lyons discounts the possibility that the 'relevant objects' part of the specification of context of situation should be taken referentially. Here, however, he is surely wrong. There is no reason why this part of Firth's contextual specification should not be interpreted as covering at least the denotation of referring expressions (where the denotation of a lexeme is 'the relationship that holds between that lexeme and persons, things, places, properties, processes and activities external to the language system' (Lyons, 1977, p.207), as opposed to the reference of an item, which is what a speaker is picking out on a given occasion of its use). Indeed, Robins (1970, pp.8-9) appears to be of the opinion that both reference and denotation are covered when, in a description of Firth's parameters of contextual variation, he writes:

> Within contexts of this sort the utterance is shown to be connected to the extra-linguistic features of the situation by a network of different relations, all of which together constitute its function, that is to say its meaning. Reference, denotation, and naming, as relations between certain words and certain things, are just one sort of relation between part of an utterance and part of its environment as formalised in a context of situation, and one sort of function, among many others, attributable to certain words.

Lyons also points out that Firth's theory has no place for 'sense relations' of the type characterized by later structural semanticists. Again, it is important to take account of the overall aims and orientation of Firth's theory. Firth would indeed have been sceptical of much of the later work on structural semantics, feeling that it forced language into the straitjackets of neat oppositions. Take, for instance, the sense relation of synonymy. As is well known, very rarely, if ever, are two or more lexical items fully intersubstitutable in all contexts. Given Firth's view of meaning as function in context, this leads inexorably to the view (expressed also by non-Firthian linguists: see, for example, Ullmann, 1962, p.141) that there are no true synonyms. Firth would certainly not have wanted to elevate 'cognitive' meaning above other types of meaning, so that for him even the notion of 'cognitive synonymy' would be unacceptable. This said, however, it could be argued that Firth's own practice was at odds with his precepts: the very nature of his concept of system forces linguistic items into the neat oppositions of which he professed himself to be wary. Furthermore, Firth did, as we have seen, make generalizations about context and, had he wished to do so, could surely have specified those ranges of context in which lexemes are indeed equivalent. We shall see in Section 7.2.3 that some of the later work on lexical patterning has provided a framework equivalent to the componential analysis of many structural approaches to meaning; within such a framework, sense relations such as hyponymy and incompatibility could easily be accommodated.

Even if Firth's theory was, as we have suggested, deficient with regard to sense relations of a paradigmatic kind, it can fairly be claimed that it paid more attention to the syntagmatic aspects of sense relations, as represented by collocation, than have most structural semanticists. Lyons remarks (1966, p.295) that Firth 'never makes clear how the notion of collocation fits into his general theory'. This is surely not true: the lexical level is one of the 'modes' into which meaning is dispersed, and some lexical items co-occur with a high degree of regularity, thus providing syntagmatic contexts for each other. Since meaning is interpreted as function in context, the function of a lexical item in a collocation is, for Firth, part of the meaning of that item.

On terminological grounds, Lyons (p.300) suggests that 'the use of the term "meaning" in some of the senses in which it is employed by Firth cannot but lead to confusion with more-established uses, and should be abandoned'. It is certainly true that Firth's use of the term is highly idiosyncratic, and this aspect of his legacy has led to an unfortunate lack of clarity in Halliday's later accounts of the relations between form and meaning. Nevertheless, it must be admitted that Firth's usage was totally consistent with his 'function in context' view.

Firth's concept of meaning has also been attacked by Langendoen (1968, 1971), who states that it 'has nothing whatever to do with the meaning of sentences in the ordinary sense of the word' (1968, p.46), and points out that Palmer, a student and staunch defender of Firth, admits that 'only a tiny fraction of what is usually meant by meaning appears to be statable in terms of context of situation' (Palmer, 1958, p.237). Langendoen also rejects Firth's concept of 'meaning by collocation', claiming that 'the goal of semantics should be, rather, to show how the meaning of such phrases as *dark night* is determinable from a knowledge of the meaning of the lexical items comprising them and the syntactic relationships that are found in them' (Langendoen, 1968, p.64). But here Langendoen has failed to appreciate the significance of a passage from Firth which he quotes only two pages earlier, and which we commented on in Section 1.3: Firth makes it quite clear that collocational meaning is merely an abstraction from the syntagmatic patterning of lexical items, and is not to be confused with other types of meaning, including the 'semantic meaning' (a perfectly proper and consistent term for Firth) which Langendoen regards as primary. Again, as with Lyons, there is a confusion of aims: Langendoen appears to assume that the only kind of phrasal meaning which is to be accounted for is the 'compositional' meaning derived from the (presumably context-independent) paradigmatic sense relations of the individual items; Firth, on the other hand, while not rejecting compositionality, is concerned to account for the function of each linguistic item in its context, and points out, correctly and relevantly, that part of this context is the linguistic environment provided by other lexical items which are co-present. Langendoen may feel that Firth's goals are not worth pursuing (though he does not give convincing reasons why they are not); but it should be recognized that if these goals are accepted, Firth was being entirely consistent in his treatment of collocational meaning.

Langendoen also objects to Firth's rejection of the 'linguistic unity' view inherent in Saussurean structuralism. He claims (Langendoen, 1968, p.47) that Firth could be taken as implying that, for example, 'the expression *Good day!* when uttered as a greeting is completely unrelated to the same *Good day!* when uttered as a farewell, and so on for countless such instances'. The case against Firth is clearly overstated: he would surely not have wished to claim that the two instances are 'completely unrelated'. There is, however, some validity in Langendoen's criticism, in that the poly-systemic principle makes it difficult to state what overlapping systems have in common. We shall voice very similar doubts concerning Halliday's development of Firth's ideas in his 'sociosemantic' model (see Chapter 5).

Further doubts about the polysystemic principle underlying the 'linguistic plurality' view are raised in relation to prosodic phonology by Sommerstein (1977, p.62), who observes that 'the hypothesis founders on the simple fact that on any reasonable analysis, different subsystems of the phonology of one language show far more similarity, on the average and in comparison with subsystems of the phonology of different languages, than can possibly be attributed to chance'. And yet, as Sampson (1980, pp.217-18) has pointed out, the polysystemic approach has reduced to the status of non-problems various phenomena which have proved problematic for phonemic analysis (see, for example, the discussion of Mandarin Chinese phonology in Chao (1934), treated further in Sampson (1980, pp.70-71, 215)). We shall see in later chapters of this book that Halliday has modified the polysystemic principle, and Hudson has argued for its complete abandonment in his models of syntax.

A fault for which Firth's work has been severely, and rightly, criticized is his lack of explicitness, and his failure to relate the various components of his theory into a tightly organized, coherent whole. Langendoen (1968, pp.37-8) notes that Firth did not attempt to define rigorously the various levels or modes of meaning, or to arrange them systematically with respect to one another. He also comments, in his review of Palmer's collection of

Firth's later papers (Langendoen, 1971, p.180) that 'it would appear that all Firth was capable of doing in syntax was to discuss isolated examples ad hoc, and to make pronouncements ex cathedra'. Haugen, in his review of Firth's earlier papers, similarly complains that Firth 'does not establish techniques or definitions which would enable others to apply his ideas with confidence' (Haugen, 1958, p.501), and that it is not clear how many levels of linguistic analysis he would wish to recognize.

1.5 The link with Halliday

A balanced assessment of Firth's work requires that we recognize the perceptiveness of many of his ideas, and their value in reacting to the monosystemic approach of the Saussureans and the meaning-excluding theories of the American structuralists. We must, however, also admit that these ideas were presented only programmatically, often obscurely, and almost never with the degree of rigour which we have come to expect of modern linguistics. It was left to Halliday to take up the task of using Firth's ideas on context of situation, on restricted languages and on system and structure, to build a linguistic theory in which the categories and their relationships would be made explicit. To what extent Halliday has succeeded in this task will, it is hoped, emerge from the following chapters.

2. Scale and Category linguistics

2.1 Introduction

We saw in Chapter 1 that the work of Firth, though insightful in many ways, lacked a coherent theoretical framework of interrelated categories. In the present chapter we shall trace Halliday's attempts, in papers published in the late 1950s and early 1960s, to build Firth's insights, often in a modified form, into an overall theory of what language is, and how it works.

2.2 The earliest work

Since, as we have seen, Halliday was trained as a sinologist, it was natural that his earliest work should relate to Chinese. In the paper 'Grammatical categories in Modern Chinese' (Halliday, 1956) a framework is provided, within which the relationships between linguistic units can be handled in a consistent manner. At this early stage of the theory, three basic grammatical categories are recognized: *unit, element* and *class.*

The *unit* is 'that category to which corresponds a segment of the linguistic material about which statements are to be made' (1956, p.180). Halliday recognizes five such units for Chinese: sentence, clause, group, word and character. To describe the units, Halliday sets up *elements* which occupy places in the structure of particular units. At each place in the structure of a given unit operates a *class* of the unit next below, consisting of an exhaustive list of the forms which can occur at that place. For instance, at each place in clause structure will operate a class of the next lower unit, i.e. the group. Primary classes are those which operate uniquely at a given place in structure; secondary classes arise by subdivision of the primary classes, and also by classifications cutting across the primary dimensions. The definition of class in terms of the operation of linguistic forms at particular places in the structure of the next higher unit formalizes Firth's notion of 'function in context', by specifying the contexts (the structural place in the next higher unit) in which particular forms can operate.

It will be noted that 'system' is not a primary category of the theory at this stage. System is, in fact, regarded as secondary to class, in that 'the system of terms operating at a particular place in the structure of a given unit is a system of classes of the unit next below' (p.180). Halliday here maintains Firth's polysystemic principle, since systems are set up for particular places in structure.

Let us now exemplify Halliday's use of the terms unit, element, class and system by looking briefly at his analysis of the sentence and clause in Chinese. Sentence and clause are, as we have seen, two of the *units* proposed for the analysis of Chinese (and also English, in later papers): they are, in fact, the 'highest' units of the grammar. Halliday recognizes two

structural *elements* in the Chinese sentence, which he labels O and X. At each of these elements operates a particular primary *class* of the unit next below (i.e. a particular class of clause). At O, we have the class of 'free' clauses; at X, the class of 'subordinate' clauses. These two classes of clause form a two-term *system* of clause classes in sentence structure. We can also recognize secondary classes of clause within the primary classes 'free' and 'subordinate': 'free' clauses are either 'disjunctive' or 'conjunctive', so that there is a two-term secondary system operating at O; 'subordinate' clauses are either 'conditional' or 'adjectival', so that there is also a two-term secondary system operating at X. The secondary classes of clause can be justified in terms of their different distributional probabilities in different types of sentence.

Having related the units of sentence and clause by means of the categories of element (of structure) and class (and, secondarily, system), Halliday can now go on to relate clauses to groups in a similar way. The basic clause structure has the elements V and N, an element A also being needed in subsidiary structures. At V operates the primary group class 'verbal group'; at N 'nominal group', and at A 'adverbial group'.

In addition to setting up the basic framework of what was to become known as 'Scale and Category linguistics', the early work on Chinese affords pointers towards areas developed later in Halliday's thinking. The comment (p.182) that 'one could set up a unit of contextual statement features of which would determine grammatical features' echoes Firth's insistence on the crucial role of context of situation in linguistic study, and adumbrates Halliday's own work on diatypic variation. In the distinction between 'given' and 'new' information in the Chinese clause (p.188), Halliday brings into play aspects of language structure which are to assume considerable importance in later work. We may also note the use of probabilistic weightings for systemic choices in particular environments (p.179), an early indication of Halliday's rejection of the 'all-or-none' view of language in favour of a statistical approach.

2.3 Further development of the theory

The most comprehensive account of early Hallidayan theory (though not the most readable: the newcomer would be well advised to read first the potted version in Halliday, McIntosh & Strevens, 1964) is to be found in the article 'Categories of the theory of grammar' (Halliday, 1961). In what follows, we shall discuss in some detail the main claims made in this and related work, though postponing until Chapter 7 a consideration of the place of lexis within the model. Halliday's points are often inadequately exemplified, and therefore additional illustration will be provided where necessary.

2.3.1 The requirements of a linguistic theory

In the early part of his 1961 article, Halliday sets out what he takes to be the necessary characteristics of a general linguistic theory. The theory is held to consist of 'a scheme of interrelated categories which are set up to account for the data, and a set of scales of abstraction which relate the categories to the data and to each other' (p.243). It is assumed that the data consist of observed linguistic events: the approach is thus strongly

corpus-based.

The processes of abstraction involved differ among themselves in kind, so necessitating the postulation of different levels of analysis. The primary levels are those of *form, substance* and *context*. 'Substance' refers to the phonic or graphic manifestation of language. 'Form' is the organization of this substance into patterns which carry meanings; it consists of the two 'demi-levels' of grammar and lexis. Grammar is defined as 'that level of linguistic form at which operate closed systems' (p.246); any other formal patterning belongs to lexis. We shall discuss this distinction further in Chapter 7; meanwhile, it should be noted that the concept of system plays an important role in this definition (see further Section 2.3.2.4 below).

'Context' is, strictly speaking, an 'interlevel', relating form to situational features, and to linguistic features other than those being studied. Halliday prefers 'context' to 'semantics' as a label for this interlevel, because of the 'conceptual' orientation of much semantic theorizing; nevertheless, it would be fair to say that Halliday's contextual relations are semantic in a wider sense of the term, taken as including variations of focus and emphasis, formality, and the like, as well as 'cognitive' meaning. Phonology and graphology (or orthography) are likewise interlevels, relating form to phonic and graphic substance respectively.

Halliday differentiates between two types of meaning, which he labels 'formal' and 'contextual'. Formal meaning is the relationship between the item concerned and other items in a network of formal relations; it thus encapsulates Firth's view of meaning as function in context. Halliday equates formal meaning with 'information', in the information theory sense; this, however, has been challenged by Lyons (1966, pp.298-9). Contextual meaning refers, more narrowly, to the relationship between a linguistic item and extra-textual features, and can be assigned only after the place of the item in the network of linguistic relations (i.e. its formal meaning) has been established.

2.3.2 Grammar: scales and categories

Four categories (unit, structure, class and system) and three scales relating them (rank, exponence and delicacy) are proposed. Several differences from the 1956 version of the theory are immediately apparent: system is now one of the fundamental categories, rather than secondary to class; the concept of structure, hitherto subsidiary to that of element, is now given full recognition; and the relationships between the categories, and between these and the data, are more explicitly accounted for in terms of the three scales, which were merely implicit in the earlier work.

2.3.2.1. Unit and rank

Units are set up to account for the stretches of language carrying grammatical patterns. They are arranged hierarchically on a scale of *rank*, successive units on the rank scale displaying a 'consists of' relationship, such that in the simplest case each unit consists of one or more of the unit next below on the scale. The theory also allows for 'rank shift' in more complex structures: a unit can be, as it were, transferred to a unit of lower rank, and can then be included (in terms of the 'consists of' relationship) in a unit of equal or lower rank. A unit may not, however,

behave as if it were a unit of *higher* rank; that is, there is no 'upward rank shift'.

Halliday's article is unfortunately very poor in exemplification, and we shall therefore take examples of rank shift from the discussion in a later publication (Halliday, 1965) concerned with types of structure. In 2.1 below, the clause 'that Jack built' is rank shifted into the structure of the group 'the house that Jack built'; while in 2.2 the group 'in the garden' is rank shifted into the structure of the group 'the tree in the garden', and the group 'the garden' is in turn rank shifted into the structure of 'in the garden'.

2.1 The house that Jack built.
2.2 The tree in the garden.

An important aspect of Halliday's rank-based theory is the principle of 'total accountability', which requires that every item must be accounted for at all ranks. We may not, therefore, claim that 2.3 is a sentence consisting of a single morpheme; rather, we must say that it is a sentence consisting of a single clause, which itself consists of a single group, this in turn consisting of a single word, which itself consists of a single morpheme.

2.3 Yes.

Such a sentence thus exemplifies to a remarkable degree the phenomenon of 'singulary branching', whereby a linguistic item consists of just one constituent. As we shall see later, the principle of total accountability, and indeed the whole concept of a rank-based grammar, has come under quite heavy attack from outside systemic linguistics.

2.3.2.2 Structure and delicacy

Structure is 'the category set up to account for likeness between events in successivity' (Halliday, 1961, p.59). It is thus an abstraction describing patterns of syntagmatic relationship at the grammatical level. Consider, for example, 2.4–2.8 below (these are not Halliday's examples: here too the article is sadly lacking in illustrative material).

2.4 John	kicked	the cat	rather violently.
2.5 The old man	has spent	fifty pounds	during the last fortnight.
2.6 Everyone in the room	would have made	their excuses	immediately.
2.7 Good boys	don't tell	lies	about anything.
2.8 My father	was	ill	yesterday.

The similarity in syntagmatic patterning shown by these five sentences (and countless others like them) can be captured by the recognition of four basic elements of clause structure, which Halliday labels S(ubject), P(redicator), C(omplement) and A(djunct). Note here that Halliday uses the terms Complement and Adjunct more widely than in some other accounts: the former covers the direct and indirect objects of traditional grammar as well as complements of copula-type verbs; the latter covers a wide range of groups with 'adverbial' function (cf. the more restricted interpretation of the term in, for instance, Quirk et al. 1972, p.268 ff.).

Elements of structure are defined with reference to the unit next below on the rank scale, in the sense that 'each element represents the potentiality of operation of a member of one *grouping* of members of the unit next below' (p.256). For instance, the element P in clause structure is that element at which a certain grouping of items (in fact, that which we refer to as 'verbal groups': see Section 2.5.2.3 below) can operate.

The elements of structure of a given unit are 'ordered' in 'places'; where there are alternative orderings, a variety of structural types may result. For example, the four elements of clause structure, S, P, C and A, may be combined in various ways, and C and A may appear at more than one structural place, giving structures such as SPC, ASP, SAPA, ASPCC, and so on. Halliday is careful to point out that 'order' and 'sequence' are not the same thing. This had already been recognized by Wells (1947), and by Firth when he wrote:

In these structures one recognises the place and order of the categories. This, however, is very different from the successivity of bits and pieces in a unidimensional time sequence. (Firth, 1957a, p.173 in Palmer, 1968)

and again: 'Elements of structure, especially in grammatical relations, share a mutual expectancy in an *order* which is not merely a *sequence*,' (Firth 1957d, p.186 in Palmer, 1968).

Halliday's illustration (1961, p.257, fn. 33) clarifies the distinction. He contrasts two interpretations, in spoken English, of the sequence of items shown in 2.9.

2.9 The man came from the Gas Board.

The two spoken versions differ intonationally (the symbol // represents a tone group boundary, and / the boundary of the rhythmic 'foot'; underlining shows the 'tonic' syllable, on which the main pitch change occurs; 1 is the number given to the falling tone in Halliday's account of English intonation: see Halliday (1963a and b, 1967a, 1970a), also Section 7.3.3).

2.10 //1 The /<u>man</u> /came //1 from the /<u>Gas</u> /Board //
2.11 //1 The /man /came from the /<u>Gas</u> /Board //

'From the Gas Board' occupies the same position in sequence in 2.10 and 2.11; the ordering relations of the elements of clause structure are, however, different in the two cases. The structure of 2.10 is SP, with the Subject consisting of the discontinuous pieces 'the man . . . from the Gas Board' (that is, the sentence is taken as a variant of 'The man from the Gas Board came'); in 2.11, however, we have the structure SPA. In 2.11 'from the Gas Board' represents the Adjunct element of clause structure; in 2.10 it is part of the Subject.

Sequence, then, is not the same as order, but is just one possible way in which ordering relations may be represented in the 'expounding' of abstract categories in linguistic substance. Halliday does, however, claim that sequence is important in the definition of some types of linguistic structure. He points out, for example, that in English clause structure (and presumably Halliday is here talking about the simple declarative clause, though he does not say so) 'it is a crucial criterion of the element S that it precedes P in sequence' (p.258). He indicates this essential sequential relation by placing an arrow over the inherently sequenced elements, thus: S̄P̄CA. As we shall see later, Halliday's views on this matter have been criticized by Palmer (1964).

The distinction between order and sequence is also made by Halliday in a later paper (Halliday, 1965), in which he introduces a notational convention for the two types of relation. Ordering relations are symbolized by a raised dot, representing a simple concatenation of elements, with no implications of sequence: for instance, M˙H is equivalent to H˙M. Sequence is represented by linking elements with the symbol ˆ, so that MˆH means 'M followed by H'. The sign ˆ can be omitted, by convention, so that MH is to be interpreted in the same way as MˆH, or, rather, as M˙H represented by the sequence MˆH.

The scale of *delicacy* is linked with the concept of structure (and also with class) in Halliday's 1961 account though, as we shall see, it later comes to be associated also with system. Delicacy refers to the degree of detail in which a structure is specified. Halliday distinguishes between 'primary' structures, such as the various combinations of S, P, C and A in the clause, which are 'those which distinguish the minimum number of elements necessary to account comprehensively for the operation in the structure of the given unit of members of the unit next below' (p.258); and 'secondary' structures, which are more detailed, more 'delicate' differentiations of units at the same rank. Even more delicate description would give tertiary structures, and so on.

As an example of variations in structural delicacy, Halliday discusses briefly the structure of the English nominal group (the definition of this class of group will be discussed below; meanwhile, we may take 'nominal group' to be equivalent to 'noun phrase'). The primary elements of structure here are M(odifier), H(eadword) and Q(ualifier). At primary delicacy, then, Halliday's examples given below would have the same structure, namely MMMHQ.

2.12   M M   H   Q
    all the ten houses on the riverside
2.13   M   M   M   H   Q
    the finest old houses on the riverside

At secondary delicacy, however, the structures can be shown to differ. There are several types of modifier, recognizable by their distributional properties: in the 1961 article, Halliday distinguishes three categories at secondary delicacy, D, O and E; in later work a category N (noun modifier) is added to account for modifiers such as 'stone' in 'the stone houses' (see, for example, Sinclair (1972, p.168), where the Scale and Category model is applied to a description of English for pedagogical purposes). The structure of 2.12 can be more delicately specified as DDOHQ, and that of 2.13 as DOEHQ. Further, tertiary, distinctions are possible within the D elements: in 2.12 'all' is a 'predeterminer' to 'the', these two items representing the elements D_a and D_b respectively.

The notion of structure is expanded and refined by Halliday in a later paper (Halliday, 1965) which builds on ideas presented sketchily in an article largely concerned with class (Halliday, 1963c; see also Section 2.3.2.3). Halliday postulates two basic types of structure in language: multivariate and univariate. Multivariate structures are composed of different variables, with different relationships between them, while uni-variate structures consist of repeated instances of the same type of variable, with the same type of relationship between them.

The kinds of structure we have considered so far, SPCA and its variants for the clause, and MHQ for the nominal group, are multivariate, since the relationships between the elements, in each type of structure, are of quite different kinds: the relationship between S and P is different from that between P and C, and so on. As examples of univariate structures, Halliday gives the following:

2.14 1 2   3
   cats, dogs and horses
2.15   1   2   3
   tomorrow, Thursday, the 25th of July
2.16 α β γ
   I'd have come if you'd telephoned before I left.

Univariate structures are themselves of two types, paratactic and hypo-tactic. In paratactic structures, as exemplified by 2.14 and 2.15, the relations among the elements are purely sequential: this, then, is one case where sequence does determine ordering relations in structures. 'Cats, dogs and horses' differs from 'dogs, cats and horses' only in that the relative sequence of 'cats' and 'dogs' is reversed. 2.14 exemplifies the type of paratactic structure known traditionally as co-ordination, while 2.15 illustrates the relation of apposition. In all cases of paratactic structuring, Halliday labels the constituent elements 1, 2, 3, and so on, as shown in 2.14 and 2.15 above. In both co-ordination and apposition the structural elements show what in the terminology of logical relations is called a 'transitive' patterning: if A is related to B in a particular way, and B to C in the same way, then A also bears the same relation to C. Thus 'cats and dogs' and 'dogs and horses' implies 'cats and horses', and 'tomorrow = Thursday' and 'Thursday = the 25th of July' implies 'tomorrow = the 25th of July'.

Now consider 2.16, which illustrates a hypotactic structure, whose elements are labelled α, β, γ, and so on, by Halliday. Here, in traditional terminology, we have a series of clauses, each of which is dependent on (or subordinate to) the preceding clause. As with paratactic structures, only one kind of relationship is involved, since each clause is directly subordinated to one other. The relation is not, however, transitive since, for example, 2.16 does not imply 'I'd have come before I left'. Further-more, hypotactic structural relations, unlike paratactic relations, need not be represented by sequence. In 2.16 the clauses are indeed sequenced in such a way that each is dependent on the one which precedes it. This is not, however, invariably the case: 2.17 shows the same subordination relations as 2.16, but is differently sequenced.

2.17 If before I'd left you'd telephoned I'd have come.

One important difference between univariate structures (both paratactic and hypotactic) and multivariate structures is that the former are recursive, but the latter are not. That is, univariate structures can be extended indefinitely (at least in theory), while multivariate structures are closed rather than open-ended. The recursive nature of univariate structures can be illustrated by adapting Halliday's examples as follows:

2.18 cats
2.19   1   2
       cats and dogs
2.20   1   2   3
       cats, dogs and horses
2.21   1   2   3   4
       cats, dogs, horses and pigs
2.22 tomorrow
2.23   1   2
       tomorrow, Thursday
2.24   1   2   3
       tomorrow, Thursday, the 25th of July
2.25   α
       I'd have come.
2.26   α   β
       I'd have come if you'd telephoned.
2.27   α   β   γ
       I'd have come if you'd telephoned before I left.
2.28   α   β   γ
       I'd have come if you'd telephoned before I left
              δ
       to go to the doctor's.

Huddleston (1965, p.579), in a detailed discussion of univariate and multivariate structures, points out that in a univariate structure such as is exemplified by the Subject nominal in 2.29 below, a single element of structure (here, an element of clause structure) is represented by more than one unit of the next lower rank. (Halliday's example, reproduced here as 2.14, is similar, except that each nominal group has just a head noun, with no modification.)

2.29 The vicar, the bank manager, and the doctor are coming this afternoon.

Huddleston introduces the useful idea of 'unit complexes' to handle such relationships. The Subject of 2.29 is represented by a nominal group complex, consisting of three nominal groups in co-ordinative paratactic relationship. Similarly, 2.15 is a nominal group complex consisting of three nominal groups in appositional paratactic relation. The concept of unit complex can be extended to cover hypotactic relations, so that 2.16 is a clause complex consisting of three clauses in αβγ relationship. Note that since clause co-ordination and subordination can both be handled in terms of complexes, the unit 'sentence' on the rank scale is thereby made redundant, being replaced by 'clause complex', parallel to complexes needed at all other ranks. Examples of word and morpheme complexes are italicized in the following:

2.30 Sue has *washed and dried* the dishes.
2.31 Many *pro- and anti-*abortionists attended the meeting.

Huddleston points out that the notion of complex should be invoked only where strictly needed: it would be pointless to claim that 'Sue' in 2.30

represents a group complex which consists of a single group. That is, the principle of total accountability is to be adhered to only in respect of the 'basic' ranks.

We saw earlier that multivariate structures are not themselves recursive. They are, however, enabled to operate recursively by means of rank shift. The following examples are taken from Halliday (1965).

2.32 This is the cat that killed the rat that nibbled the malt that lay in the house that Jack built.
2.33 The tree in the garden of the house near the gasworks.

Associated with the discussion of types of structure, in the work of both Halliday and Huddleston, are the concepts of 'layering' and 'depth'. Halliday introduces the term 'depth' to mean the extent to which recursion applies in the specification of the structural relations of a given item (Halliday, 1963c, p.11). Thus, for instance, the γ clause in 2.16 would have a greater depth than the β clause. The term 'layering' is used (Halliday, 1965, p.33 in Halliday & Martin, 1981) to mean 'the bracketing of one recursive series within another'. For example, as Halliday shows, the items 'Tom', 'Dick' and 'Harry' can be arranged in three ways, differing in their layering.

2.34 (Tom, Dick and Harry)
2.35 (Tom, and (Dick and Harry))
2.36 ((Tom and Dick), and Harry)

In 2.34 there is just a single layer, but in 2.35 and 2.36 there are two layers, as shown more clearly in the tree diagrams below.

2.37   2.38

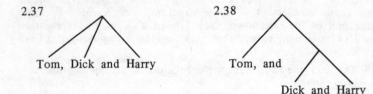

2.39

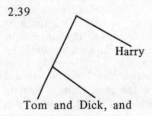

Huddleston (1965, p.577 ff.) uses the terms 'layer' and 'layering' in a rather wider way. Huddleston's layering is concerned with what, in terms of his notion of unit complexes, can be seen as the structuring of such a complex into layers of basic units. Huddleston extends the concepts of layering and depth to include the layers of constituents derived from the rank principle. Where there is no rank shift (and no recursion due to parataxis and hypotaxis), there is one layer for each basic rank (that is, minimally four layers for a simple English sentence). The occurrence of rank shift introduces a further, theoretically infinite, number of layers. The following tree diagrams are based on Huddleston's examples; however, for consistency with previous analyses, the labels used for structural elements differ slightly from Huddleston's in places.

2.40

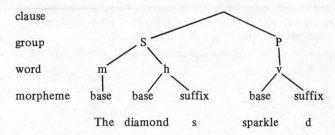

2.41

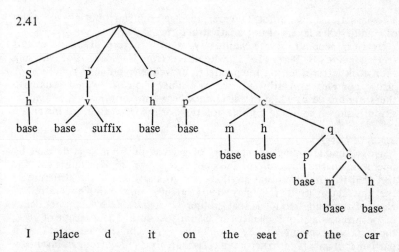

In 2.40, which displays no rank shift, the suffix '−d' is at a depth of 4, while in 2.41, which shows rank shift in the structure of the Adjunct, the item 'car' is at a depth of 7.

It will be noted that in the tree diagrams above, we have departed from our original notational conventions in one respect. Here, and in later work within the Scale and Category model, lower case letters are used to label elements of group structure. This has the advantage of differentiating such elements clearly from elements of clause structure, and avoiding ambiguity in the use of the labels P and C. These are used only for elements of clause structure, p and c being used for the preposition and its complement in a prepositional group.

As Huddleston hints, depth is one useful index of the complexity of a sentence. However, it would seem preferable, in studies of complexity, to keep the two kinds of layering (within complexes of a given rank of unit, and between ranks) separate in principle, since they are logically independent, and it is likely that some types of text will turn out to be complex in one respect but not the other. Huddleston himself confounds the two kinds of layering, and shows a basic misunderstanding of rank shift, when he writes (1965, p.585) that 'a complex may be rankshifted to an element in a larger complex' in examples such as 2.42.

2.42 The eldest went into business and earned a fortune, the second married a rich widow and consequently could retire early, and the youngest was left the family estate.

Huddleston quite properly analyses this sentence in terms of a layering of the kind shown below.

2.43

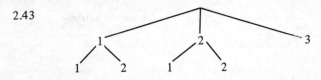

These relationships do not, however, involve rank shift, but are examples of Huddleston's layers of univariate structure.

A clear account of the various types of structure discussed in this section is given by Berry (1975), who differs from Halliday (1965) in using the Greek letter notation for paratactic as well as hypotactic structures. A clause complex consisting of two co-ordinated clauses would thus have the structure $\alpha\,\alpha$, while the difference between co-ordination and apposition is shown by using a prime notation for the latter ($\alpha'\alpha'$, for instance).

2.3.2.3 Class

Class is 'that grouping of members of a given unit which is defined by operation in the structure of the unit next above', and accounts for 'the fact that it is not true that anything can go anywhere in the structure of the unit above itself' (Halliday, 1961, p.260). For example, the 'verbal' class of the unit 'group' is that grouping recognizable by its potentiality of occurrence at the P element of clause structure. The concept of class, then, takes account of the paradigmatic possibilities associated with particular elements of structure: a class is an abstraction from an inventory of items, all of which share distributional characteristics, in being able to operate at a certain structural element, in syntagmatic association with other structural elements.

Halliday is very careful to stress that classes of items are to be defined in relation to the operation of the members in the next *higher* unit, and not in relation to their own constitution in terms of members of a *lower* unit: 'a class is *not* a grouping of members *which are alike in their own structure*' (p.261, original emphasis). Thus class, defined distributionally, is not to be confused with what Halliday in a later paper (Halliday, 1963c) calls 'type', a grouping based on the internal structure of the unit itself. Halliday brings in a terminological distinction which may seem rather odd to many readers of the 1961 article: the upward-looking definition of class in terms of operation in a higher unit is seen as a 'syntactical' definition, while a downward-looking approach in terms of the structure of the unit itself is seen as 'morphological'. Halliday feels able to use these terms in a wider way than usual, because he claims that the traditional distinction between syntax and morphology 'has no theoretical status' (p.261). For Halliday, the relationship between morphemes and words is of the same kind as that between words and groups, or between groups and clauses, all units being related on a single scale of rank.

Halliday's discussion of class is poorly exemplified, and it may be of use to include an illustration at this point. Consider the following sentences, discussed earlier in relation to their structure.

2.44 John kicked the cat rather violently.
2.45 The old man has spent fifty pounds during the last fortnight.
2.46 Everyone in the room would have made their excuses
     immediately.
2.47 Good boys don't tell lies about anything.

Each of these contains a single clause with, as we have seen, the structural elements S, P, C and A. The items which represent (or 'expound': see Section 2.3.2.5) the element S ('John', 'the old man', 'everyone in the room', 'good boys') are members of the 'nominal' class of the unit 'group'; those which represent P ('kicked', 'has spent', 'would have made', 'don't tell') belong to the 'verbal' class. It will be noted that in the examples given above, the items which operate at C ('the cat', 'fifty pounds', 'their excuses', 'lies') could also operate at S, and those operating at S could also occur at C. Halliday therefore conflates such items into a single major class. The nominal group is thus what Sinclair has referred to as a 'cross-class', in that it consists of items which can operate at either of two elements of structure. The class of items which can operate at A in clause structure (including 'rather violently', 'during the last fortnight', 'immediately', 'about anything') is the 'adverbial' class of group. This class illustrates very clearly the distinction between upward-looking and downward-looking approaches to classification: all the groups acting at A in the above examples are of the adverbial class, but they differ in their own structures, 'rather violently' and 'immediately' having a word of the 'adverb' class as their head, while 'during the last fortnight' and 'about anything' consist of a preposition followed by a rank shifted nominal group in one case and a pronoun in the other.

So far, we have discussed class only in relation to the major groupings which stand in direct relationship to primary elements of structure. The scale of delicacy applies to class as well as to structure, so that in addition to primary classes such as the nominal, verbal and adverbial classes of group, Halliday recognizes secondary classes, derivable from structures in two ways.

If the same element can occur at two places in a grammatical structure, it may be that the grouping of items which can occur at one of these places is not co-extensive with the grouping which can operate at the other place in structure. We then have two secondary classes, differentiated more delicately within the primary class of items which can represent the element of structure concerned. The example given by Halliday is abstract and not very illuminating; a more concrete illustration has, however, been offered by Berry (1979, p.51), who points out that 'the primary class adverbial group which realizes the element of structure adjunct can be subdivided into secondary classes on the basis of the positions in the sequence of elements of the clause at which its members most naturally operate'. As shown in the detailed discussion of Quirk et al. (1972, Chapter 8), certain kinds of adverbial element favour clause-initial position (that is, before the Subject), others prefer a medial position, others an end position, while some are quite mobile. Such positional tendencies would, for Halliday, serve as criteria for the establishment of secondary classes of adverbial groups.

A second way in which Halliday's secondary classes are derived from structures is by one-to-one correspondence with the elements of secondary structure into which primary elements may be more delicately divided. Halliday gives the example of the nominal group: the primary elements of structure are Modifier, Headword and Qualifier, but modifiers can be more delicately described in terms of the secondary elements D, O, E (and, in later work, N), to which correspond secondary classes of word (deictic at D, adjective at E, and so on). Halliday himself appears to see this way of deriving secondary structures as distinct from that based on positional preferences. Since, however, the evidence for secondary elements such as D, O, E is, at least in part, positional, it is surely preferable to regard this as essentially similar to the phenomena discussed earlier.

Halliday also recognizes a special kind of secondary class, which he calls a 'sub-class'. Sub-classes differ from the secondary classes we considered above in that they are not derived from more delicate structural descriptions, but are recognized where there is 'a relation of mutual determination, or "concord", between two classes; each divides into two sections such that a member of one section of one class is always accompanied by a member of one section of the other class' (p.260). Again, Halliday's example is abstract and unrevealing, and again Berry (1979, p.51) provides a more enlightening illustration, pointing out that countable nouns are a sub-class of the primary class representing the head element of a nominal group, since they show a relationship of mutual determination with deictics. For instance, count nouns can co-occur with 'a', 'each' (if singular), 'these' and 'those' (if plural), while non-count (mass) nouns cannot. Furthermore, Berry could have pointed out that mass nouns, but not count nouns, can co-occur with 'much'. We can thus regard 'count' and 'mass' as sub-classes of noun, and can also recognize sub-classes of deictic which are in concord relation with the sub-classes of noun.

In a paper (Halliday, 1963c) closely related to the concerns of the 'Categories' article, Halliday discusses a further dimension along which classes can vary. He distinguishes between 'chain' classes, derived from elements of structure, and 'choice' classes, related to the paradigmatic patterning encapsulated in the category of system (see Section 2.3.2.4). The primary classes, and those secondary classes derived from elements of secondary structure, are chain classes. On the other hand, classes such as 'singular nominal group' and 'plural nominal group' are not derived from structures, but are the exponents of terms in grammatical systems. These choice classes appear to be closely related, if not identical, to the sub-classes of the 1961 account, but the relationship is not made clear by Halliday.

2.3.2.4 System

As we saw earlier, system is now treated as one of the four central categories of the theory, rather than as subordinate to class. It is the category set up to account for 'the occurrence of one rather than another from a number of like events' (Halliday, 1961, p.264). System is defined in an essentially Firthian way as follows (p.247):

A closed system is a set of terms with these characteristics:
  (i)   the number of terms is finite: they can be listed as ABCD, and all other items E . . . are outside the system;
  (ii) each term is exclusive of all the others: a given term A cannot be identical with B or C or D;
  (iii) if a new term is added to the system this changes the meaning of all the other terms.

The reference to 'meaning' here relates to formal meaning, the place of an item within the overall network of relationships. Although the addition of a term to a system may well change the contextual meaning of the other terms as well, this is not itself a property of the system in its present formulation. The relationship between system and class in the 1961 model is that the more delicate classes into which primary classes can be divided form a system of classes operating at a particular place in structure.

It is unfortunate that Halliday's examples of the important category of system are either too abstract or too sketchy to afford the uninitiated reader a sufficient grasp of the concept. For a simple, and rather more revealing, illustration let us again consider the nominal group. We have seen that the nominal group can be divided into singular and plural sub-classes on the basis of the concord relations of subject nominal groups with corresponding sub-classes of verbal group. These two sub-classes form a two-term system operating at those elements of structure where nominal groups can occur.

2.3.2.5 Exponence

The scale of exponence has been left to the end of our discussion of scales and categories, because it is what brings the categories of the theory together, relating them to each other and to the linguistic data they are set up to account for. Halliday points out that although we could relate any abstract category to what finally represents it at the formal level (that is, to its ultimate 'exponents' in form), we should thereby lose a large number of significant generalizations. For instance, in the following sentence, discussed earlier in relation to structure and class, we could say that the element S of clause structure is expounded by the sequence of items 'the old man'.

2.45 The old man has spent fifty pounds in the last fortnight.

This would, however, miss the fact that 'the old man' shares with 'fifty pounds', and many other items, the characteristic of being an example of the nominal class of the unit group, but differs from 'fifty pounds' in having selected the term 'singular' from the number system. It also ignores the fact that this nominal group (like many others) itself has structure in terms of the elements m, m, h (more delicately: d, e and h), which are in turn expounded by certain classes of word. Only when no further grammatical structure can be proposed do we allow the structural elements to be expounded by 'formal items', such as 'the', 'old' and 'man'. Exponence relations, then, taking the longest route through the formal apparatus, relate terms in systems, units, classes and structures, and allow the analysis to achieve maximum generalization. Eventually, of course, formal items are themselves expounded by elements of phonic or graphic substance, via the interlevels of phonology or graphology.

2.3.3 Scale and Category theory and Bloomfieldian linguistics

At the end of the 'Categories' paper, Halliday points to what he sees as some shortcomings of the body of linguistic theory which he subsumes under the label 'Bloomfieldian'. Here we shall merely note some of the more interesting points of contrast with Halliday's own theory.

Halliday first objects to Bloomfield's (1933, p.161) claim that morphemes 'consist of' phonemes. He points out that there is a confusion of rank with level here: the morpheme is a unit on the grammatical rank scale, the phoneme a unit on the phonological rank scale, and the kind of abstraction relating one unit to another on the same rank scale is very different from that relating one level to another. Related to this confusion is another, that between grammatical and phonological phenomena and criteria in general. According to Halliday, the criteria for grammar should come from within grammar, and it is not a requirement that a grammatical category be identifiable by reference to its phonological exponents.

Halliday also criticizes the confusion of rank with exponence: although one may relate elements of structure at a particular rank of unit to their ultimate exponents via successive moves down the rank scale, we can, as we have seen, also relate an abstract category directly to its formal exponents, though many generalizations are missed by so doing. The point is that the scales of rank and exponence express different kinds of abstraction, just as do rank and level.

A further criticism levelled by Halliday at Bloomfieldian linguistics is its overemphasis on the smallest units of grammar and phonology, the morpheme and phoneme respectively. These smallest units are often called upon to account for phenomena which would be better handled in terms of a higher unit: Firthian prosodic phonology provides an obvious example of the approach favoured by Halliday. Halliday also criticizes the strongly directional nature of Bloomfieldian analysis, starting from the morpheme at one end, with the sentence at the other, and describing language by means of a combination of morphemics and immediate constituent analysis. Halliday prefers to see 'shunting' between ranks as an essential part of a linguistic theory, required in order to give a unified description of the links between the smallest and the largest units on the rank scale at a particular level.

Halliday also attacks the black-and-white, yes/no nature of much preceding work, feeling that probabilistic statements should be built into the theory, rather than being regarded as a theoretical embarrassment. This view relates in an obvious way to the concern shown by Halliday, and by some other systemic linguists, for the relationship between the abstract categories of the theory, on the one hand, and textual data, on the other.

Finally, Halliday is critical of an overuse of the notion of redundancy in linguistic theory. He observes that in putative cases of multiple exponence of a given category, it may be difficult to demonstrate that it is indeed the same category which is being expounded more than once. In any case, the distinction between single and double exponence itself has formal meaning.

2.4 Criticisms of Scale and Category theory

Certain aspects of Scale and Category theory came under fire from other linguists soon after their initial presentation. In this section we shall review, and at times supplement, these criticisms.

2.4.1 Criticisms concerned with rank

The concept of a rank-based grammar, and the associated principle of total accountability, have attracted severe criticism from Postal (1964) and Matthews (1966).

Postal (1964, p.107) claims that certain types of rank shift do not occur in natural language, and that Halliday has made no provision for appropriate constraints to deal with this. Postal's criticisms are invalid on two counts. Firstly, some of his facts are incorrect. He claims that sentences and clauses do not occur rank shifted to elements of word structure; however, examples such as 2.48 occur in at least some kinds of English:

2.48 the never-to-be-forgotten-ness of that day

Secondly, and more seriously, Postal appears to misunderstand the consequences of Halliday's theoretical position when (1964, p.107) he castigates him for not constraining his model in such a way that it will prevent the domination of sentences by morphemes. In order for a sentence to be embedded into a morpheme, it would have to be rank shifted to a unit smaller than the morpheme. Since, as Postal himself recognizes, there is in Halliday's theory no such smaller unit, the phenomenon Postal wishes to bar is indeed barred as an automatic consequence of Halliday's proposals.

Matthews' criticisms are of a rather different kind, and much more worthy of attention. He points out that in 2.49, since 'after we left Henry's' is a clause, 'after' must, according to Halliday's theory, be a group (Matthews actually uses the more traditional term 'phrase', which Halliday (1961, p.253) gives reasons for replacing), as well as a word and a morpheme.

2.49 I therefore remember nothing after we left Henry's.

The only alternative, says Matthews, would be to treat 'after we left Henry's' as a group rather than a clause, with 'we left Henry's' as a rank-shifted clause within the group structure. This would, however, be an unwise expedient: not only, according to Matthews, is this solution overcomplex (though similar analyses have been adopted in the literature: see, for instance, the elegant treatment in Jackendoff 1977, p.276); it also suffers from the disadvantage that the class of items which can introduce a temporal subordinate clause is not identical with the class of items which can introduce a group with temporal function, as witness Matthews' examples:

2.50   during the night
2.51   *during I was there

Matthews goes on to claim that similar arguments apply to 'therefore' in 2.49: it is a sentence-introducing element, and would thus have to be treated as a clause, as well as a phrase and a word, in a Hallidayan grammar. A parallel problem, says Matthews, occurs in the case of 'and' linking two clauses, as in 2.52 below:

2.52 I play the flute and my brother plays the piano.

If sentences consist of clauses, and every item is to be accounted for at all ranks, then 'and' must be treated as a clause. The position is made worse by the fact that 'and' can also join units at other positions on the Hallidayan rank scale, as in Matthews' examples, given below:

2.53 fish-and-chips
2.54 the walrus and the carpenter

Indeed, 'and' can join stretches of language which do not correspond to any whole unit on the rank scale, as in 2.55, where the co-ordinated elements are parts of clauses.

2.55 after the rains had started and the blackout was enforced

Matthews' view is that these problems could be solved, within a Hallidayan framework, only by amending the theory to allow 'upward rank shift', so that, for example, 'after' in 2.49 could be treated as a word (or perhaps simply as a morpheme) rank shifted upwards. This, Matthews claims, would mean that the concept of rank would no longer have any theoretical significance, since no constraints could be associated with it.

Matthews' criticisms provoked a reply from Halliday (1966a). He concedes that items such as 'and' and 'or' can 'float' between ranks, and so may be best regarded as not having constituent status, and as being outside the scope of the total accountability requirement. This does indeed appear to be a reasonable position, since Matthews' arguments here are convincing. However, we need to determine just what constraints there are on the types of item which have to be excluded from the constituency relations, and this important area remains neglected in the later work of Halliday, although we shall see in Section 6.2 that it has been taken up again by Fawcett.

With the above exceptions, however, Halliday continues to defend the rank concept and the total accountability principle. He points out that the rank scale allows us to say what 'size' of item normally occurs as a constituent at a given place in structure, and that (downward) rank shift then permits us to specify departures from this most usual pattern. Rank shift operates with the concept of 'rank 1 used as rank 2', but this does not necessarily imply that the item used as rank 2 *is* of rank 2. The relative clause of 2.56, for instance, is being used *as if it were* a word, in the sense that it functions within the environment of (nominal) group structure, its clause-like properties being lost (for example, it cannot contract normal interclausal relations outside the nominal group into which it is rank shifted).

2.56 The man who came to dinner (left at nine).

This does not mean, however, that a defining relative clause *is* simultaneously a word. On the other hand, when an item such as 'Yes' is used alone, there is a sense in which it not only acts *as* a clause, but also *is* a clause.

For instance, it takes intonation patterns which, in the unmarked case, map on to clause units, so that if we were to characterize it simply as a word (or even a word acting as a clause), as Matthews would wish, we should have to repeat the clausal intonational choices for just that class of words which can occur in such circumstances. If we accept Halliday's view of the relationship between grammar and intonational choice, then this does appear to be a strong argument against Matthews' proposals, and in favour of total accountability in such cases. However, we shall see in Section 7.3.4 that Halliday's position on the relationship between grammar and phonology, including his view on the unmarked correspondence between clauses and tone groups, has been challenged.

Halliday also makes a number of points which, although not specifically concerned with the issues raised by Matthews, argue for the adoption of a rank-based theory. In assessing these points, it is important to bear in mind the overall aims of Halliday's theories. As was mentioned briefly in Section 1.1, and will be discussed in Chapters 9 and 10, Halliday wishes his models to be applicable to the description of texts, for purposes of stylistic analysis, language teaching, and so forth. Such descriptive activities are often essentially comparative, so that the foci of interest are the respects in which linguistic items are similar, and the respects in which they differ, on both the syntagmatic and the paradigmatic axes.

Halliday argues that the demonstration of both similarities and differences is facilitated by a rank-based model. The assignment of items, and also of structures and systems, to a particular rank is the first stage in showing the syntagmatic and paradigmatic relations entered into by items, and the relationship of a given system to other systems. Syntagmatically, rank offers a way of generalizing about the bracketing of constituents: when, for example, we recognize certain classes of group as constituents of the clause, we are making a generalization about the units which characteristically act as such constituents. The rank scale can also aid in stating distinctions between similar structures. For instance, a defining relative clause such as that in 2.56 is rank shifted into the structure of the nominal group whose head it defines, while a non-defining relative clause, such as that in 2.57, is not rank shifted in this way.

2.57 The man, who came to dinner, (left at nine).

Halliday also suggests various interesting questions which are raised by a rank-based theory. Some of these would appeal to linguists whose aims are purely theoretical: for instance, whether the number of units on the grammatical rank scale is a universal, or perhaps a variable of use in typological classification; whether certain kinds of pattern are characteristically associated with particular ranks. Other questions are more applied in their orientation: for example, whether in some kinds of speech loss there is progressive deterioration of grammatical structures rank by rank.

Halliday further observes that the grammatical rank scale 'provides a point of reference for the description at other levels, such as phonology' (1966a, p.112). It is not entirely clear what Halliday means by this. He may simply mean that organization at the phonological level can also be described in terms of a rank scale (tone group, foot, syllable, phoneme). Alternatively, he may mean that although, as we saw in Section 2.3.3, we must not expect a one-to-one relation between units or other categories at different levels, we can specify at least the most usual ('unmarked') mapping of some phonological units on to grammatical units (see Halliday 1970a, p.3, also Section 7.3.3).

A further point in support of the rank concept is made by Anderson (1969). He points out that systems are, in all but the lack of a binarity requirement, equivalent to subcategorization rules, but that the rules of a Hallidayan grammar differ from those of the type of transformational grammar current in the mid-1960s (see Chomsky, 1965), in allowing subcategorization of non-terminal nodes in structural trees, such as those for clauses, noun phrases (nominal groups), and so on (we shall take up this point again in Section 6.3.3.3). Anderson shows that such a scheme provides a more plausible way of accounting for certain phenomena (classification of process types; number relations in mass nouns, count nouns and collectives) than a model which allows subcategorization only for terminal nodes. Anderson's main point in relation to rank is that by handling relationships in terms of subcategorization or systemic choice, one can eliminate many nodes in the structural trees for sentences, and that the nodes which are still required are those, such as clausal and phrasal nodes, which correspond to ranks in a Hallidayan grammar. Anderson, then, unlike Matthews, does not believe that the rank concept is invalid; he does, however, agree with Matthews that there is no strong motivation for the total accountability requirement imposed by Halliday.

There is a further point which could be made in defence of a rank-based grammar. Given that one of Halliday's aims is to develop a model which will be applicable to text analysis, the rank concept is extremely useful as a search aid in such a study. Breaking a text up into units of a particular rank, with no (or little?) residue, and then further division of these units into units of lower rank (while mindful of the possibility of rank shift) is a way of making sure that every bit of the text is accounted for, and that both its larger-scale and smaller-scale patterns can be recorded. This is of particular importance in, for example, stylistic analysis: in Section 9.2.1 we shall see how, especially in the work of Sinclair, a rank-based analysis has proved illuminating in the linguistic investigation of poetic styles. Such arguments will cut very little ice with those linguists whose aims are purely theoretical; however, within the context of a theory which has as a priority a 'renewal of connection' (to use Firth's phrase) with textual data, it makes very good sense.

A more general, but no less important, point is that it is of great value to pursue a theoretical concept to the point where it begins to break down, so that we find out just how much it will account for and how much remains to be explained. It may be that the residue can be accounted for by extensions or minor amendments to the theory, or it may be that the intractable cases are so fundamental, and perhaps numerous, as to call into question the whole basis of the proposal. In either case, the proposal will have been worth making. We have seen that there are considerable advantages to be gained from a rank-based grammar, if we accept the aims of Halliday's theorizing. There are, however, points at which it breaks down. We have seen that certain elements need to be considered as outside the rank-based hierarchy of constituents. Furthermore, Halliday has not provided an answer to Matthews' observation that certain con-joinable elements are not constituents at all in Halliday's theory (see 2.55).

A further difficulty, not raised by Matthews, is that the theory offers no place for a 'Predicate' or 'Verb Phrase' constituent (in the transformational grammar sense of these terms), although the recognition of such a constituent would seem necessary in view of the substitution relations in sentences such as 2.58.

2.58   I ate a peach and so did Laura. (did = ate a peach)

These facts suggest that as a theoretical construct, the rank hierarchy faces serious problems, which have still not been satisfactorily solved. They do not, however, lessen the contribution which a rank-based grammar can make to, for example, the study of naturally occurring texts.

2.4.2 Criticisms concerned with class

One problem concerns the relationship between the categories of structure, class and system. Halliday (1961, p.264) claims that terms in systems consist of the secondary classes into which primary classes can be divided. It will be remembered from our discussion in Section 2.3.2.3 that secondary classes may be derived from structures, or from sub-groupings which are in concord relation, in which case they are more specifically designated sub-classes. Halliday's abstract diagrammatic representation of the relations among the categories of structure, class and system (p.264, fn. 54) clearly implies that structure-derived secondary classes can constitute terms in systems. However, the membership of such classes can overlap, and it is a condition of a system that its terms shall be mutually exclusive. It would therefore seem that only sub-classes, whose membership does not overlap, should qualify as candidates for the status of terms in systems, and this is indeed what we assumed in our example in Section 2.3.2.4. Halliday himself comments (pp.264-5) that the concept of sub-class is important because 'whenever a choice among a finite number of mutually exclusive possibilities is found to occur within a class one can recognize a system whose terms have the nature and degree of abstraction of the "class"'. The implications of this statement are, however, at odds with Halliday's own exemplification of the category of system, which, as we have seen, involves structure-derived secondary classes.

There are further problems connected with the concept of class. We saw in Section 2.3.2.3 that Halliday (1963c) makes a sharp distinction between class (the upward-looking, 'syntactic' classification of items, in terms of their potentiality of occurrence at structural elements of the next higher unit), and type (the downward-looking, 'morphological' classification based on the internal structure of a unit), regarding the former as of greater theoretical importance than the latter. Halliday is, however, inconsistent in his allocation of linguistic items to classes, in two ways.

Firstly, he allows (as we saw earlier) for the conflation, into one primary class, of groupings of items which are very similar but not identical. Thus, for example, items which can occur at S in clause structure can also occur at C; but there are some kinds of item (notably adjective-headed groups) which occur regularly at C, but are not normally found at S. Halliday treats such items as 'very happy indeed', at primary delicacy, as nominal groups, so putting them in the same primary class as those items which readily act at S. Therefore, although class is supposed to be based on potentiality of occurrence within the next higher unit, the same primary class can contain members with different potentialities of occurrence. Note that this is not parallel to the conflation of, for example, count and mass nouns into one primary class 'noun': both count and mass nouns can occur as the head element of a nominal group.

A second inconsistency in Halliday's approach to class is revealed by his discussion (Halliday, 1963c, p.6) of groups such as 'this morning'. As his examples, given below, illustrate, such groups can operate at S (as in 2.59), C (as in 2.60) or A (2.61).

2.59 This morning promises to be fine.
2.60 I've set this morning aside for it.
2.61 I came this morning.

If classes of group are to be defined in terms of the operation of items at elements of clause structure, 'this morning' must be treated as a nominal group in 2.59 and 2.60, but as an adverbial group in 2.61. Halliday recognizes this, but then goes on to say:

> Morphologically, however, it clearly resembles other nominal groups (*the morning, this man*, etc.) rather than other adverbial groups (*quickly, on the floor*, etc.) and this can be allowed to determine its primary syntactic assignment.

Halliday is thus prepared to let the 'morphological' classification take over in such cases, and this runs counter to the whole basis on which classes are supposed to be assigned. Such difficulties seriously weaken the position taken by Halliday on class, and have led certain other sytemicists to abandon the syntactic definition in favour of the morphological criterion, based on the internal structure of units (see Fawcett, 1974, pp.9-10, also the discussion in Chapter 6). This redefinition will then allow us to say that the groups 'this morning', 'quickly' and 'on the floor' all belong to different structural, 'morphological' classes, but that each can act as A in clause structure.

Summing up the position we have reached on the problem of class, we may say that if we are to account for the variety of structures available in a language, we shall have to elevate structural type (that is, 'morphologically' defined class) to a more central position in the theory than Halliday suggests, for we shall have to show explicitly that a given syntactically defined class may contain members from more than one structurally defined class. This is basically the position taken by Huddleston (1966) and Hudson (1967); however, although these authors appear to think they are operating within Halliday's own framework, their use of the term 'class' in fact differs from that in Halliday's 1961 article, and this is a source of potential confusion for the unsuspecting reader. Although neither Huddleston nor Hudson actually define class, their discussion suggests that their criteria for classification are those of internal constituency. This is particularly clear in Huddleston's paper, where 'energetically' and 'well' are labelled as adverbial groups, but 'by the roadside' as a prepositional phrase (sic).

2.4.3 Criticisms concerned with structure

Huddleston (1977), in a rather unfavourable review of Berry's (1975) textbook on systemic linguistics for students of English, appears to reject his own earlier work (Huddleston, 1965, discussed in Section 2.3.2.2), on which part of Berry's account of grammatical structure is based. Huddleston's argument, which is brief and not always clear, is concerned with the distinction between univariate and multivariate structure. He points out that any co-ordination of three or more elements can show contrasting bracketings (see the discussion of layering in Section 2.3.2.2):

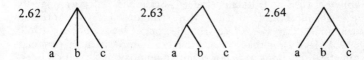

2.62   2.63   2.64

    a   b   c   a   b   c   a   b   c

Only a two-way contrast, however, is available in a hypotactic structure with three components: Halliday's example, repeated as 2.65 below, contrasts only with 2.66.

2.65   I'd have come if you'd telephoned before I left.
2.66   I'd have come before she left if you'd telephoned.

Hypotactic structures, Huddleston argues, should therefore be analysed, initially, into only two constituents, as in 2.64. But this means that it is difficult to draw a clear distinction between univariate and multivariate structures: it is trivially true that hypotactic structures can have only one type of relation between the elements, since there are only two immediate constituents; but there are two-element structures which would be regarded as multivariate (for instance, a clause with SP structure), although here too there can be only one type of relation between the parts. Huddleston, who by 1977 had shifted his sympathies from the systemic to the transformational model, claims that no other syntactic model makes a distinction between recursion in univariate structures and recursion due to rank shift in multivariate structures. It is perhaps worth noting that Huddleston's criticisms of Berry are to some extent unfair. Berry's intention was to write an introduction to Scale and Category grammar, and to certain aspects of later developments in systemic theory, which would provide an applicable model for students of English wishing to analyse texts. She specifically disclaims any intention to provide a full theoretical treatment. Huddleston recognizes this, and yet criticizes Berry for not providing thorough theoretical justification for the points she makes.

Further criticism in the area of structure has come from Palmer (1964, p.127), who has attacked Halliday's view of the relationship between order and sequence. He claims that if, as Halliday suggests, sequence is a crucial criterion in defining the Subject of a clause, and so is in this case 'built into' order, two separate symbols for Subject and Object (Halliday's Complement) are unnecessary, since the mere writing of two identical symbols in an ordering relation to the Predicator would differentiate the two elements if we allow that sequence may determine order to some degree. Such a proposal would obviate the need for Halliday's arrow convention, as in S̄PCA, showing the sequence relation between S and P. There are, of course, other respects, apart from sequence, in which Subject and Object differ (for example, the Subject shows concord with the finite verb in English, while the Object does not), but if we allow separate symbols on such grounds, then the ordering relation is no longer needed.

Postal (1964, p.111), going even further than Palmer, has suggested that element of structure labels are not needed at all in the grammar. To understand this position, we must consider the model of transformational generative grammar which was current in the mid-1960s. In this model, as presented by Chomsky (1965) in *Aspects of the Theory of Syntax*, categories such as Subject are regarded as grammatical *functions*, expressing the *relations* between constituents. Indeed, Scale and Category linguists also came to abandon the term 'element of structure' in favour of (grammatical/structural) 'function' (see Huddleston, 1966; Hudson, 1967; Halliday, 1968, 1969a). In the *Aspects* model of transformational grammar such grammatical functions were not specified on nodes in structural trees, but were deduced from dominance relations. Consider a simple sentence such as 'Tom hit Dick', which might be represented in a simplified transformational grammar tree diagram as follows:

2.67

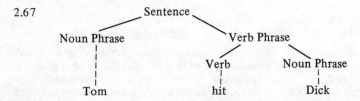

The Subject, 'Tom', is that noun phrase which is immediately dominated by the Sentence node, while the Object, 'Dick', is that noun phrase which is dominated immediately by the Verb Phrase node, and only indirectly by the Sentence node. It was argued that since these structural functions could be deduced from the shape of the tree, they would be redundant in a structural representation. Compare the diagram in 2.67 with the Scale and Category equivalent in 2.68:

2.68

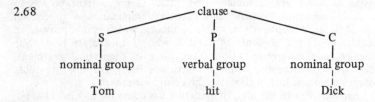

It will be noted that while the tree in 2.67 first splits the sentence (or clause: the difference here is purely terminological) into two parts, one of which is then split again, the Scale and Category tree in 2.68 has an immediate three-way division. The transformational grammar analysis takes a 'few immediate constituents' approach, the Scale and Category analysis a 'many immediate constituents' approach. The 'few immediate constituents' approach is crucial to the deduction of grammatical functions from the tree structure, since this involves the distinction between immediate and remote domination of a noun phrase by the Sentence node. If we adopt a 'many immediate constituents' approach this mechanism is not available to us, and we must therefore label the nodes explicitly with grammatical functions, if our grammar requires reference to the items which carry those functions. It is easy to show that the grammar does indeed need to make reference to items with particular functions: for instance, we must be able to pick out the item acting as Subject in order to state the rule for inversion in interrogatives:

2.69 The old man with the grey beard is Mr Smith.
2.70 Is the old man with the grey beard Mr Smith?

Hudson (1965) has argued against a 'few immediate constituents' approach, and in favour of a 'many immediate constituents' model. He points out that the 'few immediate constituents' model needs extra nodes in order to provide a mechanism for the deduction of functional relations (for instance, the tree in 2.67 has five nodes, whereas that in 2.68 has only four). This is not a very convincing argument, however, since what is presumably important (at least to those linguists whose goals include simplicity and elegance) is the overall complexity of a theory, so that other components, such as transformational rules, would also have to be taken into account.

The choice of a model with many or few immediate constituents is, of course, connected with the question, discussed earlier, of whether we can justify a rank-based grammar. A structure of the 'many immediate constituents' type, such as that in 2.68, divides the clause into its constituent groups, as viewed in a Scale and Category grammar. We have seen, however, that there are some theoretical problems with such an approach, one of which is highly relevant to the present discussion. The fact that 'hit Dick' in 2.67/2.68 can be replaced by 'did', as in 2.71 below, suggests that it is a constituent, and so favours the 'few immediate constituents' analysis in 2.67.

2.71 Tom hit Dick and so did Harry.

If, then, there is no compelling evidence that a model with many immediate constituents has any theoretical advantages over an approach with few immediate constituents, should we not opt for the latter, and leave functional relations to be deduced from structural configurations? Whether or not we decide to abandon the 'many immediate constituents' approach (and such a decision would need to take into account the arguments about rank discussed earlier), there are two lines of argument which might lead us to retain the explicit labelling of grammatical functions. The first is concerned with the goal-related considerations discussed earlier in relation to rank. It may be highly relevant, in a model oriented towards the description of text, to include labels for the functions which grammatical constituents have, since the qualitative and quantitative distribution of these functions in texts may be a major point of comparison. The second argument is a theoretical one. Consider a pair of sentences such as 2.72 and 2.73.

2.72 Behind the door would be the best place to put it.
2.73 Would behind the door be the best place to put it?

The rule for inversion in the interrogative needs to refer to the constituent 'behind the door', just as it needs to refer to 'the old man with the grey beard' in 2.69/2.70, discussed earlier. However, the rule for the formation of polar questions in a transformational grammar normally refers to 'that noun phrase which is immediately dominated by the Sentence node'. Since there would seem to be no independent motivation for labelling 'behind the door' as a noun phrase, it is difficult to see how such a rule could be made to apply to the generation of the structure of 2.73: putting this another way, it is hard to see how the correct constituent for inversion can be picked out merely in terms of dominance relations. In this type of case, at least, it seems necessary to have a grammatical function label of some kind to which the rule can refer. For a summary of the treatment of functional relations in various approaches to language (not including Scale and Category grammar) see Stockwell (1980, pp.363-70).

2.4.4 Criticisms concerned with the taxonomic nature of Scale and Category linguistics

A further criticism of Scale and Category linguistics is that it is purely taxonomic, providing a number of labels for the analysis of sentence structure, rather than predicting in an explicit manner exactly what strings of elements constitute the possible grammatical sentences of a language. Postal (1964, p.106) comments:

> There is no attempt to specify the form of rules which must assign SD [structural descriptions] and their elements to infinite sets of sentences, consequently no attempt to specify the principles of structure assignment for these rules, their possible interrelations (ordering, mutual dependency, etc.); in short no real attempt to specify the notion 'grammar of a language' in the sense of a theory which can describe exactly what utterances are and are not sentences of the language and which can assert what structure the sentences have.

This is basically a just criticism. Halliday states his aim in writing 'Categories of the theory of grammar' as 'to suggest what seem to me to be the fundamental categories of that part of General Linguistic theory which is concerned with how language works at the level of grammar' (Halliday, 1961, p.242). It is reasonable to expect that a theory of 'how language works' should state clearly how well- and ill-formedness can be predicted. We shall see later that as Halliday's thinking developed in the 1960s, the theory became rather more predictive (see Section 3.2).

There is one important point which should be made in defence of the taxonomic nature of the Scale and Category approach. Halliday saw his theory as giving rise to descriptive methods which were applicable to the analysis of texts, and there is no doubt that Scale and Category linguistics does provide a useful set of categories for this purpose, and has for this reason proved to be a highly suitable model in, for example, stylistic studies (see Section 9.2.1).

Conclusion

We have seen, in this chapter, that Halliday's work in the early 1960s built the Firthian interpretation of structure and system into a grammatical theory based on four major categories (unit, structure, system and class) and three scales (rank, delicacy and exponence) relating the categories to one another and to the textual data to be accounted for.

There are certainly some important theoretical weaknesses in Scale and Category linguistics: the taxonomic, non-predictive nature of the theory and the adoption of a rank scale as a basic principle of organization have been seen as particularly problematic. As we shall see in the following chapters, there was a considerable shift in the emphasis of Halliday's work after about 1965, and because of this the problems inherent in Scale and Category linguistics have never been satisfactorily worked out. However, it must be said that from the point of view of the descriptive application of the theory, there is much in favour of it. The set of categories it provides, including the theoretically controversial scale of rank, has proved highly applicable in textual studies, and this is an important factor for an approach which places great value on the potential of linguistic theories to give rise to methods for the description of natural language texts.

We shall see in Chapter 6 that the Scale and Category theory, in a considerably revised form, has been adopted as the basis of proposals for systemic syntax by Fawcett. Meanwhile, however, we turn to more recent developments in Halliday's own models.

3. Towards a deep systemic grammar

3.1 Introduction

The mid-1960s saw an important shift in the emphasis of Halliday's work, which led to the emergence of a model most naturally referred to as 'Systemic Grammar'. At this time, linguists had begun to realize that an examination of surface patterning in language was insufficient: in order to provide a satisfactory account of many phenomena, it was necessary to probe the 'deeper' aspects of linguistic patterning. Thus Chomsky (1964, 1965) proposed a 'deep structure' for sentences, which provided information for semantic interpretation, and was related to the 'surface structure' by a series of 'transformations'. Halliday, too, was aware of the need for a more abstract approach to the grammar, although, as we shall see, the path he took was very different from Chomsky's, being based on the concept of system as representing deep paradigmatic relations, and on a more abstract interpretation of syntagmatic (structural) relations than had hitherto appeared in his work. We shall begin by considering an important development in the concept of system.

3.2 Systems and networks

We saw in Chapter 2 that system rose from its humble beginnings in the 1956 article on Chinese, to become one of the four principal categories of the Scale and Category model. In the 1961 version of the model, systems appear to be regarded as single sets of choices available at particular places in structure. This is, of course, fully in accordance with the Firthian polysystemic principle. In the 1960s, however, the concept of system was developed further. From this time on, we find the paradigmatic patterning of language described in terms of sets of systems, or system 'networks', operating with a particular rank of unit, and sometimes a particular class of a given rank, as their 'point of origin'. Certain system networks are selected from at clause rank, others operate at the nominal class of the unit group, and so on.

The organization of sytems into networks became possible once the concept of delicacy was extended from structural relations (see Section 2.3.2.2) to systemic relations (Halliday, 1964a, p.16ff.; 1966b, p.61ff.). Delicacy ordering of systems is of two major kinds: simultaneity and dependence. Two (or more) systems are simultaneous if choices must be made independently from the systems concerned; dependence occurs where terms in different systems are hierarchically ordered, such that a selection from one system can be made only if a particular term (or terms) has been chosen from an 'earlier', less delicate system. The network diagram in Figure 3.1 shows the notational conventions which were elaborated in the 1960s to indicate systemic relations of this kind.

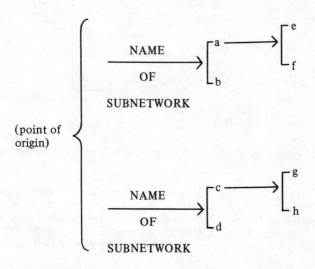

Figure 3.1: Notational conventions for simple dependence

Here we have a hypothetical system network, with a particular point of origin, in which there are two simultaneous systems (a *or* b, c *or* d) at the least delicate end of the network, simultaneity being shown by the right-facing bracketing of the systems. For any given instance of the unit (or class of unit) specified as the point of origin, a selection must be made from each of the two simultaneous systems, giving the four possible combinations of terms ac, bc, ad, bd. The terms selected by a particular clause, nominal group, or whatever, are often referred to as the 'features' of that clause, etc. We thus talk of a clause selecting, or choosing, the feature [interrogative], or a nominal group selecting the feature [singular], and so on. It is conventional to put feature labels in square brackets, and we shall adopt this convention from now on. The arrows from the feature [a] to the [e]/[f] system, and from [c] to the [g]/[h] system, indicate dependence relations: if, and only if, [a] is selected from the [a]/[b] system, then a further choice must be made between [e] and [f]; likewise, if, and only if, [c] is chosen, a choice must be made between [g] and [h]. The network thus allows nine possible combinations of 'terminal' systemic features: [eg], [eh], [ed], [fg], [fh], [fd], [bg], [bh], [bd].

The network in Figure 3.1 shows only simple dependence relations, where entry into a given system is dependent on the selection of a particular term in just *one* less delicate system. There is also the possibility of complex dependence, of two kinds, as shown in Figures 3.2 and 3.3.

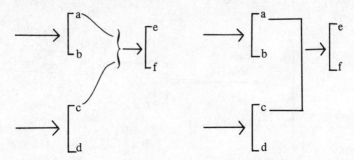

Figure 3.2: Conjunctive dependence   *Figure 3.3: Disjunctive dependence*

In Figure 3.2, the left-facing curly bracket indicates a conjunctive type of complex dependence: if the [e]/[f] system is to be entered, *both* [a] *and* [c] must have been selected from their respective systems. In Figure 3.3, the square bracketing shows a disjunctive relation: that is, *either* [a] *or* [c] must be chosen in order for a further choice to be made between [e] and [f].

In some of Halliday's system networks, the realizations (or, in terms of the earlier model, 'exponents': the term 'realization' will be discussed later) of terms in systems are shown by means of an oblique arrow leading from the term concerned. Thus in Figure 3.4 the feature [a] is realized, or expounded, as p, and [b] as q.

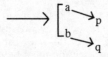

Figure 3.4: A convention for realization

We shall now consider briefly two examples of system networks illustrating the various possibilities for delicacy ordering. The network in Figure 3.5 below is based on Halliday's early account (Halliday, 1964a, pp.18-19) of 'theme' in the English clause, concerned with the function of clause-initial elements (see also Section 8.2.4).

The point of origin for this network is specified as the major clause, that is, a clause containing a Predicator (note the appeal to a structural classification of clauses here: see Section 2.4.2). There are two simultaneous systems at the least delicate end of the network: independent choices are made between (i) predicated and unpredicated theme, the former being realized by 'highlighting' of the element concerned, by means of the 'it' + 'be' + relative clause construction, as in 3.2, and (ii) the Subject or Complement as the initial, 'thematic' element (Adjunct theme is also possible,

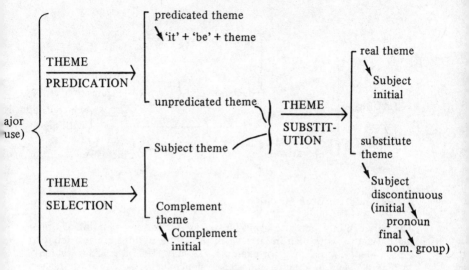

Figure 3.5: A network for theme

but is not catered for in the above network). This gives four initial possibilities, illustrated in Halliday's examples given as 3.1 - 3.4 below.

    3.1   The Smiths are having a party this evening.

                                     ([Subject theme, unpredicated])

    3.2   It's the Smiths that are having a party this evening.

                                       ([Subject theme, predicated])

    3.3   A party the Smiths are having this evening.

                                ([Complement theme, unpredicated])

    3.4   It's a party the Smiths are having this evening.

                                ([Complement theme, predicated])

As Halliday points out, 3.5 has the same systemic description as 3.1, up to
the point in delicacy given by the two simultaneous systems so far discussed.

    3.5   They're having a party this evening, the Smiths.

We can, however, differentiate between 3.1 and 3.5 if we propose a further
system of 'theme substitution', entry to which is dependent on the selection
of both [unpredicated theme] and [Subject theme] from the initial,
simultaneous systems. 3.1 then has [real theme], with the Subject initial
in the clause, while 3.5 has [substitute theme], the Subject being discontin-
uously realized as a pronoun ('they') in initial position and a nominal
group with a noun as head ('the Smiths') in final position.

    For an example of disjunctive complex dependence we turn to a network
for the 'mood' options of English, which were inserted into the text of an
article (Halliday, 1966b) when this was reprinted in a collection of
Halliday's papers (Kress, 1976). Further discussion of mood can be found
in Section 8.2.3.

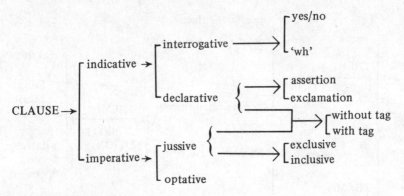

Figure 3.6: A network for mood

The network in Figure 3.6 again illustrates the notions of point of origin (here, 'clause', although in later work the mood options are restricted to independent clauses: see, for example, Halliday, 1971a, p.173 = Halliday, 1973a, p.56), simultaneity and simple dependence. A clause (or rather, more accurately, an independent clause) is either [indicative] (having an expressed Subject) or [imperative] (having no expressed Subject). Clauses which are [indicative] go on to select either [interrogative] or [declarative]. Interrogative clauses are either [yes/no] (polar interrogatives) or ['wh'] (introduced by wh-words such as 'who', 'what', 'where'); declarative clauses select either [assertion] or [exclamation]. Clauses with the feature [imperative] can be either [jussive] or [optative], the latter type having non-permissive 'let' and a non-second person nominal. Jussive imperatives are either [exclusive] or [inclusive], the latter being realized as 'let' plus a second person pronoun (that is, 'let us' or 'let's'). The disjunctive entry condition to the [without tag/with tag] system expresses the generalization that declarative clauses (whether assertions or exclamations) or jussive clauses (whether exclusive or inclusive) can, but need not, have a tag. Examples of the combinations of features permitted by the network (not provided by Halliday) are given below.

3.6   Did John go to London?   ([yes/no])
3.7   Who went to London?   (['wh'])
3.8   John went to London.   ([assertion, without tag])
3.9   John went to London, didn't he?   ([assertion, with tag])
3.10 What a long time John spent in London!   ([exclamation,
                                                                  without tag])
3.11 What a long time John spent in London, didn't he!
                                                         ([exclamation, with tag])
3.12 Go to London.   ([exclusive, without tag])
3.13 Go to London, will you.   ([exclusive, with tag])
3.14 Let's go to London.   ([inclusive, without tag])
3.15 Let's go to London, shall we?   ([inclusive, with tag])
3.16 Let him go to London.   ([optative] – non-permissive interpret-
                                                           ation of 'let')

It should be noted that a system network in fact constitutes a set of hypotheses about what is and what is not possible in the language under description. For instance, the networks discussed above are claimed to operate at the rank of clause, and not, or not necessarily, at other ranks. Further, the dependence relations predict that certain combinations of features are permissible, but that others are impermissible. We shall, it is claimed, find declarative and jussive clauses with question tags attached, but interrogative and optative clauses are barred from accepting such tags. The ungrammaticality of the following sentences is thus correctly predicted for the variety of English for which the network was written (Standard English English), though not necessarily for other varieties.

3.17 *Did John go to London, didn't he?
3.18 *Let John go to London, shall we?   (non-permissive 'let')

A further point worthy of note is that the concept of a system network involves some degree of deviation from the Firthian interpretation of the polysystemic principle, though it certainly does not entail the abandonment of the principle. For Firth the environment of systems was wholly syntagmatic, individual systems being set up for particular places in structure. For Halliday, on the other hand, the environment is at least partly paradigmatic, in that the 'entry conditions' for a system may, as we have seen, involve the selection of other features from less delicate parts of the network. The syntagmatic environmental conditioning still remains, however, in the concept of 'point of origin': each system network operates at a particular rank of unit, so that a fresh set of choices is available each time we meet another instance of this rank (and perhaps, also, a particular class) of unit in progressing along the syntagmatic axis.

3.3 'Deep' grammar and the priority of systemic relations

In a short but seminal article (Halliday, 1966b), which could be taken to mark the emergence of 'Systemic' Linguistics out of the previous Scale and Category model, Halliday reinterprets the distinction between 'deep' and 'surface' aspects of linguistic patterning, which plays such a large part in transformational generative accounts of that period.

Halliday takes up the point, made in his 1961 'Categories' article and discussed in Section 2.3.2.2, that the relation of *order* between the elements of structure of a given unit is different from, and more abstract or 'deeper' than, the *sequence* relation between surface exponents in syntagmatic combination. Indeed, as we have seen, sequence is only one possible way in which structural relations may be expounded. Thus exponents of particular grammatical classes, in sequence relation, may be said to represent the 'surface' structure, while structural relations between abstract elements such as S, P, C and A in the clause (now seen as structural *functions:* see the discussion in Section 2.4) represent the deeper aspects of syntagmatic patterning. The two are connected by realization (formerly exponence).

Halliday then goes on to generalize the notion of deep grammar to the paradigmatic axis. Just as structures represent deep syntagmatic relations, so systems, it is suggested, represent deep paradigmatic relations. Systems embody sets of options available in a given functional environment (for example, the function Subject provides one environment for the systemic choice between singular and plural nominal groups). The specification of systems thus presupposes a representation of deep syntagmatic relations, and for that reason systems themselves are at a relatively deep level.

Halliday now takes the most crucial step in the development of his model, by suggesting that paradigmatic relations are, in fact, primary, in that they constitute the basic, underlying relations of language:

> . . . it might be useful to consider some possible consequences of regarding systemic description as the underlying form of representation, if it turned out that the structural description could be shown to be derivable from it. (Halliday, 1966b, p.62)

Structural relations would, then, be derived by the process of realization from a specification of the selections made from systems. The according of priority to paradigmatic relations stands in sharp contrast to the contemporary transformational generative approach, which concentrated almost exclusively on syntagmatic patterning.

Not only is system now the most fundamental category of the theory; Halliday also makes it clear that terms in systems are viewed as being closely related to their underlying semantic properties:

> . . . underlying grammar is 'semantically significant' grammar, whether the semantics is regarded, with Lamb, as 'input', or, with Chomsky, as interpretation. What is being considered, therefore, is that that part of the grammar which is as it were 'closest to' the semantics may be represented in terms of systemic features. (Halliday, 1966b, pp.62-3)

This is an extremely important statement. Halliday's work had, from the beginning, always insisted on the meaningfulness of linguistic elements, building as it did on the work of Firth; but here we have an explicit claim that grammars can be written so as to reflect, at least in part, the specifically semantic meaning (to use a Firthian distinction) of formal choices, and that such a grammar can and should take the system as its most fundamental category.

3.4 The functional components hypothesis

From about 1967 onwards, the concept of deep paradigmatic and syntagmatic relations became linked with what was to become a key feature of Halliday's theory, namely the postulation of 'functional components' of the grammar. Halliday (1968, p.207) observes that the multiple functions of language have often been referred to in the literature, for example in the work of Malinowski, in the classification of function by Bühler (1934) into 'representational', 'expressive' and 'conative' types, and in the development of Bühler's classification by the Prague School linguists (see Vachek, 1966). What is needed, according to Halliday, is a functional theory which, rather than being directed towards sociological or psychological investigations, is intended to illuminate the internal structure of language itself, explaining why language is patterned as it is, and not in one of the many other possible ways. It is in this sense, primarily, that Halliday uses the term 'functional' in formulating a theory of language.

Halliday's claim is that the grammar of a language (which, as we have seen, is regarded as 'semantically significant' grammar, and is indeed often referred to by Halliday as the 'meaning potential' of the language) is itself organized along functional lines. Specifically, the claim is that 'when we examine the meaning potential of the language itself, we find that the vast numbers of options embodied in it combine into a very few relatively independent "networks"; and these networks of options correspond to certain basic functions of language' (Halliday, 1970b, p.142). Similarly, in a slightly earlier article we find the following:

> If we represent the set of options available to the speaker in the grammar of the English clause, these options group themselves into a small number of subsets, distinct from one another in that, while within each group of options there is a very high degree of interdependence, between any two groups the amount of interdependence, though by no means negligible, is very much less. This provides a syntactic basis for the concept of language functions, and suggests how the diversity of functions recognizable at the semantic levels may be organized in the course of realization. (Halliday, 1968, p.207).

Thus, although the functions themselves are semantic in origin, they are said to be reflected in the grammar as blocks of options with very few connections between the blocks.

In his earliest exposition of the theory (Halliday, 1968) Halliday recognizes four functional components of the grammar, which he calls experiential, logical, discoursal and speech-functional or interpersonal. Later (for instance in Halliday, 1970b, 1973a) there is a certain amount of renaming: the experiential and logical are now seen as subsumed under the label 'ideational', and the discoursal component is renamed as 'textual'; the 'interpersonal' component remains.

The *ideational* component 'serves for the expression of "content": that is, of the speaker's experience of the real world, including the inner world of his own consciousness' (1970b, p.143). Within this, the *experiential* subcomponent is concerned with the expression of processes, participants in those processes, circumstances, qualities, and the like. The *logical* subcomponent 'provides for the linguistic expression of such universal relations as those of "and", "or", negation and implication' (1968, p.209).

The *interpersonal* component 'serves to establish and maintain social relations: for the expression of social roles, which include the communication roles created by language itself – for example the roles of questioner or respondent, which we take on by asking or answering a question; and also for getting things done, by means of the interaction between one person and another' (1970b, p.143). The interpersonal component also includes the speaker's comments on the probability, relevance, etc. of the message, and his attitude towards it.

The *textual* component 'enables the speaker or writer to construct "texts", or connected passages of discourse that is situationally relevant; and enables the listener or reader to distinguish a text from a random set of sentences' (1970b, p.143). Through the textual function, language provides 'for making links with itself and with features of the situation in which it is used'.

No single one of these functions is considered by Halliday as more basic than any other, nor as more abstract.

It is not necessary to argue that one function is more abstract, or 'deeper' than another; all are semantically relevant. (Halliday, 1970b, p.165)

Halliday's emphasis on the equal importance of the non-ideational aspects of language function contrasts with the attitude prevalent among the more traditional approaches, viz. the primacy of 'cognitive' meanings. In Halliday's scheme, the construction of an utterance (except perhaps in the case of ritualistic utterances such as greetings) involves simultaneous selection of options from all the functional components.

At the rank of clause, the relevant options are those in transitivity (ideational), mood and modality (interpersonal), and theme (textual). We shall discuss Halliday's accounts of these areas in Chapter 8; a very brief summary will therefore suffice at this point. Transitivity is 'concerned with the type of process expressed in the clause, with the participants in this process, animate and inanimate, and with the various attributes and circumstances of the process and the participants' (Halliday, 1967b, p.38). In the area of mood 'the principal options are declarative, interrogative (yes/no and wh- types), and imperative, etc' (Halliday, 1970b, p.160 – see also the network given in Figure 3.6 earlier). Modality, closely related to mood, is concerned with the expression of degrees of probability. The area of theme, as we saw from the network given in Figure 3.5, is concerned with the structuring of the clause as a message. It is closely linked to, though distinct from, a second kind of information structuring, into 'given' and 'new' information, as signalled by intonational means in English.

So far, we have considered the functional components only in relation to the paradigmatic axis, as represented by system networks. Halliday also proposes that the deep syntagmatic relations embodied in structure are functionally organized. Whereas his earlier work had proposed a structural description of the clause in terms of just one set of elements, S, P, C and A, Halliday now suggests that structures are composed of several strands, which are integrated in the process of realization, to give the final 'surface' structure. Halliday sometimes uses the analogy of polyphonic music, in which several strands or lines are interwoven to form the complete musical fabric. Each strand in the linguistic structure is contributed by one of the functional components, and consists of a complex of 'functions', 'functional roles' or 'micro-functions'. We have now used the term 'function' in three related, but distinct, senses: the non-technical meaning which can be glossed as the overall uses to which language can be put; a component of the grammar (ideational, interpersonal, textual) reflecting external function; and a role forming a structural element in a strand contributed by one of the functional components. It will be as well to look at this potentially confusing set of meanings in rather more detail, and particularly at the relationship between the last two.

In Chapter 2, it was pointed out that the elements of structure proposed in the Scale and Category model (for example, S, P, C and A for the clause) were more accurately regarded as grammatical 'relations' or 'functions'. We have also seen that from 1966 onwards the semantic orientation of the grammar becomes clearer. It is not surprising, then, that other functional relations, of a semantically orientated kind, became incorporated into the grammar. Such relations are proposed for each of the key areas, of transitivity, mood and theme, which constitute the functional component networks at clause rank. These 'functional roles', which we shall now discuss, are the elements making up the strands of structure contributed by each functional component.

Transitivity is, as we have seen, concerned with the relations between processes and their participants. There is a functional relationship between types of process (for example, action process) and types of participant involved in such processes (for instance, the Actor performing the action, and the Goal towards which the action is directed). The ideational (or, more narrowly, the experiential) function (or functional component) thus provides a strand of structure consisting of functional elements such as Actor, Process and Goal.

The mood systems distinguish initially between the clause types indicative and imperative, and then between declarative and interrogative types of indicative clause. The functional role Modal, contributed by the interpersonal component, has the function of carrying these distinctions, that part of the clause which is not concerned with showing mood distinctions being the Residual (in Halliday, 1968) or Propositional (in Halliday, 1973b) element. Within the Modal element, the mood distinctions are shown by the presence or ordering of the Subject and the finite verb. Consider Halliday's example (1973b, p.362, p.43 in Halliday, 1973a) given in 3.19 below.

3.19

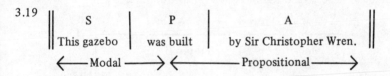

The fact that the clause is indicative in mood is signalled by the presence of the Subject; further, the fact that S precedes the finite verb shows that the clause is declarative rather than interrogative (see the mood network in Figure 3.6). Compare Halliday's example with the following:

3.20

P	(S)	A	
Was (this gazebo) built		by Sir Christopher Wren?	

←— Modal —→ ←———————— Propositional ————→

Here, the Subject follows the finite part of the Predicator, being sandwiched between the two halves of P (inclusion in a discontinuous structure being conventionally indicated by round brackets). The Subject is, then, 'that nominal which, together with the finite verbal element, fulfils a modal role in the realization of speech function; the two together form a constituent specified by the mood systems' (Halliday, 1967c, p.213). There is thus an intimate relation between the functional roles Modal/Propositional and the SPCA functional structure of the clause: indeed, Halliday appears to regard SPCA structure as an interpersonal matter (see Halliday, 1969a, p.87; 1973b, p.362 = 1973a, p.43). As he makes clear (1967c, p.213; 1970b, pp.159-60) it is the 'surface' or 'grammatical' Subject which is derived from the interpersonal component: the 'deep' or 'logical' Subject is the Actor of an action clause, and is derived, as we have seen, from the transitivity relations of the ideational component; the so-called 'psycho-logical' Subject is the Theme, derived from the textual component, to which we now turn.

The textual component contributes the functional roles Theme and Rheme, the Theme being 'what is being talked about, the point of depart-ure for the clause as a message' (1967c, p.212), and the Rheme constituting the rest of the clause. Also derived from the textual component are the functional roles Given and New, representing a distribution of information into that which the speaker assumes to be available to the hearer and that which is being presented as new. These roles, however, strictly operate in the structure of the phonological unit 'tone group' rather than in that of the clause.

Let us now return to Halliday's example, 3.19, in order to consider more fully the functional strands of which the overall clause structure is composed. A fuller analysis (adapted slightly from that given by Halliday (1973b, p.362 = 1973a, p.43)) is given in 3.21: it is assumed that the clause is spoken as one tone group, with the tonic on the last syllable, for the purpose of allocating the Given/New elements of functional structure.

3.21   This gazebo was built by Sir Christopher Wren.

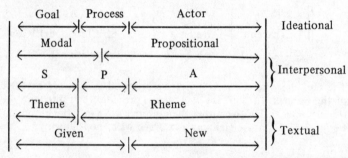

Such an analysis shows clearly that each part of the clause serves a number of functions, derived from the different functional components. The group 'this gazebo', for instance, has the complex of functional roles: Goal/ (part of) Modal (S)/ Theme/ (part of) Given. These functional roles are themselves reflexes of the systemic choices made by the clause in the networks of transitivity, mood and theme, and by the tone group in the information distribution network. The realization of these systemic choices, ultimately as a single integrated structure, involves the 'hooking up' of the functional roles, that is their conflation into bundles and the mapping of these bundles on to surface constituents. There are certain 'unmarked' conflations of functional roles, which correspond to the selection of unmarked features from the system networks, that is, those 'default' options which are chosen if there is no good reason to do other-wise. For instance, the unmarked counterpart of the passive clause in 3.21 is the active clause in 3.22.

3.22 Sir Christopher Wren built this gazebo.

In 3.22 the functions of Actor, (part of) Modal and Theme are all carried by the Subject 'Sir Christopher Wren', and this is the most 'neutral' combination of functional roles. The difference between active and passive, in functional terms, is thus that Modal and Theme are conflated with Actor in the active, but with Goal in the passive.

3.5 Realization

We have seen that the path from systemic choice to the formation of the final grammatical structure involves the specification of the conflation and ordering of functional roles derived from the components of the grammar. We must now consider this realizational process in more detail.

The term 'realization' was borrowed by Halliday from Lamb (1964), to replace 'exponence' in the Scale and Category model. Halliday's own discussion of realization is somewhat scanty. The only serious attempt to specify formal realization rules (or 'statements', as Halliday calls them) for the functional component networks is to be found in an article (Halliday, 1969a) in which three types of rule are explicitly proposed.

> In some cases [. . .] the realization statement merely specifies the presence of a certain structural function; but in other cases it may have the effect of ordering one function with respect to another or to initial or final position in the syntagm. But it may also specify the conflation of two functions into a single element of structure. (Halliday, 1969a, p.82)

A further type of rule is implicit in the statement that certain systemic features can be realized by the specification of a particular class of unit.

In this article Halliday considers the structural derivation of the clause in 3.23, taken from a recording of spontaneous informal conversation (notational conventions for intonation as in Halliday, 1970a: see also examples 2.10 and 2.11 in Chapter 2, and the discussion in Section 7.3.3).

3.23 //1 well then *surely* //1 he must have made a fair amount
of *mo*ney //

Halliday presents networks of transitivity, mood and thematization, as well as two other textual networks, for information distribution and cohesion. He also gives a table of realization statements, showing exactly how any given systemic choice is reflected in the insertion, concatenation and conflation of functions. Here we shall consider just two portions of these networks, and some of the associated realization rules, as an illustration of the three types of rule proposed.

Halliday expands the mood network to include options in the area of 'modalization' (later to be called 'modality' – see Chapter 8), that is, the choice of expressions relating to the speaker's assessment of probabilities (modal verbs such as 'may', 'must', adverbs such as 'possibly', 'surely'). He also expands the thematization network to account for the possibility of a 'complex theme' such as 'well then surely' in 3.23. These parts of the network are given overleaf in Figure 3.7.

From the portion of the network shown in Figure 3.7, the clause in

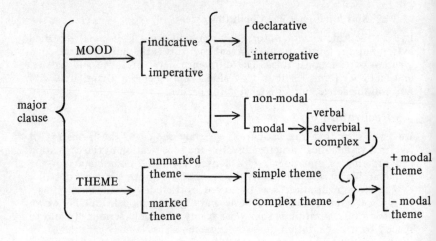

Figure 3.7: A network for clause options

3.23 selects the following features (non-terminal features are given in round brackets) : [(indicative), declarative, (modal, complex, unmarked theme, complex theme), modal theme]. Certain structural functions are present by virtue of choices made outside that part of the network considered here: for instance, the fact that the clause is [major] means that Predicator and Process have been inserted and conflated into the same constituent, and that an initial Theme has been inserted.

Let us now consider the realization rules for the mood and modalization options.

Feature	Realization rule
[indicative]	insert Subject
[declarative]	concatenate Predicator with Subject
[modal]	insert Modality
[complex]	insert Modality$_1$, conflate with Predicator

The application of these rules gives rise to a partial structure as follows:

Subject ˆ Predicator/Process/Modality$_1$ · Modality

where ˆ represents an ordered relation and · an unordered relation between the functional roles (see also Section 2.3.2.2), and / represents conflation of the functional roles on either side of it. The functional role introduced by the modalization option is thus split into two, one part being conflated with the Predicator, the other being as yet unordered with respect to the other functional roles.

The realization rules for the thematic options selected by 3.23 are as follows:

Feature	Realization rule
[unmarked theme]	conflate Subject with Theme
[complex theme]	insert $Theme_1$ initially (concatenate tone group boundary with it)
[modal theme]	insert $Theme_2$, concatenate with $Theme_1$, conflate Modality with it

The application of these rules to the partial structure generated so far yields the new structure below:

$$// \hat{} Theme_1 \hat{} Theme_2 / Modality \hat{} Subject/Theme \hat{} Predicator/Process/ Modality_1$$

This does indeed give us the correct arrangement of functional roles, as seen in 3.24.

3.24   well   then   surely   he   must have made ...

$// Theme_1$ $Theme_2/$ Subject/   Predicator/Process/
      Modality   Theme $Modality_1$

Halliday's account gives all the realization rules for the complete generation of the structure of 3.23 in terms of bundles of functional roles; our limited exemplification will, however, have sufficed to show the principles involved. It should be noted that the order of application of realization rules in Halliday's scheme is determined by the delicacy ordering of the systemic features being realized. For instance, [indicative] must be realized before [declarative] (otherwise there would be no Subject for the realization rule associated with [indicative] to operate on), but the rules for [declarative] and [modal] may be applied in either order, since the two features are from simultaneous systems.

Halliday's realization rule types have been expanded by Berry (1977) into six types, which must apply in a fixed order. Certain important differences between Berry's account of realization and Halliday's arise from the fact that Berry (1975, p.77ff.) does not consider elements of structure, such as S, P, C and A, as themselves being structural functions. Rather, she attempts to marry the non-functional approach of Halliday's 1961 account with the concept of strands of functional structure, by treating elements such as S, P, C, A as generalizations from the unmarked conflations of functions. Thus the Subject, in the unmarked case of an active declarative clause, represents Actor, Mood Marker[1] (corresponding to the first half of Halliday's Modal functional role) and Theme. In cases where one or more of these functions is carried by a different surface constituent (as, for instance, in the passive, where, as we have seen, the Goal is Subject), we must decide which strand of structure to take as defining the Subject, the normal solution being to take the mood-derived strand as primary.

There is certainly something to be said for Berry's approach. The definition of Subject as a mood indicator in Halliday's work betrays a somewhat anglocentric approach: attempts to characterize the notion of Subject cross-linguistically (see Comrie, 1981, p.98ff.) have led to the proposal that prototypically the Subject is the intersection of what, in terms of functional roles as discussed here, would be Actor and Theme. Furthermore, it could be argued that the mood function may not be the best way of characterizing the Subject even for English: for instance, dependent clauses may have a Subject, which does not, however, mark mood. There are other syntactic properties which could equally well be taken as criteria for Subject in English: in finite clauses, the Subject shows person and number concord with the finite verb, and can participate in relations of the type illustrated by 3.25 and 3.26, where the Subject, 'John', of the dependent clause in 3.25 is, in transformational generative grammar terms, 'raised' to give 3.26.

   3.25 I believe that John is a fool.
   3.26 I believe John to be a fool.

The existence of such criteria for Subject in English contrasts with the lack of syntactic (as opposed to semantic) criteria for functional roles such as Actor, Goal and the like. This point will be taken up in greater detail in Chapter 5; meanwhile, we should note that, if substantiable, it provides evidence for a separation between categories such as Subject, which we may regard as syntactic functions, and categories such as Actor and Goal which, we shall argue, are semantic functions.

   Correlated with the distinction between elements of structure and functional roles is Berry's differentiation between the *inclusion* of functions in a partial structure, and the *insertion* of elements of structure to realize bundles of functions. Such a distinction is especially important in accounting for the fact that although particular types of process have particular numbers of inherent roles associated with them, there is sometimes a choice of whether to represent a given role in the surface structure or not. Thus, for example, the functional role of Goal, as well as that of Actor, is inherently associated with the process of 'throwing' (in that we conceive of this action as involving both someone who is throwing and something which is thrown), but the Goal may either be explicitly represented in the surface structure as in 3.27, or implicit as in 3.28 (Berry, 1975, p.158).

   3.27 Cover point threw the ball wildly to the wicket-keeper.
   3.28 Cover point threw wildly to the wicket-keeper.

Inclusion statements must, of course, be ordered before insertion statements. There are, in fact, two other types of rule which operate on functions before we reach the stage of inserting elements of structure. Firstly, any functions which appear in two or more discontinuous parts in the final structure must be split up by means of *discontinuity* realization statements. This addition to Halliday's scheme (apparently suggested by remarks made by Halliday in a lecture in Nottingham – see Berry, 1977, p.136) has the advantage of showing explicitly that the discontinuous parts belong to the same function. It will be remembered that Halliday (1969a) simply added a further function in cases of discontinuity, indicating its relationship with related functions only by the labelling (for example, Modality/Modality$_1$, Theme/Theme$_1$/Theme$_2$). Once the functions have been introduced, and split up if necessary, certain functions are brought together into a single bundle by *conflation* realization statements identical in kind to those proposed by Halliday. Next comes the *insertion* of elements of structure to realize conflated bundles of functions, as mentioned above. Only at this stage does *concatenation* occur: in order to parallel Halliday's statements concerning, for example, the ordering of Subject and Predicator, Berry must, of course, consider concatenation rules as applying to elements of structure rather than to functions as such. The final stage in the realization process at the grammatical level is the application of *particularization* realization rules, which specify the particular classes or sub-classes of linguistic unit which realize the elements of structure. This is an important development of the possibilities hinted at in Halliday's scheme: the realization process as formalized by Halliday stopped short at the stage of generation of the correct ordering of bundles of functions (including, of course, those which might be thought of as elements of structure), although the possibility of more detailed rules was adumbrated by the claim that certain transitivity choices 'specified' the class of verb used. In order to complete the generation process, we need rules which tell us precisely what the realization of the functions will be, in terms of formal items. This can be achieved by particularization rules of greater and greater refinement.

In order to illustrate the six types of realization rule proposed by Berry, let us now consider again the realization of the mood and modalization options selected in the generation of example 3.23. The system network for mood and modalization given by Berry is very similar to Halliday's, despite differences in labelling. The following version is based on the

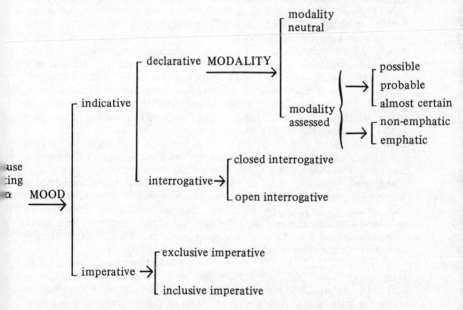

Figure 3.8: A network for mood and modality based on Berry's work

network given by Berry (1975, p.190), augmented by a distinction which she discusses elsewhere (Berry, 1977, p.34), between 'emphatic' and 'non-emphatic' modality, corresponding exactly to that between Halliday's 'verbal' and 'complex' modalization (that is, modality expressed as modal verb, or as modal verb plus adverb). In this network, [modality neutral] parallels Halliday's [non-modal]; and [possible], [probable] and [almost certain] are more delicate specifications of degrees of modality.

The clause in 3.23 has the following features from Berry's network: [(indicative, declarative, modality assessed), almost certain, emphatic]. All independent (that is α) clauses will have the Process and Mood Marker functions introduced by inclusion rules. The selection of the feature [modality assessed] triggers an inclusion rule which introduces the function Degree of certainty. This function is then split into Degree of certainty[1] and Degree of certainty[2] by a discontinuity rule sensitive to the feature [emphatic]. Degree of certainty[1] is then conflated with the Process function. Next come the insertion rules, which insert the element S in response to the feature [indicative], and an Adjunct to realize the second half of the modality function, Degree of certainty[2]. The element P will also be inserted in response to the feature [major], which is not of concern to us here. The feature [modality assessed] specifies the insertion of an auxiliary element in the structure of the verbal group realizing P. A concatenation rule now ensures that since the clause is declarative, S will be ordered before P. Finally, particularization rules will specify that the auxiliary verb is realized as one of the class of modal verbs expressing the degree of certainty [almost certain], and the Adjunct as one of the class of adverbs also expressing this degree of certainty. Note that more delicate distinctions within the modality network would be needed for us to be able to specify the actual lexical items, 'must' and 'surely', as opposed to, for example, 'should' and 'certainly' (see Halliday, 1970c, also Chapter 8).

The development of Halliday's proposals by Berry has certain implications for the relationship between realization and the delicacy ordering of systems. In Halliday's scheme, the order of realization is identical with the order of delicacy relations between systems: a less delicate choice is realized before a more delicate choice, but simultaneous choices can be realized in any order. There is, of course, an intrinsic order imposed on the realization processes relating to any one function: clearly, a function cannot be conflated or concatenated with another function until it has itself been introduced by an appropriate insertion statement. As we have seen, Berry's six types of statement are viewed as applying in a fixed order, and again the order is constrained by logical considerations. Berry (1977, p.41) does, however, make one important additional point, namely that 'a term specifying the inclusion of one function may well be more delicate than terms specifying the inclusion, insertion and particularisation of another function'. For instance, the term in the transitivity network specifying the inclusion of Actor and Goal in particular types of clause is more delicate than the term which includes the function Process.

Berry (1977; p.35 ff.) also expands considerably on brief comments by Halliday (1966b, p.66) concerning the relationship between realization and rank. As we have seen, particular ranks of unit provide the point of origin for particular system networks. Further, the realizations of systemic features have particular ranks of unit as their domain. The rank providing the point of origin for a system may, but need not, be identical with the rank providing the domain of realization for terms in that system. For instance, as Berry points out, the mood network containing the system [declarative]/[interrogative] has the clause as its point of origin, and the terms in the system are also realized within the clause as domain, by the relative ordering of elements of clause structure. The system [possible]/ [probable]/[almost certain] is also in a network with the clause as point of origin, but the realization of its terms involves the specification of a particular class of auxiliary verb, at the rank of word. Other examples of the relationship between realization and rank can be found in Berry's account.

3.6 Concluding remarks

We have seen in this chapter that the period from 1964 to about 1971 was a crucial one in the development of the Hallidayan model. An important advance on Firth's interpretation of the category 'system' was the linking of systems into networks, with dependency relations, simple or complex, between the individual systems. Such networks came to be seen as representing those deep paradigmatic relations of language which were 'semantically relevant'. Deep syntagmatic relations were now encapsulated in multi-layered structures consisting of functional roles, each strand of the structure being contributed by one of the 'functional components' of the grammar. The concept of realization, linking systemic choices to structures, was developed more fully, so that the grammar became at least partly generative, in the sense of assigning an explicit structural description (albeit a *functional* description) to sentences. The model current in 1970 can thus be described, if somewhat inelegantly, as 'semantically orientated systemic functional grammar'.

We shall see, in the next chapter, that Halliday's more recent work has continued to centre around a functional model in which semantic phenomena play an increasingly important part. For this reason, we shall delay presentation of a critique of the model until Chapter 5.

4. Sociological semantics

4.1 Introduction

We saw in Chapter 3 that one of the most important characteristics of Hallidayan linguistics in the late 1960s was its functional orientation, and in particular the claim that the very design of the grammar itself reflects the basic needs which language is called upon to serve, namely the expression of experience (ideational function) and the expression of social roles and attitudes (interpersonal function), together with the language's internal function of organizing messages into coherent texts (textual function). In the 1970s Halliday has continued to emphasize the functional basis of language, but has attempted to integrate this approach into a wider perspective on the language system.

As might be expected from the Firthian origins of Hallidayan linguistics, the perspective is sociological: the language system is regarded as one component of a sociolinguistic complex which also includes the concepts of text, register (varieties of language differentiated according to the characteristics of the user: see for example Halliday, McIntosh and Strevens, 1964; Gregory, 1967; Ellis & Ure, 1969; Hasan, 1973; Gregory & Carroll, 1978), code (see for instance Bernstein, 1971) and situation type, all related to, and deriving from, the social structure of the culture. This emphasis on *function* in a *sociolinguistic* perspective is apparent in the titles of two of Halliday's publications which will form the main material for the discussion in this chapter: *Explorations in the Functions of Language* (Halliday, 1973a) and *Language as Social Semiotic* (Halliday, 1978). The title of a further publication to be discussed here, *Learning How to Mean* (Halliday, 1975a), highlights two more aspects of Halliday's thinking in the 1970s: the increasing emphasis on the centrality of meaning, and an interest in the child's learning of his native language, again seen in functional and semantic terms rather than in the more familiar psycholinguistic perspective.

In this chapter, we shall first examine Halliday's proposal for a layer of sociosemantic networks 'above' the lexicogrammatical stratum. We shall then consider the relationship between the linguistic system and the other components of Halliday's sociolinguistic model. Finally we shall discuss briefly Halliday's work on child language acquisition. The aim here will be to present the main features of the model without much critical comment; in Chapter 5 we shall attempt a critical appraisal of the sociologically oriented semantic functional approach.

4.2 Sociosemantic networks

As we saw in Chapter 1, Malinowski considered language as 'a mode of action', and Firth, developing Malinowski's ideas into a more specifically linguistic theory, saw language primarily in relation to its place in the social life of man. Halliday's work in the 1970s is descended directly from this Firthian tradition (note the title of his contribution to the Schools Council Programme in Linguistics and English Teaching Papers, *Language and Social Man* (Halliday, 1974, reprinted in a slightly modified form as Chapters 1 and 13 of Halliday, 1978)). Language is seen from an '*inter*-organism' perspective, concerned with behaviour in social interaction, rather than from the '*intra*-organism' perspective of contemporary Chomskyan linguistics, which is concerned chiefly with the linguistic 'knowledge' stored in people's heads (see Halliday, 1974, pp.8-12 = 1978, pp.12-16; Parret, 1974, pp.84-5, 112 = Halliday 1978, pp.37-8, 56-7). These matters will be discussed further in Chapter 10.

Two of the papers in *Explorations in the Functions of Language* are particularly important in setting out Halliday's ideas on how we might characterize language as behaviour; these are 'Language in a social perspective' (Halliday, 1971a = 1973a, pp.48-71) and 'Towards a sociological semantics' (Halliday, 1972 = 1973a, pp.72-102). The basic position can be summarized as follows. As members of a particular culture, with a particular social structure, each of us has available to him a range of behavioural options (a 'behaviour potential') for use in certain types of social context. This behaviour potential constitutes what we 'can do', and encompasses non-linguistic as well as linguistic behaviour. What Halliday wishes to study is what we can do with *language*, and this he equates with what the speaker 'can mean', that is with the range of 'meaning potential' available to him. This meaning potential is thus the linguistic realization of part of the 'higher' behaviour potential. The meaning potential (or, rather, a given selection from it) is in turn realized in the actual forms of language (lexical items and syntactic constructions), as what the speaker 'can say'. Finally, of course, the lexicogrammar is itself realized as combinations of phonological, and ultimately phonetic, elements.

> The potential of language is a meaning potential. This meaning potential is the linguistic realization of the behavioural potential; 'can mean' is 'can do' when translated into language. The meaning potential is in turn realized in the language system as lexicogrammatical potential, which is what the speaker 'can say'. (Halliday, 1971a, p.168 = 1973a, p.51)

An important shift of position is implicit in this quotation: the term 'meaning potential' was originally used for the functionally based networks of the lexicogrammar (those of transitivity, mood and theme); now, however, it is being used for the potential available at a new, sociosemantic level. In the new model, the sociosemantics is related both 'upwards' to a network of behavioural options which are themselves outside language, and 'downwards' to the syntax and lexis of the language, the relations involved being realizational in nature:

'can do' behavioural potential	realized by	'can mean' sociosemantics (*linguistic* behaviour potential)	realized by	'can say' lexicogrammatical potential

In order to ensure a sound basis for his sociological semantics, Halliday insists (1971a, pp.169, 180 ff. = 1973a, pp.52, 63 ff.; 1972, p.79 ff. in 1973a) that the meaning choices should relate to behavioural options which are interpretable, and are predicted to be important, on the basis of some social theory. In other words, 'in sociological linguistics the criteria for selecting the areas of study are sociological' (Halliday, 1972, p.80 in 1973a). The theory on which Halliday bases his discussions is that of Bernstein (see for example Bernstein, 1971), in which language is held to play a crucial role in the socialization of the developing child. What Halliday is aiming to do, then, is to provide accounts of the meaning potentials available in behavioural environments defined in terms of the categories of a social theory. The categories may relate to generalized social contexts of importance in the culture (for example, the context of mother/child inter- action which is central to Bernstein's theories of socialization), or to situation types or settings in which structured units of social interaction can be identified (such as shop transactions, doctor/patient interviews). The requirement that the social contexts and settings studied should be significant in terms of some social theory imposes a severe restriction on the scope of such investigations, in that by no means all of the linguistic activity engaged in by adult speakers in the course of their everyday lives takes place in such definable contexts and settings (see Halliday, 1971a, p.179 = 1973a, p.62; 1972, p.92 in 1973a). We shall see in Chapter 5 that this aspect of the sociosemantic model has attracted criticism.

The social input to the semantics, then, is a set of contexts and settings. The linguistic output is seen in terms of the functional component net- works of transitivity, mood and theme which constitute the lexicogrammar and, as we have seen, are claimed to underlie all the many specific uses to which language can be put. The task, as envisaged by Halliday, is thus to specify both the meaning options available in a given context or setting, and the possible combinations of lexicogrammatical options which can realize the semantic choices.

The options at the sociosemantic and lexicogrammatical levels, and indeed also those at the phonological level and at the non-linguistic level of behavioural choice, are seen in terms of system networks (1971a, p.172ff. = 1973a, p.55 ff.; 1972, p.93 ff. in 1973a). At the sociosemantic level, such networks show relations of contrast and dependency between meaning choices available in a particular social context, just as the parallel networks at the lexicogrammatical level show contrasts and dependency within the options in transitivity, mood and theme. The task is to identify which combinations in the lexicogrammar act as systematic realizations of parti- cular options in the sociosemantic networks. As Halliday points out (1971a, p.174 = 1973a, p.57; 1972, p.93 in 1973a), we shall not expect a one-to-one correspondence between semantic and grammatical options: rather, the norm will be for a given meaning to be expressed by a number of lexicogrammatical features together. Nevertheless, Halliday claims, it is possible to work out the mappings concerned. The model thus involves 'preselection' of combinations of lexicogrammatical features by features in sociosemantic networks, just as features from phonological networks are preselected by lexicogrammatical choices. It is perhaps helpful to think of preselection in terms of a kind of wiring diagram: given a particular sociosemantic choice, we can trace 'wires' through to one or more lexicogrammatical options which systematically realize that meaning, and thence to the combinations of sounds and prosodic features which in turn realize the lexicogrammatical features.

Let us now see how Halliday's model might work in relation to the meaning potential available in one particular social context. Halliday himself (1971a, pp.175-9 = 1973a, pp.58-62; 1972, pp.76-92 in 1973a) discusses the social context of mother/child control and in particular the linguistic means available for the expression of disapprobation. The fully developed sociosemantic network (1972, p.89 in 1973a) covers threats and warnings, with or without explicit conditions such as 'if you do that again'. For each feature in the sociosemantic network, Halliday provides a preselection statement giving the realization of that meaning in terms of choices in the lexicogrammatical areas of transitivity, voice, mood, theme, aspect and person, also lexical categories, specified as selections from particular sections of Roget's Thesaurus. Here, we shall consider just that part of the network concerned with the subclassification of threats (see Figure 4.1).

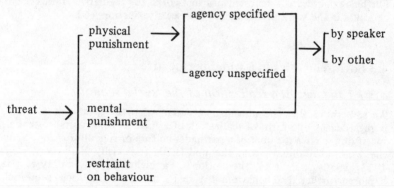

Term in sociosemantics	Lexicogrammatical realization
Physical punishment	Clause: action: voluntary ('do' type); effective (2-participant): goal = 'you'; future tense; positive; verb from Roget § 972 (or 972, 276)
Agency specified	Voice: active
Agency unspecified	Voice: passive
By speaker	Actor/Attribuend = 'I'
By other	Actor/Attribuend = 'Daddy' etc.
Mental punishment	Clause: relational: attributive: Attribute = adj. from Roget § 900
Restraint on behaviour	Clause: action: modulation: necessity; Actor = 'you'

Figure 4.1: Halliday's network and realization rules for threats

Examples of threats described by the network and associated realization rules are as follows (Halliday, 1972, p.85 in 1973a). All could be accompanied by explicit conditions such as 'if you do that again' or 'if you go on doing that'.

4.1 I'll smack you. [physical punishment, agency specified, by
speaker]

4.2 Daddy'll smack you. [physical punishment, agency specified,
by other]

4.3 You'll get smacked. [physical punishment, agency unspecified]

4.4 I shall be cross with you. [mental punishment, by speaker]

4.5 Daddy'll be cross with you. [mental punishment, by other]

Halliday gives no example of the [restraint on behaviour] type of threat, but presumably the following would qualify:

4.6 You'll have to come in (if you keep kicking the ball into next door's garden).

Further examples of sociosemantic networks for regulative contexts can be found in the work of Turner (1973) (see also Section 9.3).

4.3 Sociosemantics in a wider perspective

4.3.1 Language as a realization of the 'social semiotic'

We saw above that the meaning potential, what the speaker 'can mean', is regarded as one form of realization of a 'higher' behavioural potential, specifying what a member of a particular culture or subculture 'can do'. In the work of Halliday from the mid-1970s (especially Halliday, 1975a, 1978, 1980a, b and c), the notion of a higher behavioural system is explored further. The behavioural system is now seen as a 'social semiotic', a system of categories with their own values relative to each other, their own functions in the overall social system, and thus, in a Firthian sense, their own meanings:

> The social system, viewed in these terms, is a system of meaning relations; and these meaning relations are realized in many ways, of which one, perhaps the principal one as far as the maintenance and transmission of the sysem is concerned, is through their encoding in language. The meaning potential of a language, its semantic system, is therefore seen as realizing a higher level system of relations, that of the social semiotic, in just the same way as it is itself realized in the lexico-grammatical and phonological systems. (Halliday, 1975a, p.60)

Other kinds of symbolic system through which the social semiotic can be realized include, according to Halliday (1975a, p.121; 1980a, p.5), art forms, social structures and institutions, educational and legal systems.

The total picture of language as a realization of the higher social semiotic has various components, which Halliday integrates into an overall sociolinguistic model. These components are: the linguistic system itself, text, situation, register, code and social structure. We shall consider each in turn.

4.3.2 *The linguistic system*

In the work of the mid- to late 1970s, there is an important shift in Halliday's position with regard to the level at which the functional component networks of transitivity, mood and theme operate. We shall take this point up again rather more critically in Chapter 5; here, we shall simply trace rather briefly the changes involved.

As we saw in Chapter 3, the functional components were originally said to be components of the lexicogrammar. In the papers of *Explorations in the Functions of Language* there is considerable ambiguity on this matter: it appears that the functional component networks are still to be regarded as lexicogrammatical, but side by side with such claims there are indications that the functional components (or 'macrofunctions', as they are often called at this time) are essentially semantic, a position which would be consistent with the change, noted earlier, in the application of the term 'meaning potential' to the sociosemantic rather than the lexicogrammatical stratum.

In the paper (Halliday, 1975b) which provides the title for Halliday's (1978) book *Language as Social Semiotic*, the functional components are treated as components of the *semantic* system, but are still said to be reflected as discrete networks of options in the lexicogrammar. A later paper (Halliday, 1977), an extract from which also appears in the 1978 book, shows a further shift, in that the functional component networks of transitivity, mood and theme are now seen as *constituting* the semantic level, rather than as lexicogrammatical. This position is finally confirmed in Halliday's latest writings (1979, 1980b), where transitivity, mood and theme are seen as relatively independent blocks of *semantic* options.

4.3.3 *Text*

The concept of text, always important in Halliday's thinking, has assumed special prominence in his more recent work. A text is constituted by 'any instance of language that is operational, as distinct from citational (like sentences in a grammar book, or words listed in a dictionary)' (Halliday, 1975a, p.123). The term thus refers to 'any passage, spoken or written, of whatever length, that does form a unified whole' (Halliday & Hasan, 1976, p.1). A text could thus be as short as a one-sentence public notice, or as long as a whole committee meeting or a novel. Texts are distinguishable from non-texts in terms of the property of 'texture', conferred by two factors: their internal cohesiveness, and their consistency with respect to the context of situation (Halliday & Hasan, 1976, p.23). Cohesion (see Halliday & Hasan 1976, also Chapter 8) is achieved through phenomena in the text whereby 'the interpretation of some element in the discourse is dependent on that of another' (Halliday & Hasan, 1976, p.4). Consistency of text meaning in relation to situation is a matter of register, and will be discussed further in Section 4.3.5 below.

Halliday stresses that text is not to be regarded in terms of an extension of the grammatical rank scale upwards from the sentence. It is rather a semantic unit (indeed, according to Halliday (Halliday, 1975b, p.24 = 1978, p.109; Halliday and Hasan, 1976, p.25), *the basic* semantic unit), which is realized by, rather than consisting of, sentences (Halliday, 1975a, p.123; 1975b, p.24 = 1978, p.109; 1977, p.194 = 1978, p.135; 1980a, p.10; Halliday & Hasan, 1976, p.2). A text, produced in a particular context of situation, is a product of the actualization of various choices made from the meaning potential available in that type of context (Parret, 1974, p.113 = Halliday, 1978, p.57; Halliday, 1975a, p.123; 1975b, pp.24, 37 = 1978, pp.109, 122; 1977, p.195 = 1978, p.137). However, a text is not only a *product* of the various choices made, but also represents an interactive *process*, an exchange of meanings between participants, whether they are speakers engaging in a dialogue, or writer and reader (1977, p.198 = 1978, p.139; 1980a, p.11). Indeed, the process of creating texts continually modifies the linguistic system which allows their production. The interactive nature of text is neatly expressed by Hasan (1978, p.229): 'a text is a social event whose primary mode of unfolding is linguistic'.

4.3.4 Situation

We saw in Chapter 1 that Malinowski's concrete view of the context of situation of an utterance was modified in the direction of greater abstraction by Firth. Halliday points out (1975b, p.24 = 1978, p.109) that if we are to relate social context to a general sociolinguistic theory, we must characterize situation in still more abstract terms, as situation *types*, which are essentially semiotic structures, each of which is 'a constellation of meanings deriving from the semiotic system that constitutes the culture'. It is from the properties of a particular situation type, as defined by the values of variables in the semiotic structure, that hearers can predict what their interlocutors are likely to say (or, more fundamentally, mean), and so are able to negotiate verbal interactions and even, for example, adjust to a conversation which they have entered half way through. In other words, it is through the analysis of situation types as complexes of values for variables in the semiotic structure that Halliday is able to make the link between situations and the texts produced in those situations.

Halliday's framework for the description of the semiotic structure of situation types is based on earlier work, by Halliday himself and also notably by Gregory, on language variety (see especially Halliday, McIntosh & Strevens, 1964; Spencer & Gregory, 1964; Gregory, 1967; also the useful discussion and exemplification of situation types in Gregory & Carroll, 1978). Three dimensions are proposed: field, tenor and mode. Discussion of these dimensions can be found not only in the early work just cited, but also in various of Halliday's more recent publications (Halliday, 1974, pp. 34, 48-54 = 1978, pp.33, 221-7; 1977, pp.200-3 = 1978, pp.142-5; 1980a, pp.12-15; Halliday & Hasan, 1976, p.22).

The *field* of discourse is 'that which is "going on", and has recognizable meaning in the social system; typically a complex of acts in some ordered configuration, and in which the text is playing some part, and including "subject matter" as one special aspect' (Halliday, 1977, pp.200-1 = 1978, pp.142-3). It is 'what the participants in the context of situation are actually engaged in doing' (1974, p.49 = 1978, p.222). Thus, for example, although in a transaction involving the buying and selling of a newspaper we may talk about the weather, the field of discourse is 'buying and selling a newspaper', and not meteorology, conversation about the weather simply forming part of one strategy appropriate to this field.

Tenor is concerned with 'the cluster of socially meaningful participant relationships, both permanent attributes of the participants and role relationships that are specific to the situation, including speech roles, those that come into being through the exchange of verbal meanings' (1977, p.201 = 1978, p.143). This set of relations 'includes levels of formality as one particular instance' (1975b, p.25 = 1978, p.110). Halliday's examples of the kinds of role relation which would be echoed in the language used include teacher/pupil, parent/child, child/other child in peer group, doctor/patient, customer/salesman, and casual acquaintances on a train.

Mode is concerned with 'the particular status that is assigned to the text within the situation; its function in relation to the social action and the role structure, including the channel or medium, and the rhetorical mode' (1977, p.201 = 1978, p.143). Underlying the concept of mode, then, is the question

> what function is language being used for, what is its specific role in the goings-on to which it is contributing? To persuade? to soothe? to sell? to control? to explain? or just to oil the works, as in what Malinowski calls 'phatic communion', exemplified by the talk about the weather, which merely helps the situation along? (1974, p.49 = 1978, p.223)

Halliday differentiates between 'mode' and 'medium', although recognizing that considerations of medium (basically spoken/written) are fundamental to mode. Certain modes, such as persuasive uses of language, can be realized through either the spoken or the written medium, but what is said will be at least partly dependent on the medium used. For a more detailed discussion, demonstrating the inadequacy of a simple spoken/written dichotomy for the analysis of medium, see Gregory (1967), also Gregory & Carroll (1978, Chapter 4).

As examples of the specification of situation type in terms of field, tenor and mode, we may take Halliday's analyses of two particular instances: a child play situation, for which a specific text is provided (1975b, p.30 = 1978, p.115), and the instruction of a novice in the rules of a board game (1974; pp.52-3 = 1978, p.226).

	Child play	Board game instruction
Field	Child at play: manipulating movable objects (wheeled vehicles) with related fixtures, assisted by adult; concurrently associating (i) similar past events, (ii) similar absent objects; also evaluating objects in terms of each other and of processes.	Instruction: the instruction of a novice – in a board game (e.g. Monopoly) with equipment present – for the purpose of enabling him to participate.

	Child play	Board game instruction
Tenor	Small child and parent inter-acting; child determining course of action, (i) announcing own inten-tions, (ii) controlling actions of parent; con-currently sharing and seek-ing corroboration of own experience with parent.	Equal and intimate: three young adult males; acquainted – but with hierarchy in the situation (2 experts, 1 novice) – leading to superior – inferior role relationship.
Mode	Spoken, alternately mono-logue and dialogue, task-oriented; pragmatic; (i) referring to processes and objects of situation, (ii) relating to and further-ing child's own actions, (iii) demanding other objects; interposed with narrative and exploratory elements.	Spoken: unrehearsed Didactic and explanatory, with undertone of non-seriousness – with feedback: question-and-answer, correction of error.

As we noted earlier, in proposing the analysis of situation types accord-ing to values of the field, tenor and mode variables, Halliday is attempting to show in what ways the context of situation influences the selection of meanings for the construction of a text. The link is made through an inter-esting hypothesis, namely that each component of the semiotic structure of situation types tends to be reflected in the types of choice made from one particular functional component of the semantic system:

> . . . the type of symbolic activity (field) tends to determine the range of meaning as content, language in the observer function (ideational); the role relationships (tenor) tend to determine the range of meaning as participation, language in the intruder function (interpersonal); and the rhetorical channel (mode) tends to determine the range of meaning as texture, language in its relevance to the environment (textual). (Halli-day, 1975b, p.36 = 1978, p.117)

Halliday is claiming, then, that if we compare texts differing in field, the most likely differences in the meaning choices made will be those concerned with the types of process, participant, circumstance, and the like, includ-ing the lexical characterization of relevant objects, persons, and so on; while if we compare texts differing in tenor, it is more likely that the dif-ferences in meaning will be in the areas of speech role, styles of address, lexical and intonational expression of attitude, and other such inter-personal features; and if we compare texts differing in mode, the semantic differences will tend to be located in the areas of theme, information structure and cohesion. For examples in which Halliday claims to demonstrate such correlations, the reader is referred to the following: 1975b, p.30 ff. = 1978, p.115 ff., repeated in 1980c (analysis of the child play text referred to above); 1977, p.203 ff. = 1978, p.145 ff. (analysis of a short extract from a literary text, much more detailed in the original article than in the excerpted version); 1980b, p.38 ff. (analysis of part of a poem, and of a broadcast talk on a religious theme).

4.3.5 Register

The term 'register' has been widely used to mean a variety of language distinguished according to the *use* to which it is put, as opposed to a variety characterized in terms of the properties of its *users*; the former type of variation is sometimes called 'diatypic', the latter type 'dialectal' (see Halliday, McIntosh & Strevens, 1964, p.87; Gregory, 1967; Halliday, 1980c, pp.66-74). Originally, registers were thought of in terms of their lexical and grammatical characteristics; however, consistently with his shift to a semantically based theory, Halliday now proposes that the defining features of registers are semantic:

> A register can be defined as the configuration of semantic resources that the member of a culture typically associates with a situation type. It is the meaning potential that is accessible in a given social context. (Halliday 1975b, p.26 = 1978, p.111)

The concept of register, conceived of as a subset of the total semantic potential, provides the final link between situation type and text: a register is that set of semantic resources which is activated by a given combination of field, tenor and mode values; and any text is an instance of a particular register. For further discussion and exemplification of the concept of register, see Ellis & Ure (1969), Ure (1971), Ure & Ellis (1974), Chiu (1973), Hasan (1973), Gregory & Carroll (1978, Chapter 6), Halliday (1980c).

4.3.6 Code

The concept of code, as taken over by Halliday from Bernstein, refers to 'types of social semiotic, or symbolic orders of meaning generated by the social system' (Halliday, 1975b, p.26 = 1978, p.111). Examples would be the 'elaborated' and 'restricted' codes proposed by Bernstein (see, for instance, Bernstein (1971) and the summary of Bernstein's views in Halliday (1975c, p.872 ff. = 1978, p.87 ff.)). Codes are not themselves varieties of language; rather, they are said to act as filters, regulating access to particular classes of variety. Thus Halliday (1975b, p.27 = 1978, p.111) claims that 'when the semantic systems of the language are activated by the situational determinants of text — the field, tenor and mode — this process is regulated by the codes'. In other words, codes, representing particular subcultural angles on the social system, and transmitted during the socialization of the child, determine the repertoire of register types available to speakers and hearers.

Such a proposal would, of course, have important implications for the educational process if it turned out that children socialized within family role systems favouring a particular code were denied access to registers demanded by the school system as we know it. But this is to enter the minefield of discussions on educational deprivation and deficit, an area which is peripheral to the scope of the present book: for a critical discussion of Bernstein's ideas, see Stubbs (1976, 1980). It should be emphasized that codes are related, in Halliday's model, to register rather than to social dialect: registers, as we have seen, constitute subsets of meaning potential, and it is meaning potential whose availability is regulated by code; social dialects, on the other hand, are different lexicogrammatical and phonological ways of representing the same meaning potential. For full discussion of the relationship between code, register and social dialect, see Hasan (1973). For a brief discussion of educationally important work on language and code, see Section 9.3.

4.3.7 The social structure

The social structure, that is the specific form of organization of a given society, is the source of several of the sociolinguistic components discussed above (see Halliday, 1975b, pp.28-9 = 1978, pp.113-4). It is the social structure which determines which types of social context will be of central importance: the status and role relations (tenor), the types of activity (field), and even the available media and types of rhetorical function (mode). Through its reflection in types of family role system, the social structure also gives rise to the codes which are claimed to regulate access to registers. The hierarchical systems (of class and caste) set up by the social structure give rise to a range of social dialects, as well as affecting family role systems, status relationships and the differentiation of codes. Halliday (1975a, p.128) distinguishes between the social structure and an even more general category, the social system, which is at the top of the whole tree of complex interrelationships, and is equivalent to 'the culture'.

4.3.8 Halliday's sociolinguistic model: a summary

The interrelationship of the components discussed in the preceding sections may be summarized as in Figure 4.2, taken from Halliday (1975b, p.41; 1975c, p.860 = 1978, p.69).

4.4 A semantic functional perspective on child language development

4.4.1 The general approach

We have seen that Halliday now views the adult linguistic system in terms of a central functionally organized semantics. The functional components, although reflecting and ultimately derived from, the extrinsic functions language is called upon to serve, are claimed to be built into the organization of the linguistic system itself. It is natural to ask how such a system is acquired by the developing child. How does the child's early language differ from the adult system? By what stages does learning proceed? These are questions to which Halliday addresses himself in two papers reprinted in *Explorations in the Functions of Language*: 'Relevant models of

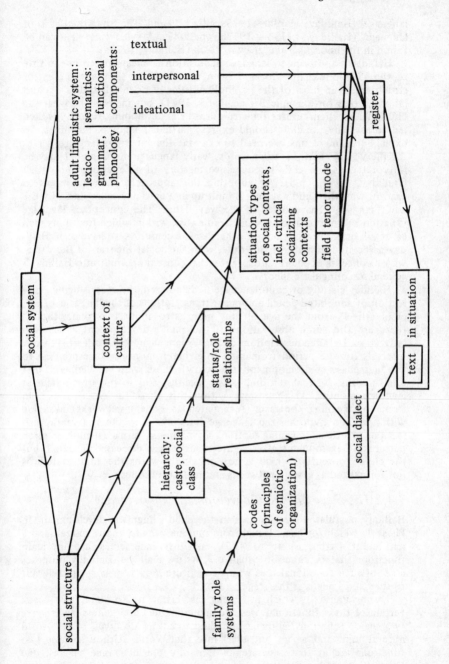

Figure 4.2: Halliday's sociolinguistic model

language' (Halliday, 1969b = 1973a, pp.9-21) and 'The functional basis of language' (Halliday, 1973b = 1973a, pp.22-47). A fuller treatment can be found in the book *Learning How to Mean* (Halliday, 1975a).

Halliday's approach to language acquisition is encapsulated in the title of the 1975 book: the process is seen, not simply as the development of structures, as in most of the psycholinguistically oriented studies of child language (see for example Braine, 1963, 1971), but in terms of what the child means when he uses the structures he is developing. Halliday is then led to ask why the child should express particular kinds of meanings. To explain this, he claims, we need to examine the functions language serves for the young child. In other words, 'early language development may be interpreted as the child's progressive mastery of a functional potential' (Halliday, 1975a, p.5). By adopting this approach, Halliday hopes to explain why the child's system is built up in a particular way, and why the adult language has evolved in the way it has. The concept of language function presupposes some social framework within which functions such as 'regulating the behaviour of others' make sense. As we have seen, Halliday associated himself, at this time, with the social theories of Bernstein, whose concepts of code and relevant social context are built into Halliday's general sociolinguistic theory.

Halliday's study of child language is data-based, the corpus being a collection of annotated pencil-and-paper transcriptions of the language of one child (Nigel) from the age of nine months to about two years, though there are also some observations of the child's development at an even later stage. Detailed descriptions of Nigel's language were made at six-week intervals for the period from nine to eighteen months, corresponding to the first phase of development (see below): these were labelled as NL0 at nine months, NL1 at ten and a half months, and so on, up to NL6 at eighteen months. At each stage within this phase the description is in terms of meaning contrasts (formulated as system networks) available within certain hypothesized language functions, and the systematic realizations of these meaning options in phonetic terms (including pitch patterns). Development after eighteen months is discussed in detail, but the child's potential, which is now moving towards the adult system, is not formalized as system networks and realization rules.

4.4.2 The three phases of development: an overview

Halliday postulates three phases in the child's linguistic development. In Phase I, which for Nigel lasted from nine months to about sixteen and a half months (that is, up to NL5), each utterance serves just one main function: that is, function equals use. As we shall see, Halliday proposes a set of such functional uses which constitute models of language relevant to the child's needs at this stage.

During Phase II, which in Nigel's case lasted up to about two years, certain of these functional uses become combined and generalized to give two major functions, allowing the child to act as 'observer' of the world around him, and as an 'intruder' into that world. Although these two functions are at first separate, in that any one utterance has just one function, Nigel later learns to combine the two in one and the same utterance. This means that there is no longer a direct one-to-one relation between content and expression: in other words, the child now needs a lexicogrammar to map the functions on to each other as a single multi-functional output. During this phase, there is also a sharp increase in the number of new words learned by the child. A further significant development is the ability to engage not only in narrative description, but also in dialogue, made possible by learning the concept of communication roles.

The process of combination and generalization of functions in Phase II is an important step on the way to the adult linguistic system in which, as we have seen, almost all utterances are seen as multifunctional. Nigel begins to approach this adult system in Phase III (two years onwards): the 'observer' and 'intruder' functions of Phase II become the ideational and interpersonal functions of the adult system, and the child's newly acquired ability to relate language to its context as narrative, dialogue, or whatever, forms the nucleus of the adult textual component.

We shall now consider each of the three phases in rather more detail.

4.4.3 Phase I

Halliday begins (1969b; 1975a, p.18ff.) by postulating a set of functions relevant to the linguistic needs of a very young child. The particular set of functions is, Halliday claims, suggested by two different types of consideration. Firstly, one can observe what a child is doing as he speaks, and so gain an idea of the functions of speech in context. Secondly, one can suggest possible generalizations about the functional use of the child's language by looking at this in the light of general hypotheses concerning the functions of language in the life of social man. This will involve a consideration of the functional organization of the adult semantic system, and also of the types of social context likely to be critical for the transmission of the culture to the child. In formulating his set of child language functions, Halliday makes considerable use of the 'critical socializing contexts' proposed by Bernstein.

The seven functions proposed are summarized below, together with Halliday's short glosses on them.

Instrumental	Language used as a means of obtaining goods and services to satisfy the child's material needs. The focus is on the goods and services themselves – it does not matter who provides them.	'I want'
Regulatory	Language used as a means of controlling the behaviour of others. The focus is on the behaviour of a particular individual.	'Do as I tell you'
Interactional	Language used as a means of interacting with others (especially, initially, the mother, but also other adults and, later, the peer group). Includes, for example, generalized greetings.	'Me and you'

Personal	Language used as a means of expressing the child's own individuality, including expressions of emotion, participation, and so on.	'Here I come'
Heuristic	Language used as a means of finding out about the environment, increasingly perceived as separate from the self.	'Tell me why'
Imaginative	Language used as a means of creating the child's own environment, through stories, games, pretences, and so on.	'Let's pretend'
Representational (in 1969b) or Informative (1975a)	Language used as a means of communicating information to someone who does not already possess it.	'I've got something to tell you'

Halliday's original hypothesis was that these seven functions would appear in the order listed. This proved not to be the case: up to and including NL2 (that is, up to one year), systematic meaning-sound correspondences were found within just four functional areas (the first four on the list: instrumental, regulatory, interactional and personal), with no developmental sequence among the four. The imaginative function appeared next (at NL3), followed by the heuristic (NL5), so reversing the predicted order. The representational or informative function was, as predicted, the last to appear (at NL9): although the passing on of new information is an important use of adult language (and is indeed probably considered by most people as the main function), it is a use definable only in relation to language itself, and this is an advanced concept which the very young child has not yet mastered.

Networks and realization rules showing the full range of Nigel's linguistic system at NL1-6 can be found in Halliday (1975a, pp.148-57). So that the reader has some idea of the kind of description he will find, the portion of the NL2 potential within the instrumental and regulatory functions (1975a, p.149) is reproduced below, together with the phonetic exponents of the meaning choices and the gloss provided in terms of the adult language. The symbol - - - represents repetition of the syllable three times.

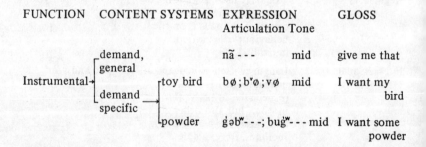

FUNCTION	CONTENT SYSTEMS	EXPRESSION Articulation	Tone	GLOSS
Instrumental →	demand, general	nã - - -	mid	give me that
	demand specific → toy bird	bɸ ; bʼɸ ; vɸ	mid	I want my bird
	powder	ġəbʷ- - -; buġʷ- - -	mid	I want some powder

4.4.4 Phase II

From NL6 onwards, Nigel learned many new words, which were actual
items of English, rather than idiosyncratic realizations of meanings, as in
the very early stages. Structures were also beginning to appear: at the start
of Phase II (NL6) Nigel could use two types of structure, a specific expression plus a gesture, or a specific expression plus a general expression from
the same functional potential. The following are among the examples given
by Halliday (1975a, p.45):

4.7 [dã:bɨ] ('Dvořak) + beating time: 'I want the Dvořak record on'
                                                                (instrumental)

4.8 [ndà] ('star') + shaking head as a negation gesture: 'I can't see
                                                        the star' (personal)

4.9 [ɛ̀ lɔ̀u] (command + 'hole'): 'make a hole' (regulatory)

4.10 [ù æyì] (excitement + 'egg'): 'ooh, an egg' (personal)

Then came two-word strings with independent tone contours, such as:

4.11 [bʌ̀bu nɔ̄umɔ̀] ('bubble, no more'): 'the bubbles have gone
                                                                away'

and lists with as many as six items.

At about the end of NL7 (nineteen to nineteen and a half months)
two-word sequences with a single tone contour appeared. These fell
functionally into two groups, corresponding to two new functions, which
Halliday calls 'pragmatic' and 'mathetic', and which arise from combination
and generalization of certain of the individual Phase I functions. The pragmatic function relates to contexts in which actions or objects are being
asked for, the mathetic function to various aspects of the child's explora-
tion of the environment, and of his own individuality in relation to that
environment. Thus the pragmatic function arises largely out of the instrumental and regulatory functions of Phase I, and the mathetic out of the
heuristic and personal functions. The interactional function of Phase I
contributes to both the pragmatic and mathetic functions of Phase II.
The pragmatic/mathetic distinction was given a very clear realization
by Nigel for some months, starting at NL7: all his utterances had either
a clearly rising or a clearly falling pitch contour; falling tone utterances
were mathetic in function, rising tone utterances were pragmatic. Examples
from NL7-8 given by Halliday (1975a, p.76) include:

4.12 chuffa stúck ('the train's stuck; help me to get it out')

4.13 high wáll ('let me jump off and you catch me')

4.14 háve it ('I want that')

4.15 play ráo ('let's play at lions')

4.16 molasses nòse ('I've got molasses on my nose')

4.17 red swèater ('that's a red sweater')

4.18 chuffa stòp ('the train's stopped')

4.19 green stick fìnd ('the green stick's been found')

Of these, 4.12 to 4.15 are seen as pragmatic, 4.16 to 4.19 as mathetic.
Halliday recognizes that certain of these utterances could be interpreted as

either pragmatic or mathetic, but points out that Nigel himself made the distinction plain, by demanding a response to any utterance with rising tone, but not to falling tone utterances.

At first, newly acquired vocabulary items were restricted to just one of the two general functions. For instance, 'more meat' (also other sequences with 'more') occurred only in pragmatic contexts, 'green car' (also 'green peg', 'red car', and so on) only in mathetic contexts. Slightly later, however, this tight form/function bond was loosened, so that, for example, 'more meat' could come to mean 'look, there's some more meat', and 'green car' could mean 'I want the green car'. This is a stage on the way to the important step of combining the two functions into a single utterance, as in Halliday's example below:

4.20 téatime . . . lúnchtime (on entering father's study – 'it's teatime – I mean it's lunchtime – so come along!')

As the functional basis of the child's language becomes more general and abstract, and as the functions begin to combine in one and the same utterance, a one-to-one form/function correspondence ceases to be an adequate system for the encoding of meanings, and under the pressure of this need a lexicogrammatical system (vocabulary items and structures) develops, to mediate between the semantic content and its ultimate expression. The various stages (holophrastic, two-word, and so on) familiar from structure-based work on child language acquisition are thus explained, in Halliday's model, in terms of the exigencies of the functions language is called upon to serve.

A further important aspect of Nigel's development in Phase II was his increasing ability to engage in dialogue (see Halliday, 1975a, pp.48-51). By NL5, Nigel could answer questions in the instrumental, regulatory and interactional functions ('Do you want . . . ?', 'Shall I . . . ?'), but had no general concept of polarity, and in particular could not answer any question which sought information, as indeed we might expect if the informative function has not yet developed. But at NL7, Nigel could respond to 'wh'-questions and commands, could signal acknowledgment of a statement or response, and could initiate dialogue by asking 'wh'-questions. However, he still could not ask, or even directly respond to, ordinary polar questions: these abilities appeared towards the end of Phase II.

4.4.5 Phase III

We have seen that by the end of Phase II, the pragmatic/mathetic distinction has begun to break down, in the sense that utterances are no longer rooted in just one or the other function, but combine the two aspects, of speaker as participant in the interaction and as observer of experience. The child's language also has texture by this stage: that is, the spoken texts produced are fitted to their context, as narratives, dialogues, or mixtures of the two, and display information structuring and cohesive patterning. In other words, Nigel has moved from the Phase I position of 'function equals use', through a transitional Phase II in which the functions become ever more generalized, to Phase III, in which they have developed into what is effectively the three-function system of the adult language, in which each utterance combines ideational, interpersonal and textual meanings. Halliday in fact distinguishes terminologically the functions of Phases I,

II and III, saying (1975a, p.77) that 'the "functions" of Phase I become "macro-functions" in Phase II, and "meta-functions" in Phase III'. (This is somewhat confusing, since, as we have seen, the term 'macrofunction' is applied elsewhere to the *adult* system; however, the term 'metafunction' does seem to be favoured in Halliday's latest work.) 'Function' has now become quite distinct from 'use', all uses of language being mediated via the functional components of the Phase III system.

The functional components of Phase III, like those of the fully mature adult system, are selectively activated by the situation type parameters of field, tenor and mode: that is, the activity in which the child is engaged will affect predominantly the ideational meaning choices, his relationship with the person he is talking to will condition interpersonal choices, and the part being played by language in the overall interaction will be reflected mainly in textual choices. For examples of child language analysed in these terms, see Halliday, 1975a, pp.132-3, also 1975b, p.30 = 1978, p.115, mentioned earlier.

4.4.6 Language and culture in mother tongue acquisition

We saw in Section 4.3 that for Halliday, the linguistic system is just one component, though a centrally important component, of a wide-ranging sociolinguistic model embracing the concepts of text, situation type, register, code and social structure. We also saw that Halliday subscribed, in large measure, to Bernstein's theories, in which linguistic interaction plays a major part in the exploitation of critical socializing contexts. Halliday points out (1975a, p.120 ff.) that although learning the language and learning the culture are different things, they are clearly interdependent: since the linguistic system is part of the social system, neither can be learned without the other. The child is thus faced with a very complex task. As Halliday puts it (1975a, p.122): 'In principle, a child is learning one semiotic system, the culture, and simultaneously he is learning the means of learning it – a second semiotic system, the language, which is the intermediary in which the first one is encoded'.

As Halliday points out (1975a, p.134 ff.), the child is at least aided by the fact that everything he hears around him is relevant to the learning process, in that it is systematically related to its context. The task of acquisition is made manageable by the filtering effect of the child's functional potential: at any stage of development, he will act upon only those linguistic elements which are within the scope of his meaning potential, and more generally, his semiotic potential. However, the filter is not so much a limitation as a means for interpreting the input in terms of the available resources, and allowing their further development.

4.5 Conclusion

With the conclusion of our exposition of the sociosemantic model, we have reached what appears to be Halliday's present position. The adult linguistic system is seen in terms of a semantic core consisting of the functional component networks (transitivity, mood, theme and associated areas). Semantic options are encoded in the lexicogrammar, by a process of preselection. The semantic options are also related 'upwards' to the social context, through the selective activating effects of the situation type parameters (field, tenor and mode) on the functional component networks (ideational, interpersonal and textual respectively). The specification of the semantic resources available in a situation type defined by particular values of field, tenor and mode constitutes a register of the language. Access to registers is controlled by Bernsteinian codes, representing particular subcultural 'angles' on the social system. Texts are produced by the actualization of the meaning selections made from the potential offered by a register, in accordance with the particular ways of expressing meanings which are available in the social dialect of the speaker. All of these components of the sociolinguistic model are related to the social structure, via the determination of availability of fields, tenors and modes, the hierarchical structuring of class and caste systems, and types of family role relation.

Whereas the adult language system is multifunctional, each utterance combining ideational, interpersonal and textual meanings, the system of the very young child is monofunctional, and function can be equated with use. Acquisition of language by the child can be seen as a process of 'learning how to mean', in which the meaning potential develops along functional lines. The initial 'functional uses' become progressively more general and abstract, until at about two years the child has developed the basis of the adult system.

5. Systemic functional grammar: a critical appraisal

5.1 Introduction

So far, we have discussed the work of Halliday from about 1970 onwards in a fairly uncritical manner. There are, however, some important issues about which serious questions have been raised. It is interesting to note that criticism of Halliday's position has come mainly from within systemic linguistics: by and large, non-systemic linguists have had little to say, either positively or negatively, about this approach to the study of language. Some possible reasons for this unfortunate state of affairs will emerge later in this chapter.

In the sections which follow, we shall take up six major areas of controversy:

(i)   relationships between syntax and semantics;
(ii)   whether the semantics should be seen as the encoding of behavioural options in defined social contexts and settings (as with Halliday) or in more general terms, not tied specifically to social behaviour;
(iii) the validity of the functional components hypothesis;
(iv)   the validity of the categories of field, tenor and mode, and the way in which they are said to correlate with the meaning potential and with the actualization of this meaning potential in the production of texts;
(v)   the relationship between the above controversies and Halliday's views on language acquisition;
(vi)   possible criticisms of Halliday's general approach to linguistic theorizing.

In the course of our discussion, work by other systemic linguists will be brought in (see especially Fawcett, 1975a, 1980; Berry, 1980, 1982; Hasan, 1978, 1980a and b; Butler, 1979, 1982).

5.2 The relationship between syntax and semantics

We have seen in the last three chapters that one of the most significant aspects of Halliday's work, from its beginnings right up to the present day, is its emphasis on the meanings underlying linguistic forms. Even in the early days of Scale and Category linguistics, language was regarded primarily as *meaningful* activity. By 1966, Halliday's theory was concerned with 'semantically significant grammar', that part of the grammar which is 'closest to' the semantics. From this point on, it is often very difficult to decide from Halliday's writings what is to be regarded as syntactic, and what as semantic. It has, of course, been suggested by some non-systemicists (for instance the generative semanticists) that the syntax/semantics distinction is misleading or unnecessary. If this were also Halliday's view, we should, of course, not expect to be able to differentiate clearly between syntactic and semantic phenomena in his work. Halliday is not, however, committed to such a position. We have seen that he has continued to maintain allegiance to a traditional tristratal model involving the levels of semantics, lexicogrammar and phonology. Let us remind ourselves of the apparent relationship between syntax and semantics, and the position of the functional component networks within these levels, in the models developed since the late 1960s.

First, consider the following quotation from Halliday's account of transitivity and theme in English (Halliday, 1967c, p.199):

> The English clause, it is suggested, can be regarded as the domain of three main areas of syntactic choice: transitivity, mood and theme. Transitivity is the set of options relating to cognitive content [. . .]. Mood represents the organization of participants in speech situations [. . .]. Theme is concerned with the information structure of the clause . . .

Thus the main systemic choices at clause rank are seen as syntactic but they 'relate to' cognitive content, speech roles and information presentation, which are referred to later in the same paragraph as 'areas of meaning'. It is not clear here whether Halliday would have wished these areas of meaning to be described at a separate semantic level, or exactly what the relationship between meaning and form is intended to be. Since, as we saw in Chapter 3, the transitivity, mood and theme networks constitute the functional component 'blocks' of options, there is a similar ambivalence about the status of these components in relation to the levels of linguistic description. Halliday claims (1968, p.207) that the partitioning of English system networks into three relatively independent blocks 'provides a syntactic basis for the concept of language functions, and suggests how the diversity of functions recognizable at the semantic levels may be organized in the course of realization'. Thus the functions are said to be semantically based, but are themselves seen as components of the lexicogrammatical level.

It will be remembered from Chapter 3 that each functional component is said to contribute a layer of structure to the clause, in terms of structural roles (microfunctions) such as Actor, Goal and so on. These are said to be 'syntactic functions, or roles, combinations of which make up structures of the clause' (1967c, p.199). It is not at all easy, however, to see how syntactic tests could be used to identify such functional roles. Consider, for instance, the tests used by Jackendoff (1972, p.32, based on Gruber, 1965) for the presence of Agent (which we may take as equivalent to Halliday's Actor for our present purposes – see also the discussion of transitivity in Chapter 8). Jackendoff points out that 'the presence of an Agentive subject correlates in part with the possibility of using purposive constructions like *in order to* and *so that* and purposive adverbials like *intentionally, accidentally*, or *on purpose*'. We may note, however, that what unites these test items is their purposive meaning, not their syntactic properties: they include subordinating conjunctions and adverbials, and even the adverbials are of different syntactic sub-classes, as indicated by their distributional potential:

5.1   John dropped the book $\begin{cases} \text{intentionally} \\ \text{accidentally} \\ \text{on purpose} \end{cases}$

5.2   John $\begin{cases} \text{intentionally dropped the book.} \\ \text{accidentally} \\ \text{*on purpose} \end{cases}$

Likewise, as Jackendoff points out, only Agentives can appear in orders:

5.3   Drop the gun.
5.4   *Understand Freud.

However, again note that it is not the syntactic form of 5.4 which itself leads us to reject it, since the same form can be used acceptably in a co-ordinate construction with an implied conditional relationship between the two halves:

5.5   Understand Freud and you've got the key to all those strange dreams you've been having.

It would seem preferable, then, to regard Actor, Goal and other 'functional roles' as semantic rather than syntactic functions. For a further example of an approach in these terms see Dik's *Functional Grammar* (Dik, 1978, 1980).

Now let us return to the development of Halliday's position on the relationship between syntax and semantics. We noted in Section 4.3.2 that Halliday's views on the nature of the functional component networks seem to have undergone an important shift from about 1970 to 1977. In *Explorations in the Functions of Language* (1973a) we find a confusing juxtaposition of statements. Compare, for example, the claims, in one and the same article, that 'these macrofunctions [. . .] take the form of "grammar"' (Halliday, 1973b, p.356 = 1973a, p.36 – it is made clear that 'grammar' here refers to the lexicogrammatical level), and that 'the ideational function [. . .] is a major component of meaning in the language system' (1973b, p.358 = 1973a, p.39). At one point in *Explorations* it looks as if the confusion is about to be resolved. Halliday writes (1972, p.100 in 1973a):

The options in the grammar are organised into general components which are internal to language. But these components are based on 'macro-functions' that are extra-linguistic in origin and orientation.

This might lead us to think that the 'macrofunctions' and 'functional components' are different, the former being (socio)semantic, while the latter are internal to the grammar, and are a more abstract reflection of the macrofunctions. This rather attractive idea is, however, contradicted by Halliday's diagrammatic representation of levels and components (1972, p.101 in 1973a), in which the terms 'functional component' and 'macrofunction' are equated, and placed between the sociosemantic and lexicogrammatical networks. We must, therefore, agree with Gregory (1976, pp.198-9) when he comments in his (generally favourable) review of *Explorations*:

> Important questions remain about Halliday's model, particularly as regards the precise relationship between meaning potential and its realization at the level of form and the nature and details of the realization rules which connect the two, and the place of both within a comprehensive social theory of language.

The position is perhaps slightly clearer in a later paper (Halliday, 1975b). Here, the ideational, interpersonal and textual functions are explicitly treated as 'functional components of the semantic system' (1975b, p.27 = 1978, p.112), and are given the name 'metafunctions' (see also Section 4.4.5). The components are, however, still 'reflected in the lexicogrammatical system in the form of discrete networks of options' (1975b, p.28 = 1978, p.113), these options being those of transitivity, mood and theme. It is surely going too far, however, to claim, as Gregory does in a review of *Language as Social Semiotic* (Gregory, 1980b, p.77) that Halliday's later work goes a long way towards removing the doubts voiced in Gregory's earlier review of *Explorations*. We still do not know, at this point, just what it is in the semantics which is functionally organized.

A further shift is implicit in a still later article (Halliday, 1977), where the functional components are themselves again treated as semantic, but the transitivity, mood and theme networks now seem to be seen as constituting the semantic options, rather than as lexicogrammatical networks. And yet, in a further paper written in 1977, though not published until very recently, Halliday (1984a) appears to contradict this view. In a discussion of speech function in dialogue, he presents yet another slightly different model, one in which behavioural options at an extralinguistic 'social contextual' level are recoded as semantic options (including categories such as 'statement', 'question', 'command', 'offer'), which are in turn recoded as mood categories (basically, declarative, interrogative and imperative), seen as lexicogrammatical. We shall have cause to return to this account later (see Section 7.4.2). Others of Halliday's recent writings (1979, 1980a and c) confirm the position implicit in Halliday (1977): transitivity, mood and theme are seen as relatively independent blocks of *semantic* options.

The position adopted in these recent articles raises two important questions. Firstly, if the semantic level now consists of the functional component networks, what is the status of the sociosemantic networks discussed in Halliday (1973a) and reviewed in Chapter 4? And secondly, since Halliday still maintains allegiance to a tristratal model, what do the lexicogrammatical networks now consist of? Halliday's position with regard to the first question is relatively clear: it would seem that he would still wish to specify the semantic potential, now considered in terms of transitivity, mood and theme choices, for specific registers (defined in terms of the social contextual parameters of field, tenor and mode), rather than for the language as a whole. Halliday has not, however, even provided us with any clues for an answer to our second question. We have a slot for a lexicogrammatical level in the model, but no syntax to fill it.

The relationship between syntax and semantics is the subject of continuing controversy, and will be discussed again in later parts of this book (see especially Sections 6.4 and 8.2). Halliday's main failing lies not so much in his refusal to recognize any clear borderline between syntax and semantics as in his reluctance to make clear the apparent shifts in his position. It is possible to find two different publications dating from the same year, or even two sentences from the same article, which appear to take somewhat different positions, and yet Halliday seems content to allow what look like incompatible claims to stand side by side, without discussion, without even any recognition that they could indeed be regarded as different claims. We shall discuss further possible criticisms of Halliday's general approach to linguistic theorizing in Section 5.7.

5.3 A behavioural or a general semantics?

We saw in Section 4.2 that Halliday's semantic networks, at least as presented in *Explorations*, are regarded as encoding behavioural options ('can do') in linguistic options ('can mean'), and that the specification of the semantic potential is tied to social contexts and settings which are predicted to be important on the basis of some social theory, such as that postulated by Bernstein. This model has been criticized from within systemic linguistics by Fawcett (1975a). In what follows, we shall review Fawcett's criticisms and assess their validity. For further discussion, see Butler (1982, pp.44-8).

Fawcett's view is that although Halliday's sociosemantic networks provide an insightful description of, for example, control strategies in mother/child interaction, they are essentially networks of behavioural options, and do not, as such, constitute a level of language. He presents five arguments in favour of this view (Fawcett, 1975a, pp.32-6).

Firstly, Fawcett objects that the least delicate options in Halliday's sociosemantic networks (such as [threat]) are not necessarily mediated through language: for instance, a threat can be made by raising a fist. In answer to this objection, we may observe that a question can be asked by the raising of an eyebrow, yet no-one would suggest that the linguistic means by which questions can be asked should be excluded from the linguist's investigations. If a behavioural option *can* be mediated linguistically, then as linguists we should try to account for the linguistic means available, though not necessarily for the devices available in other codes.

Secondly, Fawcett objects (1975a, p.35) that 'some of the most delicate options to the right of the networks are non-terminal, so that the network cannot function as a fully explicitly generative device'. Two points can be made in answer to such criticism. Firstly, the networks could presumably be extended in delicacy to the point where the final structure and lexical content of the realizations could be specified. Secondly, and perhaps more controversially, it could be claimed that generativeness, heavily stressed in Chomskyan grammars (and, as we shall see, in the systemic grammars of Fawcett, Hudson and Butler) is only one possible aim of a grammar. We may also be interested in formulating grammars for descriptive purposes, in which case there is some justification for going no further in delicacy than is required for our particular purpose. As we have seen, applicability to text description is indeed one of Halliday's aims. This point will be taken up again in Chapter 10.

Fawcett's third objection is that some of the more delicate options in a sociosemantic network (for example those specifying process types) would need to be duplicated in the lexicogrammar, so resulting in an unacceptable degree of redundancy in the model. The validity of this objection again depends on one's aims in writing grammars: if a grammar is to be purely generative, with elegance and simplicity as high priorities, then certainly duplication is undesirable; if, however, we wish to be able to give an account of linguistic phenomena at different levels, perhaps for different purposes, then some sacrifice in elegance and simplicity is probably inevitable.

Fawcett's fourth objection, that Halliday's sociosemantic networks seem to imply a rankless semantics, with no internal semantic structuring of sentences, is surely valid. Halliday does not even make clear what kind of unit might qualify as a 'point of origin' for his sociosemantic networks.

It is Fawcett's fifth and final objection which raises the most serious doubts about the sociosemantic model. As we saw in Section 4.2, Halliday's requirement for setting up sociosemantic networks, viz. that they should be constructed only for those social contexts and settings which are important in terms of a social theory, imposes severe restrictions on the comprehensiveness of the model. Halliday himself admits (1971a, p.179 = 1973a, p.62) that 'we shall not of course expect to assign anything like the whole of an individual's language behaviour to situations of this kind', and (1972, p.92 in 1973a) therefore that 'of the total amount of speech by educated adults in a complex society, only a small proportion would be accessible to such an approach'. We are thus presented with a model which embraces only a small fraction of our everyday language. Fawcett rightly feels that this is a convincing argument against equating a 'behavioural semantics' with 'the semantics of a language'.

It is worth considering an alternative to the contextually restricted semantics of Halliday's model. We could try to specify the meaning potential more generally, without reference to specific situation types, and then attempt to find out which combinations of options are most likely in particular types of social context, as defined by the values of field, tenor and mode (if, indeed, we can rely on the validity of these situation type categories – see Section 5.5). The categories of the social theory would then come into the picture as determinants of situation types, as Halliday has himself suggested.

A contextually unrestricted semantics is at the heart of the systemic model proposed by Fawcett himself (see Fawcett, 1973a and b, 1975b, 1980). His 'systemic functional generative' model has much in common with Halliday's latest position, in that the functional component networks are regarded as semantic. There are, however, several important differences.

Fawcett, while not rejecting Halliday's sociological perspective, sets his model 'within the familiar Chomskyan framework of regarding linguistics as in principle a branch of cognitive psychology' (1980, p.4). Thus Fawcett's model includes not only a linguistic component, but also other codes, affective states, and the 'knowledge of the universe' which is put to use in linguistic communication, together with a 'problem solver' which decides on appropriate strategies for communication, and integrates the other components of the model.

So central is semantics to Fawcett's view of language that he proposes to restrict system networks to this level, rather than having a set of parallel networks at each level, as in Halliday's model. The semantic options are linked to syntactic structures and to grammatical and lexical 'items' by means of a realizational component. This differs markedly from the realization statements proposed by Halliday and by Berry, and discussed in Section 3.5. Fawcett (see for example 1980, p.47 ff.) proposes a 'starting framework' for each syntactic unit, consisting of a number of 'elements' (corresponding to immediate constituents of the unit), which can appear at various 'places' in the structure. The starting framework for the clause is as follows (1980, p.48):

$$1\ 2\ 3\ 4\ 5\ \ 6\ \ 7\ 8$$

$$\#^i \ \& \ B \qquad S\ \ O \quad X^1\ X^2\ X^3\ X^4\ X^5\ M\ C^1\ C^2\ A^1\ A^2\ A^3\ A^4\ A^n\ V\ \#^f$$

where: $\#^i$ = initial boundary marker
$\quad\quad\ \#^f$ = final boundary marker
$\quad\quad\ \&$ = Linker (e.g. 'and')
$\quad\quad\ B$ = Binder (e.g. 'if')
$\quad\quad\ S$ = Subject
$\quad\quad\ O$ = Operator (carrying modal meaning, tense, polarity)
$\quad\quad\ X$ = Auxiliary verb
$\quad\quad\ M$ = Main verb
$\quad\quad\ C$ = Complement
$\quad\quad\ A$ = Adjunct
$\quad\quad\ V$ = Vocative

The elements are shown in their most typical positions, corresponding to 'unmarked' choices from the semantic networks. 'Marked' options can be realized by moving an element into one of the empty slots (numbered 1 to 8) in the starting structure. For instance, polar questions can be generated by moving the Operator (O) to slot 5, before the Subject (S). The advantages claimed by Fawcett for this realization mechanism are that it gives recognition to the psychological reality of formal patterning, and that only one type of rule is needed, with no ordering.

We shall return to Fawcett's model when discussing the validity of the functional components hypothesis in the next section. Fawcett's proposals for systemic syntax are reviewed in Chapter 6.

5.4 The validity of the functional components hypothesis

We saw in Section 3.4 that Halliday's original justification for proposing the functional components hypothesis was as follows:

> If we represent the set of options available to the speaker in the grammar of the English clause, these options group themselves into a small number of subsets, distinct from one another in that, while within each group of options there is a very high degree of interdependence, between any two groups the amount of interdependence, though by no means negligible, is very much less. (Halliday, 1968, p.207)

There are several criticisms which can be levelled at this statement. Firstly, as Berry (1982, p.77) has pointed out, it is very easy to think of cases where two sets of systems, claimed to belong to different functional components, do in fact interact. Berry observes that Halliday himself has suggested interaction between the areas of transitivity and theme, and that attempts to formulate a network for voice (treated by Halliday as textual) usually lead to considerable interaction with the transitivity network (see Halliday, 1968, p.203). She also notes that the imperative option within the mood network (interpersonal) is available only if certain types of process are selected from the transitivity systems (ideational), as illustrated by the following examples from Berry's discussion:

5.6 Go!
5.7 *Happen.

We could add here that, as discussed in Butler (1982, p.245), the imperative is also ruled out in combination with the meanings carried by modal verbs and their paraphrases, and that this is so not only for those 'epistemic' or 'modality' meanings (of possibility, probability and certainty) which Halliday allocates to the interpersonal component, but also for the 'root' or 'modulation' meanings (of permission, obligation, and so on), which are said to be part of the ideational component. Examples from Butler (1982, p.245) are given below: for further discussion of the modal area in Hallidayan linguistics see Halliday 1970c, also Chapter 8 of this book.

5.8 *Must go now. (starred *qua* imperative)
5.9 *Be obliged to go now.

Halliday could, of course, defend his position by pointing out that his claim about the discreteness of networks is phrased in more-or-less terms rather than in all-or-none terms. However, we are then left with the decision as to just how many links between the blocks of options we are willing to allow before we regard the three (or four, if the logical is treated as a separate entity) component hypothesis as untenable. As Berry (1982, p.77) says, Halliday's more-or-less position 'presumably only means that there is all the more need for him to show that there really is a statistically significant difference between the "strong internal" and the "weak external" constraints. Particularly since other parts of his theory rest on the assumption that the statements made here are true'.

A second line of criticism might run as follows. We have, of course, no reason to disbelieve Halliday's claim that partitioning into three major blocks was something which simply became apparent when he was attempting to draw networks for the grammar of the English clause. It would, however, be naive to ignore the fact that Halliday's thinking has always been heavily influenced by functional concepts (taken in the broadest sense), such as those present in the work of Malinowski, Firth and the Prague School linguists. And it would be equally naive to pretend that such an orientation could not have influenced the way in which the networks were drawn up. The crucial point here is that we need to know precisely what Halliday's criteria were (and are) for formulating networks in a particular way. It could then be demonstrated whether the criteria were indeed independent of functional bias. Unfortunately, however, Halliday has always been reluctant to specify rigorous criteria for the setting up of terms in systems, and the arrangement of systems in delicacy ordering. To be fair to Halliday, much the same criticism could be levelled at other systemic linguists, although one attempt to discuss possible criteria is being made (Martin, forthcoming).

If all systemicists were indeed operating with the same set of criteria for drawing system networks, whether explicit or implicit, then we should expect that networks devised by different linguists, for the same area of the grammar, should look alike. This is, however, manifestly not the case. Even if we confine ourselves just to the work of Halliday himself, it is not difficult to find quite different networks for the same grammatical area, constructed at round about the same time (see, for instance, the networks for theme in Halliday, 1968, p.206 and 1969a, p.84).

Nor is it the case that all systemic linguists operating within a functional framework recognize the same number of functional components. Fawcett expands the number of components to six (in Fawcett, 1973a and b), and later to eight (in Fawcett, 1980). In the latest version of his model, Fawcett follows Halliday's split of the ideational into 'experiential' and 'logical', but also splits the interpersonal (into 'interactional' and 'affective'), and the textual (into 'informational' and 'thematic'), and adds two further components, 'modality' and 'negativity'. The multiplication of components in Fawcett's work arose out of a very laudable attempt to specify criteria for the recognition of such components. Fawcett's discussion (1980, pp.34-8) is summarized briefly in what follows.

As Fawcett points out (1980, p.35):

. . . if we consider ALL the system networks that are required, rather than just the more 'central' ones that have a high statistical probability of having an overt realization (as is done in introductions to the model such as most of Halliday's better known writings are), there are very many system networks that are almost completely independent of other system networks.

We cannot, then, accept Halliday's 'relative independence' criterion by itself, although it undoubtedly enters into the total picture. Fawcett then discusses, and rejects, two further possibilities. It is not the case that if two networks are entered both simultaneously and initially they must be allocated to different components (for instance, theme and information systems are simultaneous and initial in Halliday's scheme, but are both said to belong to the textual component). Neither is it true, as might at first sight seem plausible, that any network considered to belong centrally to a functional component must have its unmarked (most typical) options overtly realized at the level of form (for example, in some accounts, such as Halliday, 1973b, p.360 = 1973a, p.40, Halliday treats the polarity system as 'central', yet the unmarked term (affirmative) has no overt realization). Finally, Fawcett proposes a criterion which relates to his view of language as intimately bound up with other components of a communication system, including our 'knowledge of the universe'. The suggestion is that options within the same functional component relate to the same kind of knowledge: for instance, the areas of 'information focus' (signalled by the position of intonational prominence) and 'redundancy balance' (striking an appropriate balance between giving too much and too little information, realized by the use or non-use of elliptical forms such as 'Ike did (so)', 'Yes', and the like) both draw on the speaker's knowledge of the addressee's state of information, and both are allocated to the informational component in Fawcett's scheme. Within the framework of Fawcett's model, such a notion is perhaps attractive; however, it must be admitted that the whole problem of the interaction of our world knowledge and our acts of meaning is a thorny one, and that this is one of the least convincing areas of Fawcett's work.

Fawcett observes, in his discussion, that systemic features are definable in three ways: by their relations to other features at the same (semantic) level, by their 'downward' relations with their realizations at the level of form, and by their 'upward' relations with aspects of our knowledge of the universe. A very similar point is made in recent work by Halliday (1979), although, as we should expect, the 'upward' relations do not involve the psycholinguistic concept of world knowledge, but rather the sociolinguistic concept of a social semiotic. Whereas the original motivation claimed for the functional components was, as we have seen, in terms of the relationships within and between networks at a given level, Halliday is now suggesting that additional support for the hypothesis can be adduced from the relationships between semantic networks and what is 'above' and 'below' them.

In terms of what is 'above' the semantics, we have seen that Halliday has proposed a selective activation (again of a more-or-less kind rather than an all-or-none kind) of certain areas of meaning by each of the three determinants of register (field, tenor and mode), these areas of meaning corresponding to the functional components. In terms of what lies 'below' the semantics, Halliday is making a new suggestion, namely that the major functional areas of meaning labelled as experiential, logical, interpersonal and textual, are typically realized by different types of lexicogrammatical structure.

A structure representing experiential meanings is, according to Halliday, typically 'a configuration, or constellation, of discrete elements, each of which makes its own distinctive contribution to the whole' (Halliday, 1979, p.64). Examples are the inclusion of syntactic elements functionally labelled as Process, Participant and Circumstance, corresponding to choices in the transitivity network, or the presence of elements functionally labelled as Epithet, Numerative and Thing in a nominal group such as 'four young oysters'. This type of structure is one for which the notion of constituency is appropriate.

Interpersonal meanings are, it is suggested, realized through 'prosodic' structures, running like a thread through a stretch of language, rather than being located in quite separate entities. Examples include the use of intonation contours to express speech function and attitude, or the comulative expression of possibility by the incorporation of markers such as 'I wonder', 'perhaps', 'might', 'd'you think' into a single stretch of language such as the Halliday example given below:

5.10 I wonder if perhaps it might be measles, d'you think?

Textual options are said to be realized through 'culminative' structures, explained as follows (1979, p.69):

What the textual component does is to express the particular semantic status of elements in the discourse by assigning them to the boundaries; this gives special significance to 'coming first' and 'coming last', and so marks off units of the message as extending from one peak of prominence to the next.

Examples include the thematic status of the first element in clause structure, and the importance of the end of a tone group as the unmarked position for information focus.

Finally, as long ago as 1974 (Parret, 1974, pp.95-6 = Halliday, 1978, pp.48-9), Halliday claimed that logical meanings are expressed by recursive devices of parataxis and hypotaxis which were discussed in Section 2.3.2.2. Examples of paratactic devices include co-ordination (with 'and', 'or'), conjunction (with 'yet', 'so', 'then') and apposition; examples of hypotactic structuring would include condition and modification (for instance in the nominal group), among others (see Halliday 1979, p.76).

Halliday's proposals are interesting, and have links (recognized by Halliday) with Pike's (1959) discussion of language as *particle* (parallel to Halliday's particulate, constituent-like structures), *field* (Halliday's prosodic structures) and *wave* (culminative structures). This new evidence for the functional components is, however, subject to the same kind of criticism as the 'relative independence' criterion. Halliday is at pains to point out (1979, p.70) that 'when we associate each of these structural types with one of the functional semantic components, we are talking of a tendency not a rule'. Apart from the undesirable implication here that tendencies cannot be expressed as rules (for further discussion of this, see Berry, 1982, also Section 5.7), the vagueness of Halliday's formulation leaves us in the uncomfortable position of not knowing how many counter-examples would suffice to invalidate the hypothesis. As with the relative independence criterion, counter-examples are not hard to find: speech function, for instance, can be realized not only by prosodic means, but also by the relative ordering of two discrete constituents, the Subject and the finite verbal element of the clause.

A further difficulty arises from Halliday's comment (1979, p.70) that although the functional components themselves are claimed to be universals, 'the structural tendencies, though clearly non-arbitrary – we can see why it is that each should take this form – may differ very considerably from one language to another'. Thus it would seem that the evidence from modes of realization applies specifically to English, but may not apply, at least with such force, to other languages.

Finally, we must note a very important point made by Berry (1982, pp.75-6). As we have seen, one of Halliday's major claims is that field, tenor and mode determine the range of semantic options activated, the three situational parameters correlating with the ideational, interpersonal and textual components respectively. Halliday has also claimed that the functional organization of the semantics is reflected in that of the lexicogrammar, though, as we have seen, the position is unclear here. If a relation of determination is proposed between two phenomena A and B, then it is clearly necessary, as Halliday himself implies (1977, p.206 = 1978, p.149) that A and B should be independently definable. We thus need some way of defining the functional components independently of either the situation type or the lexicogrammar, and we are thus thrown back on the criterion of relative independence of networks, which, we have noted, is open to serious doubt.

In conclusion, we must say that although the functional components hypothesis is attractive, its validity is open to quite serious question. As Hudson (1974a, p.7) has observed, 'Halliday's claim is an empirical one, and should be testable by writing optimal grammars for all languages, then seeing whether their rules tend to fall into relatively independent sets and whether such sets, if there are any, reflect different functions of language'. But before we can write such 'optimal grammars', we must be very clear about exactly what is meant by 'optimal', and what criteria are being used for the formulation of system networks.

5.5 The validity of the categories of field, tenor and mode, and their correlation with semantic choice

We saw in Section 4.3.4 that definitions of the situation-type parameters of field, tenor and mode have been given in Halliday's work. However, as Berry (1982, p.75) has pointed out, these definitions are not sufficiently precise for another linguist to be able to say exactly what comes under each of the headings. This problem is highlighted by differences between Halliday's interpretation and that of Gregory, the other linguist most centrally associated with the proposed tripartite classification. As Halliday himself observes (1978, p.224), Gregory places distinctions of rhetorical genre (language used to persuade, inform, and so on) under tenor, creating a term 'functional tenor' for such relationships, as opposed to the 'personal tenor' reflected partly in formality (see Gregory, 1967, p.184 ff.; Gregory & Carroll, 1978, p.53 ff.); on the other hand, Halliday treats such distinctions as variants within the mode of discourse, and Berry (1982, p.75) suggests that they might be handled under field. Again, Gregory (1967, p.186) regards technical and non-technical varieties of language as differing in field, whereas for Halliday (1974, p.50 = 1978; p.222) such varieties are to be handled under tenor. As Berry (1982, p.75) observes, 'What is worrying here is not that there are differences of opinion, but that there seems to be no principled basis for adjudicating between the different opinions'. This is surely a crucial point: much of what Halliday claims in his most recent work rests on our acceptance of the validity of the field/tenor/mode distinction and the functional components hypothesis. Because of lack of rigour in giving criteria, we cannot be sure of the validity of either.

Halliday's claim that values of field selectively activate ideational meanings, values of tenor interpersonal meanings, and values of mode textual meanings, is, like the other major claims we have discussed, couched in more-or-less terms (see for example Halliday, 1974, p.52 = 1978, p.225). Again, in the absence of a more precise formulation, the hypothesis is impossible to falsify. The position is further complicated by the existence of recent work by Hasan (1978, 1980a and b) on the structure of text, which, although said to be set within the Hallidayan framework, could, as Berry (1980) has shown, be interpreted as making rival, and incompatible, claims. Hasan (1978, p.229) proposes that 'associated with each genre of text - i.e. type of discourse - is a generalized structural formula, which permits an array of actual structures'. Certain elements of the structural formula will be obligatory, others optional. Hasan goes on to claim that the structural formula for each genre is determined by the 'contextual configuration' (CC) of the text, which is made up of particular values of the variables field, tenor and mode. For instance, Hasan (1978, p.231) considers the following contextual configuration:

Variables	Values of the variables
field	professional consultation: medical; application for appointment . . .
tenor	client: patient-applicant, agent for consultant: receptionist; maximum social distance . . .
mode	aural channel: — visual contact: telephone conversation; spoken medium . . .

Corresponding to this contextual configuration, she claims, we have the structural formula RIˆ (A · II)ˆ OˆC, where RI = Respondent Identification, A = Application, II = Initiator Identification, O = Offer, C = Confirmation, · represents an unordered relation, ˆ an ordered relation, and brackets enclose optional elements. Any given text produced in the situation described by the contextual configuration will have one of a range of structures permitted by this general formula (RIˆOˆC, RIˆAˆIIˆOˆC, and others). Other optional elements such as Greeting (G) and Documentation (D) may also occur.

It is the nature of the determination of the structural formula by the contextual configuration which is of interest here. Hasan demonstrates (1978, p.236) that the presence of the element I (composed of the two elements RI and II in the formula) is determined jointly by the features [– visual contact] and [maximum social distance]. If the participants are in face-to-face interaction, and if they know each other quite well, then identification is unnecessary, and I does not appear in the structural formula. If the contextual configuration contains [+ visual contact] and [maximum social distance], or [– visual contact] and [minimum social distance], then at least part of I (that is, RI or II) is obligatory. Hasan discusses possible texts for three of the situation types:

5.11 (= Hasan's Tla) ([– visual contact], [maximum social distance])
  – Dr Scott's clinic (I)
  – this is Mrs Lee speaking (I) I wonder if I could see Dr Scott today (A)
  – um well let me see I'm afraid I don't have much choice of time today would 6.15 this evening suit you (O)
  – yes yes that'll be fine (C)

5.12 (= Hasan's T4a) ([– visual contact], [minimum social distance])
  – Dr Scott's clinic (I)
  – [oh Maria] it's me Julie here (I) etc.

5.13 (= Hasan's T5a) ([+ visual contact], [maximum social distance])
  – could I speak to Dr Scott's secretary (I)
  – I am the secretary (I)
  – well my name is Mrs Lee (I)

No text is offered for the [+ visual contact], [minimum social distance] situation, but it is clear that identification of either party would be superfluous.

Berry (1980, pp.24-5) demonstrates that a third situational factor may also be operative in determining the presence or absence of identification in texts. Quoting Labov's example:

5.14 (= Berry's 8)
(William Labov to total stranger in the street)
Excuse me! My name's William Labov. Can you tell me the way to the railway station?

Berry suggests that if there is no likelihood of a future transaction between the two parties in the interaction, identification is not permissible.

We may now see how Hasan's proposals might be at odds with Halliday's. It would seem that the presence of the I element is controlled by the contextual features [± visual contact] (a *mode* feature), [maximum/minimum social distance] (a *tenor* feature), and [± future transaction] (a *field* feature). If Hasan regards elements such as I as representing meanings, then it would appear that one type of meaning is determined by *all three* social contextual variables. This claim would, as Berry observes, be clearly incompatible with Halliday's proposal that each contextual variable determines a different area of meaning. Hasan might, of course, dispute the interpretation of her elements of text structure as meanings. In a later article on the same area (Hasan, 1980b, p.82), she writes of the presence of the structural elements being 'controlled by' meanings within the functional components, but does not expand on this. It is obviously important that the relationship between the contextual configuration, structural formula and functional components be made clear.

5.6 A brief critical appraisal of Halliday's work on 'learning how to mean'

There can be no doubt that Halliday's view of language acquisition as the learning of meaning potential and its realization offers many insights which are not to be gained from the better-known 'structural' work in this area. Halliday's work is not, however, without its problems.

Firstly, as we have seen, Halliday's approach to language acquisition is based on the premise that the organization of the adult linguistic system is functional, so that the child's progress is seen in terms of successive modifications of his own functional potential, leading ultimately to the mature system. We have seen that the functional components hypothesis, though attractive, cannot yet be regarded as very firmly supported. Even Dore (1977, p.114), in a generally very favourable review of *Learning How to Mean*, feels that Halliday 'is somewhat less successful, or at least puzzling, in supporting some basic claims; for example, that "the internal organization of the grammatical system is also functional in character" (p.16)'. Dore also observes, correctly, that Halliday does not actually demonstrate that language functions determine case-like structures (that is, the relations between functional roles such as Actor, Process and Goal).

Secondly, Halliday provides no evidence for the 'relevant models of language' (instrumental, regulatory, interactional, personal, heuristic, imaginative and representational) which he claims the child internalizes.

Furthermore, although Halliday tells us that these become combined and modified to give the 'pragmatic' and 'mathetic' macrofunctions during Phase II of language development, and that this distinction in turn breaks down in favour of the tripartite adult functional system, there is again no concrete evidence for this particular interpretation of the changes in meaning potential. As Dore (1977, p.117) says:

> . . . although it is clear that Halliday describes how the functional system changes, it cannot be confidently stated that he explains why it does or why the grammar should have the form it does. The child's achievement of greater meaning potential no more explains the change than does the structuralist argument about disambiguation explain the change from one-word to syntactic utterances.

Thirdly, Halliday's interpretation of language acquisition as a socio-semiotic development rests on the acceptance of the sociolinguistic model discussed in Section 4.3. We have now seen that certain of the key concepts of this model are open to some doubt. In particular, the interesting idea that components of the meaning potential are selectively activated by features of social context, as defined by values of field, tenor and mode, is made problematic by the lack of clear definition of, and motivation for, not only the functional components, but also the situation-type variables (see Section 5.5).

Finally, we must question whether the methodology of Halliday's project was really adequate for the task at hand. It is, as Dore (1977, p.116) comments, a tribute to Halliday's virtuosity as a linguist that he managed to record so much interesting data simply by the use of pencil and paper, often when acting also as a participant in the linguistic inter-action. However, the most adept transcriber is prone to error and, more insidiously, to selectivity, and it would surely have been wiser (if more difficult) to make audio recordings of the child's language. Indeed, in view of the heavy reliance placed on contextual information in the allocation of function to utterances, a video recording would have been extremely helpful.

5.7 Further comments on Halliday's general approach to linguistic theorizing

In the course of the present chapter, certain general criticisms of Halliday's approach to the presentation of his theories have emerged. In particular, we have suggested that Halliday has not been sufficiently concerned to make clear the apparent shifts in his theoretical position, or to give detailed reasons for these shifts. In the present section we shall consider further critical comments on Halliday's general approach, made by Berry (1982) in her review of *Language as Social Semiotic*.

Concentrating on Chapter 6 of *Language as Social Semiotic* (the shortened version of Halliday, 1975b), Berry points out that Halliday's theory has, potentially, some important contributions to make to both linguistic and educational theory, but that it still remains merely an outline of a theory, which has not since been filled in, whether by Halliday him-self or by other systemic linguists. Berry's main point is that Halliday makes it more difficult for himself or other linguists to develop his approach, because he does not present his arguments in the ways linguists normally use. She comments that Halliday is in fact proscribing the very means which linguists usually employ for developing and testing their theories, leaving himself with nothing effective to put in their place. Berry goes on to discuss five specific points of criticism.

The first criticism concerns the relationship between theory and relevant data in Halliday's presentation. There is, as Berry points out, very little data in Halliday's discussion. What data there is is also limited in range, not related point by point to the theory, and not always strictly relevant to the theoretical claims made. The last point is a particularly important one: Berry is quite right to criticize Halliday for using just a single, rather homogeneous text as data, and then claiming that certain features of texts are determined by features of social context. As Berry (1982, p.73) says, 'one cannot support a hypothesis that factor X determines feature A without showing, not only that A occurs when X occurs, but also *that A does not occur when X does not occur*. Halliday's discussion of a single homogeneous text does not show what it claims to show'. A consideration of even two texts would have been sufficient to justify the setting up of a hypothesis, although systematic testing of the hypothesis would, of course, require analysis of a statistically valid sample of texts. A further, related point made by Berry is that Halliday does not use types of data other than textual (for instance, intuitions about, and reactions to, texts), and does not even discuss what different types of data would be relevant to his theory.

Berry's second criticism is one that has been made throughout the present chapter, namely that Halliday fails to define his terms adequately. She gives examples from *Language as Social Semiotic* of terms (such as *meaning, semiotic*) whch are undefined, others (such as *semantics*) which are defined in different ways in different parts of the book without explanation, and yet others (such as *field, tenor* and *mode*) which are not defined precisely enough for Halliday's analyses to be replicable. Furthermore, as we noted in Section 5.4, Halliday often defines one category in terms of another, and yet claims that one of the categories determines the other. It is, as Berry observes, essential that categories be independently defined if a relationship of determination is to be proposed.

Berry's third criticism is that Halliday fails to distinguish clearly between fact and hypothesis. In other words, claims are often made authoritatively, as if based on systematic observation, when in fact no such objective and systematic investigation has been carried out. An example was discussed in Section 5.4, namely the claim that networks for the English clause fall into three fairly discrete blocks.

A final criticism concerns two types of linguistic description which Halliday denies himself, but which Berry considers would make it much easier to develop his theory. Firstly, Berry feels that the shift away from syntagmatic relations towards paradigmatic relations, which we have noted in Chapters 3 and 4, has gone so far that syntagmatic phenomena have now all but disappeared from the theory, when in fact such relations would provide a useful way of defining some of the categories whose definitions are at present too imprecise. We shall consider such definitions further in our discussion of systemically orientated discourse analysis in

Chapter 7, and one example will therefore suffice here. Berry's suggestion is that categories such as 'ask' and 'demand', as used in *Language as Social Semiotic*, could be defined in terms of what they predict in the structure of the following discourse: thus an act of asking predicts a syntagmatically related answer, and a demand predicts a non-verbal response to satisfy that demand. Berry also considers that Halliday's failure to take syntagmatic relations into account means that he cannot explain why only part of the total meaning potential can appropriately be activated at any particular point in the structure of a discourse – for instance, that an answer is appropriate only in response to someone else's act of asking.

The other type of linguistic description which Halliday opposes is one in terms of rules. Halliday himself says (1978, pp.191-2) that for him it is important 'to interpret language not as a set of rules but as a *resource*'. The idea appears to be that rules are inappropriate for describing how people actually interact verbally. But, as Berry (1982, p.86) points out, there is in fact no clash between the concept of a rule and the desire to account for the ways in which people talk to one another. System networks can be regarded as collections of rules, just as structural formulae can, and the notion of 'variable rule', central to much recent work in sociolinguistics, allows a flexibility which is well suited to the kind of investigation Halliday wishes to pursue. The essential characteristic of rules is explicitness, and this is precisely what Halliday's work so often lacks.

5.8 Concluding remarks

Since the present chapter has been quite severely critical of many aspects of Halliday's recent work, it is important to point out that the inadequacies we have discussed matter greatly only because the ideas Halliday puts forward have such great potential for a theory of how language structure relates to the structure of the social context and, more widely, to the culture. For this reason, it is very much to be hoped that criticisms such as those voiced by Berry will be taken in the spirit in which they are intended, and, even more importantly, acted upon, so that we may develop a precise and rigorous systemic theory which will be truly open to falsification and modification.

6. Systemic syntax

6.1 Introduction

In Chapter 2 we discussed the Scale and Category model of language expounded most completely by Halliday in his article *Categories of the theory of grammar* (Halliday, 1961). In subsequent chapters we have seen that since about 1966, Halliday's own model has given increasing prominence to semantic phenomena. Although it is frankly difficult to know what counts as semantic and what as syntactic in this later work, Halliday's most recent proposals do at least make it clear that the functional component networks are to be regarded as semantic, but we are given very little idea of what the lexicogrammar might now consist of.

Other systemic linguists have, however, been concerned to remedy this gap in later systemic linguistics. In particular, Fawcett (1974, 1975c, 1976) and Hudson (1971, 1974a, 1976, 1978) have proposed models of syntax within a systemic framework. As we shall see, Hudson's later work marks a considerable departure from Hallidayan approaches: indeed, his most recent model is not recognizably systemic at all. The present chapter will summarize Fawcett's and Hudson's models of systemic syntax.

6.2 Fawcett's 'iconoclastic approach to Scale and Category grammar'

We saw in Section 5.3 that Fawcett's systemic model is firmly centred on the semantics, to the extent that only at that level are system networks postulated. Syntactic 'choices' are seen simply as contrasts, and not given systemic status. Paradigmatic patterning at the syntactic level is thus not formalized. Fawcett has, however, made detailed proposals for the description of the structure (that is, syntagmatic patterning) of English. His approach to the recognition of syntactic categories is dictated by his commitment to the centrality of semantics:

> The main criteria that I consider have validity are *semantic* criteria, in the sense that the syntactic categories that I shall make use of are those that seem to be needed to state with the greatest economy the realisation rules that express the options in the semantics. Criteria that *seem* syntactic, such as those relating to the internal and external relationships that a unit may enter into, are in the last analysis themselves dependent on semantic criteria. In other words, if you don't need to recognise a unit or element of structure to state a realisation rule, that unit or element should have no place in the syntax. (Fawcett, 1974, pp.4-5, original emphasis)

Applying this rule, Fawcett sets out to modify Halliday's Scale and

Category model (the term 'iconoclastic' in the heading of this section is Fawcett's own) in such a way that it will be applicable to the detailed description of naturally occurring texts in English. We have already seen that the category of *system* is removed to the semantics; the categories of *unit* and *element of structure* retain a similar role to that in Halliday's model; the criteria for defining *class* are changed; the *rank* scale is reduced in extent and importance; the scale of *exponence*, as used in Halliday's 1961 paper, is developed further; and the scale of *delicacy*, though viewed as in Halliday's work, is not seen as central to the theory. We shall now look briefly at Fawcett's treatment of exponence, class and rank.

Fawcett (1974, pp.7-9) splits Halliday's scale of exponence into three parts, of which *exponence* proper is one, the others being *componence* and *filling*. Componence is the relation between a unit and the elements of structure of which it is composed. For example, a clause may be composed of the elements S, P, C and A. Each of these elements of structure may be (but need not be – see below) filled by groups. In the specification of a syntactic structure, componence and filling alternate until, at the bottom of the structural tree, the smallest elements of structure are not filled by other units. It is at this point that we need the concept of exponence, as used by Fawcett: the lowest elements of structure are expounded by 'items' which, as we shall see, are more or less equivalent to 'words' and 'morphemes' in Halliday's model. Exponence thus takes us out of syntax, as viewed by Fawcett. The concepts of componence, filling and exponence are illustrated in the following example from Fawcett (1974, p.7). The elements of group structure will in part be unfamilar, and will be explained later.

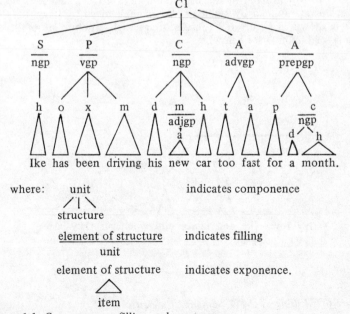

Figure 6.1: Componence, filling and exponence

The notion of 'filling' leads Fawcett to propose a definition of class of unit which is quite different from Halliday's. We saw in Section 2.3.2.3 that Halliday defined the class of members of a unit in terms of the part played by the unit in the structure of the unit next above on the rank scale. Thus, for example, a verbal group is one which acts at P in clause structure. It was shown in Section 2.4.2 that this approach runs into difficulties when we examine the kinds of group which can act at A in clause structure: as Fawcett (1974, p.10) points out, if 'too fast' and 'for a month' in Figure 6.1 above are to be recognized as adverbial groups, on the basis that they typically act at A, then surely groups such as 'last week' should also be regarded as adverbial when they act as Adjuncts. As was noted in Section 2.4.2, Halliday (1963c, p.6) is inconsistent in his treatment of such groups, allowing their structural similarity to other nominal groups to determine their primary syntactic classification, and so going against his own definition of class.

Fawcett completely rejects the 'function in the higher unit' criterion for classification, his own classification of units being based purely on internal structure (cf. Halliday's 'type', see Section 2.3.2.3). As Fawcett points out, this allows him to account in a simple and elegant way for the complexity and flexibility of the grammar: 'a relatively *small* number of units can carry a very *large* number of complex meanings precisely because there is *not* a one-to-one relationship between unit and element of structure' (1974, p.10, original emphasis). Thus, for example, the Adjunct element of clause structure can be filled by adverbial groups such as 'very quickly', prepositional groups (or, as Fawcett calls them, 'prepend groups') such as 'for a month', or nominal groups such as 'last week'. Fawcett also allows the A element (as well as the S and C elements) to be filled by a clause, so dispensing with the distinction between α β and rank shifted structures maintained by Halliday. An example given by Fawcett (1974, p.9) is shown in Figure 6.2 (details of internal structure are omitted; L stands for Linker — see below).

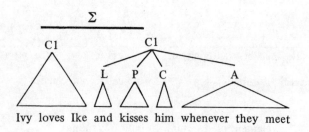

Figure 6.2: Filling of the A element by a clause

Provided that we accept the explicit labelling of structural functions in the grammar (see Section 2.4.3), Fawcett's proposals are simpler and more consistent than Halliday's. The definition of class in terms of constituency, together with the recognition of elements of structure representing structural functions, allows us to account for much of the complexity of language in terms of many-to-many relations between the two categories. In proceeding in this way, we are doing no more than recognizing the dual nature of traditional labels such as 'noun phrase': a noun phrase or nominal group consists minimally of a head noun or pronoun; it can act as the Subject or Complement of a clause, but can also perform other syntactic functions (for instance, as the complement, or 'completive', of a preposition).

Fawcett's model makes extensive use of the concept of rank shift, in postulating the filling of elements of clause or group structure by other clauses, and elements of group structure by other groups. The rank scale is, however, reduced to just clause and group, together with a new unit, the cluster, which will be described briefly later. In abandoning the sentence as the highest syntactic unit, Fawcett is simply following the ideas of Huddleston (1965) reviewed in Section 2.3.2.2, later accepted by Halliday (see, for example, Halliday 1977, p.177 = 1978, p.129). More controversial are his proposals for removing 'word' and 'morpheme' from the grammatical rank scale, so hiving off morphology in a reversion to the more traditional approach which was abandoned in Halliday's integrated rank scale.

Fawcett observes (1976, p.50) that some elements of group structure are typically *not* filled by 'words': for instance, qualifiers in nominal groups are almost always rank shifted groups or clauses. Furthermore, when an element of group structure *can* be filled by a single word, it can equally well, in many cases, be filled by a higher unit: for example, the completive to a preposition can be a single word (as in 'in cities'), but this can be expanded into a nominal group with more than one element of structure (as in 'in all the largest cities'). Another problem is that some elements of group structure can be filled by items which are not obviously 'words' in any meaningful sense, and yet have to be treated as 'functioning as a word' in a Hallidayan model. Examples include complex prepositions such as 'in spite of', 'because of', and complex conjunctions such as 'in order that'.

In order to resolve these problems, Fawcett removes from the theory any expectation that elements of group structure will be filled by a particular kind of unit, or indeed by any kind of unit at all. Some elements of group structure are indeed filled by units, but others may be expounded directly by items (for instance, the element p could be expounded directly by the item 'in spite of'). Fawcett's proposal also involves a relaxation of Halliday's principle of 'total accountability' (see Section 2.3.2.1), by which every linguistic item must be accounted for at all ranks. As Fawcett (1976, p.54) remarks, in Halliday's theory an Adjunct such as 'moreover', 'therefore' or 'however' would have to be treated as the head of an adverbial group. There is, however, no possibility of expanding such Adjuncts by the addition of other elements of adverbial group structure, as there is with an Adjunct such as 'quickly' (expandable as 'very quickly', 'very quickly indeed', and so on). Fawcett therefore proposes that Adjuncts such as 'moreover' are expounded directly by the items concerned. Similarly, the clause structure elements Binder and Linker are directly expounded by items such as 'because', 'if', 'as soon as', or 'and', 'or', respectively; such items thus operate outside the rank scale (see also Section 2.4.1).

If, then, words and morphemes are no longer to be regarded as grammatical units, we may ask how Fawcett proposes to deal with the internal structure of words. His answer to this question is brief, inexplicit and somewhat unsatisfactory (Fawcett, 1976, pp.51-2). Morphs representing certain inflectional morphemes (such as the possessive 's) are regarded as 'items', just as are whole words. We are told, however, that 'morphemes such as *n't*, the plural morpheme and the suffixes on auxiliaries are handled as simple affixes on items that fill elements of structure, and we have not discussed these in detail'. Derivational morphology 'is assigned to the student of historical linguistics', and no more is said about it. Clearly, we need more detailed proposals for how morphological phenomena might be handled in the context of a model such as Fawcett puts forward.

Furthermore, the elimination of word and morpheme from the rank scale has one especially undesirable consequence, in that it forces Fawcett to propose a new syntactic unit, the *cluster*, to handle certain phenomena such as possessive constructions. Examples of the 'genitive cluster' given by Fawcett include the following:

6.1 the King of England's own (hat).
6.2 the play's (climax).
6.3 those boys' (feet).

Clusters, unlike groups, cannot fill elements of clause structure directly. For instance, 'the King of England's' cannot fill the S, P, C or A element of clause structure (unless, of course, the headword is ellipted, as in 'The King of England's contains the biggest diamond'). Clusters also differ from groups in that they fill only one element of structure: a genitive cluster can fill only the 'deictic determiner' element of nominal group structure. Clusters are tentatively proposed also for the structure of proper names (such as 'Mr George Bernard Shaw') and certain elements (called 'temperers' — see below) which can premodify adjectives and adverbs (as in 'much too soon'). The postulation of a new unit to handle so few phenomena seems an unsatisfactorily *ad hoc* solution, and is made necessary, at least in the case of possessive constructions, only because Fawcett denies himself the simpler and more general solution involving rank shift. In a Hallidayan model, we can regard 'the King of England', 'the play', and so on, as nominal groups rank shifted to the rank of word, to combine with the possessive morpheme realized as ''s'. Since there is no rank of word in Fawcett's grammar, this solution is not available.

We conclude this discussion of Fawcett's model with a brief illustration of the range of group structures proposed, using examples taken from Fawcett's own work. Space does not permit detailed discussion of the justification for individual categories.

The elements of nominal group structure are as follows (Fawcett, 1975c, p.46):

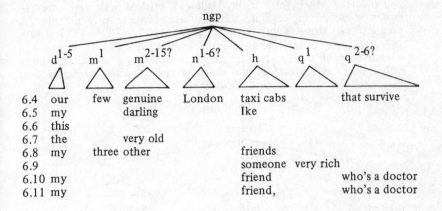

	d$^{1-5}$	m^1	m$^{2-15?}$	n$^{1-6?}$	h	q^1	q$^{2-6?}$
6.4	our	few	genuine	London	taxi cabs		that survive
6.5	my		darling		Ike		
6.6	this						
6.7	the		very old				
6.8	my	three	other		friends		
6.9					someone	very rich	
6.10	my				friend		who's a doctor
6.11	my				friend,		who's a doctor

Here, d = determiner, m = modifier, n = nominator, h = headword, q = qualifier. More delicate distinctions are also recognized at d.

Fawcett's model does not actually regard the 'verbal group' as a single clause constituent, but follows certain transformational generative approaches in suggesting that the individual auxiliary verbs and main verbs are clause constituents in their own right (Fawcett, 1975c, p.59). Evidence for this view includes the fact that 'verbal groups' are easily interrupted by adverbials, and also the observation that this 'group' is redundant in that it has a one-to-one relation with the element P in clause structure. Nevertheless, for pedagogical purposes Fawcett does make use of the Scale and Category concept of verbal group, and proposes the following structure:

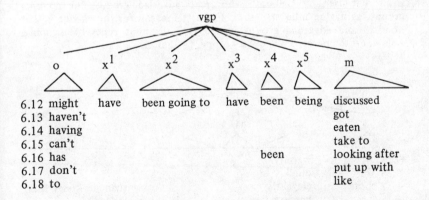

	o	x^1	x^2	x^3	x^4	x^5	m
6.12	might	have	been going to	have	been	being	discussed
6.13	haven't						got
6.14	having						eaten
6.15	can't						take to
6.16	has					been	looking after
6.17	don't						put up with
6.18	to						like

The symbol o represents the 'operator' (for discussion see Quirk *et al.*, 1972, p.65); x represents an auxiliary verb, and m the main verb. Fawcett does not discuss in any detail the problem of 'verb + particle' constructions such as 'take to', 'look after', 'put up with'.

Fawcett's model differs from Halliday's original Scale and Category model in recognizing separate classes of adverbial and 'prepend' (that is, prepositional) group (see, however, Halliday, 1977, p.177 = 1978, p.129, which does recognize a class of prepositional group). This is, of course, a consequence of the decision to base classification on structural criteria rather than on function in the clause. Prepend groups are regarded as having the following structure (Fawcett, 1975c, p.60):

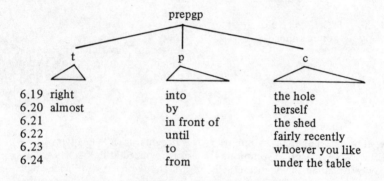

	t	p	c
6.19	right	into	the hole
6.20	almost	by	herself
6.21		in front of	the shed
6.22		until	fairly recently
6.23		to	whoever you like
6.24		from	under the table

Here, t stands for 'temperer', the label being chosen to show the similarity of this element to the identically named element of adverbial and adjectival group structure (see below); p is prepend, and c completive. The completive can be a nominal group (as in 6.19-6.21), an adverbial group (as in 6.22), a clause (as in 6.23) or another prepend group (as in 6.24).

The structural labelling of adverb-headed groups (Fawcett, 1974, pp.11-13) is adapted from the account given by Muir (1972), and differs from that used by Halliday, who treats adverbial groups, like nominal groups, as having mhq structure. Fawcett's reason for the change is that nominal and adverbial groups realize very different types of meaning. Below, t = temperer, a = apex, s = scope, l = limiter.

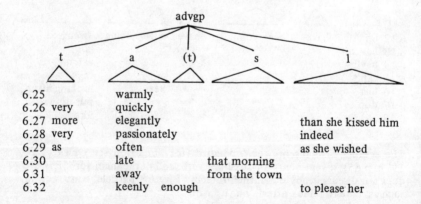

	t	a	(t)	s	l
6.25		warmly			
6.26	very	quickly			
6.27	more	elegantly			than she kissed him
6.28	very	passionately			indeed
6.29	as	often			as she wished
6.30		late		that morning	
6.31		away		from the town	
6.32		keenly	enough		to please her

The temperer usually precedes the apex, but the item 'enough', acting as temperer, follows. Limiters typically realize meanings whose realization starts in the temperer; scope elements realize a rather different type of meaning, defining the scope of some quite general meaning expressed in the apex. Both scope and limiter are typically filled by rank shifted groups or clauses.

Adjectival groups are recognized as a separate class by Fawcett. This approach again differs from that of Halliday, who regards adjectival groups, such as 'very quick indeed', as a sub-class of nominal group, on the grounds that they can act at C in clause structure (see Section 2.4.2). Structurally, however, adjective-headed groups have more in common with adverbial groups than with nominal groups (compare 'very quick indeed', 'very quickly indeed'), and this is reflected, in Fawcett's scheme, in the use of the same structural labels for adjectival and adverbial classes (Fawcett, 1974, p.14). The reason for recognizing these classes as separate is that they realize different types of semantic choice.

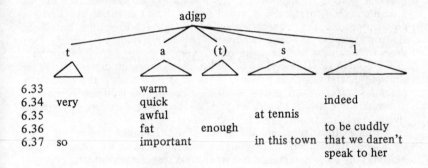

	t	a	(t)	s	l
6.33		warm			
6.34	very	quick			indeed
6.35		awful		at tennis	
6.36		fat	enough		to be cuddly
6.37	so	important		in this town	that we daren't speak to her

The 'genitive cluster' (1975c, p.66) has the following structure:

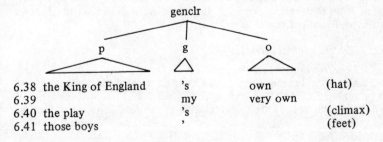

	p	g	o	
6.38	the King of England	's	own	(hat)
6.39		my	very own	
6.40	the play	's		(climax)
6.41	those boys	'		(feet)

Here, p = possessor, g = genitive, o = owner.

Even the brief overview presented here will have demonstrated that Fawcett's model allows a much more detailed description of English structures than Halliday's original Scale and Category model. Fawcett (1976, p.65) makes it clear that he, like Halliday, wishes the model to be applicable to text analysis: indeed, the proposals are themselves the result of successive modifications necessitated by problems raised during the analysis of texts. The model is at present being used in a study of children's language being supervised by Fawcett.

6.3 Hudson's work on systemic syntax

6.3.1 Stages in Hudson's work

Four major stages can be recognized in Hudson's work. His first large-scale contribution to systemic linguistics was *English Complex Sentences: An Introduction to Systemic Grammar* (Hudson, 1971), in which he set out a systemic model which, although clearly derived from Halliday's work, yet had a very distinct character of its own, as can be judged merely from the fact that it was applied to the description of phenomena, such as clausal complementation, which had received scant attention in Halliday's publications. A considerably modified model was presented briefly in Hudson's paper 'Systemic generative grammar' (Hudson, 1974a). Two years later came a further major book, *Arguments for a Non-Transformational Grammar* (Hudson, 1976). This presented a model which, while showing clear links with previous work by Hudson and others, was sufficiently different to merit a distinct name, 'daughter dependency grammar'. This model has, as we shall see, been hailed as a serious alternative to transformational generative grammar.

Although these three models show major differences, they are all based on a set of fundamental underlying assumptions, and we shall discuss these before going on to summarize the salient features of each model.

Recently, Hudson has developed daughter dependency grammar in a new direction, into a model which he calls 'word grammar' (see especially Hudson, 1982, 1984). This model marks a break with some of the underlying assumptions of the earlier accounts. Since it is no longer recognizably systemic (and is not regarded as such by Hudson), we shall not deal with it in any detail; however, since it shows a clear line of development from daughter dependency grammar, we shall summarize its main features at the end of this chapter.

6.3.2 General characteristics

6.3.2.1 The autonomy of levels

In all his work, Hudson adopts the view that syntax and semantics (and also phonology, though his work is concerned very little with this end of the linguistic hierarchy) are to be treated, in the first instance at least, as separate levels:

What I shall be assuming [. . .] is that the linguistic description of an utterance-type will consist of four separate representations, each corresponding to a different level of language: phonological, grammatical, lexical and semantic. (1971, p.11)

The GRAMMAR has to provide a set of descriptive categories such as 'interrogative', 'noun-phrase', 'transitive verb', 'conditional', 'subject' and 'restricted'. These would be related 'upwards' to the sentence's meaning in a more or less direct way [...]. The grammatical categories are also related 'downwards' to phonological categories, however. (1974a, p.8)

. . . it is only if you start from the assumption that syntax and semantics are separate that you can really find out how closely they are related, and be impressed by the many points at which they are in almost a one-one relationship. (1976, p.7)

Given the view of semantics that I am advocating, there is no reason to assume in advance that semantic and syntactic structures must be in a simple relation to one another, . . . (1984, 136)

Although Hudson does not discuss the autonomy of levels in any detail, he does offer a number of brief observations in support of his view. One is that 'the elements that we isolate on the different levels can cut across each other' (1971, p.10). Hudson gives the example below:

6.42 They're pulling your leg.

'They're' consists phonologically of a single syllable, but grammatically represents subject NP + auxiliary. 'Pulling your leg' is grammatically parallel to 'pulling your arm', but in its idiomatic interpretation the lexeme is presumably 'pull - - - 's leg', which has no status as a grammatical element. Further arguments are presented in Hudson (1976, pp.4-7). There exist noun phrases which are syntactically but not semantically plural, such as 'these bathroom scales', 'these oats' (compare 'this wheat'); others are semantically but not syntactically plural, so that, for instance, 'committee' can co-occur with a singular verb, but also with verbs such as *disperse* which require a subject referring to a group of individuals, noun phrases such as 'a large heap of logs' can occur in reciprocal constructions, as in 'A large heap of logs were piled on top of each other', and so on.

6.3.2.2 The goals of a grammar
Unlike Halliday, Hudson accepts many of the goals of transformational generative approaches to language (we saw in Section 5.3 that some of these goals are also accepted by Fawcett). In particular, Hudson places great emphasis on *generativeness*, and has, more than any other linguist, been responsible for introducing into systemic linguistics the degree of explicitness which a generative grammar requires.

. . . a grammar should consist of rules that can be used in a completely mechanical way to decide whether or not any given object is well-formed [...]

The reason for wanting a grammatical description of a language to be generative, in the sense of explicit, is that this is the only way of finding out precisely what one has to know in order to be a native speaker of that language – we must take none of this knowledge for granted, so we must spell everything out in a completely explicit way. (1971, p.7)

Hudson (1971, p.4) aligns himself with the 'God's truth' view of linguistics rather than the 'hocus-pocus' view: that is, he believes that in writing a grammar we are trying to capture 'the truth' about that language. He sees this 'truth' as having to do with the way in which a native speaker's linguistic knowledge is stored in the brain: it follows, of course, that Hudson's theories are seen as postulating a set of linguistic universals of a formal kind. Hudson's view of language is thus uncompromisingly mentalistic, and in this respect contrasts sharply with Halliday's approach. It was indeed under the influence of Hudson that Fawcett developed his cognitive approach to language, reviewed in Section 5.3.

Hudson also follows the Chomskyan tradition in his evaluation criteria for grammars. These include 'generality, comprehensiveness, elegance, simplicity, economy, and so on' (1971, p.4), the last three, in particular, being criteria which have been accorded a very low priority in Hallidayan grammars. We shall see, in what follows, that Hudson has 'played the transformational game' in that he has attempted to construct grammars which will account for the range of phenomena with which transformational generative linguistics has been concerned, but in what he believes to be a more natural and revealing manner. Hudson again contrasts with Halliday, who appears to feel that his own aims differ so greatly from those of transformational generative linguists that comparisons are unhelpful.

6.3.2.3 The content of a grammar

Hudson's grammars (with the exception of his recent, wide-ranging 'word grammar') deal specifically with the syntactic properties of linguistic items. As Hudson points out (e.g. 1976, p.14, 23 ff.; 1978, p.2), the structural trees generated in his systemic grammar differ from those of a transformational grammar in one very important respect: in the systemic account, a single structural representation includes information which in a transformational model would be captured in separate 'deep' and 'surface' representations, linked by a series of transformationally related intermediate stages.

This has a number of important consequences, which are discussed by Hudson (1971, p.18 ff.; 1976, p.24 ff.; 1978, p.2). Firstly, it means that no transformations are needed, since their function is to link deep and surface structures. Secondly, the difficulties of deciding whether deep sequence should differ from surface sequence are avoided. Thirdly, all rules relating semantic and syntactic structures can refer to the same syntactic structure. This contrasts with the position in Chomsky's 'Extended Standard Theory' (see Chomsky, 1970), which postulates that both deep and surface structure representations need to be referred to in semantic interpretation. Fourthly, there are certain rules mapping syntax on to phonology which require both deep and surface information, and this is all available in the single structure generated by Hudson's grammars. Fifthly, lexical insertion is much easier in a model with only one structural representation, since it can simply apply at the end of a syntactic derivation, rather than in stages, as in transformational grammar. Sixthly, a single integrated structure has advantages from a psycholinguistic viewpoint, since there is considerable doubt over which of the structures generated by a transformational grammar have any psychological validity. Finally, testing of the model by the mechanical generation of structures by computer should be easier if there is a single structure to generate rather than a chain of structures.

A second general gain of Hudson's grammars over transformational grammars is that they are more concrete: they do not allow the generation of underlying elements which never reach the surface structure, or of underlying sequences of constituents which differ from the surface sequence (see Hudson, 1974a, p.21; 1976, p.23). The ability to dispense with deletion and reordering rules is largely a consequence of a further important property which marks off systemic grammars in general from most versions of transformational grammar (see Hudson, 1971, p.47; 1974a, p.11; 1976, p.16; 1978, p.1 ff.). In a transformational grammar of the *Aspects* type, only the terminal nodes are classified by means of features. In a systemic grammar, on the other hand, higher nodes also bear features: that is, clauses and phrases, as well as words, are all sub- and cross-classified. This means that 'the rules which introduce immediate constituents [. . .] can be sensitive to quite specific sub-classifications of clauses and phrases, and only introduce immediate constituents of the right kind to fit the particular subclass in question' (1978, p.1). It is this which enables a systemic grammar to generate structures without deleting or permuting 'underlying' elements.

Like other systemic grammars, Hudson's grammars provide an account of the two major types of patterning, syntagmatic and paradigmatic. Syntagmatic relations can be broken down into three components: constituency, sequence and dependency relations (1971, p.29 ff.). Constituency and sequence relations are shown by the tree diagrams used for structural representation. By dependency, Hudson means relations of the type exemplified by subject-verb concord, concord between demonstrative determiners and head nouns ('this plate'/'these plates'), the relationship between 'have' and the '-en' form of the succeeding verb in the English perfect construction, and so on. The explicit discussion of such relations is one of Hudson's major contributions to systemic theory (it is not entirely clear how Halliday would handle, for instance, subject-verb concord), and we shall see that dependency relations become a cornerstone of Hudson's later daughter dependency model.

Paradigmatic relations are shown by means of systems as in other systemic grammars. For Hudson, terms in systems are simply classes of syntactic item, as defined by distributional criteria and by those internal constituency properties which are relevant to distribution (1971, p.45 ff., 1976, p.20; 1978, p.3). Each system must be locatable in a network of relations by defining what set of classes it subdivides; further, each term in the system must have an overt realization or contrast with a feature which has such a realization, or give rise to sub-classes which are realized positively. This approach clearly echoes early Scale and Category grammar, rather than later Hallidayan models. However, Hudson goes further than Halliday, in treating *all* classification and subclassification relations as paradigmatic. This decision has some important consequences. Firstly, it entails the total abandonment of the Firthian polysystemic principle. We saw in Section 1.3 that in Firth's work, systems were set up for specific places in structure. In Chapters 2 and 3 we saw that Halliday modified this principle so that systems were set up for generalized structural environments specified in terms of the rank (and sometimes class) of unit acting as the 'point of origin' for systems (for example, systems at clause rank, systems operating at the nominal group, and so on). Hudson, however, treats even the units themselves (clause, phrase (Hudson uses the more generally accepted term rather than 'group'), word, etc.) as being in paradigmatic relation since, as he points out (1971, p.70) they are simply names for classes of item, defined in distributional and structural terms. This means that Hudson's classification relations are embodied in just one large 'super-network' which subclassifies the basic feature [grammatical item]. A second consequence of the decision to treat all classification relations as paradigmatic is, then, that unlike Halliday's grammars, Hudson's do not treat rank as a separate scale; rather, the concept of rank is built into the network, and also into the constituency relations shown in the structures generated (since clauses are shown to have phrases and other embedded clauses as their constituents).

Hudson's reasons for not tying paradigmatic relations to places in structure are basically those mentioned briefly in Section 1.4, namely that this approach misses important generalizations across environments. Even Halliday's tying of systems to ranks of unit may miss generalizations across ranks. It might be objected that Hudson's abandonment of the poly-systemic principle leaves him unable to account for the facts which the principle was intended to account for, namely that there are indeed differences between the selections available at different points in structure. This can, however, be shown in a Hudson-type grammar, though in a different way. As Hudson observes (1978, p.13), 'within the system network one can decide to which larger classes any given system should apply, and the realisation rules can specify which features are obligatory in any environments which do impose restrictions'. It is interesting to note that there is one point (Parret, 1974, p.87 = Halliday, 1978, p.41) at which Halliday seems to be accepting Hudson's position, though in later work he still refers to clause networks, nominal group networks, and the like.

6.3.3 The form of the grammar: Hudson's three systemic models

6.3.3.1 The 'English Complex Sentences' model
In the *English Complex Sentences* (henceforth ECS) model, as in Hudson's later systemic models, paradigmatic relations are shown in classification rules expressible in systemic network form. Figure 6.3 shows the network presented in Chapter 2 of ECS. From the selection expression of systemic features for a given linguistic item (say a clause), a structure for that item is constructed by means of a set of structure-generating rules. The final structure shows explicitly the constituency relations and the sequence of constituents. It does not show explicitly the dependency relations between, for example, perfective 'have' and '-en', or between transitive verbs and their object nominals: these relations are, however, implicit in the *functional* relations of the constituents. The syntactic function of an item 'has to do with the way in which it is being used in a particular sentence, whereas its form has to do with its own "shape" ' (1971, p.33). For instance, one and the same noun phrase can act as Subject or Object, in different sentences. As Hudson points out, most discussions of functions have centred around those with clear semantic significance, such as Actor, Goal, Subject, Topic and Comment. However, it can be argued that *every*

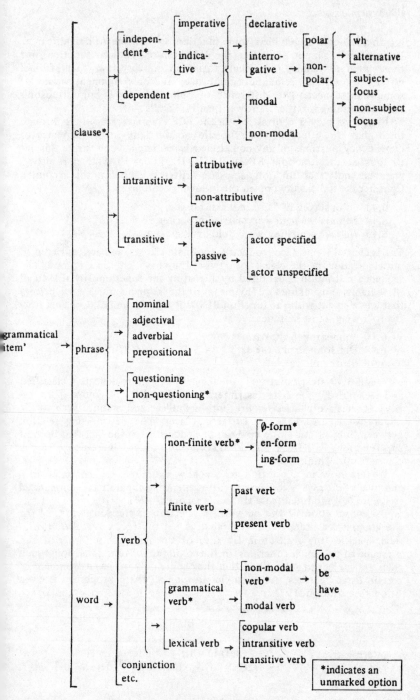

Figure 6.3: Basic system network in ECS

grammatical constituent bears some function, so that semantic significance, Hudson feels, cannot be part of the definition of syntactic function. For those, such as Halliday, who claim that there are very few, if any, formal differences without semantic significance, Hudson's argument would be somewhat suspect. The difference of opinion arises because Hudson's view of meaning is rather narrower than Halliday's.

Functions play a central role in the ECS grammar, since it is through them that the effect of the syntactic environment on the sequence or dependency relations of any constituent is mediated. To illustrate this, let us look at the functions BINDER, SUBJECT and FINITE in Hudson's grammar (note that function names are written in capitals in this account). Consider the italicized words in the following sentences:

6.43 John stayed in *because* it was raining.
6.44 John is the man *who* married my sister.
6.45 *Had* we seen him, we should have spoken.

The italicized items all introduce subordinate clauses, and are restricted to initial position in the clause; otherwise, they have little in common. The sequence restriction is captured by allocating the function BINDER to all these items, and making sure (by means of the 'sequence rules — see below) that any element with the function BINDER is clause-initial. Consider now the following set of sentences:

6.46 John stroked the cat.
6.47 Did John stroke the cat?
6.48 Stroke the cat.

6.46 and 6.47 are [indicative], the former being more delicately classified as [declarative], the latter as [interrogative] ; 6.48 is of course, [imperative]. Indicative clauses require both a Subject and a finite verb, while imperative clauses have no surface Subject. The dependency relation between Subject and finite verb can be deduced from the fact that both of the functions SUBJECT and FINITE are introduced in response to the clause feature [indicative].

We are now in a position to see how structures are generated in a grammar of the ECS type. The structure-generating apparatus is summarized in Figure 6.4, modified from Hudson's account (1971, p.103)

By consultation of the network, a selection expression is formed for the grammatical item to be generated. A set of *feature realization rules* then specifies the realization (if any) of the features in terms of the presence of particular functions, or the conflation of functions. Some such rules are subject to a condition that they apply only in the environment of certain listed features. An example showing all these properties is given below (see Hudson, 1971, p.84).

Feature	Realization
interrogative	+MOOD-FOCUS / / [independent] +QUESTION = BINDER / / [dependent]

(where + means 'add', = means 'conflate', / / means 'in the environment').

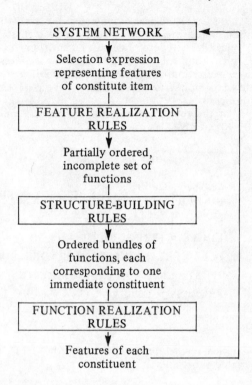

Figure 6.4: Components of Hudson's ECS model

MOOD-FOCUS is the function which brings together the 'focus' elements of independent interrogatives: the finite verb in a polar question, and the 'wh'-word in a 'wh'-question. The rule states that this function is to be introduced in the environment [independent], if [interrogative] has been selected. In the environment [dependent], on the other hand, the function QUESTION is to be introduced, and conflated with the function BINDER (which will already be present as a realization of the feature [dependent]). The output of the feature realization rules is thus a set of functions, some of which are conflated, but which are otherwise unordered.

The *structure-building rules* now take the set of functions generated so far, and put them in the right order, also adding further functions in some cases. There are two types of structure-building rule: absolute and conditional. The absolute rules apply whenever their explicitly stated conditions are satisfied, whereas the conditional rules apply only if this will not lead to a conflict with the absolute rules. The absolute rules are of two kinds: the *sequence rules* restrict the sequences in which functions can occur; while the *compatibility rules* prevent certain functions which are incompatible from conflating. The conditional rules are also of two kinds: the *addition rules* ensure that certain functions which are needed in the generation of the final structure are present although they have not been introduced by the feature realization rules; the *conflation rules* specify the conflation of functions which would not be conflated by the feature realization rules. Each type of rule can be environmentally conditioned, the necessary environment being stated in terms of functions, not features as for feature realization rules. The structure-building rules are not extrinsically ordered, although, as we saw above, there is priority of absolute over conditional rules.

Examples of the four types of structure-building rule (from Hudson, 1971, pp.89-90) are given below.

Sequence: $\left.\begin{array}{l}\text{MOOD-FOCUS}\\\text{BINDER}\end{array}\right\} \rightleftarrows \text{(PRE-SUBJECT} \rightarrow \text{SUBJECT)} \longrightarrow$

POST-SUBJECT $\rightleftarrows$ PROCESS $\longrightarrow$ POST-VERB

FINITE = (PRE-SUBJECT = (MODAL $\rightarrow$ PASSIVE) $\rightarrow$ PRO

Compatibility: POST-VERB $\neq$ QUESTION, BINDER, SUBJECT

Addition: +POST-VERB = ATTRIBUTE, ACTOR, GOAL

Conflation: PROCESS = COPULAR, TRANSITIVE, INTRANS

Certain notational conventions here are as for the feature realization rules; others illustrated above are:

F $\longrightarrow$ F	The first function must come before the second if both are present
F $\rightleftarrows$ F	The first function must either precede or be conflated with the second, if both are present
$\left.\begin{array}{l}\text{F}\\\text{F}\end{array}\right\}$	Whichever of the two functions is present will be at the position indicated
F = (F $\longrightarrow$ F)	The first function is conflated with whichever of the two in brackets comes first, and the latter must come in the order shown
F $\neq$ F	The two functions must not be conflated
+F = F,F	If any of the functions separated by commas are present, they must be conflated with the first, which may have to be added to make this possible.

The output of the structure-building rules is an ordered sequence of bundles of functions, each bundle corresponding to one immediate constituent in the structure of the item being generated.

The *function realization rules* now operate to allow the functions of the immediate constituents to determine some of their features. Some examples are shown below (see Hudson, 1971, p.96).

Function	Realization
FINITE	[finite verb]
PROCESS	[lexical verb]
INTRANS	[intransitive verb]
QUESTION	[questioning]
SUBJECT	[nominal] *or* [dependent]

Only some of the features of an immediate constituent are determined in this way. Others will be added because they are 'unmarked' features in the network (see the asterisked options in Figure 6.3), to be selected where there is no reason for making a 'marked' choice; yet other features are 'free' choices (for example [past verb] or [present verb] for a finite verb).

This completes one cycle of the structure-generating process. The cycle is now repeated for each immediate constituent: the feature list is checked for compatibility by consultation of the network, and unmarked and free choice features added as explained above. The feature realization, structure-building and function realization rules then operate to generate features of the next layer of immediate constituents, and this cycling continues until the whole structure has been generated.

We shall now demonstrate how the various types of rule outlined above operate in the generation of structure for a particular sentence. Hudson's own example (1971, p.91 ff.) is somewhat complex, and we shall use a simpler sentence here:

6.49 He fled.

The features selected from the network (see Figure 6.3) are: [clause, independent, indicative, declarative, non-modal, intransitive, non-attributive]. The relevant feature realization rules are as follows:

Feature	Realization
[clause]	+PROCESS
[indicative]	+SUBJECT
	+FINITE
[non-attributive]	+ACTOR = SUBJECT
	+INTRANS

The relevant structure-building rules are those quoted earlier. The first sequence rule tells us that SUBJECT must precede PROCESS, and the second that FINITE is to be conflated with PROCESS. Note that the addition rule

+POST-VERB = ATTRIBUTIVE, ACTOR, GOAL

does not apply. This is because if it did, POST-VERB would be introduced and conflated with ACTOR, but we know that ACTOR is to be conflated with SUBJECT, so that SUBJECT and POST-VERB would also be conflated, and this is prevented by the following compatibility rule which, being an absolute rule, takes precedence over any conditional rules:

+POST-VERB ≠ QUESTION, BINDER, SUBJECT

The conflation rule

PROCESS = COPULAR, TRANSITIVE, INTRANS

indicates that PROCESS is to be conflated with INTRANS. At the end of the structure-building rules, then, we have the following pair of ordered bundles of functions, each corresponding to one immediate constituent of the clause:

SUBJECT   PROCESS
ACTOR   FINITE
                INTRANS

The function realization rules given earlier tell us that the Subject must be either a nominal or a dependent clause, and that the second immediate constituent must have the features [lexical verb, finite verb, intransitive verb]. At the end of the cycle, we have:

[clause, independent, indicative, declarative, non-modal, intransitive, non-attributive]

SUBJECT	PROCESS
ACTOR	FINITE
	INTRANS
[nominal] or [dependent]	[lexical verb, finite verb, intransitive verb]

Consulting the network, we choose the feature [nominal] for the Subject (presupposing the feature [phrase]), and add the features presupposed by those already attached to the finite verb (that is, [word, verb]). We also make the free choice of [past verb] for the second constituent. The result is as follows:

[clause, independent, indicative, declarative, non-modal, intransitive, non-attributive]

SUBJECT	PROCESS
ACTOR	FINITE
	INTRANS
[phrase, nominal]	[word, verb, finite verb, past verb, lexical verb, intransitive verb]

Hudson does not discuss here the details of how noun phrase structures are generated; nevertheless, it is clear that a further cycle could operate to show that the Subject nominal consists of just a pronoun as head.

The main body of ECS consists of a very detailed account of non-finite clauses and noun clauses in English, in terms of the model outlined above. ECS certainly constitutes the most detailed and explicit account of a systemic generative grammar yet available. There are, however, some reservations which might be expressed about it, especially concerning the role of grammatical functions in the model. Some 80 functions are proposed in ECS, and Hudson claims (pp.35-6) that 'this should not worry us, however, since the large number of functions that we recognize simply reflects the fact that a grammar contains a very large number of different rules relating constituents to their environments, and that each rule tends to apply to a different range of functions'. We might perhaps accept this, if Hudson's criteria for setting up new functions were clear and well-constrained; they are not, however, as is obvious from the statement (p.34) that 'we shall justify functions with reference to their effect on the grammar of the language as a whole. This means that we shall assign different functions . . . [to the italicized items in a sentence under discussion] . . . if this improves the grammar, but not if it does not'. Hudson himself later became aware of the dangers of a proliferation of functions, and recognized that it made the grammar too powerful (1974a, p.12). This realization led Hudson to propose the modified and rather simpler model which will be described briefly in the next section.

Further criticisms of Hudson's model are made by McCord (1975), who firstly points out that the structure-building rules allow the production of different structures from the same functional input, depending on the order in which the rules are applied. Secondly, McCord criticizes the fact that if a conditional rule is applied at a certain point in a derivation, but the condition becomes invalid later in the derivation, then the application of the rule must be cancelled. This leads to the undesirable possibility of 'backtracking' through the derivation. Thirdly, the separation of the feature realization rules from the structure-building rules is somewhat unnatural: some of the structure-building rules, like the feature realization rules, add functions; and some feature realization rules conflate functions, this type of action being more typical of structure-building rules. McCord therefore proposes that the two types of rule should be amalgamated into a single component, consisting of a set of linearly ordered rules, some of which differ somewhat from Hudson's own rule types. McCord's rules are either 'actions' or 'conditional rules'. Actions involve processes such as the addition or deletion of a function, the adjoining of one function to the right or left of another, the moving of functions and features so that they are associated with a different node, the assignment of a set of features to a node having a particular function, or the blocking of a derivation. Conditional rules consist of a condition which may be true or false, and a list of rules to be followed, in order, if the condition is true. A further difference between McCord's work and Hudson's concerns the interpretation of system networks as 'feature networks', which are directed graphs with labelled nodes and arcs, such as are used in much work on artificial intelligence. Indeed, one of McCord's major concerns is to develop a model which will lend itself to computer representation (see also Section 9.4 of this book).

6.3.3.2 The 'Systemic generative grammar' model
The main difference between Hudson's 1974 sketch of a systemic generative model and the earlier account is the decision to dispense entirely with the explicit inclusion of function labels. Instead, functional properties are derived by interpreting configurations of features. For instance, the Subject

is defined as that item (which will be either a nominal phrase or a dependent clause) which is required in the realization rule for the feature [clause], and the Object as that item which is required in the realization of the feature [two participants]. This fundamental change makes the new theory less powerful, in that it must be possible to refer to any function required in the grammar by means of the features it relates: it is no longer possible simply to postulate a new function just because it makes the grammar simpler, as in the 1971 model. (See, however, Section 2.4.3, where it was suggested that explicit labelling of functional categories might be necessary.)

The exclusion of functions necessarily has effects on the form of the realization rules linking system to structure. One set of rules, which must be applied first, states what features of an immediate constituent can be specified as direct realizations of features of the constitute. For instance, any clause other than one marked as [copular] will have an item classified as [lexical verb] as one constituent; if the clause is also [perfect], it will have the item 'have' as a constituent; and so on. The rules in this first set can be applied in any order. The second set of rules is grouped into ordered subsets. These rules concatenate constituents with particular features, and conflate other sets of features into one constituent. Rules are applied here only if they do not conflict with earlier rules in the ordered sequence. Examples of these rules are those which state that an auxiliary must precede a lexical verb, that a modal auxiliary must precede a non-modal auxiliary, and that the feature [finite verb] must be conflated with the feature [first verb]. In addition to the realization rules, certain 'output constraints' are necessary to block the generation of structures (such as sequences of two '-ing' forms) which are ungrammatical, but would otherwise be generated by the grammar.

The presentation of the model in Hudson's paper is unfortunately rather sketchy, and does not allow us to show how a complete sentence structure might be generated. However, the new model is clearly simpler and more highly constrained than its predecessor. Hudson also demonstrates (1974a, p.22 ff.) that it can cope with phenomena such as embedding, discontinuity and co-ordination in a natural and elegant manner.

6.3.3.3 The 'Arguments for a Non-Transformational Grammar' model: daughter dependency grammar

As the title suggests, *Arguments for a Non-Transformational Grammar* (henceforth ANTG, Hudson, 1976) is concerned largely with the presentation of a model which offers considerable advantages over transformational models. The general advantages are those common to all Hudson's models, and discussed in Section 6.3.2.3. More specific empirical arguments are presented during the book's detailed discussion of particular points of syntax. We shall examine some of the more important issues later.

The main difference between the ANTG model and Hudson's previous models is that dependency relations are made explicit, rather than left implicit in either functional relations or configurations of features. The model combines elements of dependency grammars (see Tesnière, 1959; Heringer, 1970; Vater, 1975; Werner, 1975) with the constituency grammar approach of previous systemic models, to create a model whose distinctiveness is mirrored in a new name, 'daughter dependency grammar'. The advantages and disadvantages of constituency and dependency grammars as seen by Hudson at this time are clearly summarized in an article comparing daughter dependency grammar with other systemic grammars (Hudson, 1978, p.5 ff.). Briefly, in a constituency grammar, only part–whole relations (or, in current terminology, relations between 'mothers' and their 'daughters') are shown explicitly; in a dependency grammar, on the other hand, only part–part relations (that is, relations between 'sisters') are shown explicitly, and constituency is implicit. Daughter dependency grammar, by recognizing both daughter and sister dependencies, achieves the best of both worlds, as shown in the following structural diagram from Hudson (1976, p.16).

6.50

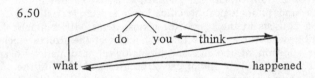

Here, the vertical and diagonal lines represent daughter dependency relations (between the main clause and its constituents, and between the embedded clause and its constituents), while horizontal arrows show the direction of sister dependency relations (both 'you' and 'what happened' depend on 'think'). Note that although 'what happened' is a constituent of the whole sentence 'What do you think happened?', it does not have a direct link to the top node representing the sentence. This is because its presence depends, not on the features of the mother (that is, the classification of the whole sentence), but on the properties of 'think'.

The ANTG model is, in one important respect, intermediate between the ECS and the 1974 model. Although in most cases grammatical functions are implicit in the configurations of features, as in the 1974 model, there is a set of properties of items occurring at the left hand end of clauses which cannot be satisfactorily accounted for in terms of features, because the items which share the relevant properties do not share any features which could be used to mark them off as a set. This leads Hudson to propose that a small set of functions should be introduced to capture the relevant generalizations. Those included in his grammar are SUBJECT, TOPIC (to deal with topicalized complements and the like, which Halliday would handle in terms of marked theme), RELATOR (to deal with a class of items such as 'that', relative pronouns and 'wh'-items in embedded clauses, which do not allow a fronted adverbial before them), and SCENE-SETTER (associated with fronted adverbials).

The structure-generating apparatus of the ANTG model, like that of previous models, contains a set of rules for classification of linguistic items (which can be expressed in network form) and a set of rules for the realization of selection expressions as syntactic structures. These sets of rules operate cyclically, one cycle corresponding to each layer of immediate constituents, as in the ECS model, as shown in Figure 6.5, taken from Hudson (1976, p.22).

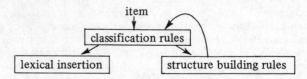

Figure 6.5: Components of the ANTG model

In ANTG, however, it is made clearer how lexical items are slotted into the grammatical structures generated. We shall return to Hudson's views on the lexicon later (see Section 6.3.4, also Section 7.2); here, we need only note that the lexicon in daughter dependency grammar is similar to that of a transformational grammar (that is, it contains a semantic, syntactic and phonological specification for each lexical item): lexical insertion consists in the search for lexical items with syntactic features compatible with those of the terminal nodes of the structure generated, and the addition of the relevant phonological information to an independently generated phonological structure, and also of the semantic information to a semantic structure.

Let us now consider the six types of structure-building rule (the term being used in a wider sense than in the ECS model) proposed by Hudson. We said earlier that the new departure in ANTG is the explicit recognition of dependency relations of the sister–sister as well as the mother–daughter types. Hudson puts forward two types of structure-building rule introducing such dependencies. *Daughter dependency rules* show what features of the constituents (daughters) arise in response to features of the item (mother) whose constituents we are concerned with. An example is the following rule (p.189):

+ interrogative, – nominal ⟶ + finite, + Aux

The arrow below the line shows that this is a daughter dependency rule, and the rule can be read as: any clause which is [+ interrogative] and [– nominal] (that is, a non-embedded interrogative clause) has, as a daughter, a finite auxiliary verb. *Sister dependency rules* define dependency relations between constituents (sisters), as shown by the following example (p.190):

+ transitive ⟶ + nominal

The arrow above the line indicates that this is a sister dependency rule, and the rule may be read as: every item which is [+ transitive] (and must therefore, from the classification relations, be a verb) must have a nominal as sister. This nominal will in fact act as the Object in an active clause.

The dependency rules say nothing whatever about the sequence of elements; this is the job of a separate set of ordered *sequence rules*, operating in conjunction with *peripherality rules*. The latter, which are referred to by some sequence rules, specify which elements of the sentence will be closest to the verb, and are not worked out in detail in Hudson's book. As an example of a sequence rule, we may take the following (p.195):

[+ article] ⟹ [– article]

Since [- article] is a feature of ordinary nouns, this rule serves to place articles before nouns in noun phrases.

The remaining two types of structure-building rule are concerned with the addition to nodes of further labels, which can be either features or functions. *Feature addition rules* are needed where features of a particular constituent cannot conveniently be introduced by daughter dependency rules. An example is the rule:

[item] : - nominal, + moody

This rule (p.193) says that any grammatical item must be given the features [- nominal, + moody] (the properties defining main clauses) unless there are other features already attached to the item which are incompatible with these features. The rule is necessary, as Hudson (p.90) points out, to make sure that the very top node in a structure is shown to represent a main clause. The features of this top node clearly cannot be introduced by a daughter dependency rule, since there is no mother to refer to. Items which are not main clauses must, of course, not have this rule applying to them, but this is taken care of by the fact that they have features attached to them which are incompatible with the specification [- nominal, + moody].

Function assignment rules assign the functions SUBJECT, TOPIC, RELATOR and SCENE-SETTER to appropriate items. An example is the rule for introducing SUBJECT (p.193):

SUBJECT is present as daughter of [+ sentence] if:
    (i)   another daughter is [+ finite]
or (ii)   [+ sentence] is [+ optative, - interrogative, + nominal]
or (iii)   [+ sentence] is [+ relative, - optative]
or (iv)   [+ sentence] is *not* [+ optative], with another daughter
              as TOPIC, *nor* [+ object-raising, + nominal, - optative];
              if only condition (iv) is satisfied, SUBJECT is optional.

The first part of this rule says that a finite verb needs a Subject. The feature combination in the second part of the rule defines clauses such as that italicized in 6.51:

6.51 I recommend *that John be appointed*.

The features in part (iii) define relative clauses other than those involving infinitives. Part (iv) states that Subjects *cannot* occur in main or embedded imperatives with topicalized Objects, or in clauses with 'raised' Objects, such as:

6.52 Money is hard *to borrow from this bank*.

Otherwise, SUBJECT is optional, as in 6.53:

6.53 I don't like *(John) smoking cigarettes*.

Let us now see how the ANTG model would generate the sentence used for exemplification of the generative apparatus of ECS:

6.49 He fled.

The derivation begins with the topmost node, which is given the features [- nominal, + moody] by the feature addition rule discussed earlier. The classification rules tell us that [+ moody] can apply only to an item which is also [+ sentence, - phrase] (the combination [+ sentence, + phrase] is intended to account for gerund clauses - see later). From the subnetwork for [+ moody] sentences, we choose the features [- interrogative, - optative]. A daughter dependency rule states that every sentence must have at least one daughter, and a feature addition rule says that this must be a finite verb. The feature [+ verb] is a subclassification of [+ predicate], and there is a sister dependency rule which specifies that every predicate must have at least one sister which is [+ nominal]. The classification rules tell us that we can choose [+ phrase] to combine with this feature. So far, then, we have the following structure, without, as yet, any ordering of the constituents:

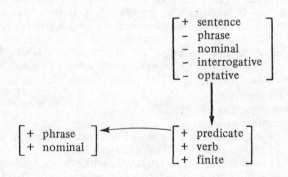

Consulting the classification rules for verbs, we add the features [- transitive, - sentence-complement, - verb-complement, - Auxiliary] to the verb node (that is, the verb which will finally appear in the sentence, 'flee', is here intransitive, does not take a sentence or another verb as complement, and is not auxiliary). Similarly, the nominal phrase is further specified as [- 'wh'-phrase, + definite-NP], since 'he' is definite and not a 'wh'-word. The function assignment rule discussed earlier tells us that since there is a finite verb there must be a Subject, and a further rule says that the function SUBJECT must be assigned to the least peripheral nominal. In our sentence, since there is only one nominal, SUBJECT is attached to that. Further daughter dependency rules specify that the nominal must contain a daughter which is [+ noun] (a feature of both nouns and pronouns), and that since the nominal phrase is [+ definite-NP] it must also have a daughter which is [+ definite]. The classification rules tell us that [+ definite] is a sub-class of [+ article], and that both [+ article] and [+ noun] can be attached to the same node in order to generate pronouns, as in the present case. Finally, we apply a sequence rule which states that any constituent bearing a function label must precede anything without such a label, so that the constituent marked as SUBJECT must precede the verb. Our final structure is thus as follows:

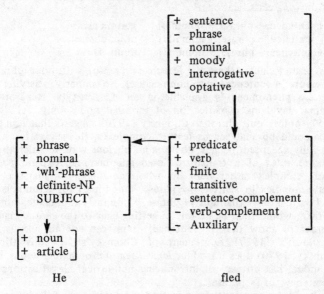

$$
\begin{bmatrix}
+ & \text{sentence} \\
- & \text{phrase} \\
- & \text{nominal} \\
+ & \text{moody} \\
- & \text{interrogative} \\
- & \text{optative}
\end{bmatrix}
$$

$$
\begin{bmatrix}
+ & \text{phrase} \\
+ & \text{nominal} \\
- & \text{'wh'-phrase} \\
+ & \text{definite-NP} \\
 & \text{SUBJECT}
\end{bmatrix}
\qquad
\begin{bmatrix}
+ & \text{predicate} \\
+ & \text{verb} \\
+ & \text{finite} \\
- & \text{transitive} \\
- & \text{sentence-complement} \\
- & \text{verb-complement} \\
- & \text{Auxiliary}
\end{bmatrix}
$$

$$
\begin{bmatrix}
+ & \text{noun} \\
+ & \text{article}
\end{bmatrix}
$$

He   fled

We are now in a position to consider briefly some of the advantages claimed for daughter dependency grammar as compared with transformational generative models of syntax. This area is covered in a very clear and succinct manner in a review of ANTG by Schachter (1978), on which the following summary is based.

Some of the general arguments in favour of daughter dependency grammar are those which can be claimed for all Hudson's models, and which were discussed in Section 6.3.2.3. In particular, the postulation of a single integrated structure in daughter dependency grammar obviates the problems of motivating underlying elements which are later deleted, or underlying constituent orders differing from the surface order; it also means that there is no question of different structures being involved in semantic and phonological interpretation, or in lexical insertion.

Furthermore, the classification of higher nodes (corresponding to clauses and phrases) as well as terminal nodes allows daughter dependency grammar to capture a number of generalizations which are not easily accounted for in Chomsky's model. For instance, as Schachter (1978, p.355 ff.) observes, gerund clauses such as those in 6.54 below are like noun phrases in that they permit an optional initial possessive (compare the noun phrase in 6.55), but like noun clauses in that both can take 'not' and can include auxiliary verbs (compare 6.56 and 6.57).

6.54 (= Schachter's 13)   We talked about (John's) distributing
                                                                    leaflets.
6.55 (= Schachter's 14)   We talked about (John's) leaflets.
6.56 (= Schachter's 15)   That John has not been arrested is
                                                                    surprising.
6.57 (= Schachter's 16)   John's not having been arrested is surprising.

Daughter dependency grammar accounts for these facts satisfactorily by the following classifications:

[+ sentence, + phrase, + nominal]   gerund clause
[– sentence, + phrase, + nominal]   noun phrase
[+ sentence, – phrase, + nominal]   noun clause

Thus gerund clauses share the feature [+ phrase] with noun phrases, and the feature [+ sentence] with noun clauses. No similarly satisfying account of these phenomena is available in an *Aspects*-type transformational grammar involving classification of terminal nodes only. As Schachter (p.357) points out, although Chomsky (1970) suggests that non-terminal nodes could be analysed as feature complexes, this suggestion has never been fully accepted, because there is no obvious way in which the phrase structure rules of a transformational grammar can expand *parts* of a feature complex rather than the whole complex. For instance, given a feature complex [+ sentence, + phrase, + nominal] for gerund clauses, we could write a rule expanding [+ phrase, + nominal] to include determiners, but there would then be no way of getting back to the gerund clause node in order to show that [+ sentence] items can contain auxiliary verbs. Jackendoff's (1977) refinement of Chomsky's 'X̄ convention' (see Chomsky, 1970) does introduce *lexical* features on higher nodes, but even this model has no way of introducing non-lexical classifications such as [+ sentence] or [+ phrase].

Schachter singles out three further characteristics of daughter dependency grammar which confer advantages over transformational approaches: the formal recognition of sister dependencies, the formal recognition of a small set of functions, and the strict separation of constituency and sequence rules. We shall deal briefly with each of these.

The chief advantage of the formal recognition of sister dependencies is that it enables us to show just which structural properties reflect dominance (mother–daughter) relations, and which reflect head-dependent (sister–sister) relations (Hudson, 1976, p.83-4; Schachter, 1978, p.359 Schachter considers the example of transitive verbs and their Objects: the structure generated by the phrase structure rules of a transformational grammar, 6.58, simply shows that the verb and the Object noun phrase are daughters of the sentence node (though the strict subcategorization frames of the lexical entries will show which verbs can be followed by a noun phrase). The daughter dependency grammar structure 6.59, on the other hand, clearly shows that the presence of an Object nominal depends on the properties of the verb, and so predicts that the verb properties will depend on the type of mother clause involved, but that those of the verb complements (including Objects) will depend on the type of verb. This prediction seems to be correct since, as Schachter points out, it is the clause type which determines whether the verb will be finite, infinitive, gerundive, and the like, while the range of complements allowed will depend on whether the verb is transitive or intransitive, and so on.

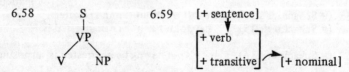

6.58   S
       |
       VP
      / \
     V   NP

6.59   [+ sentence]

$\begin{bmatrix} + \text{ verb} \\ + \text{ transitive} \end{bmatrix}$ [+ nominal]

The postulation of a small set of functions also enables daughter dependency grammar to explain phenomena which are puzzling for a transformational approach. Both Hudson (1976, p.100 ff.) and Schachter (1978, p.360 ff.) exemplify these advantages by considering the function TOPIC. It is a fact about English that complements or 'wh'-items, but not both, can be fronted, as shown by Hudson's examples:

6.60   He bought the other one for somebody else.
6.61   The other one he bought for somebody else.
6.62   For whom did he buy the other one?
6.63   *The other one for whom did he buy?

Hudson explains this by postulating that there can be only one TOPIC per clause, so that, since both the 'wh'-phrase and the complement are fronted in 6.63, the sentence is ill-formed. This restriction could not, of course, be formulated in terms of features, since the features of 'wh'-items, and also of complements, are identical whatever their position.

A second phenomenon which is readily explained in functional terms is the unbounded movement of constituents into positions much higher up the structural tree than the clause in which they originate. Examples are the italicized elements in the following sentences:

6.64   (= Schachter's 22) *What* did Mary say that John claimed that he
                                                                                    saw?
6.65   (= Schachter's 23) *Tomorrow* I think that I promised Mary that
                                                                                    I would help her.
6.66   (= Schachter's 24) *John* seems to be likely to succeed.

We shall not go into the details of how such structures would be generated in a daughter dependency grammar (for further information see Hudson, 1976, p.115 ff.; Schachter, 1978, pp.360-61). Briefly, all constructions allowing unbounded movement of a constituent involve 'double mother-hood': that is, the movable constituent has two mothers, a situation which is not possible in standard transformational models. The only way in which double motherhood can come about in a daughter dependency grammar is by the operation of function assignment rules. The model thus predicts that only items which can bear functions (for instance the 'wh'-TOPIC in 6.64, the SCENE-SETTER adverbial 'tomorrow' in 6.65, the SUBJECT 'John' in 6.66) will be able to move unboundedly. Furthermore, the model explains why all unbounded movement in English is leftward rather than rightward: as we saw earlier, there is a sequence rule which states that all items bearing functions must precede items without functions.

The separation of daughter and sister dependency rules from sequence rules is an advantage in accounting for free constituent order in languages such as Tagalog (for examples see Schachter, 1978, p.362). Where the ordering of elements is syntactically unconstrained, we can simply omit any specification of ordering in the sequence rules for these elements. Schachter also observes that ordering regularities which cut across grammatical categories, and have been suggested as typological characteristics (see Greenberg, 1963; Comrie 1981) can be expressed in a natural way in daughter dependency grammar. For instance, many languages show the orders verb + Object, auxiliary + main verb, preposition + nominal, noun + genitive and noun + adjective, while other languages have precisely the reverse ordering of these elements. This can be expressed generally in a model with explicit dependency relations, by saying that in languages of the first type dependent sisters follow their heads, while in languages of the second type dependent sisters precede their heads.

We could have spent considerably more time on a discussion of further advantages of daughter dependency grammar over transformational models. For instance, both Hudson (1976, p.78) and Schachter (1978, pp.363-4) show that daughter dependency grammar can explain quite easily certain constructions for which transformational grammarians have been forced to postulate powerful 'global rules', which are able to relate the properties of non-contiguous phrase-markers in derivations. It is hoped that the rather brief treatment made necessary here by space considerations will stimulate the reader into a detailed reading of the original work.

Finally, we should mention certain criticisms of the daughter dependency grammar model made by Schachter (1978, 1980), and certain enhancements Schachter has proposed to overcome these points of difficulty. We shall discuss briefly Schachter's points relating to three aspects of the model: Hudson's ban on disjunctions of features, the criteria for deciding whether to introduce a constituent by means of a daughter or a sister dependency rule, and the relations between syntax and other levels.

Aware that any model which makes use of features runs the risk of being too powerful, Hudson (1976, p.31 ff.) proposes a constraint on classification by features, namely that 'the left hand side of a classification rule never contains a *dis*junction of features, although it can contain a conjunction of them'. That is, the left hand side of a classification rule never says 'if the item has such-and-such features *or* such-and-such other features'. Thus the classes set up by Hudson's rules are 'natural' in the sense normally applied in phonology: they are defined on the basis of shared features, and a class never needs more features to define it than any of its members. Schachter (1978; pp.368-9) makes two points relating to this constraint. Firstly, it is empirically incorrect, in that, as Schachter shows, certain constructions not discussed by Hudson do require disjunctions of features. Secondly, Schachter points out that the ban on disjunctions in *rules* can, if desired, be preserved, by simply subcategorizing two categories separately for the same feature. For instance, Schachter shows that both auxiliary verbs and determiners need to be subcategorized for a feature [+ pro], and suggests the rules:

$$[+ \text{auxiliary}] \longrightarrow [\pm \text{pro}]$$
$$[+ \text{determiner}] \longrightarrow [\pm \text{pro}]$$

The generalization across categories can be achieved by using [+ pro] in rules concerned with the proform-like properties of auxiliary verbs and determiners.

We turn now to the criteria for deciding whether a given constituent should be introduced by means of a daughter dependency or a sister dependency rule. In the case of head constituents, the position is clear: they must be introduced by daughter dependency rules, since sister dependency rules are, by definition, concerned only with the specification of head-dependent relations. Schachter (1980, p.282) suggests a fairly straightforward principle for deciding how to introduce sister nodes:

Nonhead nodes must be introduced into structures by sister-dependency rules alone whenever their properties depend exclusively on properties of their heads, by daughter-dependency rules alone whenever their properties depend exclusively on properties of the nodes that dominate them, and by the interaction of sister-dependency and daughter-dependency rules whenever their properties depend on properties of both the head and the dominating node.

Thus, for instance, sentence adverbials such as 'certainly' must be introduced by daughter dependency rule, since they can occur in declarative but not interrogative clauses (that is, they depend, for their presence, on the class of the mother clause); Objects of transitive verbs will be introduced by sister dependency rule since, as we have seen, their presence depends on the verb being [+ transitive]; while determiners involve the interaction of daughter and sister dependency rules, because it can be shown that the form of the determiner depends both on the classification of the head noun (as count or non-count) and that of the noun phrase of which it is a constituent.

With regard to inter-level relations, Schachter points out that Hudson does not present evidence for the adequacy of his syntactic structures for mapping on to the semantic and phonological levels, though it seems likely that semantic rules could be built up together with the syntactic rules in a manner similar to that employed in Montague grammar (see Partee, 1975; Cooper, 1980). We shall see below that Hudson has recently made clear his views on this area.

6.3.4 Recent developments in Hudson's work: 'word grammar'

In a series of mimeographed working papers produced in 1979-80, some of which have been published, Hudson develops daughter dependency grammar in a new direction, which eventually leads to a distinctly different model, based on the word as the fundamental unit. Since the model is not recognizably systemic, and is not claimed as such by Hudson, it is, strictly speaking, outside the scope of this book, and we shall therefore merely indicate its relationship to daughter dependency grammar. Since some rather fundamental linguistic issues are involved (for instance, whether constituency is needed at all in grammars), it is hoped that readers will be interested enough to follow up the references to published work given here.

Hudson (1981) is impressed with the advantages which have accrued in transformational grammar through the move towards 'lexicalism', involving a progressive increase in the role of the lexicon, at the expense of the syntactic rules, including transformations (see Bresnan, 1978). For instance, 6.67 and 6.68 below would be related, not by a 'dative movement transformation', as in earlier models, but by allowing verbs such as 'give' to have either two noun phrases (Direct and Indirect Objects) or a noun phrase (Direct Object) and a prepositional phrase (Indirect Object) after them.

6.67 John gave Mary a book.
6.68 John gave a book to Mary.

Hudson (1980a, 1981) argues for a similar approach to the lexicon in daughter dependency grammar. In other words, rather than generating a complete syntactic structure into which matching items from the lexicon can be inserted, as in the 1976 model, Hudson now allows the lexicon to contribute to the syntactic structure by specifying the frames in which verbs can occur, and thus what sisters they can take.

Hudson goes further than this, however, in suggesting that the lexicon need not be simply a repository for idiosyncratic information about lexical items, but can be generalized to cover regular patterns too, so that in effect the lexicon swallows up almost the whole of the grammar. Hudson (1981) offers strong arguments in favour of this 'panlexicalist' position. Firstly, since the lexicon associates the syntactic properties of an item with its meaning (and also its phonology), the model offers a way of building up the semantic structure of a sentence at the same time as its syntactic structure. This, together with Hudson's concrete proposals for semantic structure (1980a, p.39 ff.), answers Schachter's criticism, mentioned earlier, and endorsed by Hudson himself (1981, p.68), that the 1976 model paid insufficient attention to the semantic level. Secondly, Hudson argues that the lexicon must in any case contain entries for multi-word items constituting idioms, clichés and non-canonical constructions (constructions such as 'if only' + clause with past tense verb, which are productive, yet do not conform to normal syntactic patterns). It should not, therefore, be too difficult to allow the lexicon to cope with regular multi-word units, that is phrases and clauses.

A brief sketch of a model which is still closely related to daughter dependency grammar, but builds in the panlexicalist approach, is given in Hudson (1980a). To reduce the number of lines in a structural diagram, the dependency lines in the syntactic structures of the 1976 model are now replaced by a slot-and-filler notation, in which slots are defined by function labels, and their fillers identified by index numbers. For instance, in the structure of 6.69 there is a slot in clause structure labelled HEART, which is filled by the verb, whose index number is 2 since it is the second word in the sentence.

6.69 Boys like girls.

Corresponding to each item in the structure (the whole clause, each noun phrase, the verb) there is a box which holds not only the syntactic information but also a semantic representation (consisting of 'predicates' associated with their 'arguments', and 'terms', which can fill argument slots) and a phonological representation. The boxes are thus linked by the slot-and-filler relations specified within them. The 'grammar' itself consists simply of a set of templates against which the well-formedness of a sentence can be checked according to a set of instructions. In the case of, say, a cliché, the sentence structure will be exactly the same as that of the template. For more 'normal' sentences, the checking process will have to ensure that the slot-and-filler relations in the sentence are correct.

A further development of the model is hinted at in Hudson (1980a, pp.33-4) and discussed at length in Hudson (1980b). Hudson argues that explicit dependency relations are required in the grammar, as assumed from 1976 onwards, but that constituency relations are not. This is, of course, tantamount to the claim that no unit higher than the word need be postulated in the grammar. The general form of the arguments in favour of retaining dependency is that some phenomenon applies across a wide range of constructions, and is easy to formulate in dependency terms, but cannot be explained in pure dependency terms. The areas discussed include: typologically important sequencing restrictions covering a range of categories (see our earlier summary of Schachter's discussion of Greenberg's typological features in relation to daughter dependency grammar); the fact that the position of a modifier is generally determined in relation to that of its head and not *vice versa*; the fact that when the morphological form of one word is determined by that of a second, the second will always be head; the fact that only a word's modifiers can provide fillers for its syntactic slots; and a suggestion that only syntactic modifiers of words are eligible as fillers for slots in the corresponding semantic frames.

Hudson then takes six arguments which have been advanced in favour of constituency, and shows how they can be answered within a purely dependency-based model. The arguments which he counters are: that only constituency grammars can show linear sequence; that units higher than the word are needed in order to define the position of items which occur only at the beginning of, say, a clause (for example subordinating conjunctions); Hudson's own earlier arguments for the feature classification of higher nodes in systemic grammars; the need for categories such as noun phrase and clause in order to define the domains of certain syntactic rules; the existence of putatively 'headless' constructions such as 'the poor'; and the argument that constituency is necessary in semantics, therefore needed in the syntax if we are to keep the structure-building apparatus at the two levels in step. Dahl (1980) presents some counter-arguments, and in a reply, Hudson (1980c) answers all but one of Dahl's arguments. He is, however, forced to concede that constituency is needed in the one case of co-ordinate constructions, if we are to explain the fact that, for example, co-ordinated noun phrases behave syntactically like single noun phrases.

Hudson's latest position is expounded in detail in his recent book *Word Grammar* (Hudson, 1984). Clearly, the model makes some very controversial claims, and is very far removed indeed from Hudson's earlier systemic work. Nevertheless, we can see, in Hudson's publications since 1971, a clear progression from a model with considerable Hallidayan influence, through the *Arguments* model which retained certain centrally systemic concepts (the classification rules/system networks, realization rules, the postulation of features on higher nodes), to a model in which the only similarity with Halliday's thinking seems to be a concern (new for Hudson) to handle the semantic patterning of language.

6.4 Conclusion: semantically based or autonomous syntax?

Fawcett and Hudson have much in common in their aims: both are trying to develop an explicitly generative model; both attempt to model the 'psychological reality' of language, and consider that incorporation into an automaton would provide an appropriate test of their models. They are very different, however, in the range of facts they set out to account for. Fawcett, as we have seen, attempts to model the meaning relationships of language, using a version of Halliday's functional components approach (see Sections 5.3 and 5.5). His model of syntax is explicitly restricted to just those distinctions which are needed to account for the syntactic part of the realization of semantic options. The semantics thus determines the scope and nature of the syntax in Fawcett's model. Hudson, on the other hand, favours autonomous descriptions of syntax and semantics.

Fawcett rejects approaches which assume an autonomous syntax, such as Chomskyan transformational grammar and Hudson's models, because he feels that they run 'serious danger of getting the interdependence of syntax and semantics out of balance' (Fawcett, 1980, p.6). Fawcett's main argument for adopting a meaning-based approach is that in the pioneering work of Winograd (1972) on a computer program for understanding discourse, a Hallidayan systemic model was found to be appropriate as a linguistic base, precisely because it dealt with the ways in which the syntax of a language is organized to carry meanings (see the discussion of Winograd's work in Section 9.4). In view of the cognitively oriented goals of Fawcett's model, a meaning-based linguistic component seemed appropriate there also.

However, as we shall see in Section 9.4, the later work of Davey (1978) on the generation of connected discourse by computer took as its linguistic base not the semantically oriented Hallidayan model, but the 1971 ECS model of Hudson. Fawcett (1980, p.7) claims that Hudson's networks are more semantically oriented than he admits. However, although, as we have seen, Hudson says that the syntax must be 'deep' enough to provide categories which are suitable for mapping on to those of the semantics (though not necessarily in a one-to-one manner), this is a very different proposal from Fawcett's, in which the shape and content of the syntax is entirely determined by the semantics. Most linguists would surely agree with Fawcett that our ultimate aim should be a holistic model of language in which the characteristics and relationships of various kinds of patterning are accounted for. But, as Davey's work has shown, even if one's goal is a cognitively oriented model which can be tested by incorporation into an automaton, there is no need to assume that the semantics totally determines the organization of the syntax. By making this assumption, Fawcett denies himself the possibility of demonstrating its validity.

Hudson's brief discussion of evidence for the autonomous syntax view was reviewed earlier. Additional evidence supporting the essential validity of this view can be found elsewhere in the literature. Leech, for example (Leech, 1969, p.28 ff.; 1981, p.180 ff.) has pointed out that there are rules of syntactic well-formedness in particular languages which have little to do with meaning: for instance, the English rules which stipulate that a grammatically complete sentence must contain a finite verb phrase of some kind (compare Russian, which makes no such stipulation), and that a sentence or finite clause must contain a Subject. Leech also observes that the same semantic content can be mapped on to more than one syntactic construction, as in nominalizations corresponding to subordinate clauses:

6.70 She regrets his failure to find a job.
6.71 She regrets that he failed to find a job.

There are even instances of 'zero mapping' between levels, as when 'it' is inserted as a 'dummy' Subject, with no semantic content, in sentences such as 6.72:

6.72 It is raining.

or when entities present in the semantic structure are left unexpressed, as with agentless passives:

6.73 The dinner was cooked. ('. . . by someone or other')

Ultimately, of course, such arguments revolve around the question of exactly what is to be included under the heading of 'meaning'. Leech, Hudson and the present author take a rather narrower view than either Halliday or Fawcett, who would regard 6.70 and 6.71 as expressing subtly different meanings (see Fawcett, 1980, pp.92-3). We shall be in a position to assess the merits of the two approaches properly only when detailed descriptions of both syntax and semantics, of both kinds, are available and have been evaluated in relation to particular goals. The relation between syntax and semantics will also be raised in relation to systemically based descriptions of English in Section 8.2.

7. Systemic approaches to lexis, phonology and discourse

7.1 Introduction

So far, this book has been concerned mainly with the levels of grammar and semantics. The present chapter will give an overview of systemic approaches to other kinds of linguistic patterning: the organization of the vocabulary (lexis), the sound patterning of language (phonology), and patterning above the sentence (discourse).

7.2 Lexis

7.2.1 The basic problem

In grammar we are able to make powerful statements, in that we can generalize about a large number of possible language events, abstracting properties which are common to particular language events, and which thus allow the classification of those events. Because of this, linguists try to describe as much as possible in terms of grammatical patterning. However, we need to ask whether *all* formal patterning can be accounted for in terms of grammar. Consider Example 7.1:

    7.1   The little girl was sitting on a low stool.

Grammatically, we can state the classes to which each item belongs, and the structures into which the classes enter. But we must also be able to account for the contrast between those items which have been chosen, and other items, from the same large grammatical class, which could have been chosen, for instance 'little' versus 'big', 'pretty'; 'girl' versus 'boy'; 'sitting' versus 'standing'; 'low' versus 'high'; 'stool' versus 'chair'; and so on. We must also account for the likelihood of 'sitting on a low stool' as against the unlikelihood of, say, 'flying on a delicious table'. The question is whether such matters can be subsumed under grammatical patterning, or whether some other type of formal pattern is involved.

There are two main schools of thought on this issue. The first maintains that grammar and lexis represent two kinds of linguistic patterning which are qualitatively as well as quantitatively different. This view would seem to be implied by Firth's concept of collocation (see Chapter 1), which was intended to account for purely formal patterning (rather than semantic selection restrictions) in lexis. The second view considers lexis as simply 'most delicate grammar': that is, grammar and lexis are on a 'cline' with no sharp cut-off point, being quantitatively but not qualitatively different. The first view predominated during the period of Scale and Category linguistics, although the possibility of the second approach was not ruled out. Those, such as Hudson, who have continued to be concerned with syntactic patterns as such, still hold this view. However, as we saw in

Chapters 3 and 4, Hallidayan linguistics became ever more semantically oriented during the 1970s, and with this development came a change in the position of lexis in the model. We saw earlier that Halliday now often refers to the 'lexicogrammar', and this reflects his current view that lexis is best regarded as the most delicate extension of the grammar. In what follows, the two positions will be discussed in turn. In the course of the discussion, a metalanguage for talking about lexis will emerge.

7.2.2 Lexis and grammar as distinct forms of patterning

There is a brief discussion of lexis in Halliday's seminal article 'Categories of the theory of grammar' (Halliday, 1961). Here, the position taken is that:

> [when] . . . the description yields a class where no further breakdown by grammatical categories is possible, a class whose exponents make up an open set [. . .] we must leave the grammar; the relations between the exponents must be accounted for as lexical relations. (Halliday, 1961, p.266)

The question is how far the 'breakdown by grammatical categories' can go:

> The grammarian's dream is (and must be, such is the nature of grammar) of constant territorial expansion. He would like to turn the whole of linguistic form into grammar, hoping to show that lexis can be defined as 'most delicate grammar'. The exit to lexis would then be closed, and all exponents ranged in systems. No description has yet been made so delicate that we can test whether there really comes a place where increased delicacy yields no further systems . . . (Halliday, 1961; p.267)

Halliday's conclusion in this article is that 'for the moment it seems better to treat lexical relations [. . .] as on a different level, and to require a different theory to account for them' (p.267). This is also the position adopted in Halliday, McIntosh and Strevens (1964), where the fundamental distinction between grammar and lexis is expressed as follows:

> . . . grammar deals with closed system choices, which may be between items ('this/that', 'I/you/he/she/we/they') or between categories (singular/plural, past/present/future); lexis with open set choices, which are always between items ('chair/settee/bench/stool', etc.) (Halliday, McIntosh & Strevens, 1964, p.23)

The most detailed arguments for regarding lexis and grammar as distinct though related kinds of linguistic patterning are presented in a later paper (Halliday, 1966c). Here, Halliday notes (p.150) that 7.2 below is an acceptable sentence of English, and that 'powerful' could be substituted for 'strong' in this context:

7.2   He put forward a strong argument.

He also notes, however, that 'strong' and 'powerful' do not always stand in this equivalence relation, as shown by the acceptability of 7.3 and 7.4, but the relative unacceptability of 7.5 and 7.6.

7.3 a powerful car
7.4 strong tea
7.5 ? he drives a strong car
7.6 ? powerful tea

In terms of the grammatical structure, all these nominal groups are of the same (m)mh type. We could, of course, postulate a subclassification of modifiers such that 'strong' and 'powerful' are members of a class which can combine with the class to which 'argument' belongs, while 'powerful' (but not 'strong') also belongs to a class which can occur with the class containing 'car', and so on. But we have no good reason for doing this unless such classes are needed at other points in the grammar, and there is in fact no evidence that this is the case. It seems, then, that we have a kind of patterning which is separate from, and superimposed on, grammatical patterns.

This argument is strengthened by the fact that the same patterns of co-occurrence can be seen with different grammatical structures. The first sentence of this paragraph contains the words 'this argument is strengthened'; an alternative would have been 'this argument is made more powerful': as Halliday notes, we can say 'the strength of his argument', 'he argued strongly', also 'the power of his argument' or 'he argued powerfully'; we can say the 'power of his car', but 'the strength of his car' is at least more marked, while 'the strength of her tea' is unremarkable, but 'the power of her tea' odd.

What is needed, then, is the abstraction of a category which represents the lexical content of 'strong', 'strength', 'strengthen', 'strongly', and other related items, or of 'power', 'powerful', 'powerfully' and so on. This category is the *lexical item*, and the range of grammatical forms in which the item can occur is termed the *scatter* of that item. The defining feature of a lexical item, by which such an item is recognized, is its pattern of co-occurrence with other items, that is its *collocational* behaviour. A lexical item is recognized as different from other lexical items because its total pattern of collocation is unique.

An example may be useful at this point. In investigating a large sample of text, we might find that the item spelled 'ball' collocates rather frequently with the items 'play', 'field', 'match', 'goal'. We might also find that in certain other cases 'ball' is not found in collocation with any of these items, but tends to occur instead with items such as 'dance', 'waltz', 'dress', 'band'. We should then have evidence for the provisional identification of two different lexical items, which we could call 'ball$_1$' and 'ball$_2$', and which are in fact homographs.

In a lexical study, we usually focus on the collocational behaviour of one item at a time: this item Halliday terms the *node*. We also need to fix a limit on either side of the node, the *span*, within which an item will be counted as a collocate of that node. (The problems involved in deciding on an appropriate span will be discussed later.) The total list of collocates of a particular node, within whatever span is used, is termed the *cluster* of that node. For a particular node, some members of the cluster will occur quite frequently; others may appear only once, or just a few times. We can apply statistical techniques to find out which collocates of a node occur significantly more frequently than would be predicted for a text in which the items present are randomly ordered. These significant collocates form the central core of the cluster.

By examining the clusters of many separate nodes, or by testing the degree of association of each lexical item with each other item, we can group clusters into *lexical sets* whose members show similar (though not, of course, identical) collocational behaviour. For instance, as Halliday (1966c, p.158) has pointed out, if we investigated a large sample of text, and isolated all collocates occurring within a span of three items from the node 'sun', we might obtain a list among which the items 'bright', 'hot', 'shine', 'light', 'lie' and 'come out' are frequent. These items are presumably central members of the cluster of 'sun'. If we then took 'moon' as the node, we might find 'bright', 'full', 'new', 'light', 'night', 'shine', as central members of the cluster. Taking the common items 'bright', 'shine' and 'light', we obtain a lexical set with greater generality than either of the clusters from which it is derived. If we could find other nodes whose clusters included these items, the case for treating them as a set would be further strengthened.

Let us now consider in rather more detail the similarities and differences between the categories proposed for grammar and lexis. The discussion is based on brief comments by Halliday (1966c), expanded by Berry (1977, pp.51-61).

In lexis, as in grammar, we need to distinguish between syntagmatic and paradigmatic patterning. Since Halliday's discussion is framed in terms of a Scale and Category approach to grammar, we shall compare lexical categories with those discussed in relation to grammar in Chapter 2. There, we saw that syntagmatic patterning in grammar was accounted for by *structures* carried by *units* arranged hierarchically on a *rank* scale. In lexis, syntagmatic patterns are accounted for in terms of *collocation*, but it is doubtful whether any lexical unit at a higher rank than the lexical item can be isolated. Halliday (Halliday, 1966c, p.156; Halliday, McIntosh & Strevens, 1964, p.34, 35) recognizes this, but Berry (1977, p.58, 60) maintains that there must theoretically be a rank scale with two or more units on it, although she admits the difficulty of isolating any higher unit. It is surely unnecessary to assume, as Berry seems to, that because there is a rank scale for grammar there must also be one for other levels. There are, as Berry points out, important differences between grammatical structure and lexical collocation: position is involved in grammatical structure, but unimportant for the definition of collocations; further, whereas structures are composed of 'elements' which are abstracted from large numbers of individual items, collocations are themselves made up of individual lexical items, so that statements made about them are less general than statements about structures.

It will be remembered that grammatical *classes* in the Scale and Category model bring together items with the same potentiality for occurrence as exponents of particular elements of structure, and thus the same potentiality for co-occurrence with items representing other elements of that structure. Halliday (1966c, p.153) finds no need for a parallel category in lexis since, as stated earlier, collocations are made up of individual items rather than classes of item. Berry (1977, p.61), however, draws a parallel between the grammatical category of class and the lexical categories of cluster and set. She points out that clusters, like classes, are lists from which we select in order to fill a slot in a pattern. Furthermore, just as grammatical classes which share certain environments can be conflated to form a cross-class, so the common members of two or more lexical clusters can be conflated to form a set.

The parallel drawn by Halliday (1966c, pp.152-3) is between cluster/set and grammatical *system* rather than class (although, we might argue, class is indeed involved indirectly, since terms in systems were in effect classes in the Scale and Category model — see Section 2.3.2.4). Just as a system represents the list of grammatical choices available in a particular structural environment, so a lexical set contains those lexical items which can be selected for a collocation. The essential difference is that systems are finite, closed lists of options, whereas lexical sets are open-ended. Berry's views on the relationship between lexical patterning and the category of system will be discussed in Section 7.2.3, since they are arguably set not within a Scale and Category framework, but within a model which regards paradigmatic (but not syntagmatic) patterning in lexis as being the most delicate extension of grammatical patterning.

There are, then, important differences, as well as similarities, between the categories appropriate for the description of lexis and grammar. A further reason for regarding lexis and grammar as complementary but different forms of patterning is the fact that lexical and grammatical items are not always co-extensive, on either the paradigmatic or the syntagmatic axis. As Halliday (1966c, p.153) observes, the two lexical items 'make up'$_1$ (collocating with 'face', 'complexion', and so on) and 'make up'$_2$ (collocating with 'team', 'committee', and the like), which are in paradigmatic lexical contrast, belong to the same grammatical class. Furthermore, the scatter of a given lexical item covers a number of different grammatical forms. If we turn now to syntagmatic patterns, most lexical items, as defined collocationally, turn out to be co-extensive with words at the grammatical level (that is, the unit between morpheme and group on the grammatical rank scale). This is, however, only the unmarked correspondence, as pointed out by Halliday (1961, pp.273-4; 1966c, p.154) and Berry (1977, p.60). Consider the following sentences:

7.7 The horse that won the last race is called Pink Panther.
7.8 You're a dark horse, having a PhD and not saying anything about it.
7.9 That's not the way to do it — you're putting the cart before the horse.

A lexical item 'horse' can be isolated, as in 7.7, by its collocation with items such as 'win', 'race', 'stable', 'hay', and so on. 'Horse' as it appears in 7.8 does not collocate significantly with any of these items, but might well be associated with a lexical set concerned with 'hidden merit'. Furthermore, we should no doubt find that when 'horse' occurs in this type of environment, it is always in the combination 'a dark horse'. It is thus this combination, co-extensive with a group at the grammatical level, which is the lexical item here. This is clearly one type of idiom: a second idiom involving 'horse' is shown in 7.9. Here, the lexical item is 'put the cart before the horse', which is more than a group but less than a clause. Thus we can say not only that lexical items are not always co-extensive with words at the grammatical level, but also that they need not even correspond to any complete grammatical unit.

To summarize the approach taken in the 1960s, we may say that since statements about the patterning of individual items can be made without reference to the grammatical classes into which the items can be grouped or the grammatical structures into which they enter, and since we can abstract lexical items which are not necessarily co-extensive with grammatical items, it seems best to regard grammar and lexis as two different kinds of linguistic patterning, working in parallel.

Halliday is careful to point out, in this early work, that every item in a language can be looked at both grammatically and lexically. This point is of particular relevance to discussion of the often-posited distinction between so-called 'grammatical' words (sometimes called 'empty' or 'function' words) and 'lexical' ('full' or 'content') words. The former are items such as 'a' or 'the' which serve a primarily grammatical function, while the latter carry the burden of the 'content' of the message. This distinction is, Halliday feels, best viewed in terms of which type of patterning, grammatical or lexical, is more important in determining the restrictions on the occurrence of the items concerned. Items such as 'a' and 'the' are restricted in the grammatical structures into which they can enter, but are largely unrestricted lexically, in that they collocate with an extremely wide range of other items. Items such as 'strong', on the other hand, show greater collocational restriction, but the lexical item concerned can enter, via its scatter of grammatical forms, into a number of grammatical structures. Also, although we can specify the items 'a' and 'the' within a very few steps in delicacy in grammatical systems, we cannot specify uniquely an item such as 'strong' in this way: all we can do grammatically is specify the class to which 'strong' belongs. The items 'a' and 'the' represent terms from closed systems: an item such as 'strong', on the other hand, is a member of an open lexical set.

There are, however, difficulties with such a simplistic approach, as Halliday himself recognizes. Firstly, as we shall see when we discuss the results of practical work on lexis, items such as 'the' are not entirely neutral collocationally (indeed, this possibility is allowed for in Halliday's discussion). Secondly, there are some items which do not fit neatly into the two-way classification into 'grammatical' and 'lexical' words. For instance, as Halliday, McIntosh and Strevens (1964, p.22) have pointed out, it is difficult to say whether the English prepositions constitute 'a small set of fixed possibilities'. There is certainly a fixed total number of them, but this number is fairly large, of the order we might expect for a lexical set. And although the prepositions are structurally restricted, they are, as we shall see, not entirely neutral collocationally. Considerations such as these led to the suggestion, even in the early accounts (see Halliday, McIntosh & Strevens, 1964, p.22), that grammar and lexis may form a cline, a continuous gradation with clearly grammatical patterns at one end and clearly lexical ones at the other. In other words, the possibility of lexis as most delicate grammar remained open.

7.2.3 Lexis as most delicate grammar

Even in Halliday's earliest formulations (see Halliday, 1961, p.273) the possibility is put forward that as linguists make more and more detailed classifications of language events, it may eventually prove possible to reach the stage where each formal item in a language is specifiable as the only member of a class, defined by the intersection of a number of extremely delicate classes. If this were indeed possible, it would mean that by an extension in delicacy of the principles of grammatical classification we could arrive at a point where individual items could be uniquely specified. The suggestion is, then, that grammar and lexis are not different in kind, but only in degree.

This rapprochement of grammar and lexis has been favoured by developments in the systemic model during the last 15 years or so. As we saw in Chapters 3 to 5, there was in the 1970s a shift in the centre of gravity of the model from form to semantics, so that in Halliday's recent formulations the core of the linguistic potential is the complex interlocking set of options represented as semantic systems. Within such a model, the concept of lexis as most delicate grammar takes on a new relevance, since both grammar and lexis can now be seen as realizing semantic choice. Functionally, then, there is no essential difference between the two: classes of (grammatical) item and individual (lexical) items are both important as ways of realizing meaning options. Delicacy now comes into the picture in that the less delicate options in semantic networks tend to be realized by grammatical structures and items, while the very delicate options at the extreme right of a semantic network will be realized largely by lexical items. This was clearly Halliday's position even at a time when his networks were conceived as lexicogrammatical rather than semantic: 'The lexicon . . . is simply the most delicate grammar. In other words, there is only one network of lexicogrammatical options.' (Parret, 1974, p.90 = Halliday, 1978, p.43). By 1976, Halliday is talking of meanings being realized partly through the grammar, partly through lexis:

Within this [lexicogrammatical] stratum, there is no hard-and-fast division between vocabulary and grammar; the guiding principle in language is that the more general meanings are expressed through the grammar, and the more specific meanings through the vocabulary. (Halliday & Hasan, 1976, p.5)

A rather more detailed working out of this position can be found in work by Fawcett (1980) and Berry (1977). Fawcett (1980, p.57) regards the lexicon as an extremely large and complex network of semantic features, integrated into the overall semantic network, and realized by lexical items. He produces tentative networks and realization rules for certain kinds of action process in English (1980, p.153) and for what he calls the 'cultural classification of things in English' (1980, p.218). There is, however, no attempt to justify the particular shapes the networks take.

The discussion by Berry represents a laudable attempt to examine the theoretical status of lexis within a systemic model in which systems are taken to consist of options in grammatical and lexical meaning. Berry (1977, p.62) presents a system network which will distinguish items relating to the animal kingdom: the item 'bull', for instance, would be specified by the features [masculine, bovine, adult], and the item 'heifer' by the features [feminine, bovine, youthful]. Such a network is, of course, a formalization of the familiar componential approach to lexical meaning.

Berry regards terms in lexical systems, like those in grammatical systems, as being associated with realization statements. The realization statements proposed for lexis are similar to the 'particularization' realization statements she suggests for grammar (see Section 3.5), in that they narrow down the choice of formal item. The differences between grammatical and lexical particularization statements are firstly that the former narrow the choice to a specific class or sub-class of item, whereas the latter specify a unique individual lexical item; and secondly that lexical realization statements usually operate on a combination of features, whereas grammatical realization statements often operate on a single feature. These appear to be differences of degree rather than of kind. Berry does, however, recognize (1977, p.72) that the differences between the formal categories of grammar and lexis, and the lack of co-extensiveness of their units (see Section 7.2.2) suggest a difference of kind rather than of degree. One partial solution to this problem, she suggests, might be to regard lexis as intermediate, on the realization scale, between grammatical structures and phonology/graphology, rather than as parallel to, but separate from, the whole of the grammatical apparatus. However, there would still remain the problem of mapping between grammatical units and lexical units which might not be co-extensive with them. Berry suggests that if we accept a position for lexis intermediate between grammatical structure and phonology/graphology, one solution could be

. . to allow terms from lexical systems to specify functions as we do with terms from grammatical systems. We could then map the functions specified by the terms from lexical systems onto the functions specified by the terms from grammatical systems, by means of discontinuity and conflation realisation statements at different ranks of unit, at the same time as we are mapping the functions specified by grammatical terms onto each other. (Berry, 1977, p.74)

She recognizes, however, that this would cause an unwelcome proliferation of functions.

Berry's discussion does not provide us with any cut-and-dried answers to the theoretical problem of integrating lexis into a semantically based model. It does, however, constitute the only serious attempt in the literature to examine the possibilities available. In particular, it gives due consideration to both the similarities and the differences between grammatical and lexical patterning. Halliday's own rather sparse comments on lexis in the 1970s and 1980s tend to emphasize the unity of the lexico-grammar, and to play down the formal differences between collocation and grammatical structure which were central to his earlier discussions. Hudson (1976, p.8), on the other hand, dismisses the 'delicate grammar' view of lexis, saying that 'it is hard to reconcile this view with the view that lexical and grammatical items need not be coextensive'. Berry's proposals, though programmatic and fraught with problems, do at least offer the possibility of synthesizing the similarities and differences between grammar and lexis into a coherent whole.

7.2.4 The practical study of lexis

The most detailed practical study of collocation so far reported is that of Sinclair and his colleagues (Sinclair, Jones & Daley, 1970; Jones & Sinclair, 1974). This work illustrates a number of problems in such practical studies, which will be discussed briefly.

Firstly, since lexis deals with the properties of individual lexical items, rather than those of classes of item as in grammar, very large volumes of lexical data are required in order to obtain statistically significant results. Halliday (1966c, p.159) suggests that a 20 million word corpus (1,500-2,000 hours of conversation) might provide sufficient data for interesting results to be given. Sinclair's basic corpus of spoken text, recorded during conversations on various topics, runs to only 135,000 words (supplemented, where necessary, by 12,000 words of written scientific text). Even this amount of data, however, is too great for collocations to be studied conveniently by manual sorting. Fortunately, sorting and counting tasks can be carried out extremely quickly and accurately by computer, and programs are now available for counting both individual occurrences of items and co-occurrences of pairs of items in a text (for a review of such techniques, see Butler, forthcoming a). Sinclair's work took full advantage of the computational techniques available at the time.

A second problem is the difficulty of deciding on the extent of the item to be treated as a node for collocational analysis. Readers will probably have noticed that our definition of the lexical item is such as to make it apparently impossible to isolate such items. We defined a lexical item as a stretch of language which shows unique collocational behaviour with respect to other items. However, if we have no other operational definition of a lexical item, how are we to recognize the other lexical items whose collocation with a particular bit of language we wish to test? The way taken out of this impasse in Sinclair's work is to treat each orthographic word as a potential lexical item. A study of the collocations entered into by orthographic words as nodes will, it is hoped, throw up instances where the assumption breaks down, for example where a particular orthographic form represents a pair of homographs, or is part of an idiom. When instances of this kind are discovered, the node items can be adjusted accordingly, and further collocational analyses performed. In this way, progressive refinement of the analysis can be achieved. Again, it becomes obvious that the computer is an almost essential tool in collocational analysis. As Sinclair himself has noted (1966a, p.417), it would probably be best to treat the morpheme as potentially co-extensive with the lexical item, but such an analysis would be an even more ambitious undertaking than studies based on the orthographic word.

A third problem is deciding on the span, on either side of a node, within which co-occurring items will be accepted as collocates. As we saw earlier, there is no obvious lexical unit higher than the lexical item, so that there is no natural cut-off point for collocations. An artificial span must be chosen such that a maximum of lexical information is obtained from a minimum of computational effort. By pilot studies on a 50,000-word sample of text, Sinclair was able to determine that very few new collocates were picked up when the span was extended beyond four items on either side of the node. A span of four was therefore taken in the detailed studies which followed.

A fourth problem arises in the determination of which collocations are to be regarded as significant, and which as purely casual. Here, statistical techniques come into their own: the task is to determine which collocates occur significantly more frequently than would be the case in a text in which the order of words had been randomized. Decisions as to what counts as a significant difference are essentially arbitrary (for full discussion of statistical testing in linguistic research see Butler, forthcoming b). Even statistical measures of association between two words do not tell us the extent to which each of a pair of words predicts the other. For instance, Sinclair found that there was a high probability that when the (infrequent) item 'cathode' occurred in the scientific text, it would be preceded by the item 'the'; on the other hand, given an occurrence of 'the', the probability that it will be followed by 'cathode' is low. To overcome this problem, Sinclair and his colleagues developed an 'indicator of predictiveness', equal to the ratio of the number of collocations of the two items to the number of occurrences of the node being considered. The indicator will thus have a lower value for the high-frequency item (for instance, 'the') than for the low-frequency item (for example, 'cathode').

The work of Sinclair and his colleagues is more interesting for its investigation and solution of methodological problems than for its results, as is perhaps to be expected in view of the relatively small size of the sample. By consideration of a set of items within a mid-range frequency band, Sinclair was able to construct graphical representations of patterns of collocational relationship, indicating two lexical sets, related to 'time' and 'language' respectively. They were also able to show that so-called 'grammatical' words, such as pronouns, articles, prepositions and conjunctions, are not collocationally neutral, but in fact attract a large number of significant collocates. The pattern of collocational relationship for such items was, however, determined by the grammatical class to which the items belonged, rather than by purely lexical factors. For the item 'the', for example, there was, as expected, a concentration of nouns and adjectives at the following position, and of prepositions at the preceding position.

Since Sinclair's work, no really large-scale collocational analyses appear to have been published, although a number of limited studies have been undertaken (see, for example, Berry-Rogghe, 1973, 1974; Geffroy, Lafon, Seidel & Tournier, 1973; Haskel, 1971). This is a pity, since there is no doubt that subtle and interesting patterns of lexical association remain to be discovered, and that information about such patterns would be extremely useful for lexicography and language teaching. As the power and capacity of computers increases, and as corpora of language data are amassed, it is likely that such information will become available.

7.3 Phonology

7.3.1 Introduction

As was mentioned briefly in Chapter 1, Firth is probably best known for his prosodic model of phonology, with its concentration on phenomena which operate over more than one phonological segment. This prosodic approach as such has found few echoes in later systemic linguistics. It is, however, true to say that Halliday has paid much more attention to the suprasegmental phenomena of stress and (particularly) intonation than to segmental phenomena.

A phonological rank scale is implied, though not discussed, in a footnote in 'Categories of the theory of grammar' (Halliday, 1961, pp.282-3), which assumes the units phoneme, syllable, foot (a rhythmic unit) and tone group (an intonational unit). In later accounts (for instance Halliday, 1967a, p.12) the hierarchical relationship of these units is made explicit. Halliday has also made it clear that he would model contrasts in phonology, as at other levels of description, in terms of system networks (see, for example, Parret, 1974, p.87 = Halliday, 1978, p.40).

7.3.2 Segments and syllables

The adoption of the phoneme as the lowest phonological unit runs counter to the views of Firth, and it is therefore surprising, and regrettable, that there has been almost no discussion of the status of the phoneme, or of the relationship between segmental phonology and phonetics, within systemic linguistics. Apart from a brief mention by Berry (1977, p.91) of the distinction between vocalic and consonantal phonemes, the only published account of patterning at the rank of phoneme seems to be that of Hudson (1974a, pp.34-6), in which a very incomplete system network is given for phonemic contrasts. The initial distinction is between vowel and consonant; vowels are then subclassified as tense or lax, and as peripheral or central, with more delicate distinctions based on the type of formulation used by Chomsky and Halle (1968). There is no subclassification of consonants and no discussion of the network; furthermore, no realization rules are supplied. Hudson points out that an approach which classifies phonemes by means of features has some similarity to prosodic analysis, in that it draws a clear distinction between the abstract features and their phonetic 'exponents'. Further, since phonemes themselves are viewed by Hudson as less central than their defining features, the disadvantages of phonemic analysis to which prosodic phonologists objected are circumvented. Hudson himself observes (1974a, p.36) that 'these suggestions are regrettably tentative and programmatic'. He reasonably sees no bar to a fruitful working out of these ideas; unfortunately, however, no such development has occurred.

At the rank of syllable there is again very little discussion available. Hudson (1974a, p.36) comments that:

> The realisation rules for the syllable will reflect the general constraints on consonant and vowel sequences. For instance, they will probably introduce up to three instances of 'consonant' before the vowel, and then automatically add the relevant features to each instance of 'consonant' to show that it must be *s* if there are two consonants after it, and so on.

Berry (1977, p.91) suggests that two choices are available at syllable rank: strong (that is, stressed) versus weak (unstressed), and long versus short. We shall see below that the latter distinction is too simple.

7.3.3 Stress and intonation

Systemic accounts of stress are based on the work of Abercrombie (1964a & b, 1967), who claims that 'English utterances may be considered as being divided by the isochronous beat of the stress pulse into feet of (approximately) even length' (1964b, p.217). Thus the sentence 'This is the house that Jack built' would, Abercrombie claims, normally be stressed as shown in 7.10, where the slanting lines indicate the boundaries of the rhythmic unit he calls a *foot* (Abercrombie himself used vertical lines, but obliques are used in Halliday's accounts).

7.10 /This is the /house that /Jack /built

English is a 'stress-timed' language, in which, it is claimed, the strong 'sentence stresses' come at roughly equal intervals of time (the isochronous stress mentioned in the above quotation).

The foot consists of two structural elements, which have been given the traditional names of *ictus* and *remiss*. The ictus is always present, and may consist of a sounded stressed ('salient') syllable, as in each of the feet in 7.10, or of a 'silent stress', symbolized by the caret ⌃, as in 7.11 (an example from Halliday 1970a, p.5).

7.11 /⌃ it's /Arthur

The remiss element is optional (for instance, the foot /Jack/ in 7.10 has no such element), and consists of one or more weak (unstressed) syllables. The presence of a silent stress does not disrupt the rhythm: there is a clear analogy here with the silent beat or 'rest' that can occur at the beginning of a bar of music. Furthermore, just as a whole bar can be silent in music, so a whole foot can be silent in speech, as in the middle of 7.12 (from Halliday, 1970a, p.2).

7.12 /each /foot in /turn con/sists of a /number of /syllables/⌃ /
one or /more / ⌃ and the /first /syllable in the /foot is /
always /salient

Example 7.12 illustrates a further point: foot boundaries do not always coincide with word boundaries in English, because word stress in English is irregular, and is usually (though not always) preserved in the stress pattern of the sentence.

Abercrombie (1964b) discusses the various combinations of syllable quantity which can occur in di- and trisyllabic feet. For a disyllabic foot there are three basic patterns: short plus long, medium plus medium (compare Berry's postulation of just two syllable lengths), and long plus short. The possibilities for trisyllabic feet are rather more diverse. There is an important interplay between syllable length and word division, in that the long plus short type of disyllabic foot occurs only where a word boundary comes between the two syllables. Similar factors operate in longer feet. For a more detailed discussion of the relationships between grammar and rhythm see Albrow (1968).

Berry (1977, p.89) has attempted to formalize Abercrombie's distinctions as systemic contrasts, proposing that there are three sets of oppositions at foot rank. The first of these relates to the location of foot boundaries. The unmarked position for a boundary is before a 'lexical' word such as a noun, lexical verb, adjective or adverb. Foot boundaries may also occur in marked positions, before 'grammatical' words such as pronouns, auxiliary verbs, articles and conjunctions, for purposes of contrast. Two of Berry's examples are given below. 7.13 has unmarked boundary locations, while 7.14 has one foot (/me in my/) with marked boundary location.

7.13 (= Berry's 4.11)   /Come and /see me in my /office to/morrow
7.14 (= Berry's 4.15)   /Come and see /me in my /office to/morrow

A second set of contrasts relates to sounding: a foot may, as we have seen, be fully sounded, partially sounded or fully silent. The third set of contrasts is concerned with the pace of the foot, and is correlated with the number of syllables in the foot. Berry suggests a system of three terms: hurried, neutral and leisured. A hurried foot would contain more than three syllables, a neutral foot two or three, and a leisured foot would be monosyllabic.

Halliday takes over Abercrombie's model of rhythmic patterning in English without modification. His treatment of intonation is, however, more original. Theoretical discussion of this area can be found in two papers by Halliday (1963a and b), which were later revised (Halliday, 1966d, 1967a); a more practical emphasis is present in the course on intonation prepared by Halliday (1970a) for learners of English. The examples given in the following discussion are taken from the course on intonation.

Halliday postulates two elements of structure for the tone group: the *tonic* or *tonic segment* is present in all tone groups, and the *pretonic* or *pretonic segment* in some but not all. The tonic is the most prominent part of the tone group, and begins on a salient syllable, the *tonic syllable*, which often differs from other salient syllables in the tone group in being longer and possibly louder, and also carries the main pitch movement of the intonation pattern used. The tonic segment continues up to the end of the tone group. The pretonic, if present, consists of one or more feet placed before the tonic. Thus in 7.15 the pretonic is 'Peter spends his weekends at the' and the tonic is 'tennis club'. Double obliques are used by Halliday to indicate tone group boundaries, and the tonic syllable is underlined.

7.15 //Peter spends his /weekends at the /<u>ten</u>nis club//

Although there may be only one foot in a segment, there must be at least one foot which contains a sounded salient syllable rather than a silent stress. Thus 7.11, which we may now rewrite as in 7.16 below, has no pretonic, even though there is a weak syllable before the tonic.

7.16 // ⌃ it's /<u>Ar</u>thur//

A further complication is Halliday's proposal that certain tone groups should be regarded as compound, having a double tonic, as in 7.17.

7.17 //<u>Rob</u>ert can /have it if /<u>you</u> don't /want it//

Halliday's reason for not regarding this as consisting of two separate tone groups is that the second tonic cannot have a separate pretonic, although the whole complex may indeed be preceded by a normal pretonic, as in 7.18.

7.18 //Arthur and /Jane may be /<u>late</u> with /all this /<u>rain</u> we're/ having//

We should also note that Berry (1977, p.78) regards the tonic as just that foot containing the tonic syllable, and proposes a further element of tone group structure, the *post-tonic*, which consists of any feet following this redefined tonic. She does not, however, argue for her analysis as against that of Halliday, who explicitly excludes any separate post-tonic element because no additional sets of choices are available after those operating at the tonic.

Halliday (1967a) has discussed in some detail the systemic contrasts available at tone group rank. A brief summary can be found in Berry (1977, pp.83-9). We can do no more than give a bare and oversimplified account here. The examples are all from Halliday (1967a). Tone group systems are of three types, which are termed tonality, tonicity and tone.

Tonality relates to the number of tone groups allocated by the speaker to a given stretch of language. Halliday views the tone group as representing one unit of information, as presented by the speaker. In the most usual, unmarked case, the information unit, and hence the tone group, is at least roughly co-extensive with the clause (taken as including any rank shifted clauses which may be contained in it), as in 7.19. Sometimes, however, the speaker chooses to allocate more than one tone group to a clause, as in 7.20: in such circumstances the tonality is marked.

7.19 //I saw John yesterday//
7.20 //I saw John//yesterday//

Tonicity relates to the position of the tonic syllable within the tone group. The unmarked position for the tonic syllable is on the stressed syllable of the last lexical word in the tone group, as in 7.21. Any other position for the tonic syllable (on an earlier lexical word or any grammatical word), as in 7.22, constitutes marked tonicity.

7.21 // ⌃ I /<u>saw</u> him//
7.22 // ⌃ I /saw /<u>him</u>//

The most complex contrasts are those of *tone*, which relate to the meaningfully distinct pitch patterns found in the tone group. For English, Halliday distinguishes between primary and secondary contrasts within the tonic. He postulates five simple primary tones (fall, high rise, low rise, fall-rise and rise-fall) and two compound primary tones (fall plus low rise, rise-fall plus low rise). The secondary contrasts available at the tonic depend on which primary tone is chosen; all, however, are concerned with the height of the falls and rises. For the fall and high or low rise primary tones, there are further secondary contrasts at the pretonic, any term of which may combine with any secondary tone at the tonic. A useful summary in the form of a network for tone can be found at the end of Halliday's (1967a) monograph.

Although the system networks for tonality, tonicity and tone are phonological, since they apply to a phonological unit, the tone group, they are involved in the realization of meaningful options in what Halliday, in this 1967-70 period, regarded as the lexicogrammar. Halliday's position at this time (1967a, p.10) is that 'all *contrast* in meaning can be stated either in grammar or in lexis' and that since intonationally realized contrasts are obviously not lexical (in contradistinction to those realized by pitch phenomena in 'tone languages'), they must be part of the grammar. This leads Halliday to postulate 'grammatical' systems consisting of terms such as 'reserved', 'uninvolved', 'involved', 'confirmatory', 'contradictory', when analysing the attitudinal function of intonation. The realization relationships between these 'grammatical' options and the phonological options are discussed in detail in Halliday (1967a), and from a more pedagogical viewpoint in Halliday (1970a). Networks for the grammatical options realized by intonation can be found at the end of the 1967 monograph. Further discussion of intonation in relation to the grammar of English can be found in El-Menoufy (1969).

Tonality choices realize choices in information distribution within the clause. If the speaker chooses to make just one main point in a clause, he may opt for unmarked tonality, with one tone group for the clause. If, on the other hand, he wishes to bring out more than one point of information, he may choose to split the clause into two or more tone groups.

Tonicity choices realize choices in information focus within the clause. In the case of unmarked tonicity, with the tonic on the last lexical word in the tone group, the speaker need not be assuming any knowledge shared between himself and the hearer. With marked tonicity, however, some shared knowledge is assumed. For instance, 7.22 would normally be used only where the content of the 'I saw' part of the clause can be assumed as already 'given', while the 'new' information is contained in the contrastive 'him'. The 'given' element is 'that part of the message which is shown, in English by intonation, to constitute a link in the chain of discourse', while the 'new' element is what the speaker 'explicitly offers as non-recoverable information' (Halliday, 1970c, p.354). For further discussion of the given/new distinction and its relationship with 'thematization' options in the clause, see Section 8.2.4.

Tone choices are seen by Halliday as realizing options which depend on the mood systems: that is, tone selections have different meanings in declarative, interrogative and imperative clauses. Tone may realize what Halliday calls 'sentence function': for instance in a grammatically declarative clause, with SP ordering of elements, a high-rising tone indicates question function. Tone can also realize a wide range of speaker attitudes. Some examples, with Halliday's (1970a, p.24) glosses, are given below. The figures 1–5 indicate a fall, high rise, low rise, fall-rise and rise-fall respectively.

7.23	//1 ∧ he /could do//	(simple statement)
7.24	//2 ∧ he /could do//	('is that what you think? could he?')
7.25	//3 ∧ he /could do//	('I think he could, but it's of no importance')
7.26	//4 ∧ he /could do//	('but he won't', 'but it won't help you', etc.)
7.27	//5 ∧ he /could do//	('so don't you imagine he couldn't!')

7.3.4 Problems and counter-proposals

Apart from the lack of discussion of segmental phenomena, noted earlier, there are a number of problems associated with Halliday's phonological theory.

Halliday's proposals are made within the context of a description of

English (indeed, but for the fact that the descriptions contain the only theoretical exposition available, they would have been more appropriately discussed, together with other descriptive work, in Chapter 8). The model thus suffers from an anglocentric bias. For instance, it is not at all obvious that the foot is appropriate as a unit in those languages (such as French) which are syllable-timed rather than stress-timed. This is not, however, a serious theoretical problem, since Halliday could simply claim that for such languages the rank scale involves only three units: tone group, syllable and phoneme.

More serious is the dubious theoretical validity of the foot as a unit, even for English. It will be remembered that Abercrombie set up this unit to account for the isochronous nature of stress-timing in English. Neither Abercrombie nor Halliday pretends that feet are precisely equal in length: Halliday (1967a, p.12) refers to experimental evidence for a ratio of 5:6:7 for the lengths of mono-, di- and trisyllabic feet in samples of loud-reading in English. However, as Brazil, Coulthard and Johns (1980, p.5) have noted, it is not at all clear that in casual conversation, as opposed to the loud-reading of passages, any even roughly isochronous units can be identified. Crystal (1969, p.162), too, has observed that 'even if one reduces the unit for which one posits an isochronous base to something quite small, such as the tone unit, one still finds substantial rhythmic variation'. The concept of a foot could, of course, be maintained as simply the stretch of language between two strong stresses, even if the assumption of isochrony were abandoned: such a unit would, however, be really rather different from that intended by Abercrombie and Halliday.

A further problem with Abercrombie's rhythmic theory, as pointed out by Cruttenden (1969, p.312) in his review of Halliday's work, is that it fails to account for what (borrowing musical terminology) is sometimes called 'anacrusis': that is, the theory does not allow for a group of unstressed syllables to be associated with the following stress unit, but forces us to analyse them as belonging to the foot initiated by the preceding stressed syllable. This, in turn, causes difficulties for the analysis of tone group structure. Halliday's claim that phonology, like syntax, is hierarchically organized in terms of a rank scale, combined with the principle of total accountability discussed in relation to grammar in Section 2.3.2.1, leads inevitably to the proposal that tone groups consist of an integral number of feet. Put another way, this means that a tone group boundary must coincide with a foot boundary. As Cruttenden (1969, p.313) points out, this means that in the following example (from Halliday, 1967a, p.19), the second tone group excludes the words 'on the'.

7.28 //1 this of course de/<u>pends</u> on the //1 country where they/ <u>live</u>//

This is regrettable for two kinds of reason. Firstly, as Cruttenden shows, there are phonetic cues which suggest that a boundary occurs before 'on the' rather than after it. Secondly, it will be remembered that for Halliday 'the tone group is one *unit of information*, one "block" in the message that the speaker is communicating' (Halliday, 1970a, p.3, original emphasis). Yet clearly, 'on the' belongs with the information in the second tone group, not the first.

The phenomenon of anacrusis also poses problems for the distinction between tonic and pretonic. As we saw earlier, a pretonic is said to be present only where there is at least one foot, before the tonic, containing a sounded salient syllable, so that in cases such as 7.16, discussed earlier, the unstressed syllables before the tonic do not form a pretonic. Presumably, then, they are part of the tonic: but this clashes with the definition of the tonic as beginning on the prominent syllable which initiates the main pitch movement. In any case, as Cruttenden (1969, p.310) has shown, it is sometimes difficult, using Halliday's rather inexplicit criteria for identifying the tonic, to distinguish between a pretonic segment in which there is considerable pitch movement, and a separate tonic or series of tonics. In general, as Cruttenden says, there is a need in Halliday's work for much more discussion of phonetic detail which might allow the recognition of tone groups and their tonic segments. This lack of phonetic explicitness also extends to the specification of tone contrasts: no explicit criteria are given for distinguishing certain pairs of tones (such as one type of fall-rise and the fall plus low rise pattern) which are phonetically very similar.

Brown and Yule (1983, pp.157-60) have expressed reservations similar to those of Cruttenden. They point out that smooth contours with just one main pitch movement are comparatively rare in naturally occurring discourse, and cite a series of experiments in which a panel of judges with considerable experience in teaching Halliday's system were unable to identify tone groups reliably. Brown and Yule criticize Halliday's lack of explicit criteria for boundaries, and the odd results of insisting that tone groups, and hence information units, must begin and end at a foot boundary. They are also sceptical of Halliday's claim that tone groups are in unmarked correspondence with clauses, and present evidence that Halliday's own data suggest the phrase as a more likely candidate.

Also problematic is Halliday's insistence that intonationally realized choices are grammatical. As Brazil, Coulthard and Johns (1980, p.10) observe, some of the categories proposed (such as 'contradictory', 'with reservation', 'with commitment') 'look rather odd grammatical categories'. This problem could be circumvented in Halliday's latest model, in which, as we have seen, system networks are drawn for options in meaning: intonation can now be seen as a mode of realization of semantic options, parallel to and integrated with, but theoretically separate from, syntactic and lexical realizations. This is the position adopted by Fawcett (1980, pp.58-9).

The nature of some of the 'grammatical' distinctions proposed by Halliday is also rather disturbing, especially where attitudinal contrasts are involved. As Brazil (1975, p.2) points out

. . . there is a frequent implication of an absence of systematicness in the large area of communicative potential covered by 'attitudinal' or 'emotional'. The implication does, indeed, seem inescapable when one tries to attribute a 'meaning' to a particular intonational feature.

The attitudinal implications of a particular intonation contour may vary with the lexical content of the tone group, and also with aspects of the social context.

Brazil's own work (Brazil, 1975, 1978, 1981; Brazil, Coulthard & Johns, 1980) offers partial solutions to some of the problems raised above. It is conceived within a framework which emphasizes the interactional potential of language: it thus forms a bridge between intonation and the study of discourse patterning, to be discussed in Section 7.4. The position adopted is that:

> . . . by working in a discourse framework it is possible to reveal some underlying general truths, and that these in turn give reason to believe that the way intonation affects meaning *can* be presented in fairly simple, coherent and homogeneous terms. (Brazil *et al.*, 1980, p.xiv)

The aim is thus to produce a model which, while accommodating the various functions of intonation proposed by Halliday and others, will reveal basic underlying properties which bring order to the apparently chaotically unconstrained relationships described in earlier work.

Brazil's model is based on three sets of choices, termed *tone, key* and *termination*, operating within the *tone units* of spoken discourse. The tone unit consists of an obligatory *tonic segment* with an optional *proclitic segment* before it and an optional *enclitic segment* after it. The tonic segment begins with the first 'prominent' syllable in the tone unit (called the *onset*) and ends with the last prominent syllable (the *tonic syllable*). A prominent syllable is one which is not merely accented, but is also singled out by the speaker as having some informational value. Brazil (Brazil, 1978, p.10 ff.; Brazil *et al.*, 1980, pp.42-4) provides instrumental phonetic support for the concept of prominence, showing that prominent syllables are distinguished from other accented syllables by a change in pitch direction from rising to falling. The tonic syllable is distinguished from other prominent syllables by the fact that it carries the main pitch movement of the tone unit. An example of a tone unit containing all three segments (from Brazil *et al.*, 1980, p.39) is given below. Prominent syllables are capitalized, and the tonic syllable underlined. The 'p' at the beginning of the tone unit symbolizes the tone choice (see later).

7.29 (= Brazil *et al*'s 6) //p that's a VERy TALL STOry//

proclitic segment	tonic segment	enclitic segment

Certain important differences from Halliday's account of tone group structure are immediately apparent. Brazil *et al.* do not claim that each tone unit, and each segment of such a unit, must consist of an integral number of rhythmic units. They are thus able to treat all syllables before the onset as proclitic, and all syllables after the tonic syllable as enclitic. The tonic segment, defined in this way, is a unit whose validity can be demonstrated instrumentally as well as perceptually. It is in fact Brazil's contention that all the meaning conveyed by intonation is carried by the tonic segment: this contrasts with Halliday's model, in which, as we have seen, secondary tones at the pretonic element are proposed. Meanings concerned with key in Brazil's model are realized by the pitch level of the onset syllable of the tonic segment, while meanings concerned with tone and termination are realized in the tonic syllable.

Tone refers to the direction of pitch movement (if any) on the tonic syllable. The direction of the pitch change may be continued into the enclitic segment if there is one. The most frequent and important tones of English are the fall and the fall-rise. Brazil explains their use in terms of the interpenetrating knowledge and assumptions of the speaker and the addressee. The fall-rise, which Brazil calls 'referring' tone, and symbolizes as r, is used when the speaker wishes to present the content of the tone unit as part of the shared, negotiated common ground between himself and the addressee. The assumption of shared knowledge may be based on what has been mentioned in the preceding discourse, or on aspects of the participants' background not mentioned at all in the current interaction. This assumption can be exploited by speakers, by presenting matter as if it were shared, when in fact they know that this is not the case. The falling tone, which Brazil calls 'proclaiming' tone, and symbolizes as p, is used when the speaker wishes to present the content of the tone unit as new information for the addressee. Again, the assumptions involved can be exploited. An example, taken from Brazil *et al.* (1980, p.16) will help to clarify the claims made about the use of r and p tones.

> 7.30 (= Brazil *et al*'s 7) //r he'll be <u>TWEN</u>ty//p in <u>AU</u>gust//
> 7.31 (= Brazil *et al*'s 8) //p he'll be <u>TWEN</u>ty//r in <u>AU</u>gust//

In 7.30 the fact that the person will be twenty is taken as part of what both speaker and hearer know, and the new information is taken as being that the birthday is in August. In 7.31, on the other hand, it is the age which is presented as new information, the month being part of already shared knowledge.

Rising and rising-falling tones are seen as variants of r and p tone respectively. The rising tone (symbolized as r+) is used for matter which, although considered as shared material, is thought by the speaker to be in need of reactivation. Its use reflects the 'dominance' of one partner in certain types of interaction, by which is meant the greater freedom of that participant in making linguistic choices. It is, for example, commonly used by teachers in classroom interaction. The use of rising-falling (p+) tone rather than simple falling tone is again typically associated with dominance, and is interpreted as indicating that the content of the tone unit adds to the stock of knowledge, not only of the hearer, but also of the speaker. Brazil *et al.* suggest the gloss 'That alters my world view!' and point out that such a general meaning is compatible with the attitudinal meaning of 'surprise' often attributed to this tone.

There is a fifth, so-called neutral or 'level' tone (o), characterized by a virtual absence of pitch movement. This tone can be used to highlight the continuity of a piece of language, indicating lack of completion, but not signalling any of the assumptions of r and p tones. The o tone is particularly prevalent in certain types of loud-reading where attention is paid to what is actually printed rather than to its relationship with the surrounding discourse.

Whereas tone is concerned with pitch movement, key is concerned with pitch level. More specifically, the key of a tone unit is determined by the pitch level of a 'turning-point' in the pitch contour of the onset syllable, relative to the pitch level of the onset syllable in the preceding tone unit. There is a three-way distinction of key: high, mid, low. The definition of key as relative to the preceding tone unit suggests that there might be a phonological unit higher than the tone group. Brazil (Brazil 1978, p.18 ff.; Brazil *et al.*, 1980, p.61 ff.) postulates a *pitch sequence*, defined in terms of the choice of termination, discussed below. The function of key is chiefly to indicate the relationship holding between the content of successive units, as follows:

Key of first tone unit	Key of second tone unit	Relationship signalled
mid	high	contrastive
mid	mid	additive
mid	low	equative

The following examples are taken from Brazil *et al.*, (1980, p.65), and are also used in Brazil's earlier account (1978, p.22).

7.32 (= Brazil *et al*'s 11)

high		(a)		and <u>LOST</u>
mid	//p he <u>GAM</u>bled	(b)	//p	and <u>LOST</u>
low		(c)		and <u>LOST</u>

In 7.32 (a) the implication is that his losing was contrary to expectations; in (b) his gambling and losing are simply presented as two facts; and in (c) it is implied that gambling is equivalent to losing. Further exemplification can be found in the accounts cited. Key has a special function in the initial tone unit of a pitch sequence: here, high key often signals a change in topic, and is frequently associated with boundary markers such as 'right', 'well', 'OK', 'good', 'now', and so on, in, for example, classroom teaching.

Termination choices, like key choices, are indicated by pitch level, high, mid or low; but this time it is the pitch level of the tonic syllable which is important. All combinations of key and termination are possible in a tone unit, except high key and low termination (ruled out because all the pitch levels are relative, so that the hearer always interprets a change in level as one step up or down). The choice of low termination is what signals the end of a pitch sequence: the pitch sequence can thus be defined as extending from one instance of low termination up to and including the next tone unit which has low termination. The choice of termination in the last tone unit of a speaker's contribution to discourse has an important function in controlling the pattern of that discourse. If a speaker ends on high termination, this is heard as requesting a high key initial tone unit in the next speaker's utterance, indicating a reply involving some element of contrast. On the other hand, if a speaker ends on a mid termination, he is heard as requesting agreement by means of an utterance beginning in mid key. There is thus an element of 'concord' between the final termination of one speaker's utterance and the initial key of the next speaker's contribution. Only a low termination leaves the addressee completely unconstrained in his choice of initial key. Speakers can, of course, refuse to comply with a previous speaker's expectations. The following examples of the relationships concerned are taken from Brazil *et al.* (1980, p.75, 78); they also appear in Brazil's earlier account (1978, p.25, 28). The first two are taken from a doctor–patient interview.

7.33 (= Brazil *et al*'s 4)

```
high                DRY skin
mid   //D: p+ it's                // p ISn't it // P: p MM //
low
```

7.34 (= Brazil *et al*'s 5)

```
high               IRritating you say      VERy irritating
mid   //D: p  VERy              //P: p                //
low
```

7.35 (= Brazil *et al*'s 9)

```
high   WHY
mid   //p     DON'T // p PEOple turn     //
low                                UP
```

In 7.33, the doctor's mid termination is heard as a simple request for agreement. In 7.34, on the other hand, the doctor's high termination is heard as an attempt to elicit a response which, by exploiting the contrastive significance of high key, strongly confirms what he has said. In 7.35, no constraint is placed on the type of reply in terms of its initial key. Further examples can be found in the accounts cited.

The validity of Brazil's model can be fully assessed only when a considerable body of data has been subjected to the type of analysis he proposes. The model is certainly attractive in two particular respects. First, it brings some sense of order into what had hitherto seemed an area of almost unsystematizable complexity. Brazil *et al.* (1980, Chapter 8) are able to show that their scheme is compatible with, and acts as a more fundamental explanation of, many of the more detailed patterns of relationship described by Halliday and by O'Connor and Arnold (1973). A second advantage of the Brazil model is that it does not restrict itself to a consideration of the meanings of isolated tone groups or even pitch sequences, but integrates the functions of intonation into the wider perspective of discourse patterning. It is to this important area that we must now turn.

7.4 Discourse

7.4.1 Introduction: the background to discourse analysis

Despite the notorious difficulties of defining the sentence as a linguistic unit, linguists stuck firmly at the sentence for some two thousand years. It is only in the last 25 years or so that serious efforts have been made to investigate the suprasentential patterning of language. This upsurge in activity has been coupled with increasing interest in what we *do* with language: how we use it, not only for the exchange of information, but also for getting things done, for creating and maintaining social relationships, and so on. Clearly, such interests are central to the Hallidayan view of language which, as we have seen, builds on the ideas of Malinowski and Firth. It is also central to a movement which arose within the rather different environment of studies on the philosophy of language. A series of lectures by the Oxford philosopher J.L. Austin (published as Austin, 1962) laid the foundations for what is now generally known as *speech act theory*, and this was later developed, principally by Searle (see especially Searle, 1969). These philosophers were concerned with (among other things) what a particular linguistic act 'counts as' (its *illocutionary force*, for instance as an assertion, a question, a command), and what effects the utterance could have (the *perlocutionary force*, for example in persuading or frightening someone). Even the speech act philosophers, however, analysed single speech acts, divorced from their linguistic context. This has the important consequence that speech act theory makes no predictions about the ways in which speech acts can fit together to form larger units. This is the basis for criticisms of speech act theory by those linguists whose approach has come to be known as *discourse analysis*. Thus Coulthard (1975, p.75) writes:

> Austin's concern was not with discourse structure but simply with the isolated act, and therefore he does not discuss whether the acts are structurally as well as meaningfully distinct — that is, whether there are unique restrictions on what can follow or precede 'remarking' to distinguish it from 'telling'.

The discourse analysis approach itself is interested in exactly the kind of structural patterning mentioned by Coulthard, as is demonstrated clearly by the following quotations:

> ... the level of language function in which we are centrally interested is neither the universal functions of language, nor the detailed function of surface formal ordering within the sentence. It is rather the level of the function of a particular utterance, in a particular social situation and at a particular place in a sequence, as a specific contribution to a developing discourse. (Sinclair & Coulthard, 1975, p.13)

> The fundamental problem of discourse analysis is to show how one utterance follows another in a rational, rule-governed manner — in other words, how we understand coherent discourse. (Labov, 1972, p.252)

The discourse approach thus stresses the syntagmatic relations into which linguistic acts enter, rather than simply seeing speech acts as isolated events. Discourse analysis therefore offers the possibility of defining the communicative function of utterances within a framework which is based on the concepts of syntagmatic and paradigmatic patterning familar at other levels of description.

Discourse analysts have tended to stress the differences between their way of looking at communicative function and the speech act approach (see, for instance, Sinclair & Coulthard, 1975, p.14). They are indeed different approaches, and discourse analysis does offer a framework which relates more clearly to types of patterning at other levels. However, it will be suggested later (Section 7.4.5) that a synthesis of the two approaches is not only possible but desirable.

A full discussion of recent work on discourse would be inappropriate here, even if space permitted it: in any case, a number of introductions to the area are now available (see, for instance, Coulthard 1975, 1977; Brown & Yule, 1983; and the very clear and readable treatment in Stubbs, 1983). However, a survey of developments based on the important work of Sinclair and Coulthard is relevant to our concerns, since these studies take their theoretical origins from Halliday's Scale and Category theory of grammar. Before we consider Sinclair and Coulthard's work, however, we must look briefly at the approach to speech acts and discourse seen in the recent work of Halliday and his close collaborators.

7.4.2 Discourse patterning in Halliday's models

Halliday's most detailed discussion of patterning within discourse is to be found in a paper written in 1977, but published only recently (Halliday, 1984a) in which he aims to represent relationships in dialogue in terms of a hierarchy of three types of network. The 'highest' network, of 'social contextual' options, is recoded as choices from a 'semantic' network, which are themselves recoded as options in the 'grammatical' network.

It is at the 'social contextual' level, itself seen as outside and 'above' the linguistic code, that relationships in dialogue are modelled. The network has as its point of origin 'the "move" in dialogue', and there are two simultaneous sets of options: the 'role assignment' options distinguish between an [initiating] role (more delicately classified as [giving] or [demanding]) and a [responding] role (more delicately classified as [accepting] or [giving on demand]); the 'commodity exchanged' options distinguish between the exchange of goods and services and that of information. For example, the elicitation of information would be specified in terms of the features [initiating, demanding, information].

At the 'semantic' level, a network for 'speech function' has two simultaneous sets of options: the 'turn' options [initiate] and [respond to], and the 'orientation' options, which distinguish between [give] (more delicately specified as [offer] or [statement]) and [demand] (more delicately, [command] or [question]). The 'grammatical' networks are those of mood, basically distinguishing, for the 'major' clause type, between declarative, interrogative and imperative, and also between fully explicit and elliptical clauses. Halliday recognizes certain 'congruent' realization relations between levels, such that, for example, the feature combination [initiating, demanding, goods and services] at the social contextual level is congruently realized by [command] at the semantic level, which in turn is congruently realized as [imperative] at the grammatical level. He also recognizes that there are many non-congruent realizations, which are extremely important in the process of actual conversational interaction, but which he does not discuss.

Typically, Halliday's account is insightful, but too programmatic to be really useful. A number of problems arise in connection with the 'level of social context'. It is not clear just what this level is, or how it relates to other levels in Halliday's previous work. It is equally unclear how a 'move' in dialogue is to be defined, and whether it forms part of a hierarchical scale of discourse units. As Halliday himself admits, the distinction between 'information' and 'goods and services' is far too crude. There are problems at the 'semantic' level too: we are not told how categories such as statement, question, command and offer are to be defined, and certain semantic types, such as exclamations, which do not fit into the scheme in any obvious way, are omitted. It is not at all apparent why the 'turn' system, consisting of the terms [initiate] and [respond to], is needed in the semantics: it seems to be in one-to-one correspondence with the least delicate terms of the 'role assignment' network at the social contextual level. As we have seen, non-congruent realizations are not discussed; furthermore, Halliday fails to recognize that (as will be seen later) there are in fact systematic relationships between interlevel realization relations and social contextual parameters in this important area.

An attempt to refine and expand Halliday's account of discourse structure has been made by Martin (1981a). Martin, however, concentrates on expanding the semantic speech function network, and explicitly rejects any 'higher' level of organization such as Halliday's social contextual level, claiming that 'in the vast majority of cases there would be congruence between two, if not three, of the strata in a three-strata analysis, and the third stratum would thus be redundant' (Martin, 1981a, p.58). This is surely a misguided position: non-congruent realizations are in fact extremely important in some areas (for instance, utterances with 'directive' communicative function are rather rarely imperative-form commands in many types of social interaction); furthermore, since non-congruent patterns, even if they were rare, do form part of the language user's internalized linguistic capabilities, they should, if systematic, be taken into account in our theories.

Despite the decision to reject a higher level of options, Martin does appeal to what he regards as social contextual criteria in motivating his network for speech function. In particular, speech functions are differentiated, and their number restricted, by the expectations they set up in terms of 'adjacency pairs' in the structure of the discourse. For instance, the class of acts labelled as [address other] in the network differs from that labelled [express self] in that whereas the former set up the expectation of a second pair part, the latter do not. Terms in the speech function network are also motivated by distinctions in their congruent grammatical realizations: for example, it is claimed that responses to calls and greetings are typically realized through a minor (predicatorless) clause such as 'What?' or 'Hi!'

Although Martin's work is more detailed than Halliday's, and the criteria more explicit, it still offers nothing approaching a comprehensive model of discourse structure. We now turn to attempts to provide such a model.

7.4.3 *The Sinclair and Coulthard model*

The work of Sinclair and Coulthard (1975), carried out within the English Language Research group at the University of Birmingham, is an attempt to specify the discourse structures available in the specific social context of classroom interaction. The fundamental claim in this work is that 'the discourse value of an item depends on what linguistic items have preceded it, what are expected to follow and what do follow' (p.34). Discourse acts are, then, to be defined primarily in terms of the predictions they set up within the structure of discourse. For instance, an 'elicitation' is an act which requires a linguistic response or some non-verbal equivalent such as a nod; a 'directive' is an act requiring a non-linguistic response; and an 'informative' requires no response other than an acknowledgment that the addressee is still attending to what is being said.

Sinclair and Coulthard emphasize the lack of any necessary one-to-one correspondence between discourse categories and grammatical categories. They recognize that there may be unmarked, or in Halliday's terms 'congruent', realizations of particular discourse acts (for instance, imperative for directives), but regard the more marked, less congruent realizations as important enough to justify the proposing of a level of discourse structure separate from the grammar, though they would be willing to revise this position if discourse acts could be proved to be simply consistent arrangements of clauses.

For the formal analysis of discourse patterning Sinclair and Coulthard take over the apparatus of Halliday's Scale and Category grammar, discussed in Chapter 2. The *act* is simply the lowest unit on a discourse rank scale: it is said to correspond most closely to the grammatical unit of clause. The next rank of unit, the *move*, 'is concerned centrally with each discrete contribution to a discussion made by one speaker' (p.123), and is thus the minimal free unit of discourse. Moves from different speakers combine to form *exchanges*, which in turn combine to form *transactions*. The largest unit proposed is, in the most general terms, the *interaction*, of which the *lesson* is a sub-class specific to the teaching situation. At each rank (except possibly the highest) there are various classes of unit, each class exhibiting a particular range of structures, the elements of which are realized by classes of the unit next below on the rank scale. For example, the class of exchange which Sinclair and Coulthard label a 'teaching exchange' has three elements of structure: an obligatory Initiation (I) by the teacher, followed optionally by a Response (R) by the pupil and then, again optionally, by a Feedback (F) from the teacher. The structure proposed (p.26) is thus I(R)(F). The I element is realized by a move of the Opening class, the R element by a move of the Answering class, and the F element by a move of the Follow-up class. Each of these classes of move has its own elements of structure, each of which may be realized by certain classes of act but not by others (for details see Sinclair and Coulthard, pp.26-7). A typical IRF sequence is shown in 7.36, taken from Sinclair and Coulthard (p.48).

7.36   Teacher: Do you know what we mean by accent?   I
       Pupil: It's the way you talk.   R
       Teacher: The way we talk. This is a very broad
                 comment.   F

Acts are recognizable not only in terms of the expectations they set up in the discourse, but also by the range of grammatical structures which can realize them. Twenty-two classes of act are in fact proposed for classroom discourse, realizing structural elements in 5 classes of move, which in turn realize elements in 2 classes of exchange. Despite their different discourse values, certain of the classes of act proposed by Sinclair and Coulthard show common properties. For instance, they recognize a class of act which they call 'cue', whose funtion is to get a pupil to raise his hand if he knows the answer to a question. This is clearly an attempt to get the pupil to carry out a non-linguistic action, but it is not classified as a directive, since the action requested is not the main point of the teacher's initiation, but is a preliminary, subordinate to the main task of answering the teacher's question. Cues and directives are both attempts to secure action, but their discourse values differ. Sinclair and Coulthard recognize the common properties of such acts by proposing what they call 'situational' categories of statement, question and command (p.29ff.). The situational classification of an utterance is made on the basis of the formal properties of the sentence uttered, and the context of utterance; only then can the item be allocated a discourse function.

> It is the place in the structure of the discourse which finally determines which act a particular item is realising, though classification can only be made of items already tagged with features from grammar and situation. (p.29)

Sinclair and Coulthard propose a number of rules of interpretation which allow the deduction of situational categories from the grammar and context. An example is the following set of rules for interpreting interrogatives:

> An interrogative clause is to be interpreted as a *command to do* if it fulfils all the following conditions:
> (i) it contains one of the modals *can, could, will, would* (and sometimes *going to*);
> (ii) if the subject of the clause is also the addressee;
> (iii) the predicate describes an action which is physically possible at the time of the utterance. (p.32)

Thus, in the classroom, provided that a piano is present in the room, 7.37 is interpreted as a command, but 7.38 and 7.39 as questions (Sinclair and Coulthard's examples):

7.37 Can you play the piano, John?
7.38 Can John play the piano?
7.39 Can you swim a length, John?

The subsequent allocation of a discourse classification to these commands or questions is made on the basis of position in the discourse structure. There are certain difficulties inherent in Sinclair and Coulthard's approach, which will be mentioned in Section 7.4.5. Meanwhile, let us examine some of the more recent work inspired by this model.

7.4.4 Developments in the analysis of exchange structure

Much of the recent work based on the Sinclair and Coulthard model has focused on the rank of exchange, which has emerged as the central unit in the discourse hierarchy, for reasons which will become clear in the discussion which follows.

Sinclair and Coulthard's work was purposely limited to a single well-defined context, that of classroom interaction, because it was felt that the high degree of situational structuring (clear purposes of interaction, hierarchical status relationships, and so on) would be most likely to correlate with a high degree of discourse structuring. The ultimate aim of the Birmingham research group, however, was to provide a discourse model with more general validity. With this in mind, and in the knowledge of a number of problems thrown into relief by the work on classroom discourse, the research team began to investigate other types of discourse, with varying values for what were predicted to be key parameters: the degree of control of one participant over topic and turn-taking, status and familiarity relations, and the purposes of interaction. A survey of much of this later work can be found in an article by Coulthard, Montgomery and Brazil (1981).

Work on doctor—patient interviews revealed an exchange structure with Initiation, Response and up to three Feedback elements. Brazil's work on 'key' in English intonation, reviewed in Section 7.3.4, was found to be invaluable in determining the boundaries of the exchange. Work on transcripts of industrial committee meetings showed that the most common exchange structure was the rather simple pattern IF^n, with some complication due to embedding and discontinuity. Broadcast discussions proved somewhat problematic, often consisting of initiating moves with no response or feedback, and containing large amounts of material which resisted analysis. These difficulties led to a project which examined the structure of monologue in lectures.

An important development of Sinclair and Coulthard's work was the recognition by Burton (1980, 1981) that outside the classroom situation, discourse participants do not always behave in a polite, consensus-seeking way, but have the option of challenging a previous speaker's move, rather than supporting it. In her work on modern dramatic texts and on casual conversation, Burton builds the notion of challenge into a model which otherwise stays quite close, in all but detail, to that proposed by Sinclair and Coulthard for classroom discourse.

Further developments in the analysis of exchange structure were stimulated by the work of Coulthard and Brazil (1979, 1981), who expanded on the idea, central to the Sinclair and Coulthard model, that the discourse value of an item is determined by the predictions it fulfils and those which the item itself sets up in the discourse. The basic elements of exchange structure are defined by Coulthard and Brazil in terms of the features [± predicting] and [± predicted], as follows:

	Predicting	Predicted
Initiation	+	−
Response	−	+
Follow-up	−	−
R/I	+	+

The fourth logical combination, [+ predicting, + predicted], defines a new element, labelled R/I, which, as it were, looks both ways, being predicted by a previous Initiation, and itself setting up the prediction of a following Response. This element is intended to account for items such as the pupil's reply in 7.40 (Coulthard and Brazil 1981, p.96).

7.40 (= Coulthard and Brazil's 34)
Teacher: can anyone tell me what this means
Pupil: does it mean danger men at work
Teacher: yes

R/I moves are said to be distinguished from R moves by a high 'termina-tion' intonation choice (see Section 7.3.4) or by interrogative syntax. The maximal structure proposed for the exchange is

(O) I (R/I) R (F) (F) (C)

where brackets indicate optionality, and O and C are Open and Close moves, postulated in the 1979 work, which (where present) act as exchange boundaries.

A further important proposal made by Coulthard and Brazil is that 'the exchange is the unit concerned with negotiating the transmission of information' (Coulthard & Brazil, 1981, p.101), and that its boundaries are set by the restriction of information-carrying to four elements, each of which can occur only once in an exchange, and which must occur in the following order:

e_1 eliciting move seeking major information and polarity
e_2 eliciting move seeking polarity information only
i_1 informing move asserting major information and polarity
i_2 informing move asserting polarity information only

As soon as a second occurrence of any of these elements appears, a new exchange is begun. An example, taken from Coulthard and Brazil, will illustrate the intended distinction between 'major' and 'polarity' information.

7.41 (= Coulthard and Brazil's 48)
I e_1 where's the typewriter
R/I e_2 is it in the cupboard
R i_2 no
F ack oh dear
F ack yeh

The I move requests specific non-polarity information, whereas the R/I and R moves request or assert polarity information only. 'Ack' stands for 'acknowledgment'.

Stubbs (1979) has pointed out certain problems inherent in the Coulthard and Brazil model of exchange structure. As he observes, Coulthard and Brazil provide no way of distinguishing between Open and Initiation, or between Close and Follow-up, in terms of the features [± pre-dicting] and [± predicted]. He also points out that the R/I element is claimed to be both predicted and optional, which is intuitively rather odd. Stubbs proposes an alternative exchange structure

I (R ⟨ R/I R) (F)

where overlapping brackets indicate that one or both of the bracketed elements must be present. Stubbs' proposed structure, but not Coulthard and Brazil's, allows well-formed exchanges of the following kind (attested data, from Stubbs, 1979, p.127).

7.42	A.	what time is it	I	e_1
	B.	five fifteen	R	i_1
	A.	is it	R/I	e_2
	B.	yes	R	i_2
	A.	thanks	F	ack
	B.	ok	F	ack

In later work (Stubbs, 1981, 1983), dealing with ways of motivating exchange structure, Stubbs expands upon Coulthard and Brazil's scheme in rather more detail. He points out that although Coulthard and Brazil clearly intend that Initiation should be regarded as initial in the exchange, and Follow-up as terminal, these features do not follow from the definition of the elements in terms of the features [± predicting] and [± predicted]. Stubbs therefore adds the features [± initial] to the specification of the elements, where 'an utterance is − initial if its lexis or surface syntax requires to be expanded from preceding utterances, and could not otherwise be understood in isolation' (Stubbs, 1981; p.116). He is now able to recognize two further logically possible combinations: [− predicting, − predicted, + initial] and [+ predicting, − predicted, − initial]. The first of these, labelled Inf for Inform, corresponds to an initiation which does not predict a response, as in certain kinds of lecturing. The second corresponds to a 're-initiation', Ir. In terms of this model, the move coded as R/I in 7.42 is best recoded as Ir, since it is not predicted by the preceding moves. The model of exchange structure finally proposed by Stubbs generates the basic structures Inf, I R, I R/I R, each of which can be followed by any number of Ir R pairs, and/or any number of F moves. Stubbs also discusses how any given analysis of exchange structure can be further motivated by informant testing and the collection of additional naturally occurring data.

Coulthard and Brazil's work was also the springboard for the extremely interesting proposals for exchange structure made by Berry (1981a, 1981b). Berry recognizes the importance of Coulthard and Brazil's work in suggesting that the exchange has a unity related to its role in information transmission, and that the need to conform to this unit constrains the later moves in an exchange, so that there is a progression in terms of restriction in the number of options available. However, she claims that their detailed proposals are unsatisfactory, both from the point of view of coding texts and in terms of predicting discourse well-formedness. Berry also questions Coulthard and Brazil's view that the sentence remains the highest unit of grammar, above which a separate level of discourse is needed. These claims will be examined in turn.

Berry (1981a) observes that Coulthard and Brazil's distinction between 'polarity' and 'major' information is not as clear cut as it might seem, although it does appear that polarity information can be interpreted as information which could be paraphrased by 'yes' or 'no'. Berry presents pairs of pieces of data, such as 7.43 and 7.44 below, each member of which has an internal coherence which should be accounted for by any valid model of exchange structure.

7.43 (= Berry's 1)
    A. What's the time?
    B. Six o'clock.
    A. Is it?
    B. Yes.

7.44 (= Berry's 2)
    A. Is it six o'clock yet?
    B. Yes.
    A. Is it?
    B. Yes.

If polarity information is to be interpreted as that which is paraphrasable as 'yes' or 'no', then there is only one move in 7.43 (A's second move) which requests polarity information only, so that Coulthard and Brazil can regard 7.43 as a single exchange, with elements e_1, i_1, e_2, i_2. In 7.44, however, there are two moves requesting polarity information (both of A's moves), and since only one such move can occur in an exchange, Coulthard and Brazil would be forced to regard 7.44 as two exchanges. They would thus fail to capture the fact that the two examples are parallel in their internal coherence. Berry also shows that Coulthard and Brazil are similarly unable to account for the intuitively clear parallels between pairs of ill-formed pieces of discourse. Berry's own data suggest that the distribution, and constraints on distribution, of 'polarity' and 'major' information moves are very similar. She therefore concludes that a different basis may be required for the definition of 'major' information.

Berry bases a new definition on Stubbs' (1981, p.116) comment that his definition of [± initial] 'suggests a way of defining the exchange as an information unit, in which major information is introduced and then supported by elliptical syntax in the rest of the exchange'. Berry goes on to differentiate degrees of ellipticity involving the components of the proposition being transmitted (a 'component' here being equivalent to a participant, process or circumstance in Halliday's account of transitivity – see Sections 3.4 and 8.2.2).

Class 1: no components, or just one component, of original
          proposition ellipted.
Class 2: all but one of the components ellipted.
Class 3: all components ellipted.

This classification cuts across Coulthard and Brazil's distinction between major and polarity information, and also across the informing/eliciting distinction. Berry now reformulates Coulthard and Brazil's proposals as follows: each ellipticity class may be represented only once in a given exchange, in the order 1, 2, 3; Class 1 is obligatory and Class 2 occurs if and only if the Class 1 move is eliciting; follow-up moves may occur, and are, in Berry's terms, extra Class 3 moves, which must follow all the others. Berry shows that these rules, unlike Coulthard and Brazil's, correctly group together pairs of texts, such as 7.43 and 7.44, whose coherence is intuitively of the same kind, and also group together pairs of texts whose deviance is intuitively parallel.

Berry goes on to criticize Coulthard and Brazil's categories of eliciting and informing, pointing out that their glosses 'requesting a verbal response' and 'providing new information' are notional and rather difficult to apply rigorously. Berry substitutes formal categories which she calls question (Q, defined as an utterance with interrogative syntax and/or rising intonation) and statement (S, an utterance having neither interrogative syntax nor rising intonation, which may thus be declarative or moodless). Imperative form utterances are excluded from the discussion in Berry's paper. She shows that the permissible sequences of Q and S are generated by the phrase structure rule:

$$\text{Exchange} \longrightarrow \left((Q) \ \left\{ {Q \atop S} \right\} \right) \ S \quad (\text{Oh})$$

where (Oh) shows that a follow-up move, realized by a class of utterances containing 'Oh', can but need not be present. Thus every exchange must contain a statement, as defined in Berry's terms. Berry can now reformulate Coulthard and Brazil's e and i categories as follows:

e_1 : move represented by a question for which a statement cannot be substituted.

e_2 : move represented by a question for which a statement can be substituted, or a statement for which a question can be substituted.

i: move represented by a statement for which a question cannot be substituted.

If 'a' represents a move realized by an 'Oh'-class item, then the permissible exchange structures are generated by the rule

$$\text{Exchange} \longrightarrow ((e_1) \ e_2) \ i \ (a)$$

Berry shows that these proposals, like those for ellipticity, solve the problems of accounting in similar ways for the coherence or deviance of related pairs of examples.

Berry now puts the two sets of proposals together by relating different sequences of ellipticity classes to the nature of the initial move in an exchange.

Initial move	Sequence of ellipticity classes
e_1	1 2 3 (3)
e_2	1 2 (3)
i	1 (3)

These rules are supported by all the straightforwardly well-formed examples in Berry's data. We shall give just three examples here.

7.45 (= Berry's 19)

Teacher:	What are eight twelves?	e_1	Class 1
Pupil:	Ninety-six?	e_2	Class 2
Teacher:	Right.	i	Class 3

7.46 (= Berry's 15)

Casual acquaintance A:	Was it your daughter you were telling me the other day had just gone to Oxford?	e_2	Class 1
Casual acquaintance B:	Yes.	i	Class 2

7.47 (= Berry's 18)

Teacher:	Eight twelves are ninety-six.	i	Class 1

Other rather more problematic cases, and also certain cases of ill-formedness, are accounted for by postulating embedded exchanges, for which independent evidence is given.

Berry also discusses a further kind of progression in the exchange, which Coulthard and Brazil do not deal with at all: exchanges must be well-formed not only 'syntactically' (that is, in terms of Berry's ellipticity classes and sequences of S and Q) but also semantically. For instance, a question about time is not appropriately answered by giving information about place, even though the structure of the exchange, in terms of the categories and rules discussed so far, may be perfectly well-formed. Berry relates the semantic or propositional development of the exchange to the work of Sperber and Wilson (for an introductory account see Smith & Wilson, 1979, p.158 ff.), in which the 'grammatically specified entailments' of a sentence (those derivable by the operation of substitutions on the surface syntactic structure) are arranged to form a 'semantic skeleton', in an order that shows which propositions entail which others. Berry's claim is that if the utterer of the first move does not commit himself immediately to a completed proposition, the propositional content of the second move in the exchange must entail that of the first move, and must be one step up from it on the semantic skeleton. For instance, consider 7.48:

7.48 (= Berry's 40)

    A. Who stole three horses?
    B. John (stole three horses).

Assuming that the propositional content of A's move is 'someone stole three horses', B's move is an appropriate reply because it entails 'someone stole three horses' and is in fact one step up from it on a Sperber—Wilson type of semantic skeleton.

Berry suggests that since the ellipticity and question/statement sequence rules she proposes are very similar to standard syntactic rules, and since the semantic rules developed for the sentence find an application to the propositional development of discourse, it would seem that syntax, semantics and pragmatics can be extended up to the rank of exchange: in other words, exchanges do consist of ordered arrangements of particular classes of sentence, and Coulthard and Brazil are incorrect in claiming the need for a shift to a different level between sentence and exchange, although Berry concedes that a new level may be needed above the rank of exchange.

In a second paper (1981b), Berry extends in an extremely interesting way her ideas on propositional development, outlined above. As we have seen, the work of Sinclair and Coulthard and their colleagues has been heavily dependent on the Scale and Category theory of grammar put forward by Halliday in the early 1960s. Berry's latest proposals bring discourse into a close relationship with the Hallidayan models of the 1970s and 1980s, by suggesting that exchange structure, like the structure of clauses and groups, is best seen not in simple linear terms, but as a complex of three strands, corresponding to the ideational, interpersonal and textual components of Halliday's clause grammars. A simple linear structure is, Berry claims, too limited to allow us to describe all the similarities and differences between stretches of discourse, or to generate well-formed discourse structures and block ill-formed ones. She argues that new layers of structure are required rather than a new level or rank, because the units carrying the patterns concerned are co-terminous and co-extensive. Each layer of exchange structure is seen as contributing a set of functions precisely analogous to the microfunctions (or functional roles), such as Actor, Process, Goal, Theme and Rheme, set up by Halliday for the clause. The functions contributed by the three layers are mapped on to each other by means of realization rules, to give bundles of functions which correspond to the elements of exchange structure.

The propositional structure of the exchange, already outlined in Berry (1981a), is seen as constituting the ideational layer of structure. One element of ideational structure, the 'propositional completion' (pc), is obligatory under all circumstances, and other elements, the 'propositional base' (pb) and 'propositional support' (ps) may also be present, and indeed must occur under certain circumstances.

The interpersonal layer of functions is concerned with the knowledge relationships between participants. In all exchanges involving information transmission, there is a 'primary knower' who is in possession of the information, and a 'secondary knower' to whom the information is imparted. The exchange contains an obligatory functional slot (k1) where the primary knower reveals his knowledge and stamps his authority on it. There may (and in some circumstances must) also be a functional slot (k2) where the secondary knower indicates his own state of knowledge. There may also be functional slots where the primary knower delays confirmation of his own knowledge (for instance, in the asking of questions by teachers or quizmasters, who already know the answers, but do not issue their knowledge authoritatively until after the addressee has replied), and where the secondary knower follows up the authoritative confirmation of the knowledge imparted: these are labelled dk1 and k2f respectively.

The textual layer of functions is concerned with the turn-taking patterning of the exchange, and consists of alternate contributions from each speaker, thus: ai, bi, aii, bii, . . . an, bn. The initial contribution of the first speaker is, by definition, obligatory. The reader may find a couple of examples of this multi-layered analysis of exchanges useful. The following are taken from Berry's paper.

7.49	(= Berry's 1)				
	Quizmaster:	in England, which cathedral has the tallest spire	pb	dkl	ai
	Contestant:	Salisbury	pc	k2	bi
	Quizmaster:	yes	ps	k1	aii

7.50 (= Berry's 8)

Son:	which English cathedral did you say			
	had the tallest spire	pb	k2	ai
Father:	Salisbury	pc	k1	bi

Space does not permit full discussion of the many detailed proposals made by Berry in this paper: for instance, we have said nothing about the system networks which are claimed to operate at the various functional slots. Clearly, the exhaustive testing of her proposals will require the analysis of considerable quantities of spoken text. However, this is certainly some of the most detailed and rigorous work on discourse yet published, and is particularly stimulating because of the way in which it links the study of discourse patterning to that of clause patterning, as in the work of Halliday and others. In the next section we shall examine a further, quite different, attempt to integrate the study of discourse into a general systemically oriented framework.

7.4.5 Discourse, speech acts and semantics in a systemic perspective

The author's own work on discourse (see Butler, 1982, forthcoming c, in press) was carried out within the context of a study of modalized directives in English: that is, the major focus of the study was the ways in which a wide variety of sentences containing modal verbs can be used in English to get people to do things (see also section 8.2.6). A major part of the work was concerned with the development of a model in which the discourse function of directives could be related, via the semantics, to the syntax.

The Sinclair and Coulthard model of discourse was taken as a starting point for the description of discourse properties, and it soon became apparent that certain aspects of the model were inadequate. As was mentioned in Section 7.4.3, Sinclair and Coulthard recognize a set of 'situational' categories (statement, question and command) which are intermediate between syntax and discourse. Items can only be given a discourse function after they have been tagged with features from grammar and situation. This tagging, it will be remembered, operates via interpretation rules; one such rule, quoted in Section 7.4.3, is repeated below.

An interrogative clause is to be interpreted as a *command to do* if it fulfils all the following conditions:
(i)   it contains one of the modals *can, could, will, would* (and sometimes *going to*);
(ii) if the subject of the clause is also the addressee;
(iii) the predicate describes an action which is physically possible at the time of the utterance. (Sinclair & Coulthard, 1975, p.32)

It is clear from Sinclair and Coulthard's account that different discourse acts can be represented by the same situational category: for example, directives and cues are both represented by commands. It is obvious that Sinclair and Coulthard's categories are really speech act categories, which are best seen as a stage in the interpretation of discourse function from surface form. Edmondson (1981), working towards a rather different model, reaches a similar conclusion.

Sinclair and Coulthard's interpretation rules suffer from one serious defect, which is well illustrated by the rule quoted above. Because Sinclair and Coulthard are attempting to link their situational categories directly to surface forms, they are forced to specify particular modal verbs in the rule. However, their rule provides no explanation for why the particular modals 'can', 'could', 'will', 'would', and not, say, 'must', 'may' or 'should', can signal that an utterance is to be interpreted as a command (or, better, a request). To do this, we must examine the meanings of the modals concerned. Furthermore, Sinclair and Coulthard's correlation of function directly with lexicosyntactic categories is unable to account for the ways in which the variety of modalized directives found in English pattern with respect to the social context. It can in fact be shown (see Butler, 1982, also Section 8.2.6) that the acceptability of certain combinations of modal verb and mood, and the unacceptability of others, as directives, also the relative politeness of acceptable modalized directives in a given social context, can be predicted, not from surface form directly, but from the meanings of particular modals and mood categories. We may argue, therefore, that Sinclair and Coulthard's situational categories, which we have reanalysed as speech act classes, should be related to the syntax only indirectly, via a semantic level. (This assumes, of course, that speech acts themselves do not belong to the semantic level: this position is argued in some detail in Butler (1982, forthcoming c), but space does not permit discussion of this issue here.) The speech act classes are further interpreted in terms of specific discourse functions, by consideration of their position in the stretch of discourse concerned. We thus have the following model of the interpretation relations involved.

Surface form ⟶ semantics ⟶ speech act ⟶ discourse function
classes

In Butler (1982, in press) system networks and realization rules for the discourse level (and also for certain parts of the semantics) are developed. It was found that Hudson's daughter dependency model of syntax (see Section 6.3.3.3) was applicable also to patterning in both discourse and semantics. The use of daughter dependency rules allows us to specify those features of (for example) moves which depend directly on the features of the 'mother' exchange; while sister dependency rules allow the specification of dependency relations between moves within an exchange, for instance the relationships between directing and reacting moves, or between eliciting and replying moves, which, although discussed informally in work by the Birmingham group, are not given any formal specification there.

7.4.6 Discourse in systemic linguistics: concluding remarks

There can be no doubt that the systemic orientation of the Birmingham group has proved an extremely fruitful one, and has produced highly original and illuminating work. Three aspects of the recent developments are particularly noteworthy: Brazil's work on intonation provides powerful new tools for the analysis of exchange structure; Berry's multi-layered approach draws fascinating parallels between the exchange and the clause in functional terms; and both Berry's and the present author's work suggest that discourse patterning can be usefully described in terms of system networks and structures, connected by explicit realization rules. It is very much to be hoped that the near future will witness a synthesis of these exciting developments, leading to an even fuller understanding of how people talk to one another.

8. Descriptions of English and other languages

8.1 Introduction

Systemic linguists, mindful of Firth's insistence on 'renewal of connection' with actual linguistic data, have generally shown more interest in the analysis of text than many of their colleagues working within other models. For many kinds of textual analysis, a comprehensive description of the language concerned is essential. Furthermore, there has always been among systemic linguists considerably more interest in the properties of individual languages (chiefly, though not exclusively, English) than in possible universal characteristics of human language. It is not surprising, then, that systemic models have given rise to a fairly large body of descriptive work. In the present chapter, descriptions of English by Halliday and others will be reviewed in some detail, and work on other languages will be summarized.

8.2 Descriptions of English

8.2.1 The scope of Halliday's descriptive work

Halliday's own descriptive work has focused on the systemic and functional relations shown at the rank of clause. It will be remembered from Section 3.4 that the ideational, interpersonal and textual components are represented in the clause by the system networks of transitivity, mood and modality, and theme, respectively. Each of these will be considered in turn.

8.2.2 Transitivity

Transitivity, as we saw in Section 3.4, is concerned with the types of process expressed in the clause, and with the numbers and types of participants and circumstances associated with them. Halliday's main published accounts of this area are to be found in Halliday (1967b, 1968) and in a hitherto unpublished article in Kress (1976, pp.159-73). These accounts contain a wealth of theoretical and descriptive detail, and it will be impossible to do full justice to them here. In what follows, the most fundamental areas of Halliday's descriptions are summarized, and problems with the analysis discussed.

It is important first of all to clear up some matters of terminology which may be somewhat confusing to those unfamilar with Halliday's work. Despite Halliday's choice of the term 'transitivity', this area is concerned with much more than just the distinction between transitive and intransitive verbs. As might be expected of a model which, by the late 1960s, had become quite heavily semanticized (see Section 3.3), Halliday's account explores the 'deeper' aspects of the relations between verbs and the phrases associated with them. Indeed, it does not focus specifically on verbs as a syntactic category at all, but rather on the types of 'process' expressed in the clause, where the term 'process' 'is understood in a very broad sense, to cover all phenomena to which a specification of time may be attached — in English, anything that can be expressed by a verb: event, whether physical or not, state, or relation' (Halliday in Kress, 1976, p.159). The full characterization of a process, as thus defined, will encompass relationships between that process and the participants involved in it, where 'participant' is to be understood as covering linguistic representations of non-human, inanimate and even abstract entities, as well as of human beings. Transitivity, in Halliday's terms, thus involves the whole clause: it 'refers to the "content", or factual-notional structure of the clause in its entirety' (Halliday in Kress, 1976, p.159).

The semantic orientation of Halliday's proposals is brought out clearly in the distinction between 'inherent' and 'actual' participants. Each process can be specified in terms of the number of participant entities inherently associated with it, even though some of these essential participants may not be actualized in the surface structure of the clause. The following examples are taken from Halliday's article in Kress (1976, pp.159-60).

8.1   He pelted the dog with stones.
8.2   He pelted the dog.
8.3   The dog got pelted.

'Pelt' is inherently a three-participant process: it involves someone who pelts, someone or something to be pelted, and something to pelt with. This is so even when, as in 8.2 and 8.3, one or more of these participants is not present in the structure of the clause. Many linguists would wish to say that the inherency relates to semantic rather than to syntactic entities, and we shall see, in the critical discussion which follows, that the merging of syntactic and semantic aspects of patterning is at the root of a number of problems with Halliday's account (see also the general discussion of this topic in Sections 5.2 and 6.4).

The basic framework of Halliday's early analyses of transitivity is illustrated by the network in Figure 8.1, taken from Halliday (1967b, p.47).

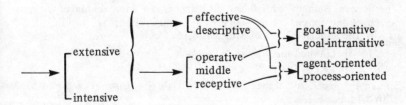

Figure 8.1: A basic network for transitivity

Halliday's own examples of the permitted combinations of features are given in 8.4-8.12 below.

8.4 She washed the clothes. [effective, operative, goal-transitive]
8.5 The clothes were washed. [effective, receptive, agent-oriented]
8.6 The prisoners marched. [descriptive, middle]
8.7 She looked happy. [intensive]
8.8 He marched the prisoners. [descriptive, operative]
8.9 The prisoners were marched. [descriptive, receptive]
8.10 She washed (sc. 'herself'). [effective, middle]
8.11 She washed (sc. 'the clothes'). [effective, operative, goal-transitive]
8.12 The clothes washed. [effective, receptive, process-oriented]

[Extensive] clauses express actions, and are subclassified as [effective] (expressing action directed towards a Goal participant which may, however, be absent from the surface structure of the clause) or [descriptive] (involving non-directed action). Intensive clauses express ascription of some attribute to a given participant. Extensive clauses are further cross-classified as [operative], [middle] or [receptive]. In an effective operative clause the Subject represents the Actor, while in a descriptive operative clause the Subject represents the Initiator of a non-directed action performed by some other participant. An effective operative clause may have its Goal expressed ([goal-transitive]) or not ([goal-intransitive]). In an effective receptive clause the Subject remains the Goal, while in a descriptive receptive clause the Subject represents the Actor who performs the non-directed action. Effective receptive clauses can express a characteristic of the process itself ([process-oriented]) or can focus on the agency involved ([agent-oriented]). The middle type of clause is intermediate between operative and receptive: in an effective middle clause the Actor and Goal are identical, the process being reflexive, while in a descriptive middle clause Actor and Initiator are identical.

The basic distinctions outlined above are extended (Halliday, 1967b, pp.51-81) to account for four kinds of 'circumstantial' element, which are called Beneficiary, Range, Attribute and Condition. The Beneficiary is the element representing someone who benefits from an action, for instance the italicized parts of Halliday's examples given as 8.13 and 8.14.

8.13 He gave *John* the book.
8.14 Pour a cup of coffee for *John*.

The Range element which can be attached to some kinds of process 'specifies the extent of its scope or relevance' (Halliday, 1967b, p.58), as with the italicized parts of 8.15 and 8.16.

8.15 He climbed *the mountain*.
8.16 He played *five games*.

Unlike the Goal, the Range cannot be a reflexive. Contrast 8.4 and 8.17 with 8.15 and 8.18.

8.4 She washed the clothes.
8.17 She washed herself.
8.15 He climbed the mountain.
8.18 *He climbed himself. (where 'himself' is to be taken as reflexive, not emphatic)

Attributes and Conditions are distinguished from other nominal elements of clause structure by certain syntactic characteristics: they can only be Complements, never Subjects; they can have adjectival realizations; they cannot be realized by a nominal group with a proper noun, personal or non-personal pronoun or determiner as its head. Attributes are exemplified by the italicized parts of 8.19 and 8.20 (again Halliday's examples).

8.19 He drinks his coffee *black*.
8.20 She brought him up *an honest man*.

Condition elements are exemplified in 8.21 and 8.22:

8.21 It'll sink *full*.
8.22 It could be made stronger *level*.

The sense of 'full' and 'level' here could be made explicit by adding 'if' before them; this is not the case with Attributes.

In Halliday (1968) the earlier description of transitivity is refined. Halliday points out a problem with the analysis of certain highly favoured types of process in English. First consider the following (Halliday's examples):

8.23 John threw the ball.
8.24 John marched the prisoners.

In terms of the earlier analysis, 8.23 has the features [effective, operative, goal-transitive], with 'John' as Actor and 'the ball' as Goal, whereas 8.24 has the features [descriptive, operative], with 'John' as Initiator and 'the prisoners' as Actor. Now consider 8.25:

8.25 John opened the door.

It is not clear which of the two analyses is to be assigned here, since both seem appropriate: 8.25 can be seen in terms of John performing an action whose influence extends to the door, or in terms of John initiating an action on the part of the door. Note that the opening of the door can be divorced from the initiator, as in 8.26:

8.26 The door opened.

As Halliday points out, many processes in present-day English are of this type: they are equally comfortable with either one or two participants. In order to solve the problem, Halliday develops a suggestion made in an earlier paper (Halliday, 1967e), namely that side by side with the 'transitive' Actor–Goal patterning there is an 'ergative' pattern of relations, in which the central concept is causation. Whereas the transitive analysis distinguishes between two kinds of process, one goal-directed, the other not, the ergative analysis postulates just one kind of action, which may be associated with either one or two participants. The single participant in a middle process is the 'Affected'. This participant function also occurs in non-middle clauses, in which, however, there is also a second inherent participant (which may or may not be expressed), the 'Causer'. This proposal gives rise to the following analyses of 8.23-8.27:

```
         Causer      Affected
8.23  John           threw the ball.
```

      Causer   Affected
8.24 John marched the prisoners.

      Causer   Affected
8.25 John opened the door.

      Affected
8.26 The door opened.

      Affected   Causer
8.27 The door was opened by John.

The kind of process typified by 'open', which can have one or two inherent participants, is now regarded by Halliday as the 'nuclear' type, so that the distinction between [effective] and [descriptive] is now replaced by a three-way distinction of [effective], [nuclear] and [descriptive].

A further advantage of the ergative analysis is that it can be extended to other types of clause, where an Actor–Goal analysis is inappropriate. Halliday distinguishes three main types of clause in terms of their transitivity relations. [Action] clauses are derived from the [extensive] class of the earlier network, but are now seen as excluding [mental processes], which constitute a separate class, and are of four subtypes: [reaction] (exemplified by 8.28), [perception] (8.29), [cognition] (8.30) and [verbalization] (8.31).

8.28 He liked the play.
8.29 He heard a noise.
8.30 He believed the story.
8.31 He said he was coming.

The third class of processes is now labelled [relational], and subsumes the [intensive] class of the earlier network (as in 8.32), together with [equative] clauses in which 'be' is used to signal an equivalence between two entities, as in 8.33.

8.32 Mary is a teacher.
8.33 John is the leader.

Mental processes involve a human 'Processer' (later called the 'Cognizant') and something which is processed (the 'Phenomenon'), which may be a physical entity (as in 8.34), a fact (8.35) or a report (8.36).

8.34 He saw (= watched) John.
8.35 He saw (= took in) that John was fighting Bill.
8.36 He saw (= read) that John had been fighting Bill.

In such cases, it is inappropriate to regard the Processer as an Actor and the Phenomenon as a Goal: in 8.34 John is not having anything done to him. An analysis in terms of Causer and Affected is, however, possible: John in 8.34 can be regarded as causing a visual perception in the Processer referred to as 'he'. This is clearer in an example such as 8.37 (still from Halliday, 1968):

8.37 The play pleased everybody.

Here, the play causes a positive reaction in the Processer 'everybody'.

Again, with relational processes, the Actor–Goal analysis is inappropriate:

in 8.32 and 8.33 Mary and John are clearly not doing anything, and equally clearly 'a teacher' and 'the leader' are not Goal. However, Halliday argues that 'Mary' in 8.32 can be treated as an Affected participant, and that the ergative analysis can also be applied, though in a rather complex fashion, to equatives such as 8.33.

The paper published in Kress (1976) was originally written in 1969, and adds little to the description summarized above, except that in a diagram in the text Halliday differentiates, within 'actions', between true actions (with animate Actors), events (with inanimate Actors) and natural phenomena (with no Actor, as with 'rain', 'snow', and so on). Actions are also classified as concrete or abstract, and these categories are then sub-divided into smaller classes, with broad correspondences to the lexical verbs in particular sections of Roget's *Thesaurus*.

Let us now consider briefly some aspects of Halliday's accounts of transitivity which are unsatisfactory, in that they leave certain important relations unexplained. Firstly, Halliday's preoccupation with 'semantically significant grammar' leads him to reject those aspects of the syntax of transitivity which are not obviously meaning-bearing. There is no detailed discussion of the syntax of complementation, involving such issues as the determination of complementizer type, about which so much has been written in the transformational generative literature. It is conceivable that certain matters relating to complementation could be dealt with under the heading of textual relations. It might, for instance, be argued that 8.38-8.40 differ, not in the transitivity choices made, but in the mapping of transitivity functions on to other functions in the realization of systemic options.

8.38 I suspect that John is a fool.
8.39 I suspect John is a fool.
8.40 I suspect John to be a fool.

Even so, such a proposal would not account for the syntax of these sentences as such. Similarly, Halliday's account has nothing to say about the differences in the complementation patterns of 'order' and 'suggest' shown by the following data:

8.41   I order you to go.
8.42   *I suggest you to go.
8.43   ?I order that you go.
8.44   I suggest that you go.
8.45   *I order you go.
8.46   I suggest you go.

As developed so far, then, Halliday's model is inadequate to deal with the specifically syntactic aspects of transitivity. Unfortunately, it also fails to capture some important semantic generalizations. One problem is concerned with the relationship between action and non-action types of process. In his earliest account, Halliday includes under action processes mental phenomena such as those represented by the verbs 'see', 'hear' and 'speak'. This was clearly misguided, as is recognized by Halliday's later admission that an analysis in Actor–Goal terms is inappropriate for such processes. However, there are processes which are related semantically to these processes, but which are truly actions: they answer the question

'What did X do?'; they easily take imperative mood; they co-occur with volitional adverbials such as 'on purpose' or 'deliberately'. Consider the following pairs of sentences:

8.47 John saw the cat.
8.48 John looked at the cat.

8.49 John heard the noise.
8.50 John listened to the noise.

8.51 John felt a sharp pain.
8.52 John felt the cloth with the fingers of his right hand.

The first member of each pair is a non-action (more specifically, each involves a change of state of some kind), while the second is an action. Furthermore, verbal processes such as 'say', 'speak', are clearly actions. At certain points in his discussion, Halliday indicates that he would treat 'look (at)', as well as 'see', as a mental process (see, for example, Halliday, 1968, p.195; Kress, 1976, p.166). There is, however, no obvious mechanism in Halliday's account which would allow him to express the generalization that these are action and non-action counterparts of the visual perception process. Indeed, in Halliday's discussion, the terms 'mental process' and 'action process' are opposed. In an account which took the underlying semantic properties fully into consideration, the action/non-action distinction would need to be kept separate from the distinction between 'material' processes (such as 'hit', 'run', and the like) and mental processes.

A further problem is concerned with Halliday's treatment of causation. As we have seen, causation is now built into Halliday's account of transitivity, in the form of the ergative analysis. However, Halliday (1968, p.198) makes certain ill-founded claims about the differences between what he calls 'first degree causatives', such as 8.24, and 'second degree causatives', such as 8.53.

8.24 John marched the prisoners.
8.53 John made the prisoners march.

Halliday claims that in 8.53 the relationship between 'the prisoners' and 'march' is one of 'doing', while in 8.24 it is one of 'happening'. This is surely not the case: in both sentences, the prisoners are performing the action of marching, and it makes little sense to ask 'What happened to the prisoners?' and supply the answer 'They marched', though a passive answer can be given in either case, 'They were marched/made to march'. Halliday is right to insist that the two sentences are not identical in meaning: some of the differences are discussed by Shibatani (1976b), from whom the following examples are taken.

8.54　I didn't stand the child up, but I caused him to stand up.
8.55　*I didn't cause the child to stand up, but I stood him up.

The meaning of the periphrastic form with 'cause' (or 'make') is clearly more general than that of the lexical causative, so that the latter entails the former, but not *vice versa*. Similarly, there are important differences between 'kill' and 'cause to die', which have been extensively discussed in the literature (for an excellent summary of the arguments on both sides of this debate, again see Shibatani, 1967b). There is, however, a basic notion of causation underlying each of the subtypes, defined by Talmy

(1976, p.51) in terms of a situation 'in which the essential event takes place and, ceteris paribus, would not take place if it were not for another event'. This basic causative element is involved in both 8.24 and 8.53.

A final problem is concerned with the relationship between sentences such as 8.56 and 8.57:

8.56 The towel dried.
8.57 The towel is dry.

Halliday would analyse 8.56 as an action clause of the event subtype; 8.57, however, would be a relational clause, with 'be' as Process and 'dry' as Attribute. Semantically, however, the two sentences have a close relationship: 8.57 represents a state, and 8.56 a change of state, both referring to the same particular state, that of 'dryness'. Semantically, the 'is' of 8.57 is empty (compare the translation of such sentences into, say, Russian): it is the adjective in 8.57 which encodes the 'semantic predicate' corresponding to that encoded in the verb in 8.56. There is no obvious way in which this relationship can be captured in terms of Halliday's proposals. One approach which does make such generalizations is that of Chafe (1970).

In summary, then, we may say that Halliday's account of transitivity, penetrating and detailed as it is in many respects, fails to do justice to either the syntactic or the semantic relationships involved. This is perhaps the inevitable consequence of adopting a model which limits itself to 'semantically significant grammar', denying itself any apparatus for investigating either those syntactic patterns which have no obvious semantic correlations, or those semantic correspondences which lie at some depth below the surface. In the next section, we shall see that the same kinds of problems arise in Halliday's account of mood and modalization.

8.2.3 Mood and modalization

The various networks for mood written by Halliday in the late 1960s and early 1970s (see, for example, Halliday, 1969a, p.84; 1971a, p.173 = 1973a, p.56; 1973b, p.360 = 1973a, p.40; and in Kress, 1976, pp.104-9) are amalgamated to show the basic options in Figure 8.2.

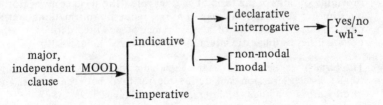

Figure 8.2: A basic mood network

In some of the earliest accounts the realizations of these options are given in terms of the insertion and concatenation of the elements of clause structure: for instance, [indicative] clauses contain a Subject, while [imperative] clauses do not; [declarative] clauses have the order SP, while interrogative clauses have P<S>, the Subject either following or being included inside the Predicator. Examples 8.58-8.61 illustrate the possibilities.

8.58 John hit the ball. [declarative] ⎫
8.59 Did John hit the ball? [interrogative, yes/no] ⎬ [indicative]
8.60 Who hit the ball? [interrogative, 'wh'–] ⎭
8.61 Hit the ball. [imperative]

Halliday has also presented further refinements of this network (see especially the networks in Kress, 1976, pp.104-9), integrating it with attitudinal distinctions carried by tone (it will be remembered from Section 7.3.3 that the significance of a particular tone selection depends on the mood of the clause on to which the tone group is mapped). Halliday also discusses:

> why the three types of indicative clause differ in just the way they do, such that the first position is occupied in each instance by one particular element: by the subject if the clause is declarative, by the finite element of the verb if it is a polar, or 'yes/no', interrogative, and by the WH-element if it is a WH-interrogative. (Halliday, 1970c, p.353)

Halliday's answer is in terms of the 'thematic' status of initial position in the English clause (see Section 8.2.4): as we shall see, Halliday regards this position as having a unique communicative function in the clause, being the 'starting point' for the message. A 'wh'-element, for instance, is in first position in the unmarked form of a 'wh'-clause because it encodes the fact that the point of uttering the clause is as a request for a particular piece of information; similarly, the finite verb comes first in a yes/no question because it carries polarity, which is precisely what is being questioned.

Halliday's accounts of the grammar of mood, and its relation to tone and thematic structure, are interesting and insightful. When, however, we examine Halliday's discussion in the wider context of his functional theory of language, problems soon emerge. Mood and its associated options, as we have seen, represent the interpersonal function as manifested in clause structure, and this function is concerned with the interaction between speakers and addressees. This is made clear in the following quotations:

> Mood represents the organization of participants in speech situations, providing options in the form of speaker roles: the speaker may inform, question or command; he may confirm, request confirmation, contradict or display any one of a wide range of postures defined by the potentialities of linguistic interaction. (Halliday, 1967c, p.199)

> The term 'mood' refers to a set of related options which give structure to the speech situation and define the relations between speaker and interlocutors in a linguistic interaction. (Halliday, 1969a, p.87)

> In the clause, the interpersonal element is represented by mood and modality: the selection by the speaker of a particular role in the speech situation, and his determination of the choice of roles for the addressee (mood), and the expression of his judgments and predictions (modality). (Halliday, 1971b, p.361 = 1973a, p.41)

It seems that mood is to be equated with the selection of a communication role by the speaker (stating, questioning, requesting, and the like), and the allocation of role choices to the hearer. Yet this is clearly claiming too much for a grammatical network such as that in Figure 8.2: we saw in Section 7.4 that the relation between grammatical mood categories, categories such as 'statement' or 'question', and the discourse roles of the speaker and addressee, is an extremely complex one. Communication roles are certainly related to mood, in a rather complex and indirect way, but they are not to be equated with it. As so often in Halliday's work, relationships between different levels of patterning are left implicit and blurred.

A rather clearer statement about the relationship between communication roles and grammatical mood categories is the following:

> . . . the relationship between, say, 'question' in semantics and 'interrogative' in grammar is not really different from that between a behavioural-semantic category such as 'threat' and the categories by which it is realized grammatically. In neither instance is the relationship one to one; and while the latter may be rather more complex, a more intensive study of language as social behaviour also suggests a somewhat more complex treatment of traditional notions like those of statement and question. (Halliday, 1971a, p.173 = 1973a, p.56)

Here, within the context of his sociosemantic model of language, Halliday does recognize the potential complexity of the relationships involved. As we saw in Section 7.4.2, a more recent paper (Halliday, 1984a) attempts a systematization of the relations between 'social contextual' options relating to 'moves in dialogue', semantic choices in 'speech function', and grammatical mood options. As was pointed out earlier, this account raises considerable theoretical difficulties, and also concentrates exclusively on 'congruent' patterns of realization (for instance, a demand for goods and services realized by a command at the semantic level, and this in turn by an imperative at the grammatical level), at the expense of the rich variety of non-congruent realizations available in English. In Section 8.2.6, work which explores the syntactic, semantic and discoursal aspects of mood and speech function will be reviewed.

Let us now turn to the area of modalization which, as implied by the network in Figure 8.2, is regarded by Halliday as closely related to mood. His viewpoint on this area is first clearly indicated by an extension of the mood network (Halliday, 1969a, p.84), where [modal] clauses are sub-classified as [verbal], [adverbial] or [complex]. Halliday is suggesting here that 'modalization' is to be taken to cover not only the use of modal verbs such as 'can', 'may', 'must', 'should', but also that of adverbs such as 'possibly', 'probably', which can carry certain of the meanings attributable to the modal verbs, and can also combine with them (as in 'may possibly'). Halliday's most detailed account of this area (Halliday, 1970c) is discussed in full in Butler (1982): only a brief critique is possible here.

Halliday's account of modalization is formulated within the framework of 'semantic functional grammar'. He distinguishes between 'modalities', which 'represent the speaker's assessment of the probability of what he is saying, or the degree to which he regards it as self-evident' (Halliday, 1970c, p.328), and 'modulations', which 'express various types of modulation of the process expressed in the clause; modulation in terms of permission, obligation and the like' (p.336). This distinction corresponds, more

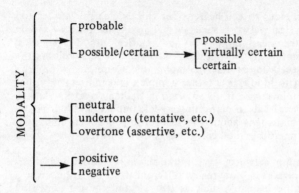

Figure 8.3: The modality network

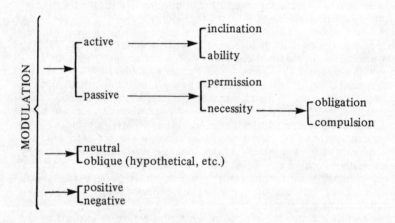

Figure 8.4: The modulation network

or less, to the epistemic/root distinction made by most writers in this area. Halliday presents system networks for modality and modulation (pp.332, 345), which are reproduced as Figures 8.3 and 8.4.

Modality is 'a strand running prosodically through the clause' (p.331): it may be realized as a modal verb or adverb, or a combination of these, or as a modal adjective ('possible', 'likely', etc.), as well as by choices in the tone systems of the phonology. Modulation, when not realized by modal verbs, is expressed by constructions such as 'be able to', 'be willing to', 'be obliged to', 'be allowed to'. Those modulations which are paraphrasable by 'be' + 'ed' form + 'to' express constraints which are extrinsic to the Subject of the clause, and are referred to as 'passive' modulations; those represented by 'be able/willing to' are 'active' in the sense that the Subject of an active clause is Actor with respect to the modulation as well as the process.

The distinction between categories such as [possible] and their realizations in a diversity of lexicogrammatical forms suggests that the networks in Figures 8.3 and 8.4 are not syntactic at all, but semantic. Halliday, as so often, is unclear about this: at times he implies that modality and modulation are indeed meaning categories (for instance, 'these meanings are what we understand by modalities' (p.328)), and yet he refers to 'the syntactic system of modality' and 'the syntactic system of modulation' (p.350). If, say, the 'can' of permission and the 'can' which realizes [possible] are truly different syntactically, Halliday should be able to demonstrate that there are significant differences in their distributional properties. He does present some arguments relating to negation and tense, but on close analysis these turn out to be unconvincing. Modulations can take negation of the main process, the modulation, or both:

8.62 You can/can't (not) go.

Modalities, on the other hand, are claimed to be inherently positive, since they represent the speaker's assessment of probability, which can never be negative. They do, however, combine with either a positive or a negative process:

8.63 That can't be John = It is certain that that isn't John.

Although there are certainly important relationships between possibility and certainty in terms of logical equivalence under negation, there are also good reasons for not claiming that the meanings of, say, 'not possible' and 'certain that not' are identical (for full discussion see Palmer, 1979, p.54 ff.) Furthermore, it can be convincingly argued that the kind of evidence Halliday is offering is not syntactic at all, but semantic: the modals show a common set of distributional properties with respect to the negative marker, whether used as modalities or as modulations; other syntactic and morphological properties which distinguish the modals from other verbs are also independent of the meaning with which the modal is being used.

Halliday's second argument for syntactic differences between modality and modulation uses of modals is concerned with the perfect tense (or, as many linguists would have it, aspect). Halliday claims that 'neutral' modals (those with present rather than past tense form, such as 'can', 'may', as opposed to 'could', 'might'), in combination with perfect 'have', can be interpreted only as modalities. Although it is true that the modality interpretation is by far the most frequent (for quantitative evidence, see Coates & Leech, 1980, p.28), a modulation reading is sometimes needed, as in the following example from the Survey of English Usage, quoted by Palmer (1979, p.94):

8.64 There is no argument for saying that in a particular locality
      nobody must have lived there who earns more than twenty
      pounds a week.

Clearly, what is regarded as syntactic and what as semantic must depend to some extent on one's overall view of the grammar. It is, however, not unreasonable to argue that a modal verb is a unitary item at the syntactic level, irrespective of the meaning with which it is being used.

A further unsatisfactory aspect of Halliday's account concerns the allocation of the networks of modality and modulation to the functional components of the grammar (it will be remembered that in 1970 these components were still said to belong to the lexicogrammar rather than to the semantics). Halliday regards this area as a clear example of functional diversity in language: he claims (pp.245-50) that the networks of modality and modulation can be (at least partially) reduced to a common network, which in the case of modality is approached from the interpersonal function, but in the case of modulation arises from the ideational function. Halliday's reasons for treating modalities as interpersonal are that they represent the participation of the speaker in the speech event and that, not being subject to polarity and tense distinctions, they do not form part of the ideational content of the clause, and are to be contrasted with modulations, which do show polarity and tense distinctions. We have already seen that these arguments are somewhat suspect. Furthermore, Halliday himself recognizes that the assignment of the networks to functional components is not clear-cut: modalities, though interpersonal, are oriented towards the ideational in that they express an opinion on the content of what is said; modulations, though ideational, are oriented towards the interpersonal in that passive modulations are concerned with the imposition of constraints on the Subject of the clause. We might add that it is not only the passive modulations which can be involved in imposing constraints: 'shall', regarded by Halliday as representing a volitional, active modulation, can be used with 'you' as a very strong form of imposition of authority.

Further doubts relating to the status of the functional components arise from the relations between the modalization options and the basic mood options discussed earlier. Halliday observes that modalities occur only in indicative clauses. However, he fails to point out that modulations too are restricted to indicative clauses. This is not wholly due to the defective morphology of the modals, since periphrastic forms such as 'be obliged to' are not normally used in the imperative either. There is thus a connection, not only between modality and mood, but also between modulation and mood — two sets of systems which supposedly belong to different components. This, as was pointed out in Section 5.4, could be seen as an embarrassment for the functional components hypothesis.

A rather different approach to modalization, still within a systemically oriented framework, is to be found in the present author's work (Butler, 1982), summarized briefly in Section 8.2.6.

8.2.4 Theme and information structure

Halliday's work on the closely related areas of theme and information structure is among his most original contributions to the description of English, and is clearly influenced by that of the Prague School linguists (for a summary see Vachek, 1966; p.88 ff.), who had distinguished between 'theme' and 'rheme' within the theoretical framework of 'functional sentence perspective'. The theme, in Prague School terms, was that element in a sentence which contributed least to the furthering of the communicative process, and so had the lowest degree of 'communicative dynamism', whereas the rheme had the highest degree of communicative dynamism. Halliday's major contribution in this area has been the demonstration that the Prague School notion of theme and rheme conflated two dimensions of patterning which are in principle independent: *information structuring* (in terms of 'given' and 'new' information) and *thematization*.

As we saw in Section 7.3.3, Halliday relates information structuring, not directly to the clause, but to a phonological unit, the tone group. The tone group encodes what the speaker chooses to present as one unit of information. In the unmarked case, the tone group is roughly co-extensive with the clause, so that information distribution options, though operating at tone group rank, do relate closely to other textual options with the clause as their point of origin. The way in which a speaker breaks up the text into tone groups represents his choice from the *tonality* systems. The distribution of information within each tone group offers an independent set of *tonicity* choices concerned with the location of the tonic segment in the tone group. It will be remembered from Section 7.3.3 that the unmarked option is to place the tonic on the stressed syllable of the last lexical word in the tone group, any other position for the tonic being marked.

Halliday (1967c, 1967d) discusses in some detail how tonicity choices determine the partitioning of information into 'given' and 'new' elements. New information is that which 'the speaker presents [. . .] as not being recoverable from the preceding discourse' (1967c, p.204), while given information is that which is presented as recoverable. This is not, of course, to say that information presented as given will in fact always be recoverable by the hearer: speakers can exploit these options in a similar way to locutions such as 'as you already know'. The information systems specify within the tone group a 'domain of focus', consisting of the highest rank constituent within which the tonic syllable is the last accented syllable. The information within this constituent is always new. In the case of unmarked focus, where the tonic is on the last accented lexical word in the tone group, the information outside the domain of focus may be either given or new. In the case of marked focus, however, all information outside the domain of focus is given. This situation is illustrated by the following examples, from Halliday (1967c, p.207).

8.65 // ⌃ I'm /looking for the /caretaker who /looks after /this /<u>block</u>//
8.66 // <u>John</u> painted the shed yesterday//
8.67 //John <u>painted</u> the shed yesterday//

In 8.65 there is unmarked tonicity, since the tonic is on 'block', the last lexical item in the tone group. The highest rank clause constituent containing the tonic syllable is 'the caretaker who looks after this block', and this is therefore the domain of focus, and consists of new information. The information outside this domain, encoded in 'I'm looking for', could also be new (in that the speaker is not expecting the hearer to reconstruct from the preceding discourse the fact that the speaker is looking for someone or something), or it could be given. In 8.66 and 8.67, however, we have marked tonicity, and the domains of focus are 'John' and 'painted' respectively. These give new information, but the rest ('painted the shed yesterday' in 8.66, 'John', 'the shed' and 'yesterday' in 8.67) are presented as recoverable information. Note that 8.66 and 8.67 correspond to specific questions ('Who painted the shed yesterday?' and 'What did John do to the shed yesterday?' respectively), and that they could not be discourse-initial, whereas 8.65 could correspond to a general question ('What are you doing?') as well as a specific one ('Who are you looking for?'), and could be discourse-initial.

Thematization, as Halliday points out, is related to information distribution, but is a different kind of choice, having the clause as its point of origin. The theme is basically what comes first in a clause: it is 'what is being talked about, the point of departure for the clause as a message' (1967c, p.212); the remainder is the rheme. What constitutes unmarked theme depends on the mood of the clause: for a declarative clause, the Subject is the unmarked thematic element; for a polar question it is the finite part of the Predicator; and for a 'wh'-question it is the 'wh'-word. In a clause with unmarked information focus and unmarked theme, such as 8.65, the given element specified by the information systems includes the theme, and this is why the two notions become conflated and confused in Prague School accounts. Examples such as 8.66, however, demonstrate that given and theme, new and rheme, do not always go together. In 8.66, 'John' is the (unmarked) theme but, as we saw above, this is the new element, not the given, since it is the domain of focus.

Halliday (1967c, pp.218-23) discusses some complications of the basic picture. For example, in addition to thematic elements representing 'cognitive' information (normally Adjuncts or Complements), there may be 'non-cognitive' thematic elements which can co-occur with the cognitive type. Examples include discourse adjuncts such as 'however' in 8.68 and 8.69, and modal adjuncts such as 'perhaps' in 8.70 and 8.71.

8.68 however John saw the play yesterday (discourse adjunct theme)
8.69 however yesterday John saw the play (discourse adjunct +
                                            cognitive adjunct as theme)
8.70 perhaps John saw the play yesterday (modal adjunct theme)
8.71 perhaps yesterday John saw the play (modal adjunct + cognitive
                                            adjunct as theme)

Halliday (1967c, pp.215-18) also discusses the relationship between thematization and the passive.

The selection of a marked thematic element is one way of emphasizing or highlighting a particular clause constituent. Halliday also discusses certain other closely related types of highlighting. One of these, 'identification', like thematization, relates to the structuring of the whole clause. It is 'the option whereby any clause may be reorganized into a "cleft sentence" with equative form, and in a number of possible arrangements' (Halliday, 1967c, p.223). Some examples from Halliday's discussion are given below.

8.72 the one who painted the shed last week was John
8.73 what John painted last week was the shed
8.74 when John painted the shed last week
8.75 what John did to the shed last week was (to) paint it

In these four examples the elements of the 'basic' sentence 'John painted the shed last week' are picked out in turn: in 8.72 'John', in 8.73 'the shed', in 8.74 'last week', and in 8.75 'painted'.

The other systems discussed by Halliday, those of 'predication', 'substitution' and 'reference', assign substructures at certain points in the clause.

Again, these mechanisms serve to highlight particular elements. Predication surrounds the highlighted element with the construction 'it/there + be . . . + who/which/that/Ø', as in Halliday's examples given as 8.76-8.78 below.

8.76 it was John who broke the window
8.77 it was in spite of the cold that he went swimming
8.78 it's his earlier novels I've read

In 8.76, the Subject of the basic clause 'John broke the window' is picked out; in 8.77 an Adjunct is highlighted; and in 8.78 a Complement. The choice of substituted theme creates a position for the highlighted element at the end of the clause, and substitutes a proform for it in the main part of the clause, as in 8.79.

8.79 they don't seem to match, these colours

In Halliday (1967c) only clauses with a substitute Subject are discussed, but in networks and examples presented in Kress (1976, pp.112, 120-23) substitution of other elements is allowed for, as in 8.80, where the Complement is substituted:

8.80 John saw it yesterday, the play

Reference is in some ways the opposite of substitution, in that it creates for the highlighted element a position at the beginning of the clause, and again substitutes a proform in the main body of the clause, as in 8.81:

8.81 Britain it's all roads

As Halliday points out, such devices are much more common in informal speech than in formal language.

The importance of message structuring has been recognized in recent years in most schools of linguistics: it appears in transformational generative grammar in the guise of 'focus', topicalization, and so on. Halliday's work on theme and information systems is, however, much more detailed than other accounts, and is particularly important because of the contribution made by such phenomena to the coherence of connected discourse. This is the area to which we now turn.

8.2.5 Cohesion

Halliday and Hasan's (1976) book *Cohesion in English* is the most detailed account yet published of the devices which contribute to the creation and interpretation of cohesive text, as opposed to a random collection of sentences. A text is defined as 'any passage, spoken or written, of whatever length, that does form a unified whole' (Halliday & Hasan, 1976, p.1). We saw in Section 4.3.3 that Halliday regards the text as a semantic unit, and its creation as the actualization of meaning potential, in a selective manner influenced by the situational parameters of field, tenor and mode. Halliday and Hasan argue that since native speakers can usually decide whether a particular passage of English constitutes a text (that is, has the property of 'texture') or not, there must be objective linguistic features which distinguish texts from non-texts, and it is these that they set out to describe.

Halliday and Hasan claim that texture is provided by cohesive relations or 'ties' between pairs of linguistic items. Such cohesive ties may be built up into chains in a text. Their initial example of a tie (1976, p.2), the focus of some critical discussion in the literature, is given as 8.82 below.

    8.82 (= Halliday & Hasan's 1:1)
          Wash and core six cooking apples. Put them into a fireproof
          dish.

Halliday and Hasan say of this example:

> It is clear that *them* in the second sentence refers back to (is ANA-
> PHORIC to) the *six cooking apples* in the first sentence. This ANA-
> PHORIC function of *them* gives cohesion to the two sentences, so that
> we may interpret them as a whole; the two sentences together consti-
> tute a text. Or rather, they form part of the same text; there may be
> more of it to follow.

The meaning of the cohesive tie between 'them' and 'six cooking apples'
is that 'they refer to the same thing. The two items are identical in reference, or COREFERENTIAL' (p.3).

Cohesion, then, 'occurs where the INTERPRETATION of some element in the discourse is dependent on that of another. The one PRESUP-
POSES the other, in the sense that it cannot be effectively decoded
except by recourse to it' (p.4, original emphasis). Halliday and Hasan are
quite clear (p.5) that cohesion belongs to the system of a language, and is
not simply something arising from outside, concerned merely with, for
example, the subject matter of the text. Being concerned with the organization of the message, it forms part of the textual component of the semantic
system. However, unlike other textual resources, such as thematic and
information distribution options, cohesion is seen as 'non-structural':
that is, cohesive ties are not properties of any structural unit such as
the clause or sentence, but can occur either within or between sentences.
Halliday and Hasan's examples are almost all of inter-sentential cohesion,
because 'cohesive ties between sentences stand out more clearly because
they are the ONLY source of texture, whereas within the sentence there are
the structural relations as well' (p.9).

As was mentioned briefly in Section 4.3.3, cohesion is seen by Halliday
and Hasan as one of two respects in which a text displays coherence.
Cohesion is coherence of the text as an entity in itself; but a text must also
be coherent with respect to the context of situation in which it is produced. In other words, consistency of register is also an important part of
texture. As Halliday and Hasan (p.23) observe, it is possible to construct
passages which are cohesive, but lack registral consistency, and also to produce passages which, though coherent with respect to register, are non-
cohesive.

The bulk of *Cohesion in English* is devoted to a description of various
types of cohesive relation. The phenomena labelled by Halliday and Hasan
as *reference, substitution* and *ellipsis* are expressed by the grammatical
resources of the language; *conjunction* is seen as partly grammatical and
partly lexical; *lexical cohesion* is realized purely through the vocabulary
of the language.

Reference (not to be confused with the 'highlighting' mechanism of
the same name discussed in Section 8.2.4) occurs where items 'instead of
being interpreted semantically in their own right, [. . .] make reference to

something else for their interpretation' (p.31). In English, personal pronouns and personal determiners, demonstratives and comparatives fall into
this category. The following examples are taken from Halliday and Hasan
(p.31).

8.83 (= Halliday and Hasan's 2:1a)
      Three blind mice, three blind mice.
      See how they run! See how they run!

8.84 (= Halliday and Hasan's 2:1b)
      Doctor Foster went to Gloucester in a shower of rain.
      He stepped in a puddle right up to his middle and never went
      there again.

8.85 (= Halliday and Hasan's 2:1c)
      There were two wrens upon a tree.
      Another came, and there were three.

According to Halliday and Hasan, the information to be retrieved for full
interpretation in this type of cohesion is 'the referential meaning, the
identity of the particular thing or class of things that is being referred to'
(p.31). The source of the additional information may be an item in the
text itself, in which case we are dealing with *endophora* (or 'endophoric
reference'), or outside the text, in the context of situation, in which case
we have *exophora* (or 'exophoric reference'). Endophoric reference is
split into two subtypes: *anaphora*, where the item needed for interpretation
is to be found in the text preceding the item to be interpreted; and
cataphora, where the item required for interpretation is in the following
part of the text. Examples 8.83-8.85 show anaphoric reference; 8.86 and
8.87 are examples given by Halliday and Hasan (pp.17, 32) for cataphora
and exophora respectively.

8.86 (= Halliday and Hasan's 1:29)
      This is how to get the best results. You let the berries dry in
      the sun, till all the moisture has gone out of them. Then you
      gather them up and chop them very fine.

8.87 (= Halliday and Hasan's 2:2)
      For he's a jolly good fellow
      And so say all of us.

In 8.86, 'this', according to Halliday and Hasan, refers forward to the
following description. In 8.87, the text itself does not make clear who 'he'
is, but the participants in the speech situation will know this from the context in which the speech event occurs.

Halliday and Hasan (p.32) insist that reference is a semantic relation, so
that there is not necessarily any correspondence between the grammatical
classes of the interpreted and interpreting items. In this respect, reference
contrasts with substitution, the second of Halliday and Hasan's major
categories (and again not to be confused with the thematic device discussed in Section 8.2.4). Substitution is 'a relation in the wording rather
than in the meaning' (p.88). It is 'a relation between linguistic items, such
as words or phrases; whereas reference is a relation between meanings'
(p.89). A consequence of this is that 'as a general rule, the substitute item
has the same structural function as that for which it substitutes' (p.89),

and may therefore be replaced in the slot created by the item to be interpreted. Halliday and Hasan distinguish three subtypes of substitution, nominal, verbal and clausal, as exemplified in 8.88, 8.89 and 8.90 respectively (taken from Halliday and Hasan, pp.89-90, with italics added to show the items involved in the cohesive ties).

8.88 (= Halliday and Hasan's 3:1a)
My *axe* is too blunt. I must get a sharper *one*.

8.89 (= Halliday and Hasan's 3:1b)
You think Joan already *knows?* – I think everybody *does*.

8.90 (= Halliday and Hasan's 3:2)
Has Barbara left? – I think *so*. (*so = that Barbara has left*)

Ellipsis is closely related to substitution: 'ellipsis can be interpreted as that form of substitution in which the item is replaced by nothing' (p.88). As with substitution, nominal, verbal and clausal subtypes are recognized, exemplified by 8.91, 8.92 and 8.93 respectively (from Halliday and Hasan, pp.148, 167 and 198, with italicization of the ellipted items).

8.91 (= Halliday and Hasan's 4:7)
Which last longer, the curved rods or the straight *rods?* –
The straight are less likely to break.

8.92 (= Halliday and Hasan's 4:54a)
Have you *been swimming?* – Yes, I have.

8.93 (= Halliday and Hasan's 4:99)
What *were they* doing? – Holding hands.

In 8.93, the 'modal element' of the clause, consisting of the Subject and the finite part of the verb (whose order shows mood) has been ellipted.

Halliday and Hasan's fourth type of cohesive relation, conjunction, is rather different from the others, in that 'conjunctive elements are cohesive not in themselves but indirectly, by virtue of their specific meanings; they are not primarily devices for reaching out into the preceding (or following) text, but they express certain meanings which presuppose the presence of other components in the discourse' (p.226). Four types of conjunctive relation are discussed, and are exemplified by the following passage (from Halliday and Hasan, pp.238-9, with the conjunctive items italicized).

8.94 (= Halliday and Hasan's 5:13)
For the whole day he climbed up the steep mountainside, almost without stopping.
a. *And* in all this time he met no one. (additive)
b. *Yet* he was hardly aware of being tired. (adversative)
c. *So* by night time the valley was far below him. (causal)
d. *Then,* as dusk fell, he sat down to rest. (temporal)

The final type of cohesion discussed by Halliday and Hasan, lexical cohesion, is achieved via the relationships between identical lexical items, or items from the same lexical field. The five subtypes of lexical cohesion are exemplified in 8.95-8.99 (taken from Halliday and Hasan, pp.279-80, 285, with cohesive items italicized).

8.95 (= Halliday and Hasan's 6:7a)
There's a *boy* climbing that tree.
The *boy*'s going to fall if he doesn't take care.

8.96 (= Halliday and Hasan's 6:7b)
There's a *boy* climbing that tree.
The *lad*'s going to fall if he doesn't take care.

8.97 (= Halliday and Hasan's 6:7c)
There's a *boy* climbing that tree.
The *child*'s going to fall if he doesn't take care.

8.98 (= Halliday and Hasan's 6:7d)
There's a *boy* climbing that tree.
The *idiot*'s going to fall if he doesn't take care.

8.99 (= Halliday and Hasan's 6:14)
Why does this little *boy* wriggle all the time?
Girls don't wriggle.

In 8.95, the same item, 'boy', is repeated; in 8.96, a near-synonym, 'lad', is used; in 8.97, the item 'child' is a superordinate of 'boy'; 8.98 uses a general word, 'idiot', which can give a cohesive link with any noun representing a human being; and 8.99 illustrates the use of items ('boy' and 'girl') which regularly co-occur (or 'collocate' – see Section 7.2.2). By discussion of a substantial passage of written English, Halliday and Hasan (p.286 ff.) demonstrate how chains of collocational patterning can be built up, providing cohesive threads which weave the text into a coherent fabric.

This summary of Halliday and Hasan's book has given only the barest outline: the wealth of detailed description of cohesive devices is unparalleled elsewhere, and has been praised even by critics of the authors' theoretical stance. The work does, however, raise some important theoretical problems, which have been discussed by Huddleston (1978), Dressler (1978), Morgan and Sellner (1980), Carrell (1982) and Brown & Yule (1983).

Several difficulties arise from the fact that Halliday and Hasan's use of the term 'reference' is non-standard, not to say idiosyncratic (indeed, one is reminded of Firth's use of the term 'meaning'). Halliday and Hasan (p.31) do recognize that they are using the term in a 'specific sense' when they talk of items not having their own direct semantic interpretation, but being dependent on 'reference' to something else for that interpretation. Morgan and Sellner (1980, p.180) point out, correctly, that in 8.82, repeated below, 'them' does not, as Halliday and Hasan claim, 'refer back to something that has gone before': rather, the speaker is using 'them' to refer to six cooking apples, not to the phrase 'six cooking apples'.

8.82 Wash and core six cooking apples. Put them into a fireproof dish.

In other words, reference, as generally defined, is a relationship between a linguistic item and an entity outside language, which it picks out on a given occasion of use. Since Halliday and Hasan are concerned with relationships between items within the text, the cohesive relation they propose is clearly not between 'them' and the six cooking apples to which this item refers. The only remaining possibility, Morgan and Sellner observe, is that the cohesive tie lies in a relation of co-reference between 'them' and 'six cooking apples'. Morgan and Sellner go on to claim that 'Halliday and Hasan give no reason to believe that this secondary kind of relation plays any direct role in understanding texts or determining properties such as coherence'. This claim, made also by Carrell (1982, p.483), is quite wrong: as was mentioned earlier, Halliday and Hasan explicitly state that the meaning of the cohesive relation between two items is that they refer to the same thing. This does not, however, save Halliday and Hasan's position, since, as Huddleston (1978, p.345) points out, 'six cooking apples' in 8.82 is not a referring expression: it is not being used to refer to six particular cooking apples, but to any six such apples. The exact nature of the cohesive tie in such cases thus remains unclear.

This basic flaw leads Huddleston to question Halliday and Hasan's claim that endophora and exophora are subtypes of a more general phenomenon of 'phoric' relations. Huddleston (1978, pp.336-7) compares the following examples.

8.100 (= Huddleston's 6)   John didn't come. – Was *he* ill?
8.101 (= Huddleston's 8)   *I* have a headache.

In 8.100 the referent of 'he' is the person John, but the 'antecedent' to which 'he' is tied in anaphoric relation is the linguistic item 'John'. In 8.101 the referent of 'I' is the speaker, but no antecedent is present, nor is one needed, since the speaker is always present in the situation of utterance. Thus Halliday and Hasan's failure to recognize a distinction between antecedent and referent leads them to regard as related what are really two quite different kinds of phenomenon.

The distinction between endophora and exophora, as made by Halliday and Hasan, is also questioned by Brown and Yule (1983, pp.199-201), though from a rather different perspective. Brown and Yule point out that since, in endophora, the reader or hearer has to search back in the text in order to establish the identity of a referent, he must, in a long text, go right back up the chain of reference to the original expression used to allude to the referent. As Brown and Yule observe, it seems unreasonable to suppose that a reader or listener is necessarily able to reconstruct the exact form of the first occurrence, when interpreting an item far into the text. They propose, instead, that 'the processor establishes a referent in his mental representation of the discourse and relates subsequent references to that referent back to his mental representation, rather than to the original verbal expression in the text' (Brown & Yule, 1983, pp.200-201). In the case of endophora, the required mental representation would be a representation of the text; in the case of exophora, it would be a representation of the world created by the discourse. In either case, the processor must relate the item to something outside language, so that the endophora/ exophora distinction becomes blurred. Brown and Yule do, however, recognize that Halliday and Hasan are not concerned to provide a description of how readers and hearers process texts. Nevertheless, we might add, in Brown and Yule's defence, that Halliday and Hasan do stress the dynamic nature of text and its creation in, for example, their discussion of the ways in which lexical relatedness contributes to cohesion.

A further distinction which is central to Halliday and Hasan's scheme, but is questioned both by Huddleston and by Brown and Yule, is that between reference and substitution. It will be remembered that according to Halliday and Hasan, reference is a semantic relation, not necessarily involving any identity of syntactic class or any possibility of direct replacement of the interpreted item by the interpreting item, whereas substitution is a grammatical relation, in which the two items are of the same class, with, consequently, the possibility of direct replacement. For instance, in 8.88, repeated below, 'one' could be directly replaced by 'axe', while in 8.102, 'John's' cannot replace 'he' directly, nor can 'John' in 8.103 replace 'his', because different word classes are involved.

8.88   My axe is too blunt. I must get a sharper one.

8.102 (= Halliday and Hasan's 2:21b)
       John's house is beautiful. He had it built last year.

8.103 (= Halliday and Hasan's 2:22 a and y)
       John has moved to a new house. His wife must be delighted
       with it.

Huddleston (1978, p.342) argues that these examples are unconvincing, depending on a purely surface treatment of the two related items. He observes that replacement is possible if the surface inflections are stripped away, and the relation seen as holding between lexemes. This reduction, however, ignores the precise point of Halliday and Hasan's distinction. Rather more damaging to their case is Huddleston's observation that similar inflectional differences occur in cases of Halliday and Hasan's substitution category, as in 8.104:

8.104 (= Huddleston's 20)
       You must tell her. – I've already done so.

Here, 'tell her' could only replace 'do so', not 'done so'. Furthermore, Huddleston discusses other cases where it is not possible to fill out a clause with a copy of the antecedent:

8.105 (= Huddleston's 24)
       What are you doing? – Trying to find my glasses.

8.106 (= Huddleston's 25)
       The chaplain visited each student who had asked him to.

These are, in fact, examples of Halliday and Hasan's ellipsis category, but since they regard ellipsis as a subtype of substitution, and since in any case Huddleston disputes some aspects of their division into the two types (see below), his argument remains valid. Huddleston's point is that the non-finite clause in 8.105 cannot be filled out by taking over 'you are' from the previous question: it needs to be changed to 'I am'. Similarly, 'to' in 8.106 cannot be filled out by 'visit each student' if the meaning of the original is to be preserved, since a given student has clearly requested a visit to himself, and not to all the other students.

Brown and Yule (1983, pp.203-204) also discuss cases where the replacement criterion proposed by Halliday and Hasan simply does not work, as in the following example:

8.107 (= Brown and Yule's 18)
       The child may set the pace. Since the literature is mostly
       anecdotal, we don't mind offering one of our own.

Here, 'one' clearly means 'an anecdote', but the item 'anecdotal' will not act as a direct replacement for the proform. Brown and Yule make a further interesting point, namely that in many texts, successive mentions of 'the same referent' actually refer to rather different entities, in that a change of state involving the referent has occurred. For instance, in the much-discussed cooking apples example from Halliday and Hasan, the apples which are to be put into a dish have undergone a change of state: they are now peeled and cored. The notion of 'co-reference', even if it were not suspect on other grounds, is thus a rather naive over-simplification.

Earlier, it was mentioned that Huddleston disputes some of Halliday and Hasan's conclusions on the distinction between substitution by some non-null element, and ellipsis, or substitution by zero. Huddleston's argument centres round examples such as 8.108:

8.108 (= Huddleston's 39)
     Has he enough money?   (i) Yes, he has.
                              (ii) No, but Tom has.

Halliday and Hasan (1976, p.201) regard such examples as involving 'self-substitution' of the verb 'has', rather than simply ellipsis of 'enough money'. They are forced into this rather counter-intuitive proposal by their general claim that ellipsis cannot involve just a single element of structure.

A further criticism made by Huddleston (1978, pp.338-41) is that it is not always clear that the 'dependent' term in a cohesive relation is quite what Halliday and Hasan claim it to be. In discussing 'reference' relations involving the definite article, Halliday and Hasan (1976, p.70 ff.) clearly indicate that 'the' is the item which has such relations. However, as Huddleston points out, in an example such as 8.109, the relationship is actually between 'Mrs Smith' and the whole nominal group 'the woman'.

8.109 (= Huddleston's 10)
     Mrs Smith has arrived. ~ I'm afraid I haven't time to see the woman.

This, as Huddleston says, is not just a matter of terminology, since it affects the analysis of sentences such as 8.110:

8.110 (= Huddleston's 11)
     The house on the corner is for sale.

For Halliday and Hasan, 'the' is cataphoric to 'on the corner', in that the identity of the house, whose definiteness is indicated by 'the', can be found only by using the information contained in 'on the corner'. If, however, 'the' by itself cannot enter into endophoric relations, then there is no endophoric relation at all in 8.110, since 'the house' has no such relation.

So far, we have discussed criticisms revolving around the grammatically realized types of cohesion proposed by Halliday and Hasan. We come now to a further area of criticism which, although bearing on the whole question of cohesion and its importance, is most easily approached through a consideration of lexical cohesion. As Huddleston (1978, p.351) has observed, lexical cohesion is quite different in kind from grammatical cohesion: it does not, properly speaking, involve any 'antecedent' to an item which is to be interpreted. However, Halliday and Hasan, while recognizing that lexical cohesion is to be delimited from other types, insist that the chains of lexical patterning exemplified earlier do not exist by virtue of any referential relationship, but that 'cohesion exists as a direct relation between the forms themselves' (Halliday & Hasan, 1976, p.284). It is not purely 'an incidental consequence of the fact that discourse does not wander at random from one topic to another but runs on reasonably systematic lines with a certain consistency of topic and predictability of development' (1976, p.288). This claim is disputed by Morgan and Sellner (1980, p.181), who believe that cohesion, rather than being a linguistic property as such, is 'an epiphenomenon of coherence of content'. In other words, the linguistic patterns are simply reflexes, effects rather than causes, of coherence, and Halliday and Hasan's claims to the contrary cannot be entertained seriously until such time as they are shown to have 'explanatory value'.

At first, it is easy to be sympathetic to Morgan and Sellner's position. In *Cohesion in English*, as so often elsewhere, Halliday is more concerned with description than with 'explanation', in the sense in which the term is often used today (a point made also by Dressler (1978) who, in his review of the book, comments that the work is almost entirely expository, with few explanations and little recourse to 'starred', ill-formed examples). There are, however, indications that the notion of lexical cohesion does have some explanatory value of a kind. As was mentioned earlier, Halliday has stressed the dynamic nature of text creation and interpretation, and has proposed that through the relationship between registral parameters and meanings, the interpreter of a text can predict what types of meaning the creator of the text is likely to express. As Halliday and Hasan (1976, p.289) point out, the preceding lexical environment of an item in a text 'frequently provides a great deal of hidden information that is relevant to the interpretation of the item concerned'. Consider the example of a person who walks into a room where two people are talking, and hears the items 'bowl', 'run', 'over' and 'gully'. Each of these items individually would not provide very much information about the nature of the text being created, but the collocation of all four immediately makes it highly probable that the conversation is about the game of cricket. Furthermore, the collocation of, say, 'bowl' and 'run' sets up a framework of expectations in the light of which later occurrences of, say, 'over' and 'gully' would be interpreted. In this sense, the cohesive patterns set up by lexical relatedness do have a predictive value when viewed from the perspective of the hearer or reader.

It remains a moot point whether the hearer or reader actually 'needs' overtly realized cohesive devices in order to interpret a text. Halliday and Hasan certainly appear to believe that this is the case. Brown and Yule (1983, p.196), however, give attested examples which demonstrate convincingly that combinations of sentences are easily interpretable as texts even when there is no explicit marking of cohesive ties. We shall note just one of their examples here.

8.111 (= Brown and Yule's 10a)
　　　　Thank you for your comments about voicing. I will eventually
　　　　get back to that lesson.

Furthermore, as Brown and Yule point out, overtly marked cohesion is no guarantee that a passage will be interpreted as a coherent text. They quote the following example from Enkvist (1978, p.110), in which there are cohesive ties between successive sentences ('Ford' — 'car', 'black' — 'Black', 'discussed' — 'discussions', and so on), yet we should not wish to say that the passage constituted a coherent text. We should note that Halliday and Hasan would probably wish to account for this in terms of inconsistency of register.

> 8.112 (= Brown and Yule's 12)
>   I bought a Ford. A car in which President Wilson rode down
>   the Champs Elysées was black. Black English has been widely
>   discussed. The discussions between the presidents ended last
>   week. A week has seven days. Every day I feed my cat. Cats
>   have four legs. The cat is on the mat. Mat has three letters.

Brown and Yule's position is that 'texts are what hearers and readers treat as texts' (1983, p.199), and that in trying to interpret a passage as a text, hearers and readers will 'try to build a coherent picture of the series of events being described and fit the *events* together, rather than work with the verbal connections alone' (original emphasis). For further discussion of the distinction between cohesion (involving surface links) and coherence (of underlying content) see Enkvist (1978), Widdowson (1978) and de Beaugrande & Dressler (1981).

Finally, we shall note a further point of criticism made by Dressler (1978), who complains that Halliday and Hasan make virtually no reference to the European tradition of 'text linguistics' typified by the work of van Dijk (1972, 1973) and of Dressler himself (1972). Dressler feels that Halliday and Hasan seem unaware of the macrostructure of texts. We might add that they also pay no attention to the kind of patterning in spoken discourse discussed in Section 7.4, some of which (for instance the signalling of boundaries between units of text, and the use of markers such as 'well', 'oh', and the like) is highly relevant to their concerns. Montgomery (1976, p.617), in an otherwise favourable review, notes that many of the problems involved in the analysis of spoken discourse are avoided by Halliday and Hasan's concentration on examples from written texts.

8.2.6 *Other descriptive work on English*

The models adopted in Hudson's *English Complex Sentences* (1971) and *Arguments for a Non-Transformational Grammar* (1976) were discussed in Chapter 6: both books contain a wealth of detail concerning syntactic patterning in English, especially in the area of complementation which, as we saw in Section 8.2.2, is neglected by Halliday in his account of transitivity. Hudson, however, has little to say about semantic process types and their relation to the syntax of complementation.

In the area of the semantics of mood, Hudson has made a valuable contribution. In an article (Hudson, 1975) concerned principally with the semantics of questions in English, Hudson demonstrates that sentences have context-independent properties which can be shown to be semantic, but which are related in a regular (though not one-to-one) way to syntactic mood categories. These 'semantic force markers', in turn, contribute to the mechanisms for working out the illocutionary force of utterances of a particular sentence, via conversational principles of the type proposed by Grice (1975), together with the hearer's knowledge of aspects of the speaker, the situation and the preceding discourse. The semantic force markers proposed by Hudson are QUESTION, STATEMENT and EXCLAMATION. QUESTION reflects a condition for all interrogative sentences, namely that 'the speaker believes that the hearer knows, at least as reliably as the speaker does, whether the proposition is true or false' (Hudson, 1975, p.11). STATEMENT reflects the fact that 'the speaker believes that the proposition is true' (1975, p.24). EXCLAMATION is a property of sentences which show that 'the speaker is impressed by the degree to which a property defined in the proposition is present' (1975, p.10). A given sentence may have more than one semantic force marker: for instance, 8.113, in its most likely interpretation, is both an EXCLAMATION and a QUESTION, whereas 8.114 is simply an EXCLAMATION.

8.113 (= Hudson's 10b)   Isn't that a pretty dress?
8.114 (= Hudson's 10a)   What a pretty dress that is!

Hudson's semantic force markers are thus based on conditions very similar to the 'sincerity conditions' on speech acts proposed in Searle's (1969) development of Austin's (1962) theory.

Taking sentences such as 8.113 and 8.114 for his discussion, Hudson shows that although they share the sincerity condition for EXCLAMATION, they have no syntactic similarity with which such a condition could be associated. Indeed, the two are very different syntactically: for instance, 8.114 but not 8.113 allows a tag ('isn't it?'); 8.113 shows the Subject/auxiliary inversion typical of interrogatives but no exclamatives; 8.114 but not 8.113 can be converted to an embedded sentence after 'He says'; 8.113 must be negative, whereas 8.114 must not be; 'pretty' can be modified by 'very' in 8.114 but not in 8.113; and so on.

Hudson's extremely persuasive arguments lead to the conclusion that the semantic aspects of communication role are separable from the syntactic features of mood and also from the illocutionary forces with which sentences may be used when uttered, although there are interesting and important relationships between all three types of patterning. A similar position on the relation between mood semantics and illocutionary force is reached by another linguist who has long been associated with systemic linguistics: Davies (1979), working within a semantic role framework derived from symbolic interactionist theory, distinguishes between the 'literal mood meaning' (LMM) of a construction and the 'significance' which the construction may have in a particular kind of context. Literal mood meaning 'attaches to a construction type irrespective of particular circumstances (including those of the speaker's actual intentions) on any given occasion of its use. It is a semantic specification which a construction type has, *per se*' (Davies, 1979, pp.38-9). Literal mood meanings are specified in terms of combinations of 'primary roles' (Speaker, Addressee, Third Party), and of 'secondary roles' (Teller, Knower, Decider, Performer). Question, statement, command and permission, among others, are seen as categories of 'first order significance', which are carried by a limited range of construction types, in contrast to other categories, such as warning, which can be conveyed by almost any construction type, and are attributable to higher orders of significance. Categories of first order significance can be derived from the literal mood meaning and features of the context of utterance.

The ideas put forward by Hudson, and in part corroborated by Davies, are developed in Butler (1982), within the context of an attempt to produce an adequate description of directively used modalized sentences in English, and to predict the speech act classification of such directives, and their relative politeness in a given social context. It is argued that a multi-level model of the type shown in Figure 8.5 is needed if all the relevant properties of modalized directives are to be accounted for.

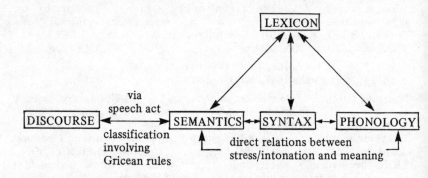

Figure 8.5: The model of Butler (1982)

Hudson's daughter dependency grammar (see Section 6.3.3.3) is shown to be a revealing model, not only for syntax, but also for the formalization of relationships at the semantic and discourse levels. The description of discourse (see Section 7.4.5) is based on the Sinclair and Coulthard model. The description of the semantics of mood extends Hudson's (1975) proposals to include imperative-form sentences and question tags. The description of modal meanings is based largely on Palmer (1979), though with contributions from many other sources. On the basis of the semantics of mood and modalization, predictions are made concerning the acceptability or unacceptablility of particular modalized sentences as directives, and about the speech act classification of the acceptable directives. The relative politeness of the acceptable directives in a particular social context is also found to be predictable from the semantic properties. These predictions are then thoroughly tested by means of informants. The informant tests corroborate very strongly the predictions made, the exceptions proving to be explicable.

In addition to the descriptions of specific areas reviewed above, several general descriptions of English grammar have taken a systemically oriented model as their basis. The grammar of Scott, Bowley, Brockett, Brown and Goddard (1968) is based on Halliday's Scale and Category model. There are chapters on word classes, group classes, clauses of various types, the sentence, aspects of the nominal group, verbal group and adverbial group, and patterning beyond the sentence. Sinclair's (1972) description of the grammar of spoken English, intended as a pedagogical tool for teachers and advanced foreign students of English, as well as for native students of the language, is also based on a Scale and Category framework, enriched by discussion of the 'deeper', functional relations of, for instance, participants in processes. The book discusses the structure of sentences and clauses (including sections on transitivity, mood and theme), and of nominal, verbal and adverbial groups. Muir's (1972) book, entitled *A Modern Approach to English Grammar,* is based on the early systemic model of the mid- to late 1960s, and contains quite detailed descriptions of the 'surface grammar' of words, groups, clauses and sentences, followed by rather less detailed accounts of the 'deep grammar', as represented by the systems of the clause, nominal group and verbal group. Berry's (1975, 1977) *Introduction to Systemic Linguistics* contains descriptions of some of the systems and structures of English, but devotes more attention to theory than does Muir. More recently, Young (1980) has produced a detailed description, within a systemic framework, of structures in the English clause. Various aspects of clause patterning are described, including mood and modality, complementation, theme, voice, and the contribution of Adjuncts. Clause complexes, bound and reporting clauses are also discussed, and structure within the verbal group treated in some detail. All the accounts of English grammar mentioned here are essentially interpretations of Halliday, although in some areas they do extend the descriptive detail found in Halliday's work. Also, as we have already seen, Berry's work, in particular, offers some important theoretical insights.

8.3 Descriptions of other languages

Like proponents of other models, systemic linguists have paid far more attention to English than to any other language. Halliday's own early work on Modern Chinese (Halliday, 1956) was described briefly in Chapter 2. Halliday (1959) also produced a description of the language of a fourteenth-century Chinese text, giving a fairly detailed account of the grammar at sentence, clause and group ranks, together with a reconstruction of the phonology and a comparison with that of present-day Mandarin.

We saw in Chapter 3 that Halliday's Scale and Category model, to which his work on Chinese was an important prelude, gave way in the mid-1960s to a model in which the system networks were regarded as the heart of the semantically oriented grammar. It was within this early systemic framework that the work of Huddleston and Uren (1969) on mood in French was conducted. Their initial network, with the clause as point of origin, is similar to those produced by Halliday for English: imperatives are distinguished from non-imperatives, and the latter are split into declarative and interrogative. Later refinements of this network lead to the inclusion of [exclamative] among the non-imperative options, and the recognition that tags can accompany non-interrogative clauses. Imperatives are then classified more delicately, and a complex network is built up for the various types of French interrogative. Examples are given, but no explicit realization rules are formulated.

Hudson's work on Beja (Hudson, 1964, 1972a, 1973a, 1973b, 1974b) was conducted within the systemic framework which was applied to English in his *English Complex Sentences* (Hudson, 1971: for discussion see

Section 6.3.3.1). In the most readily available account (Hudson, 1973b), he presents detailed system networks, feature realization rules and function realization rules for clauses, for verbs within the clauses, and for verbal morphemes in Beja.

Hudson's 1964 University of London Ph.D. thesis on Beja was later complemented by two further London theses in which systemic techniques of description were used. El-Rabbat's (1978) work on Egyptian Colloquial Arabic was concerned with the transitivity relations of Arabic clauses; Owens (1978) used a version of Hudson's daughter dependency grammar in his description of Nubi.

Finally, we should note Martin's (1981b) work on sentence connection in Tagalog. Martin adopts Halliday's latest theoretical position in that system networks are claimed to be semantic, and organized into functional components. Martin proposes a semantic rank scale consisting of the units text, message group, message and message part. Message parts are the participants, processes and circumstances of Halliday's transitivity schemas, so that the congruent realization of a message part is a group (nominal for participants, verbal for processes, adverbial for circumstances). The congruent realization of a message is thus a single clause, and that of a message group is a clause complex. Martin discusses two main system networks concerned with sentence connection: 'conjunction', said to operate at message group rank, and 'continuity', operating at message rank. Conjunction is in fact the only network located at message group rank in Martin's scheme, and he proposes that it has a functional organization of its own, rather than belonging to any of the main functional components. It is realized by a set of conjunctions, and covers consequential, temporal, comparative and additive types of relation. Continuity, realized by a set of clitic particles, is a textual network, whose meanings either reinforce, or act as an alternative to, the meanings expressed by conjunction relations.

8.4 Conclusion

Ever since the pioneering work of Firth, systemic linguists have placed considerable emphasis on the description of particular languages. This orientation has led to a body of descriptive analysis unequalled in any other approach to language. In, for example, the areas of participant/process relations, thematic relations and cohesion, Halliday himself has provided us with descriptions of unrivalled detail. This work is, as we have seen, open to serious criticism in a number of respects; without the contribution of systemic linguistics, however, our knowledge of English, and to a certain extent other languages, would be much the poorer.

9. Applications of systemic linguistics

9.1 Introduction

Halliday's writings make it quite clear that he is interested not simply in language as a system in its own right, but also in the application of linguistic techniques in the study of other related areas. In his interview with Herman Parret (Parret, 1974, p.83 = Halliday, 1978, p.36), Halliday said:

> Probably most people who have looked at language in functional terms have had a predominantly instrumental approach; they have not been concerned with the nature of language as such so much as with the use of language to explore something else.

He goes on to claim that a functional approach is also needed even if our interest is in the nature of language itself, but it is clear that the applicability of the model is never very far from Halliday's mind. Furthermore, as Halliday, McIntosh and Strevens (1964, p.139) observe, 'the applications themselves are an important source of feedback: a theory is constantly re-examined in the light of ideas suggested in the course of its application'. In this chapter three major areas of application of systemic linguistics will be considered: stylistics, educational linguistics, and the computerized understanding and generation of discourse.

9.2 Systemic linguistics in stylistic studies

We have seen that Halliday has always insisted upon the importance of studying texts, and indeed now regards the text as the basic semantic unit. It is not surprising, then, that Halliday and others working within his frameworks have applied themselves to the study of literary texts. We may divide such stylistic studies into two main groups: those which take Scale and Category linguistics as a basis for a chiefly structural analysis, and those which investigate the systemic choices made in text construction.

9.2.1 Stylistic studies based on Scale and Category linguistics

The usefulness of linguistic techniques in the study of literary texts is discussed in a paper by Halliday (1964b) in which he points out that the incomplete, ill-motivated, often Latin-based categories of many 'prelinguistic' grammars are of no use whatever for literary studies. What is needed is a more rigorous model, which may serve as a common basis for the description and comparison of all manner of texts, literary or non-literary. He observes that although no linguistic analysis will exhaust the 'meaning' of a literary text, a well-constructed grammar will at least allow the precise specification of those properties which are amenable to treatment in linguistic terms. These points are illustrated by a brief analysis of four texts. Halliday first investigates the use of the definite article in Yeats' poem *Leda and the Swan*, pointing out that this differs from the use of 'the' in another Yeats poem, *His Phoenix*, and also in most modern English prose, in that out of ten nominal groups having 'the' plus a modifier or qualifier, only one has a cataphoric use of 'the' (for discussion of 'phoric' relations see Section 8.2.5). Halliday also examines the collocational patterning of verbal lexical items in *Leda and the Swan*, concluding that those items with the greatest power to predict their collocates tend to be those in which the 'verbness' is most attenuated. He then goes on to contrast three short prose passages, each describing a room, showing differences in three areas: complexity of nominal group structure, the distribution of lexical items belonging to particular lexical sets, and types of grammatical and lexical cohesion. A shorter discussion of some of these points can also be found in Halliday (1964c). Although the analyses, both of the Yeats poem and of the prose texts, reveal interesting differences, Halliday makes no attempt to interpret these variations. He thus falls prey, in these papers, to a criticism which is often made by sceptical literary critics, namely that linguists dissect texts and display their patterns without going on to investigate the literary significance of the patterns, which should be the major point of the exercise.

The possibility of describing a literary text independently of any attempt to evaluate the literary effects of its linguistic features appears to be seen as a virtue by Sinclair (1966b). He presents a detailed analysis of the grammatical structure of Philip Larkin's poem *First Sight*, within a Scale and Category framework. The structures of sentences, clauses and groups are discussed, and the interplay of syntactic divisions and line divisions investigated. A particularly useful notion introduced by Sinclair in this paper is that of 'arrest', which occurs in circumstances where, for example, the independent clause of a sentence is delayed or interrupted, so creating a kind of tension in the structure. It is especially interesting that out of the four sentences which constitute the poem, the first three are 'arrested', while the last is not. This difference is reinforced by similar types of arresting pattern at clause rank, and also by the relative complexity of verbal group structures in the last sentence compared with the other three.

A second exercise in stylistic description by Sinclair (1968) employs similar analytical techniques in the study of Robert Graves' poem *The Legs*. The structures of sentences, clauses, nominal, verbal and adverbial groups, are all examined in some detail. In addition, the verbs of the poem are classified as 'general', 'specific' or 'rare', and the use of the definite article in phoric relationships is investigated. The distribution of these various features in the text is discussed, and related to the 'public meaning' of the poem, in that the convergence of particular patterns of grammatical and lexical organization is shown to contribute to the subjective impressions which readers frequently obtain from a reading of the text. A particularly important notion here is that of 'acceleration', 'an increase in the rate of repetition of some elements of the text' (Sinclair, 1968, p.220). Sinclair demonstrates that there is such an acceleration in the rate of change of topics as the poem progresses. This stylistic device can also be detected on a smaller scale, in that certain grammatical features show an increasing rate of repetition within stanzas. Sinclair also shows how various linguistic devices contribute to the sense of pointless movement and chaos which characterizes the poem: the breaking of linguistic symmetries; the predominance of intransitively used verbs; the presence of verbs which do not appear in the company of any of their expected collocates; and the use of definite nominal groups with no clear indication of the source of the definiteness. Many other descriptive details are discussed and related to the 'meaning' of the poem: indeed, this paper demonstrates very clearly how close attention to the minutiae of grammatical patterning can offer a more objective basis for the explanation of readers' impressions of the text. Certainly, here, Sinclair avoids the literary critics' accusation of cavalier disregard for literary interpretation.

In a recent paper (Sinclair, 1982), the notion of 'arrest', taken over from the earlier work, is developed in the course of a discussion of Wordsworth's *Lines Composed a Few Miles above Tintern Abbey*. Here, arrest is defined rather more precisely than previously: 'If, in the structure AXB, A predicts B, but not X, then X is an arresting element.' (Sinclair, 1982, p.165). Sinclair goes on to discuss some complications, and adds the following rider to circumvent some of these:

> If (in the same structure AXB) X is a regular selection in the structure (that is, in its normal position), and is of a different grammatical class from A, then it is not an arresting element. (p.166)

This prevents us from, for example, having to regard 'wild' in 'a wild secluded scene' as arresting. Arrest is one example of what Sinclair now refers to as 'focusing categories' (or 'focats'): intersection points of particular note, between linguistic details and literary interpretation. Presumably acceleration, discussed earlier, would be another such category. A third focat is 'extension', in which 'additional elements extend the structure beyond expectation' (p.166). Extension is defined more formally as follows: 'Take the case ABX_1X_2, where X_1 and X_2 are members of the same grammatical class. X_1 is an *extension* of the structure' (p.166). Examples of extension include co-ordination, juxtaposition and appositional structures. Embedding of focats (that is, the appearance of one focat within another) can occur. Sinclair goes on to analyse two sentences of the poem in detail, in terms of arrest and extension. These categories arc seen as relating to the literary impression created by the text: Sinclair proposes that

> Wordsworth's syntax accurately models his meaning; suspends itself when the meaning is in suspense; builds up a tension by repeating the same arresting devices several times, and then in the quiet last clause suggests an ultimate depth of meaning. (p.170)

There is much else in this short article which is worthy of close attention. For instance, Sinclair suggests that

> ... poetry, in common with many varieties of language, uses two routes of communication: one conventional, where words are built into phrases along accepted lines, decoded in a manner that in principle could be

automated; and the other a problem-solving system, where unique combinations are suggested that have no conventional meaning. Though they are latent in the structure of the language, the language does not typically make use of them. By this route the meaning of a latent pattern is assessed in relation to the conventional, precise and basic meaning. (p.171)

Examples of such latent patterning would include alliteration, syntactic parallelism and unusual collocations. Sinclair also discusses a useful procedure for the step-by-step analysis of a text, showing how the profusion, regularity or scarcity of linguistic patterns may be related to the 'total meaning' of the text.

Also based on Sinclair's (1972) version of Scale and Category grammar is Short's (1982) analysis of the first of T.S. Eliot's *Preludes*. Short demonstrates how the reader's impression of fragmentariness and simplicity of style can be related to the structural features of the text: there are three very short lines out of fourteen; sentence length is very variable; there are no 'bound' or rank shifted clauses; there are three nominal groups which are not related to any other elements of clause structure; no poetic inversion of Subject and Predicator occurs; each clause has a different topic; anaphora is absent; clauses with no inherent lexical-semantic relation are grouped together; the only link between clauses and between sentences is 'and', and this is in all cases followed by an Adjunct which changes the time- or place-focus. Short then goes on to show that these disparate and seemingly chaotic elements are unified by means of the rhyme system of the poem. By the device of rhyming lines which have no clear connection of content, Eliot makes the reader find such a connection for himself. This brief article is an excellent example of the power of detailed linguistic analysis when it is informed by literary sensitivity.

The integration of linguistic techniques and literary interpretation is also evident in Carter's (1982b) analysis of Hemingway's short story *Cat in the Rain*. Carter starts out from his intuitions as a reader, namely that the story is about the breakdown in a relationship between a man and his wife, and that the cat in the story is symbolic. He goes on to show how three areas of the grammar contribute to these intuitive reactions. Firstly, the nominal group structures are generally very simple, often consisting of just a determiner and a headword, or determiner, noun modifier and headword: where any complexity of nominal group structure occurs, these variations are 'foregrounded', and capture the reader's attention. Secondly, although the verbal groups of the text are usually very simple, and in the simple past or past progressive appropriate for narrative, there is one point in the story at which modal verbs and variations in tense appear. Carter shows that these features coincide with a moment of excitement in the story, and that this effect is reinforced by the occurrence of 'free indirect speech', a device which allows the author to combine authorial and character viewpoints on the dialogue. Thirdly, Carter examines the cohesive devices of the story. In the opening paragraph a sense of familiarity with the scene is conveyed by extensive use of exophoric reference to the hotel in which the man and wife are staying, the sea, the public garden, and so on. Anaphora is also used, conveying a sense of cohesive harmony. Carter also observes, however, that at times Hemingway chooses to repeat the same lexical content rather than use a pronoun or some modified expression. This, he claims, deflates the reader's expectations, giving rise to the feeling that the text is not actually going anywhere. At the end of the article, Carter draws together these three strands of the linguistic and literary analysis, relating them to the intuitive impressions from which he started out.

Finally, in this brief review of stylistic analyses based on the Scale and Category model, we turn to the work of Gregory. In an early paper, Spencer and Gregory (1964) present a valuable discussion of the role of descriptive linguistics in stylistic studies, and give a sketch of the Scale and Category model, which they consider to offer the kinds of categories and distinctions of use in the investigation of literary texts. The stylistic features of a text or body of texts may involve any or all of the levels of phonology, graphology and form (grammar and lexis); at each of these levels the Scale and Category model provides theoretical apparatus for a comprehensive description of texts. Furthermore, the categories of dialect and register (the latter related to the categories of field, tenor and mode) allow the 'placing' of a text in relation to its situation of production, and in relation to any social contexts portrayed within it. Along the field dimension, we may wish to investigate ways in which the writer draws upon the linguistic features of specialized fields for literary purposes. Along the tenor dimension, we may recognize different types of relationship between writer and reader, and between characters in the literary work. Along the mode dimension, we may study the complex relationships between spoken and written media in literature, as manifest in dialogue, monologue, interior monologue, narrative, and so on.

Gregory's later stylistic work puts into practice the principles expounded in the 1964 discussion. His study of Donne's *Holy Sonnet XIV* (Gregory, 1974) 'places' the poem in terms of its temporal provenance, its religious field of discourse, a personal tenor related to the assumption of a private audience of known readers or listeners, and a mode of discourse which could be described as 'written to be spoken' or 'written to be read with the speaking of it in mind'. Gregory's collocational analysis of the lexis of the poem reveals three sections of the text, each characterized by a particular set of lexical items. Two further instances of tripartite patterning are also demonstrated by close analysis of the text: the grammatical mood changes from imperative to declarative and then back to imperative; and there is an important interplay of first, second and third persons throughout the text. Gregory relates these patterns to the key phrase 'three person'd God' in the first line of the poem. A further example of this type of analysis is Gregory's discussion of Marvell's poem *To his coy mistress* (Gregory, 1978). A brief grammatical analysis is followed by a rather more extensive discussion of collocational patterning, and the text is interpreted as a particular kind of social event.

9.2.2 Stylistic studies based on systemic functional grammar

As we saw in Chapter 4, the systemic functional grammar developed by Halliday since the mid-1960s takes as its base the functionally organized networks of meaningful choice available to the speaker or writer. Since the process of text creation essentially consists in the selection and organization of meanings and their translation into linguistic substance, it is not surprising that the systemic functional model has been adopted as the basis for a number of studies in literary stylistics.

The seminal work in this area is Halliday's (1971b) analysis of the style of William Golding's novel *The Inheritors*. The position adopted by Halliday here is made explicit in his introduction to the analysis:

> . . . a feature that is brought into prominence will be 'foregrounded' only if it relates to the meaning of the text as a whole. This relationship is a functional one: if a particular feature of the language contributes, by its prominence, to the total meaning of the work it does so by virtue of and through the medium of its own value in the language — through the linguistic function from which its meaning is derived. Where the function is relevant to our interpretation of the work, the prominence will appear as motivated. (Halliday, 1971b, p.339 = 1973a, p.112)

Halliday stresses that it is misleading to think of style simply in terms of the 'non-cognitive' aspects of meaning: the ideational, interpersonal and textual functions all have their part to play, and 'there are no regions of language in which style does not reside' (1971b, p.339 = 1973a, p.112). Halliday also discusses the notions of deviation and statistical 'deflection' from expected patterns of frequency, pointing out that although rough statistical data are useful, perhaps even necessary, in assessing prominence, such data are not in themselves sufficient to establish foregrounding, since they do not tell us whether the patterns revealed have any interpretative significance.

The Inheritors tells the story of a small group of Neanderthal people whose world is invaded by a more advanced group. For the major part of the book, the reader perceives the activities of the Neanderthal people through their view of the world and of the new invaders. There is then a transitional passage, leading to a short final section in which the world is seen from the viewpoint of the invaders, the 'inheritors' of the title. This final world view is recognizable as that of modern man.

Through an analysis of passages from all three sections, Halliday demonstrates that the shift in world view is effected largely through changes in choices from the ideational systems of transitivity. Analysis of the first passage shows very convincingly that through his choice of transitivity relations, Golding presents the world as filtered through the limited understanding of the Neanderthal people, as represented by one of their number, Lok. The processes in this passage are almost all actions (which are always concerned with movement in space), locational-possessional, or mental processes; further, they are expressed in the most direct narrative form (simple past tense, active, finite). There is almost always only one participant, the 'Affected' in terms of Halliday's 'ergative' analysis (see Section 8.2.2). That is, the clauses contain a Subject, but Objects and Complements are rare. Processes which in our own world view would involve directed action or causation are presented as intransitive: for instance, 'he smelled along the shaft of the twig', 'a stick rose upright . . .' 'The stick began to grow shorter at both ends' (instead of 'he drew a bow'). Furthermore, half of the Subjects are not people, but are either parts of the body or inanimate objects. In contrast to the paucity of Objects and Complements, there are many Adjuncts, mainly involving location or direction. The world created for the reader is one in which there is much movement, but in which actions are not directed at anyone or anything: the life of the primitive tribe is presented as highly active but lacking in effectiveness. However, as Halliday observes, this is not simply a picture of the lives of the Neanderthal people: it is also a portrait of the limitations of their world view, and this leads us on into the deepest level of meaning in the text, at which the writer is expressing his concern with the conflicts inherent in the evolution of man. Analysis of a passage from the end of the book reveals a very different picture: most of the clauses now have a human Subject, and the majority of these clauses are transitive and of the action type. This reflects a view of the world in which the principles of cause and effect are recognized. The transitional passage between the major sections of the book is shown to be transitional also in terms of the transitivity choices made.

Halliday's analysis of *The Inheritors* is extremely persuasive and suggests that an examination of various areas of systemic choice may prove fruitful in stylistics. The principles articulated in this analysis have been taken up in later work by other systemicists. Like Halliday, they have concentrated largely on transitivity relations, though not exclusively so.

Short (1976) applies the techniques pioneered by Halliday in his *Inheritors* study, in an analysis of a passage from Steinbeck's *Of Mice and Men*. This passage gives an account of a fight between two characters, Curley and Lennie, which is witnessed by a third character, George, who constantly attempts to keep the simple-minded Lennie out of trouble. Short's principal thesis is that the transitivity options selected in the passage contribute to the reader's feeling of sympathy for Lennie, and also to the portrayal of George's lack of control over him. All but one of the clauses in which Curley is Actor have Lennie as Goal; they also contain centrally transitive verbs of a lexically powerful nature, such as 'slash', 'smash' and 'slug'. On the other hand, the clauses with Lennie as Actor have less centrally transitive verbs with less lexical power (for example, 'look (at)', 'reach (for)', 'hold on (to)'), and do not consistently have Curley as Goal, but are diverse in the persons and things towards which the actions are directed. These patterns contribute to our feeling that Curley is the attacker, and Lennie the bewildered and helpless victim. George's lack of control over Lennie is signalled in a rather different way: here, Short briefly leaves the area of transitivity and turns to that of speech function. Lennie and Curley have a distribution of sentence types ranging over statements, commands, questions and exclamations: George, however, issues only commands, the majority of which are directed at Lennie; nevertheless, George fails to control Lennie's actions.

The aim of a paper by Kennedy (1976) is to show that Halliday's techniques in *The Inheritors* article 'can be used for analysis of a much broader range of texts to bring out the significance of passages and the author's intention by revealing a semantically motivated pattern of language functions' (p.23). In pursuit of this aim, Kennedy examines two passages, one from Conrad's *The Secret Agent*, the other from Joyce's *Dubliners*. The Conrad passage is concerned with the murder of Mr Verloc by his wife. Kennedy examines the clauses which he claims have Mr Verloc as Actor, and contrasts these with those that have Mrs Verloc as Actor. The former contain largely mental process verbs or intransitives: none has Verloc as the causer of an event, suggesting that he is unable to act in the situation in order to control it. The clauses with Mrs Verloc as Actor, Kennedy claims, chiefly contain intransitive verbs of action. In clauses containing transitive action verbs, Mrs Verloc herself is not Actor; rather, parts of her body fulfil this role, or the Actor is replaced by an instrument, such as the knife used for the murder. Unfortunately, Kennedy's analysis suffers from a lack of precision in terminology: as we saw in Section 8.2.2, the role of Actor is not appropriate for mental processes such as seeing and hearing. Kennedy does sometimes use the term 'processor', but seems to regard this as equivalent to Actor for these clauses. What Kennedy in fact appears to be investigating is the set of clauses in which some action or perception connected with either Mr or Mrs Verloc is described, but in which neither person necessarily occupies the transitivity role of Actor. Given this reinterpretation, Kennedy's observations are interesting, and his arguments reasonably convincing.

In Kennedy's second analysis, of the story 'Two Gallants' from *Dubliners,* he investigates the correlation between certain linguistic features and the characters of the two main protagonists, Corley and Lenehan. Kennedy shows that most of the clauses with Lenehan as a participant contain intransitive action verbs, relational verbs or verbs of perception. Where parts of the body are Actors in the clause, the eyes are usually involved. On the other hand, clauses with Corley as a participant have approximately equal numbers of transitive and intransitive action verbs, and few relational or perception verbs. The terms 'head' and 'body', rather than 'eyes', are used in participant roles. The effect of these transitivity choices is to present Lenehan as a listener and observer, while Corley is seen as actor and speaker. The relationship between the two characters is also indicated by choices in speech function: Corley's contribution to dialogue consists largely of statements; Lenehan's utterances, on the other hand, are often questions or expressions of flattery or agreement, suggesting his subservience to the other man. Kennedy also attempts to show that the textual function is relevant to the stylistic analysis, pointing to the fact that Corley produces more utterances than Lenehan. However, although the textual function is clearly involved in the structuring of dialogue, it is not obvious that it subsumes the relative numbers of utterances made by each speaker.

Finally, we turn to the stylistic work of Burton (1982), whose contribution to the analysis of discourse was mentioned in Section 7.4.4. Writing from a feminist viewpoint, Burton claims that 'stylistic analysis is *not* just a question of discussing "effects" in language and text, but a powerful method for understanding the ways in which all sorts of "realities" are constructed through language' (1982, p.201). She illustrates this approach by analysis of a passage from Sylvia Plath's *The Bell Jar,* in which the persona of the passage describes her first experience of electric shock treatment for depression. Using the transitivity networks given in Berry (1975), Burton classifies the processes in the passage, and examines the identities of the Actors and the participants affected by the actions. She finds that two-thirds of the thirty clauses contain 'material action' processes carried out intentionally. The Actors in these clauses are the nurse (or some part of her body), the doctor, or the electricity used in the treatment. The woman undergoing the treatment makes an unsuccessful attempt at the intentional action of smiling, and later performs the action of shutting her eyes, an attempt to remove herself from the scene as far as possible. The only other successful intentional action is in the sentence 'I wondered what terrible thing it was that I *had done*': here, the action is hidden away in the past. Otherwise, any actions involving the patient are ones which are beyond her control. The picture is clear: the doctor and nurse, with their equipment, are in control, and the patient is helpless. This conclusion is strengthened by an analysis of the participant affected by the action in each clause: the nurse affects the patient, the doctor also does this via his equipment, but the patient herself affects nothing. Even if we do not wish to accept Burton's political stance (and the present author is no doubt one of those whom she would accuse of 'merely naively supporting and demonstrating the (largely unseen and unnoticed) political bias of the status quo' (1982, p.197)), it is clear that the analysis of transitivity relations can be a fruitful approach to the study of power relationships and other aspects of the construction of social reality.

9.3 Linguistics in education

Halliday's main contributions to educational linguistics have been in the area of the learning and teaching of the mother tongue, although some of his early work was done with the teacher of a second or foreign language in mind. We may recognize three strands in his work: one concerned with the explicit teaching of a language; a second with the way in which children learn their native language; and a third with the wider issues of the place of language in the socialization and schooling of the child. In a sense, such distinctions are rather artificial, since Halliday's work in all three areas arises out of, and is permeated by, his particular view of language and its place in the life of man. Since we have explored this view in some detail in previous chapters, and have discussed some of the educational implications along the way, the present section will be fairly brief.

Halliday's first substantial contribution to the field was a lecture delivered in 1960, originally published in French in 1961, and later adapted and translated into English (Halliday, 1966e). The principles discussed there are presented in an expanded form in the very influential book by Halliday, McIntosh and Strevens (1964), *The Linguistic Sciences and Language Teaching*. The authors make clear what they see as the role of the theoretical linguist in the area of language teaching:

> If linguistic theory can be used to make better descriptions of languages, as it can, then this theory has a contribution to make in any situation in which language is being taught. (Halliday, McIntosh & Strevens, 1964, p.139)

The job of the linguist, then, is to provide rigorous theoretical constructs which will account for a comprehensive range of linguistic phenomena, and will serve as a basis for describing those phenomena. If the language to be taught is foreign to the learner, there is the additional possibility of using the same theoretical framework to compare the foreign and native languages.

It is in the nature of the theoretical framework, and hence of the descriptions which result from its application, that Halliday's work has much to offer. In *The Linguistic Sciences and Language Teaching*, the framework is the Scale and Category model. It is therefore not surprising that there is an emphasis in the book on 'structural' rather than 'systemic' patterning; in this respect, Halliday's proposals at this time reflect the linguistic climate of the day. The novelty of Halliday's approach is rather in the important role given to relationships between linguistic form and the situations in which the language is produced. The first half of the book not only presents a simplified and very readable account of Scale and Category theory, but also discusses dialectal variation and register. The second half discusses the basic role of linguistics and phonetics in the teaching of the native language and foreign languages. Again, considerable attention is given to the appropriateness of the learner's language to the situations in which it is to be used. With regard to the learning of the native language, the authors comment:

> For the student learning about his own language, the picture is not complete without an account of its varieties and of the linguistic differences among them. (p.171)

The question of selecting appropriate varieties in the teaching of a foreign language is also discussed. Comments such as the following foreshadow the interest in the teaching of languages for special purposes which was to grow in the decades after publication of the book:

> There is no reason why the student of a foreign language should be required to study 'the whole language', which in any case is an aim impossible of achievement, if the uses he wishes to make of it are restricted and defined; nor why he should study certain registers, such as the language of literature, if his need is for quite other ones. There has already been a considerable trend towards language courses much more specifically related to the varying needs of the student; but the potentialities of such courses are still not widely recognised. (p.174)

In 1964-7 Halliday was involved in work, sponsored by the Nuffield Foundation, which was to form a preliminary stage for a major programme in linguistics and English teaching, under the auspices of the Schools Council. The aims of the programme were ambitious in their breadth: to look into the teaching of English from a linguistic viewpoint, to make a study of modern English in terms which would be helpful to teachers, and to offer recommendations on pedagogical aims and methods. The preparatory work led in 1968 to the publication of a series of ten papers, plus an annotated reading list. Some of these papers discussed attitudes to usage and 'correctness' in language, others dealt with the teaching of reading and writing, and with the place of linguistics in the teaching of literature. Yet others dealt with the description of particular aspects of the English language, and it is here that the Hallidayan orientation of the team is most obvious. The material in Hasan's (1968) paper on cohesion in spoken and written English was eventually incorporated into Halliday and Hasan's (1976) book on cohesion (see Section 8.2.5); Davies' (1968) analysis of clause structure is cast in a Scale and Category mould; Albrow's (1968) description of rhythm and intonation in English expands on Abercrombie's account of rhythm and presents a simplified picture of Halliday's treatment of intonation (see Section 7.3.3).

The Schools Council Programme proper was undertaken by a team of twelve teachers and linguists working at University College London between 1967 and 1971,with Halliday as director. The first major publication of this group was *Breakthrough to Literacy* (See Mackay, Thompson & Schaub, 1970), a collection of materials and a teacher manual, concerned with the initial teaching of reading and writing. The approach used does not derive from any particular linguistic model, but the influence of Halliday's functional standpoint is always clear: the aim is to develop what the child can do with language, building initially on what he can already do when he reaches school age. *Breakthrough* centres round the use of two aids, the 'sentence maker' and the 'word maker', which help the child to become more confident in constructing and reading sentences and the words of which they are composed.

The second major publication, *Language in Use,* was for the secondary level. It consisted of a collection of about 120 units on a variety of themes, which, in the words of the authors, 'aim to develop in pupils and students awareness of what language is and how it is used and, at the same time, to extend their competence in handling the language' (Doughty, Pearce & Thornton, 1971, pp.8-9). As with *Breakthrough, Language in Use* builds on what the students already know – in this case their intuitions about the nature and functions of language. It aims to inculcate a sensitivity, not only towards language, but also towards the human emotions and relationships which language helps to mediate. Again, the influence of Halliday's functional theories is apparent: the units are organized into three major sections, with the headings 'language – its nature and function', 'language and individual man' and 'language and social man'; the subsections cover topics such as 'using language to convey information', 'using language expressively', 'language and reality', 'language and culture', and so on. There is thus an emphasis on language as social and individual behaviour, embedded in and interacting with a context of use:

Language exists insofar as it is used, and its use implies the presence of particular speakers and writers, who have in mind particular listeners and readers and a particular set of circumstances that provides the context for what they say or write. In this sense, the use of language is an essential aspect of human behaviour, the means by which individual human beings relate themselves to the world, to each other, and to the community of which they are members. (Doughty, Pearce & Thornton, 1971, p.11)

The theoretical underpinning of *Language in Use* is discussed in the associated book *Exploring Language* (Doughty, Pearce & Thornton, 1972). This contains eleven chapters covering language teaching and learning; language in relation to experience, relationships and society; spoken and written media; accent and dialect, and other topics.

The final set of publications from the Schools Council project was a series of five short volumes on linguistic and pedagogical topics. The first three of these are linguistic in their orientation. The first (Thornton, Birk & Hudson, 1972) contains three papers: an account of 'the individual and his development of a language' by Thornton (1972) is heavily indebted to Halliday and Bernstein; Birk's (1972) examination of functional approaches to language discusses the work of Malinowski, Firth and Halliday as well as that of Bühler and the Prague School; Hudson's (1972b) detailed description of a single utterance is based on his *English Complex Sentences* model of systemic grammar. The second volume is Albrow's (1972) important monograph on the English writing system. The third is Halliday's (1974) *Language and Social Man* (already referred to in the present book), which gives a fairly non-technical account of his views on the functional nature of language and its relationship with context and with the social structure. The final two volumes are on examinations and on competence in English.

As we saw in Chapter 4, during the early 1970s Halliday turned towards a more explicitly sociosemantic version of the systemic model, in which the meaning potential of a language was seen as related not only 'downwards' to the lexicogrammar, but also 'upwards' to a behaviour potential. In order to provide a firm basis for the study of meaning within such a framework, Halliday insisted that the areas of meaning chosen for study should relate to those aspects of behaviour predicted to be important in terms of some social theory. The social theory which attracted Halliday was that of Bernstein. Halliday reinterpreted Bernstein's theory of code in such a way as to sidestep the controversy over 'deficit' and 'difference' theories of the role of language in educational failure. Halliday's suggestion was that Bernstein's 'elaborated' and 'restricted' codes reflect differences of orientation, in different social groups, towards the total meaning potential of language. Codes were thus seen as filters, regulating access to the functional components of the semantic system. The argument is that if those aspects of the meaning potential emphasized by certain social groups are favoured in our education system, these groups will have an educational advantage over other groups which emphasize aspects of meaning which are either irrelevant or viewed negatively within the schools (see also Section 4.3.6).

Halliday's identification with Bernstein's ideas led to work on children's language, some of which was designed to test relationships between social class and language, using Halliday's linguistic model as a descriptive basis. This work, carried out at the Sociological Research Unit of the University of London Institute of Education, was reported in a series of publications under the general title 'Primary Socialization, Language and Education', edited by Bernstein. Turner and Mohan (1970) describe the linguistic model, which was worked out in 1965 and is closely based on Scale and Category grammar, though it does take some account of the move towards a more centrally 'systemic' model which was taking place at the time. The book also describes a computer program designed to analyse the manually performed grammatical coding of speech data from a sample of five-year-old children. Preliminary analysis using this program suggested that areas of particular interest included attribution and reference in the nominal group, tentativeness and other features of the verbal group, and features associated with groups acting as Adjuncts.

In subsequent work, Turner and Pickvance (1971) examined the expression of uncertainty in the spoken language of 160 five-year-old children, selected to form 8 groups of 20 on the dimensions of sex, social class (middle/working) and verbal intelligence scores (medium/high). The language examined was produced in response to picture cards. Indicators of uncertainty investigated included egocentric sequences such as 'I think', sociocentric sequences such as question tags, as well as questions, refusals to answer the interviewer's questions, assessments of probability using modal verbs and adverbs, and suppositions based on perception (such as 'it looks as if . . .'). The authors' conclusions were that, in accordance with Bernstein's theories, 'the orientation towards the use of expressions of uncertainty is more strongly related to social class than to verbal ability. Moreover, this orientation has been shown to be mainly a middle-class phenomenon' (Turner & Pickvance, 1971, p.322).

Turner (1973) also investigated the language of control in the speech of a group of children at ages five and seven. The language was produced in response to a series of picture cards showing some boys playing football and breaking a window. As in the study of uncertainty, a sample of 160 children was used, factored into subgroups by sex, age and IQ. This work made extensive use of Halliday's concept of sociosemantic networks, and developed networks for the verbal strategies of control available within role-play and non-role-play speech. For instance, in the role-play speech, where the children acted out the roles of adults scolding the children for having broken the window, Turner recognizes two main categories of control strategy: imperative control, which suggests coercion and leaves little discretion to the child; and positional control, based on hierarchical social relations, but allowing the child rather more discretion. Imperative strategies are divided into commands and threats; positional strategies are subclassified into rule-giving, disapprobation and reparation-seeking types. Each of these categories is then subdivided. Turner's conclusions from this detailed and complex study were that verbal ability was only weakly related to control strategies, but that at both ages the working-class children were oriented towards imperative control strategies, and the middle-class children towards positional strategies. Furthermore, within these modes, the middle-class children's language was more explicit and specific than that of the working-class children. All of these conclusions were taken as supporting Bernstein's claims regarding the relationship between parental control strategies and social class.

Hawkins (1969, 1977) has concentrated on the social class correlations of linguistic features associated with the nominal group, basing his descriptions on Scale and Category accounts. Again, the speech sample was produced in response to picture cards, one set depicting the football game and the breaking of a window, and the other designed to elicit descriptive language. Initial work concentrated on a sample of 80 five-year-old children, divided into cells of five on the basis of social class (middle/working), sex, verbal IQ (high/medium/low) and a communication index rating for their mothers (high/low). Social class was found to correlate more strongly with nominal group structure choices than sex, IQ or communication index. Middle-class children used more nouns and fewer pronouns than working-class children; and in the football story task middle-class children also used more qualifiers, ordinative expressions, and more modification as a whole, than working-class. In the light of these preliminary studies, Hawkins decided to investigate a larger sample in more detail. Thirty-seven linguistic categories related to the nominal group were studied in relation to class, IQ, sex and other factors. The results are presented in detail in Hawkins (1977). Working-class children used more exophoric reference than middle-class children, but they also showed greater usage of technically anaphoric pronouns, though many of these usages were closer in their effect to the exophoric type. Overall, 'the results show working-class children oriented towards a type of reference which is less specific and takes for granted a greater degree of common knowledge shared by speaker and addressee' (Hawkins, 1977, p.183). Middle-class children used more nouns: this complements the working-class orientation towards more pronouns, although Hawkins emphasizes that both classes used a large number of nouns. Middle-class children modified nouns more frequently, and also used more first person pronouns in association with expressions of uncertainty or tentativeness. Hawkins also discusses interesting findings which emerge, not from overall generalizations, but from a detailed examination of the language used in particular contexts. His overall conclusion from this work is that there are indeed important class differences in strategies of communication which, as Halliday suggests, are more closely bound up with the functions language is called upon to serve than with matters of grammatical complexity, linguistic competence or social dialect.

The sociological theories of Bernstein also form part of the basis for Halliday's view of language acquisition as a process of 'learning how to mean'. This aspect of Halliday's work was discussed in Chapters 4 and 5, and we shall say no more about it here.

9.4 Systemic linguistics and the computer simulation of discourse understanding and production

Over the past fifteen years or so, considerable advances have been made in the simulation, by computers, of human linguistic processes. It is significant that some of the best known and most highly praised projects in this area have been based on systemic models of language. This is, of course, a highly specialized field, and we shall do no more here than indicate the scope of the major investigations, and the role played by systemic grammars in these studies. A brief non-technical review can be found in Mann (1983).

The best known work was carried out by Winograd (1972), whose SHRDLU computer program was constructed to understand English information and instructions related to a specific domain, a world of movable toy blocks on a table. The system is truly interactive: it accepts typed input, can answer questions and ask for clarifications, and also executes commands by means of a representation, on a screen, of a robot arm which can grasp blocks and move them around. Winograd's aims in writing such a program were threefold: to develop a usable language-understanding system; to gain a better understanding of how language works, and test linguistic models; and to further our knowledge of what constitutes intelligence, and how it can be modelled in computers.

In the internal workings of the program, the rules of syntax and semantics, and also strategies for problem-solving, are expressed in dynamic form as 'procedures' which are implemented by sections of the program. Since one part of the system is able to call another, complex interactions are possible, not only between different parts of one 'level' of the system (for instance, that concerned with syntax) but also between different levels (such as those concerned with syntax and with semantics). The following is a highly simplified picture of the principal components of the system, referred to by names in capital letters.

A MONITOR program oversees the whole system, calling the basic parts when they are needed: however, since the components interact directly, little overall control is needed. An INPUT program accepts typed English input, looks up words in its DICTIONARY, performs morphemic analysis, and prepares a string of the words used, with their dictionary definitions. The DICTIONARY itself consists of two parts: a set of syntactic properties for each word (used by the GRAMMAR programs), and a semantic definition for each word (used by the SEMANTICS programs). The GRAMMAR programs are an internal representation of parsing operations based on a systemic grammar of the late 1960s vintage. There is a fairly large program for parsing each major syntactic unit (clause, nominal group, prepositional group, and so on). The parsing system used (called PROGRAMMAR) can build a structural tree as it goes along, and has facilities for moving around the tree to see what is in particular branches. The SEMANTICS programs work in co-ordination with the GRAMMAR programs to interpret sentences. There is a set of such semantic programs for each basic grammatical unit. The semantic programs make use of a deductive system called PLANNER, which can draw inferences from logical representations of both the language and the world of toy blocks. The system also has a network of SEMANTIC FEATURES which are used to check semantic compatibility of various items, for example the strict subcategorization of verbs, and the compatibility between nouns and their modifiers. Further sets of programs are concerned with information about the BLOCKS world in general, about the current state of the block-world DATA, and about the MOVER needed to pick up and transport blocks.

One particularly noteworthy feature is the way in which the SEMANTICS programs can be called into play before syntactic analysis is complete, so allowing the semantics to guide syntactic parsing. For example, if (in a system dealing with a larger world) we were parsing the sentence *I rode down the street in a car,* the nominal group parsing program might come up with *street in a car* as a possible constituent. Before going on, the semantic analyser would be called in, and would reject *street in a car*, because it can work out, from the properties involved, that streets cannot occur in cars. The syntactic analyser would then reattach *in a car* as an adverbial to the whole sentence, rather than as a qualifier in the nominal group.

Previous work on natural language analysis by computer had used transformational models, and Winograd's adoption of a systemic grammar as the basis for his programs thus marks an important innovation. Winograd (1972, p.16) maintains that what is needed is an approach which is concerned with how language is organized to convey meaning, rather than with how syntactic structures are organized when viewed in isolation from semantic considerations. This is, of course, precisely the orientation of Halliday's model in the late 1960s: the emphasis, as we saw in Section 3.3, is on the meaningful choices offered by the system networks of the language, surface structures being regarded as derivable from the underlying systemic choices by means of realization rules. Systemic features, such as those of mood, are derivable from the rules of a transformational grammar, but they are implicit, and there is no attempt to distinguish semantically significant features from the numerous other features which are also also implied by the rules, and which are simply a side-product of the symbolic operations needed to produce the correct surface structure. The rank-based organization of a systemic grammar is also an advantage, since each rank of unit in the grammatical hierarchy has a particular range of roles to play in conveying meanings. Furthermore, in systemic grammar the functions of particular constituents (for instance as Subject or Object) are made explicit, whereas in a transformational grammar these are again implicit and must be derived from the configuration of the structural tree (see Section 2.4.3). For all these reasons, then, systemic grammar provides a better model than transformational generative grammar for a scheme in which the close interaction of syntactic and semantic processing is crucial. A very readable discussion of these points can be found in Winograd's impressive recent textbook (Winograd 1983), in which systemic and other functionally-oriented grammars are compared with transformational grammars in relation to their usefulness as a basis for computationally implemented cognitive models of language.

Certain aspects of Winograd's system are especially impressive. In cases of potential syntactic ambiguity it can use its knowledge of semantics, and of its limited world, to choose the most likely interpretation of an utterance: it can thus deal with the effects of linguistic and (to a certain extent) non-linguistic context. A related point is the system's ability to deal with deictic relations, ellipsis and the like, both in accepting English input and in formulating its own replies. It deals with *I/you/it*, demonstratives, indefinite pronouns, time relators such as *then*, proforms such as *one* (as in *the blue one*), and a number of other constructions, with impressive ease. It can thus cope with many aspects of natural discourse, rather than being limited to a set of uncontextualized sentences.

Winograd's program, although it did produce sentences as replies to questions, was designed essentially as a language understanding system. On the other hand, the work of Davey, carried out in 1970-73 but not published until later (Davey 1978), is concerned with the development of a computer system which will produce fluent discourse. Like Winograd's system, it deals only with a small finite world, that of the game of noughts and crosses (tic-tac-toe); also like Winograd's, it uses a systemic grammar as its linguistic base. The program accepts as input a list of legal moves in a complete or incomplete game of noughts and crosses. It can also play a game with an opponent, and remember the sequence of moves made by both players. The output is a description of the game, in continuous prose.

Davey's main interest in this work was how discourse is constructed in order to convey information from producer to receiver, the assumption being that in the simplest case, the speaker presents to the hearer a monologue conveying information he believes the hearer would like to have, while avoiding telling him anything he already knows or can easily work out for himself. Davey's decision to use a computer in his work stems from two considerations: firstly, the translation of discourse-generating procedures into computational terms forces the programmer to formulate the rules absolutely explicitly, and the output resulting from the program acts as a more reliable check on the correctness and consistency of the rules than could be achieved by human testing; secondly, Davey believes, 'a computer seems to be the most brain-like thing we have, and programs the closest analogy to the brain's processes' (1978, p.6), so that work of this nature may contribute to our thinking about psycholinguistic processes.

The program, written in the POP-2 language, and segmented into a number of modules or 'procedures', has to assess the state of the receiver's knowledge at each point in the description, and then has to decide how best to structure the information which remains to be presented. It groups together moves in the game which are tactically related, and attempts to present these in one sentence, provided that the resulting sentence length does not exceed three main clauses. Mistakes in play are commented on in the final description. The output from the sentence design procedure is a semantic specification which, however, contains all the information needed to determine the syntactic arrangement of the main clauses. The constituent structure tree for a sentence is then built up by bringing in specialist procedures for each type of constituent node (the sentence node, and nodes for the various types of clause, group and word). The operation of these specialist procedures requires attention not only to the structures of individual constituents and their arrangement in the final structure, but also to matters such as relationships (sequential, contrastive, and so on) between clauses and between sentences, the selection of appropriate forms of referring expressions (for example, nominal group with noun head, with or without modification; pronoun), and choice of suitable tense and aspect forms.

Davey's decision to base the syntactic component of his model on Hudson's (1971) *English Complex Sentences* model of systemic grammar resulted from a number of considerations. Firstly, the grammar is generative, with completely explicit rules for the formation of sentences. Secondly, the separation of the grammar into two parts is convenient from the point of view of computer implementation: the system network sets out the feature combinations which adequately characterize any item being constructed; and the combination of feature realization, structure-building and function realization rules states how decisions about the properties of items are constrained by the environment they are in. Thirdly, the explicit role of syntactic functions in systemic grammars is an advantage: the grammar states the relationship between certain properties of an item and the functions performed by that item, and so is highly suitable as the basis for a program modelling the activities of a human speaker, who presumably decides on the function of his next utterance before settling on the exact form the utterance will take.

Other advantages of a systemic base mentioned by Davey would seem to be more important for possible developments in the generation of discourse than for Davey's work itself. For instance, he points out that although his own program does not need to extend the grammar beyond the scope of Hudson's sentence-based model, systemic grammar is in principle capable of dealing with broader linguistic and pragmatic contexts, in a way not available to transformational linguists. A second potential advantage is that a discourse-generating program based on a systemic grammar can delay the specification of the precise form of any sentence constituent until a late stage: the final structure of the constituent is decided only when construction of that particular unit begins, unlike in a transformational grammar, where all the transformations needed for a given surface structure are decided before any of them is applied. This means that a systemically-based program is in principle better able to cope with the simulation of the kinds of linguistic behaviour, familiar in every-day speech, in which a sentence structure is broken off, for instance by the insertion of parenthetical material to avoid the construction of long and unwieldy referring expressions. In this respect, and in other ways considered above, a systemic grammar offers a psychologically rather more plausible model than a transformational grammar.

It is interesting that Davey chose to base his system on Hudson's grammar rather than on the Hallidayan model taken over by Winograd. One advantage which has already been mentioned is that Hudson's grammar, being generative, provides totally explicit rules. But it will be remembered that Winograd maintained the need for a linguistic base which took into account the way in which the syntax is organized to convey meaning. Davey himself says, in discussing his own work, that 'the present system, and more generally systemic grammar, is very anxious to account for the form of sentences in terms of what they are for, namely meaning things' (Davey 1978, p.32). However, as we saw in Section 6.3, this is true of Hudson's grammar only insofar as he is concerned to provide syntactic categories which are 'deep' enough to be mapped on to semantic categories, though not always in a one-to-one fashion. It seems, from the success of Davey's work, that this, combined with the functional orientation of the model, is sufficient to provide a firm basis for computational work, without having to assume that the semantics should be seen as the starting point for a view of how the syntax should be organized (see Section 6.4).

Davey's program produces perhaps the most fluent and convincing discourse yet generated by computer. Its handling of complex phenomena such as cohesive relations is impressive. It does, however, suffer from one important disadvantage, recognized by Davey himself, namely that it is not an interactive system, and so takes no account of the possibility that the addressee will not understand everything he is told, and will want to remedy this lack of understanding by asking questions. Development of Davey's work in this direction would be particularly welcome.

Although Winograd's and Davey's are the best known systemically-based programs, other recent work has also been influenced by systemic notions. McDonald's (1980) thesis on natural language production as a decision-making process under the influence of constraints, and McKeown's (1982) work on the production of discourse in response to enquiries to a database system, both embody systemic principles. Kay's 'functional unification grammar' (Kay 1979, 1983; Kartunnen & Kay 1983) also has strong systemic links. But perhaps the most exciting developments are to be found in the work of Mann and Matthiessen (see Mann 1982, Mann & Matthiessen 1983) on the 'Nigel' computational grammar. The Nigel grammar is part of a bigger project called Penman, whose aim is to generate appropriate discourse in response to a variety of 'text needs' which arise whenever language is used. It has thus been essential, not only to select, develop and implement an appropriate grammatical framework, but also to specify the means by which the grammar is controlled by particular kinds of text-producing need.

Mann and Matthiessen's reasons for choosing systemic grammar as a linguistic model were similar to those of previous workers. The functional approach specifies not only what grammatical units and constructions are possible, but also what they can be used for. Connected with this is the advantage of a model which treats paradigmatic relations as primary, and can relate them to the meanings they convey. All sources of variation are located in the system networks, and this offers considerable gains, from the point of view of computer implementation, over a 'structural' approach such as a transformational grammar, where structural variability can arise from a number of separate sources.

The Nigel program has separate parts for dealing with systemic choices, realization of these choices, and lexical items. The systemic component keeps track of the selection expression being built up for the constituent under construction, and invokes the appropriate realization procedures. In addition to systems, this part of the program uses 'gates', in which a particular grammatical feature is specified, without any options. The realization section of the program performs three kinds of operation: structure-building operations insert, conflate and expand functions and so produce function bundles; order-constraining operations deal with sequence, although much of the sequencing can be left to default function order lists; a third set of operations associates features with certain functions, for instance for lexical set membership, or even for a particular lexical item. The lexicon consists of a set of arbitrary symbols, each associated with a spelling and a set of lexical features for mapping on to the items being generated by the program. It is interesting to note that the lexicon is not seen as 'most delicate grammar' in this approach, but is more like the kind of lexicon seen in, for instance, Hudson's daughter dependency grammar (see Sections 6.3.3.3 and 7.2).

Each system in the grammar is associated with a 'chooser', which is a description of the circumstances under which each choice allowed by the system is appropriate. The knowledge upon which the choosers operate lies outside the Nigel grammar in what is termed the 'environment'. The environment is considered to consist of three parts: a 'knowledge base' consisting of information which existed even before the text need was experienced; a 'text plan' containing information created specifically in response to the text need, before the grammar was invoked; and 'text services' which hold information available at all times. The choosers have access to symbols called 'hubs', representing entities in the environment. As generation proceeds, these hubs become associated with grammatical functions, the associations being stored in a table which can be consulted at later stages of generation. Nigel is capable of determining what questions the choosers should ask of the environment, and the sequence of chooser enquiries and responses from the environment constitute a dialogue. This enables the choosers to be tested, by attempting to generate a particular clause in a way which allows the user of the program to act as the environment, providing answers to the questions asked by the choosers.

Apart from its success in generating discourse appropriate to particular tasks, the development of the Nigel program can be expected to lead to considerable spin-off for systemic linguistics as a whole, as Mann and Matthiessen (1983) observe. By running the program and examining the output, one can test the adequacy of the grammar on which it is based.

Early runs showed up a number of errors and contradictions, which could then be corrected. On a rather larger scale, the program is a test of the functional basis of the systemic framework, and of the identification of particular grammatical functions. The semantic choosers are seen by Mann and Matthiessen as particularly important, not only to the Nigel program itself, but also more generally for systemic linguistics: it is claimed that they offer a way of formalizing the semantic component of a systemic grammar, and of describing and comparing the semantics of particular languages; alternative ways of representing particular grammatical phenomena systemically can sometimes be evaluated in terms of the simplicity and elegance of the associated choosers; and the choosers also make it easier to demonstrate how grammatical options respond to discourse information.

Mann and Matthiessen operate with versions of the system networks which attempt to integrate accounts from various periods of Halliday's output: for instance, in the area of transitivity, clauses are classified simultaneously on the dimensions material/mental/verbal/relational and middle/effective. Yet they clearly regard the networks as syntactic, and the choosers as mediating between the syntax and the contextual environment, in much the same way as in Halliday's early models. The relationship with more recent accounts is, however, unclear. Mann and Matthiessen themselves comment (1983, p.55, fn. 17) that 'the organization of the grammar . . . reflects the current organization of Nigel. It does not necessarily reflect Halliday's views on what the organization of a systemic grammar and semantics should ideally be like given a particular task'. Since Halliday was closely associated with that stage of the work in which the network was being developed, he presumably feels that the particular form of the network arrived at is valid for the task of generating discourse by computer. But it is important that if, as Mann and Matthiessen claim, their work is to be seen as a test of the underlying grammar, it should be realized that the grammar is a composite one specially constructed for the task, and does not fit neatly with other proposals made recently by Halliday. Despite these reservations on the relationship of the computational grammar to the validation of the systemic functional approach, Mann and Matthiessen's work remains impressive, and will surely lead to even more exciting developments in the near future.

9.5 Conclusion

It has been claimed that over the past 25 years or so transformational generative linguistics has provided us with more fundamental insights into the internal workings of language than were achieved in centuries of previous work. The importance and value of transformational grammar are undeniable; yet it is also true that it has proved somewhat sterile as a basis for applications of linguistics. On the other hand, as we have seen in this chapter, systemic linguistics has shown itself to be eminently suitable for application to the areas of stylistics, language learning and teaching, and artificial intelligence. And there are yet other individual applications which have not been discussed because of lack of space: for instance, Rochester and Martin's (1979) study of the language of schizophrenics.

Some reasons for the greater usefulness of systemic linguistics as compared with transformational grammar will be suggested in Chapter 10, in which we attempt an overview of the characteristics of systemic approaches to language.

10. Conclusion: some salient features of systemic models

10.1 A framework for the comparison of models

In this final chapter, an attempt will be made to bring together the various strands of discussion in the preceding chapters, and to highlight some of the ways in which systemic linguistics resembles, and differs from, the transformational generative models which, though currently under attack, have been so enormously influential.

As a starting point for discussion, we shall take the stimulating paper by Moravcsik (1980), in which dimensions of similarity and difference between linguistic metatheories are proposed. Although Moravcsik's paper is concerned specifically with metatheories of syntax, much of what she says has much wider applicability to linguistic metatheories in general.

Moravcsik claims that similarities and differences between approaches can reside in any of three areas: the range of facts to be accounted for, the goals which descriptions of these facts are supposed to achieve, and the means by which these goals may be reached. She then goes on to state ways in which she assumes all syntactic metatheories to be alike. As far as the range of syntactic facts to be accounted for is concerned, Moravcsik (p.6) suggests that all metatheories will need to give an account of '(a) the MEMBERSHIP of the set of meaningful units of sound form that linguistic utterances consist of and (b) the TEMPORAL ORDER of these units within utterances'. It is less easy to propose types of fact which all metatheories of semantics or phonology might agree on: perhaps sense relations, ambiguity, and the ways in which sentence meanings are derived from lexemic and constructional meanings, might qualify for semantics; segmental contrasts and phonotactic constraints might be suggested for phonology. As far as goals are concerned, Moravcsik assumes (p.6) of all metatheories '(a) that they make assertions that are TRUE; (b) that they make assertions that COULD BE FALSE; (c) that they provide GENERALIZATIONS from which such individual assertions follow'. Although she implies that syntactic metatheories also agree on some of the means to be employed, she does not propose any specific common features.

Syntactic metatheories may differ in the range of facts to be accounted for, in various ways. Moravcsik suggests the following list:

(i) the size of constituents whose membership and order are to be defined (clauses, phrases, words, etc.);

(ii) the size of the domain within which co-occurrence and order are to be characterized (whole text, sentence, clause, phrase, word, etc.);

(iii) the size and type of utterance sets to be described (classes of languages, whole individual languages, dialects, styles, arbitrary fragments, etc.);

(iv) the nature of the linguistic utterances to be investigated (degree of idealization, competence theories versus performance theories, and so on);

(v) whether any facts other than co-occurrence and order are to be accounted for (surface/deep patterning, how far meaning considerations enter into the syntax, whether stress and intonation are included as part of the syntax, etc.);

(vi) whether any account is taken of psycholinguistic evidence, such as evidence from production, reception, judgments, etc.

Moravcsik also recognizes a number of ways in which syntactic meta-theories may differ in their goals:

(i) whether the theory is to predict all and only the grammatical sentences of a language, or all, but not necessarily only the grammatical ones;

(ii) whether maximal generality is demanded;

(iii) whether every descriptive statement must be true to fact, or just the overall description (for instance, whether 'wrong' underlying orders of elements, or inclusion and later deletion of elements not appearing in the final surface structure, are permitted);

(iv) whether any additional goals are assumed (such as simplicity, pedagogical usefulness, or applicability to translation).

According to Moravcsik, syntactic metatheories differ most in the means by which their goals are achieved. She again recognizes several types of difference:

(i) in what types of statement are permitted (for instance, are purely 'abstract' grammatical relations involved, or are syntactic patterns explained in terms of semantic/pragmatic, or phonetic, relations? is there multiple classification of items, for example functionally as well as categorically?);

(ii) in how the rules are to be used (to analyse, to generate, or both? optionally as well as obligatorily? in one direction or both?);

(iii) whether the stipulations above are to apply to all statements, or just to subtypes of statement or sub-classes of languages (are the rules universal?).

Moravcsik also points out that we usually want to know, not only that two metatheories differ, but also which is the better one. As she observes, evaluation is necessary only if the metatheories are distinct (that is, not merely notational variants) and incompatible: compatible metatheories may be equally valid, and can even be merged. Moravcsik proposes two broad types of criterion for evaluation: empirical adequacy, and what she terms external adequacy, instrumental validity, or fruitfulness. Empirical adequacy is clearly primary: a metatheory that accounts for all and only the true facts is better than one which does not. In terms of external adequacy, we may first ask how the syntactic metatheory fits in with metatheories of other kinds: concerned with other levels of language, other (for instance, functional) aspects of language, other symbolic systems (gestural codes, and so on), other social institutions, other instruments of action, other goal-directed activities, and the like. If language is an instrument, or a goal-directed activity, then an account which characterizes language in such terms is better than one which does not. Secondly, we may ask how useful the metatheory is, for example in language teaching, language planning, or translation.

10.2 Features of systemic metatheories

10.2.1 Systemic linguistics and Moravcsik's common properties of metatheories

Let us first consider whether the principles and practice of systemic linguistics satisfy the assumptions made by Moravcsik about properties which all metatheories (of syntax, at least) share. There can be little doubt that all systemicists would wish to account for the membership of the sets of units which enter into syntactic constructions, and for the ordering of such units. Halliday's early (Scale and Category) work was concerned principally with such matters, and Hudson's models still pay a great deal of attention to them. In Halliday's later work, however, the syntagmatic aspects of formal patterning have been played down at the expense of the paradigmatic aspects: this point will be taken up again later.

Turning now to Moravcsik's common goals, it is obvious that systemic linguists are concerned to produce descriptions which are true although, as we shall see later, some systemicists would not subscribe to the view that there is only one true description of any given phenomenon. It is also clear that in systemic linguistics types of statement are made which could be false: for instance, if we were to claim that the feature specification of a clause could include both [interrogative] and [+ question tag], or both [imperative] and [modalized], then we should be making a false statement, since interrogative clauses cannot (in Standard English English) take question tags, and imperative clauses cannot be modalized. However, it is not at all obvious that all statements made by systemicists in their grammars are falsifiable. It is possible to falsify a claim only if that claim is expressed in explicit, unambiguous terms. As was pointed out in Chapter 5, many of the categories which are central to Halliday's functional models of language (such as field, tenor, mode; ideational, interpersonal and textual components; semantics; semiotic; lexicogrammar) are by no means explicitly defined, and no truly reliable sets of recognition criteria are available. In the absence of such criteria, many of the statements made by Halliday and those associated with his models remain, in principle, unfalsifiable.

10.2.2 The range of facts which systemic grammars are intended to account for

Let us now consider in more detail the range of facts which systemically oriented grammars of varying complexions are meant to account for, taking Moravcsik's dimensions of difference as our guide, and comparing with transformational generative grammars wherever possible.

Most theoretical approaches to language have confined themselves to the sentence as the domain for investigation of co-occurrence and sequencing phenomena involving syntactic units. This is also true of certain systemic models, such as Halliday's Scale and Category grammar and the grammars of Hudson and Fawcett. However, as we saw in Section 7.4, there has recently been much interest, on the part of systemic linguists, in the structure of much larger stretches of language. Analysts differ as to whether they wish to extend the syntax upwards, at least to the rank of exchange in discourse structure, as suggested by Berry, or to recognize a separate level of discourse patterning, with unmarked correspondences, but not necessarily one-to-one relations, with syntactic units, as in the Sinclair and Coulthard model. There is some interest nowadays among transformational linguists in certain aspects of inter-sentential relations (such as anaphora, which can operate within or between sentences), but there has been nothing like the effort to build a coherent theory of discourse which has been the concern of discourse analysts inspired by Hallidayan models. This can truly be said to represent one of the major, and continuing, achievements of systemic approaches to language.

With regard to the size and nature of the utterance sets under description, systemic linguistics, following in the tradition of its Firthian origins, has placed a good deal of emphasis on the description of sublanguages of various kinds, and has paid rather little attention to larger-scale problems such as the typological classification of sets of languages. Firth's concept of 'restricted language' (see Chapter 1) was taken up in the early work of Halliday and of Gregory on register, which in turn became one component of Halliday's later sociosemiotic approach to language (see Chapter 4). Systemic linguists have also paid considerable attention to the study of individual texts, as linguistic objects in their own right, and as exemplars of particular registers. Far less attention has been paid to matters of dialect, although the relationship between social dialect and code is important in, for example, the work of Hasan. In all these respects, the Hallidayan mainstream of systemic linguistics contrasts with transformational linguistics, which has paid scant attention to varieties of language, preferring to study 'an ideal speaker–listener, in a completely homogeneous speech-community' (Chomsky, 1965, p.3) in the first instance at least, and placing considerable importance on the ultimate isolation of those properties which define the whole set of possible human languages.

We come now to the question of the nature of the linguistic data for which descriptions are to be provided, and in particular to the problem of how much idealization is to be tolerated. We have seen that Halliday favours an 'inter-organism' perspective on language, regarding language as behaviour, rather than an 'intra-organism' view, which treats language as a form of knowledge. Halliday's position is that although some degree of idealization is inevitable, when working within a sociologically oriented, inter-organism approach we must accept less idealization than can be tolerated in an intra-organism perspective.

> We have, in fact, to 'come closer to what is actually said'; partly because the solutions to problems may depend on studying what is actually said, but also because even when this is not the case the features that are behaviourally relevant may be just those that the idealizing process most readily irons out. (Halliday, 1971a, p.171 = 1973a, p.54)

There will always be *idealization* in any study of language, or indeed in any systematic inquiry. The point is here that we need to reduce the level of idealization, to make it as low as possible, in order that we can understand the processes of interaction [. . .] We have to impose as

low a degree of idealization on the facts as is compatible with a systematic inquiry. (Parret, 1974, p.99 = Halliday, 1978, p.52)

This area is, of course, closely linked with the Saussurean distinction
between *langue* and *parole*, and the related, though not equivalent, distinction made by Chomsky between *competence* and *performance*. Halliday's
view is that there is no need, in an inter-organism model, for clear-cut
distinctions of this kind. Rather, 'performance' is seen as the actualization
of the speaker or writer's meaning potential: what the speaker 'does'
linguistically (that is, what he 'means', in Halliday's active sense of the
word) is then related to what he 'can do' linguistically (that is, what he
'can mean'). This view is clearly expressed in the following passage, in which
Halliday is comparing meaning potential with Chomskyan competence:

The two are somewhat different. Meaning potential is defined not in
terms of the mind but in terms of the culture; not as what the speaker
knows, but as what he can do — in the special sense of what he can do
linguistically (what he 'can mean', as we have expressed it). The distinction is important because 'can do' is of the same order of abstraction as
'does'; the two are related simply as potential to actualized potential,
and can be used to illuminate each other. But 'knows' is distinct and
clearly insulated from 'does'; the relation between the two is complex
and oblique, and leads to the quest for a 'theory of performance' to
explain the 'does'. (Halliday, 1971a, pp.169-70 = 1973a, pp.52-3)

And again:

. . . in an inter-organism perspective there is no place for the dichotomy
of competence and performance, opposing what the speaker knows to
what he does. There is no need to bring in the question of what the
speaker knows; the background to what he does is what he could do —
a potential, which is objective, not a competence, which is subjective.
(Parret, 1974, p.85 = Halliday, 1978, p.38)

This approach, Halliday claims, is necessary within an inter-organism
perspective because:

If we insist on drawing a boundary between what [the speaker] does
and what he knows, we cannot explain what he does; what he does will
appear merely as a random selection from within what he knows.
(Halliday, 1971a, p.184 = 1973a, p.67)

Elsewhere, Halliday suggests that the knowledge of the speaker is not
totally irrelevant, but must be reinterpreted as 'what he knows about how
to use the language':

We do not simply 'know' our mother tongue as an abstract system of
vocal signals, or as if it was some sort of a grammar book with a dictionary
attached. We know it in the sense of knowing how to use it; we know
how to communicate with other people, how to choose forms of language that are appropriate to the type of situation we find ourselves in,

and so on. All this can be expressed as 'know how to'; as a form of knowledge: we know how to behave linguistically. (Halliday, 1974, p.9 = 1978, p.13)

In view of this, it might be expected that Halliday would recognize a close relationship between his approach and Hymes' (1971) notion of *communicative competence*. However, Halliday regards Hymes' theory as a 'theory of performance', and as an essentially intra-organism approach:

Hymes is taking the intra-organism ticket to what is actually an inter-organism destination; he is doing 'psycho-sociolinguistics', if you like. There's no reason why he shouldn't; but I find it an unnecessary complication. (Parret, 1974, p.85 = Halliday, 1978, p.38)

It seems clear, however, that the difference between the two approaches is one of viewpoint rather than one of substance. Indeed, Halliday himself says of the inter- and intra-organism approaches that

the two are, to an extent, different ways of looking at the same thing; but the former, 'inter-organism' perspective has different implications from the latter, 'intra-organism' one. (Halliday, 1973b, p.346 = 1973a, p.25)

Let us turn now to Moravcsik's final category of differences in the facts which metatheories are set up to account for: what facts, other than those taken as basic to all approaches, is the metatheory meant to account for, and what kinds of phenomenon are considered relevant to an explanation of those facts. A number of characteristics of at least some models of systemic linguistics are relevant here: the stipulation that paradigmatic as well as syntagmatic relations are to be explicitly accounted for; the relevance of meaning and phonological relations for an explanation of formal patterning; and the requirement that the theory should account, not only for relationships within language, but also for relationships between language and context. The question of psycholinguistic validation, raised by Moravcsik under this head, is also relevant to some systemic models. Each of these aspects will be examined in turn.

As was noted earlier, Halliday's early work, culminating in the Scale and Category model presented in 'Categories of the theory of grammar' (Halliday, 1961), was concerned largely with the kinds of syntagmatic patterning, at the level of form, which Moravcsik regards as fundamental facts for any syntactic metatheory to explain. Even in the early work, however, there is a paradigmatic component to the model, represented by the category of system, and this gradually assumed ever greater importance, so that by the mid-1960s Halliday was claiming that paradigmatic relations are primary, syntagmatic relations being derived from them by the operation of realization rules (see Section 3.3). In Halliday's more recent work, paradigmatic relations are still paramount: indeed, as Berry has observed, syntagmatic relations are virtually ignored, and this is detrimental to the theory, since such relations could provide much-needed criteria for some of Halliday's inexplicit categories (see Section 5.7). It is in the important role allocated to paradigmatic relations that one of the main differences between systemic grammars and transformational grammars lies. In a transformational grammar, there is no place for explicit statements of what could have been selected at a given point in place of what was actually selected: such choices must be inferred from a comparison of the structural trees for sentences related in various ways. An explicit representation of paradigmatic relations, in the form of system networks, has a number of advantages. Firstly, if systemic contrasts can be equated with (subconscious) choices made by the speaker (and this is a big assumption, not yet sufficiently discussed by systemic linguists), then it is likely that a systemic grammar will offer better possibilities as a model of language processing than a grammar which concentrates almost exclusively on syntagmatic relations. Secondly, a systemic model lends itself naturally to those applications of linguistics, such as stylistics, in which we are concerned with what a speaker or writer actually chooses to say or write, against the background of what could have been chosen but was not.

It will be remembered that the developments in Halliday's theory in the mid-1960s involved not only an increased emphasis on paradigmatic relations within language, but also the claim that systems representing such relations accounted for those aspects of the grammar which were 'closest to' the semantics (see Section 3.3). That is, the criteria for setting up systems are to be basically semantic, with the implication that any syntactic phenomena with no clear semantic import may well not be included. Halliday himself suspects that there may be very few syntactic distinctions which do not carry any meaning:

> . . . we must admit theoretically [. . .] that there is free variation in the grammatical system, with one meaning realized by two or more forms. But then I would add that we should always be suspicious when we find this, because it usually turns out that the distinction in the lexicogrammatical system does in fact express a more delicate distinction in the semantic system that we haven't yet got round to. In other words, let us not go so far as to deny free variation, but let us be highly suspicious of any actual instances of it, because very often it turns out that there is a more subtle or more 'delicate' distinction in the semantic system which is being expressed in this way. (Parret, 1974, p.91 = Halliday, 1978, p.44)

Nevertheless, in practice certain types of syntactic distinction which do not appear to correlate directly with meaning are indeed ignored by Halliday: for instance, we saw in Section 8.2.2. that his account of transitivity does not deal with differences in the complementation patterns of verbs which are closely related semantically. The part played by the semantics is even greater in Fawcett's grammars, in which the criteria for postulating syntactic distinctions are explicitly semantic (see Section 6.2). On the other hand, Hudson's grammars have never been restricted in this way, and have taken into account those syntactic phenomena, such as complementation, which are neglected by Halliday and Fawcett (see Section 6.3).

As became apparent in Section 7.3.3, certain aspects of phonological patterning are also relevant to the content of Halliday's formal networks in the 1963-70 period, in that those distinctions which are carried by intonational patterns (these patterns themselves being specified at the phonological level) rather than by syntactic patterns are nevertheless regarded as grammatical.

It was noted earlier that Hallidayan linguistics has placed considerable emphasis on the description of sublanguages, especially registers. As we saw in Chapter 4, the description of register is not regarded by Halliday as some kind of secondary activity, tacked on to the proper business of describing 'English', or whatever other language, as a whole, or solving syntactic problems arising from some variety-neutral, context-independent form of language. For Halliday, there is no variety-neutral form of language, and register is central to linguistic description. This viewpoint is particularly clear in Halliday's sociosemantic model, in which the objects to be described are the meaning potentials accessible in particular contexts and settings predicted as important by some social theory: in other words, a sociosemantic description is a description of a register. Moreover, Halliday's theory makes predictions about the relationship between social context and linguistic choice: the contextual parameters of field, tenor and mode are claimed to activate choices in the ideational, interpersonal and textual components respectively (see Section 4.3.4). Hallidayan systemic linguistics, then, has taken upon itself the task of accounting for a set of facts ignored by most, if not all, other theories: the correlations between features of social contexts and features of the linguistic output in such contexts. Indeed, Berry's view (personal communication) is that the attempt to explain these facts is the main aim of systemic functional grammar. Unfortunately, as was pointed out in Section 5.7, Halliday's own proposals rest on unsystematic, almost anecdotal observations on single texts. Furthermore, we have seen that the explanations Halliday advances for his putative facts are fraught with difficulties of defining the categories, both of social contextual variation and of the functional organization of the linguistic system. Nevertheless, the attempt to provide explanations in this neglected area is to be welcomed, and it is to be hoped that in the near future the fundamental difficulties involved will be overcome.

The question of possible psycholinguistic validation of theoretical proposals has not been raised by Halliday: indeed, his comments about psycholinguistic approaches to language are usually somewhat negative, giving the impression that he regards such approaches as valid, and as complementary to his own sociological viewpoint, but that he has no strong personal interest in what they may have to offer. Such is not the case, however, with Fawcett and Hudson, both of whom have cited psychological plausibility as an important criterion for linguistic models. Although neither linguist appears to have made use of facts about linguistic processing in the formulation of his model, it seems fair to assume that both would in principle be happy to do so. Systemic linguists have not in general relied much on judgments of grammaticality, acceptability and the like, by native speaker informants: but see the author's own work on politeness in directives, reviewed in Section 8.2.6.

10.2.3 The range of goals for systemic linguistics

Moravcsik distinguishes between metatheories which stipulate that all and only the grammatical sentences of a language must be predicted, and those which aim to predict all such sentences, but not necessarily only these. It is rather difficult to apply this criterion to Hallidayan linguistics, for two reasons. Firstly, Halliday has himself explicitly stated that systemic linguists 'don't try to draw a distinction between what is grammatical and what is acceptable' (Parret, 1974, p.85 = Halliday, 1978, p.38). Certainly Halliday's insistence on a low degree of idealization means that a much wider range of sentences is accepted than in, for example, many transformational accounts: one only has to look at, for instance, the examples discussed in Halliday's (1967c) account of thematic patterns in English to realize this. Secondly, what Halliday's recent theories are trying to predict is not so much the grammaticality/acceptability of sentences, but rather what types of meaning choice are available in particular types of social context.

Turning now to Moravcsik's suggestion that metatheories differ in the degree of generality they demand, we may say that although systemic linguists, like their non-systemic colleagues, aim to make a high number of significant generalizations, such generalizations are not made at the expense of pointing out ways in which items may differ. Very often, a systemic account of some particular set of patterns will say 'items A and B are alike in respect of X and Y, but differ in respect of Z'. It is here that the Hallidayan concept of delicacy, as applied to both structure and system, comes into its own. In 10.1, for example, 'the' and 'little' are alike in that at primary delicacy they are both modifiers of the head noun 'boy'; however, they differ at secondary delicacy, 'the' representing the d element, and 'little' the e element, of nominal group structure.

10.1 The little boy fell down.

10.1 and 10.2 are alike, systemically, in that both have chosen the feature [indicative] from the mood network; but they differ in that, more delicately, 10.1 is [declarative] whereas 10.2 is [interrogative].

10.2 Did the little boy fall down?

Sentences may also be partly alike and partly different in the combinations of systemic features they choose from different networks. For instance, the clause in 10.3 has a causative process and unmarked theme; that in 10.4 also has a causative process, but has marked (Complement) theme; 10.5 has unmarked theme, but the process is non-causative, in fact an event rather than an action.

10.3 John smashed the vase.
10.4 The vase John smashed (not the decanter).
10.5 John died.

These similarities and differences are reflected in the functions attached to clause constituents in the process of realization. 'John' in 10.3 is Agent, a Modal element (that is, one of the two elements whose position indicates declarative mood, the other being the finite verb), and Theme; in 10.4 'John' is Agent and Modal element but not Theme; and in 10.5 'John' is Modal element and Theme but not Agent.

As Moravcsik points out, metatheories may also differ in the extent to which they insist on the truth-to-fact requirement. Some metatheories allow individual statements not to correspond to the facts of the structures being generated: for instance, the Standard Theory of transformational generative grammar allows, at intermediate stages in the derivation of a sentence, underlying orders of elements which are different from those in the surface string to be generated, and also permits the postulation of elements which are deleted before the final structure is formed. In Hudson's systemic models of syntax, no such 'wrong' underlying orders or deletion operations are permitted, as we saw in Section 6.3. In Halliday's systemic functional grammar not all of the inherent roles associated with a process will necessarily be actualized in the surface structure: for instance an 'agentless passive' still has an underlying Agent in the functional structure, even though this functional role has no overt expression. However, if we regard the functional roles as semantic rather than syntactic we may still retain the strict truth-to-fact requirement for the syntax: presumably Hudson would not deny the possibility of underlying but unexpressed roles either.

As Moravcsik observes, metatheories may differ in the goals they set themselves, additionally to those common to all metatheories. In transformational generative grammar, simplicity and elegance have enjoyed a high priority, although simplicity has proved difficult to measure. These are also stated as goals in Hudson's early (1971) systemic theory, and there is no reason to believe that they have been abandoned in his later work. For Halliday, however, such matters have a low priority. For instance, he is quite content to account for a particular phenomenon at two ranks of the grammar if this results in a grammar which can capture various aspects of the patterning involved: examples would be the treatment of tense and voice at both clause and (verbal) group ranks. As was mentioned earlier, psychological plausibility is also of rather low priority for Halliday, though not for Hudson or Fawcett. Much higher on Halliday's list of priorities is the power of the theory to explain how people actually use language in social contexts: how it accounts for 'language and social man'.

10.2.4 The range of means for achieving the goals of systemic linguistics

Moravcsik's discussion of the means available for satisfying the goals of syntactic metatheories points out that some metatheories employ purely abstract grammatical relations, while others explain syntactic patterns in terms of semantic/pragmatic, or even phonetic, relations. Also, some metatheories have only one (for instance categorical) type of classification, while others have multiple classification (for example, categorical and functional). Halliday's systemic grammars certainly embody some purely abstract relations, such as the hierarchical arrangement of units on a rank scale, and the concept of the closed system. However, we have seen that Halliday, and also Fawcett and Berry, always relate the syntax of a language ultimately to its role in conveying meaning, so that syntactic patterning is explained in semantic terms. The grammars of Halliday, Fawcett and Berry are clearly multi-classification grammars, in that elements of grammatical structure have both a categorical classification (for example, as a nominal group) and one or more functional classifications (for instance, as Subject, Agent, Theme, and so on). Hudson's grammars are far less semantically motivated than Halliday's, and rely chiefly on the purely abstract type of relation (for instance dependency, in daughter dependency grammar). His early grammars relied heavily on functional as well as categorical classification, though the later versions have minimized the role of functions. We shall return to the importance of the functional orientation of systemic models when we come to discuss the usefulness of the models, in Section 10.2.5.

Moravcsik's second point concerning means is that some metatheories use syntactic rules for analysis, some for generation, others for both. Halliday's Scale and Category grammar was essentially analytical, and, by and large, this orientation continues in his work, except for minor forays into generation (see the sets of realization rules in Halliday, 1969a, 1972). The grammars of Fawcett, Hudson and Butler, on the other hand, are generative: like a transformational grammar, they consist of sets of rules which will generate well-formed sentences in as explicit a way as possible. These grammars could, of course, be used for the analysis of text, by specifying the systemic choices made and the realization rules which operate in the construction of the sentences of the text.

Optionality is built into the system networks in the work of Halliday, Fawcett and Berry: for instance, what would be seen in a transformational generative grammar as the optional fronting of, say, a Complement, would be accounted for in a Hallidayan grammar by the choice between unmarked and marked (Complement) theme in the system networks for the clause, and the realization rules would then operate obligatorily to translate whatever choice had been made into the appropriate surface structure. This difference reflects a major difference in the orientation of the two metatheories: for Halliday, the choice of a marked rather than an unmarked theme is just as important, just as meaningful, as the choice between, say, a declarative and an imperative clause, or between kinds of process; in a transformational grammar, on the other hand, matters falling under Halliday's textual component tend to be regarded as stylistic options, less central to the language than phenomena involving ideational content or 'sentence type'. We saw in Section 6.3 that Hudson's work has been much closer than Halliday's to the aims and assumptions of transformational grammar. In accordance with this general orientation, Hudson does make use of optional realization rules in some of his grammars: for instance, in his daughter dependency grammar of English (Hudson, 1976, p.191) there is a rule which optionally introduces the 'it' of extraposed clauses such as 10.6, though in an earlier account (Hudson, 1974a, p.23) extraposition is dealt with by means of systemic choice.

10.6 It's a pity you couldn't come.

There is a second, and rather different, kind of optionality which deserves mention at this point. It was observed earlier that Halliday's grammars have tended to be analytical rather than generative. He has pointed out that the analyst has a choice of how delicately to describe any phenomenon he is interested in: both systemic options and structural patterns are variable in delicacy (see Section 10.2.3), and a degree of detail which may be appropriate for one descriptive aim may be too great, or too small, for another task:

... the scale of delicacy [...] has proved of value in textual analysis because it provides a variable cut-off point for description: the analyst can go as far as he wishes for his own purpose in depth of detail and then stop. (Halliday, 1964a, p.16 = Halliday & Martin, 1981, p.22)

We come now to the question of whether the conditions on rules discussed above are to be regarded as universally valid. Firth, as we saw in Chapter 1, did not consider himself to be in the business of postulating universals of human language. Halliday, too, has always maintained a healthily empirical stand on the issue of universality, which he relates to the overall orientation of his views:

> The psychologist, concerned primarily with human constraints, or at least not culturally determined variables, may seek to make all languages look alike; the sociologist, concerned with the diversity of human cultures, is predisposed for languages to look different. Neither is wrong; all languages are alike and all languages are different. But this is not a simple dichotomy. We cannot simply say that all languages are alike underneath and different on the surface, and the work of Whorf is a useful reminder here. A grammar is not thereby less perspicuous because it embodies an empirical attitude towards the concrete universals of description. (Halliday, 1967e, pp.27-8)

Elsewhere, Halliday associates himself with a 'pseudo-Whorfian' relativist position, when he asserts that 'language lends structure to his [the speaker or writer's] experience and helps to determine his way of looking at things' (Halliday, 1971b, p.333 = 1973a, p.106). Halliday's main criticism of Whorf is that his views do not give enough weight to the social structure:

> . . . I would accept Bernstein's modification of Whorf. The weakness in Whorf's hypothesis seems to be that it has no place for the social structure; it is a hypothesis about language, culture and the individual. I think Bernstein is right in saying that the relation between language and culture is mediated by the social structure. So I would say that in the last analysis language does mirror the world, but it does so only very indirectly, through the mediation of experience which is itself mediated by the social structure. (Parret, 1974, p.118)

Halliday believes in the universality of certain linguistic categories:

> . . . general linguistic theory is a theory of formal universals; there is no dispute about the existence of such universals, however difficult it may be to characterize them at a suitably abstract level. (Parret, 1974, p. 118)

Within the Scale and Category framework, the basic categories of the model, and presumably the scales which linked them, were viewed as universals, but specific descriptive categories (such as clause, word, noun, syllable) were not:

> With these four basic categories of unit, structure, system and class it is possible to describe the grammar of all languages. What is significant here is that in order to find anything 'universal' in grammar – common, that is, to the grammar of all languages – we have to go to the very high level of abstraction represented by these categories. Only such *theoretical* categories can be treated as universal. The *descriptive* categories,

those used to talk about the grammar of any particular language, which as we have said are instances of these theoretical categories, are *not* universal and cannot be assumed to be found in all languages. Indeed, they must be redefined for each language. (Halliday, McIntosh & Strevens, 1964, p.31, original emphasis)

Within the later systemic functional model, the extralinguistic functions which underlie the functional components are regarded as universal:

By a functional theory of language I mean one which attempts to explain linguistic structure, and linguistic phenomena, by reference to the notion that language plays a certain part in our lives; that it is required to serve certain universal types of demand. (Halliday, 1971b, p.331 = 1973a, p.104)

Halliday (see Parret, 1974, p.106) also regards the functional organization of the linguistic system itself as a characteristic of all human languages, and suggests that the realization of choices in the logical component by means of recursive structures (see Section 5.4) may also be a universal. Furthermore, he claims that the developmental functions postulated for early child language (instrumental, regulatory, interactional, personal, heuristic, imaginative, representational — see Section 4.4.3) are 'universals of human culture' (Halliday, 1975a, p.33).

Hudson, as we saw in Section 6.3, has always seen his own versions of systemic theory as competing with transformational generative grammars, as ways of achieving quite similar aims. His (1971) *English Complex Sentences* model aims to produce a framework within which any natural language can be described, and defines abstract formal categories, such as 'feature' and 'function', which must appear in the grammar of any language. Hudson adds that it may be possible, at a later stage, to specify certain descriptive categories, such as noun, or clause, as substantive universals. In discussing his later, daughter dependency model, Hudson (1976, p.179) says that he would 'be both surprised and disappointed if daughter-dependency grammar were a worse framework for the search for universals than transformational grammar has been'.

Fawcett (1980, p.107) suggests that certain options at the least delicate ends of major networks such as those for mood (reinterpreted by him as an illocutionary force network) may be universal, and that 'it may further be possible to establish a set of semantic universal "primes" in which the specification of any one feature may be defined, together with a set of principles for combining them which will apply to all languages'.

10.2.5 Evaluation of metatheories

Moravcsik's (1980, pp.16-18) discussion of the means available for the evaluation of competing metatheories centres around two types of adequacy, empirical and instrumental. We shall consider each of these in relation to the systemic frameworks discussed in this book.

It is self-evident that a metatheory which leads to statements which truly describe the facts of a language is preferable to one which does not. However, metatheories can only be legitimately compared for such empirical adequacy if they are trying to account for the same range of facts, The discussion in Section 10.2.2 demonstrated that many versions of systemic theory, especially the later ones of Halliday and Berry, are trying to account for a rather different range of facts from those regarded as central by, say, a transformational generative grammarian. A systemic linguist could claim that according to his view of the 'facts', transformational grammars are not empirically adequate, since they do not account for (and are indeed not set up to account for) the relations between language and context: on the other hand, a transformational grammarian could equally claim that a Hallidayan systemic grammar is empirically inadequate because it does not account for many of the syntactic phenomena (such as complementation) regarded as central by many transformational linguists. The two metatheories have different aims. Even the stratificational approach of Lamb and his colleagues, which shares many of the premises of a Hallidayan approach, is not strictly comparable in its aims:

> For Lamb, of course, the whole point is to find out what it is the speaker has in his head [...] I am trying to characterize human interaction ... (Parret, 1974, p.98 = Halliday, 1978, p.51)

Furthermore, Halliday has never subscribed to the 'God's truth' view which admits only one 'correct' description towards which we should all aspire:

> Language may be described for a wide range of purposes [...] The question is: do these various aims presuppose different ways of using the same description, or are they best served by descriptions of different kinds? Is there one single 'best description' of a language, or are there various possible 'best descriptions' according to the purpose in view? (Halliday, 1964a, pp.11-12)

Halliday's own answer is to favour the 'horses for courses' view:

> ... I would defend the view that different coexisting models in linguistics may best be regarded as appropriate to different aims, rather than as competing contenders for the same goal. (Halliday, 1964a, p.13)

It is, then, naive and unfair to compare Hallidayan linguistics, in terms of empirical adequacy, with transformational grammar or other metatheories, unless we can develop some measure of adequacy with respect to the particular range of facts which each metatheory sets out to account for. It is, however, reasonable to compare Hudson's grammars with transformational grammars (as Hudson himself does), since the two metatheories set out to explain more or less the same range of facts (see Section 6.3).

Turning now to Moravcsik's 'external' or 'instrumental' adequacy, we have two main points to consider: the extent to which metatheories of grammar fit in with, and shed light on, metatheories of other types of linguistic and non-linguistic patterning; and the extent to which the descriptions generated by the metatheories prove useful in terms of applications.

There are certainly important and illuminating relationships between

systemic models of syntax/semantics and other types of linguistic patterning, and also the patterning of other semiotic systems. At least five kinds
of relationship can be recognized.

Firstly, the models of Halliday and Berry, in particular, show that the
apparatus of system and structure is applicable to phonology as well as
to the grammar. The work of the present author (Butler, 1982, in press)
demonstrates that a model involving systems, structures and realization
rules can be generalized to cover discoursal and semantic patterning, as
well as syntax and phonology. It seems likely that such a model might also
be appropriate for certain other codes, such as gesture. It could be objected
by transformational linguists that an apparatus which is so general in its
scope tells us little about what uniquely characterizes human language, and
still less about what is special to syntactic patterning. However, it is probably fair to say that Halliday is less interested in the distinctiveness of
language as a construct than in the special contribution it makes to communication in social situations.

Secondly, there is a close integration, in most systemic models,
between structural and functional types of pattern. As we have seen,
Halliday claims that the functions which language is called upon to serve
are reflected in the organization of the language system itself, and that
function is the ultimate basis for structure. The functional orientation of
Halliday's models is seen at a macro-level in the functional components
hypothesis (see Section 3.4), and at a micro-level in the microfunctions, or
functional roles, such as Agent and Affected, Theme and Rheme, which
are derived from the macrofunctional strands and which, during the
realization process, are conflated into bundles corresponding to elements
of the surface grammatical structure.

Thirdly, in Halliday's later work in particular, there is a close connection
between the linguistic system and other semiotic systems: language is
viewed as one of many realizations of the social semiotic, including art
forms, religious institutions, and so on.

Fourthly, the view of language as one form of realization of a behaviour
potential (derived ultimately from Malinowski's concept of language as a
'mode of action') brings into focus the relationship between language and
other types of social action. This is particularly obvious in Halliday's sociosemantic model, in which-networks were drawn for 'linguistic behavioural'
options, the meanings of which could, in some cases such as threats,
equally well be realized by other codes.

Fifthly, there is considerable emphasis, especially in the later work of
Halliday, on language as a type of goal-directed action. The process of text
creation is seen as a dynamic activity, sensitive to feedback from the interplay of meaning with the social contextual parameters of field, tenor and
mode.

Finally, we turn to Moravcsik's criterion of usefulness. Here, there can
be little doubt that systemic linguistics scores heavily over transformational
and other non-systemic approaches. As was demonstrated in Chapter 9,
systemic models have been used as the basis for much stimulating and valuable work in stylistics, educational linguistics and artificial intelligence.
There seem to be four fundamental aspects of systemic approaches which
are at the root of their applicability.

Firstly, the work of most systemic linguists pays a great deal of attention to the text as a fundamental linguistic unit. The concept of a text as an actualization of selections from a range of available options, in response to contextual factors, has proved insightful in stylistic studies based on the systemic functional model. Relations between texts and their contexts of production were also central to the construction of language teaching materials which took account of the important part played by language in the social life of man. Work in the field of artificial intelligence has also been concerned with the fitting of language to the context in which it is produced. Winograd's and Davey's programs admittedly operate within a rather narrow context, but the Penman project of Mann and Matthiessen is more ambitious in its scope.

Related to the emphasis on text as an actualization of choices in meaning is the fundamentally paradigmatic orientation of systemic models. We have seen that the style of literary texts has proved amenable to description in terms of systemic choice. The interest and value of Halliday's approach to child language acquisition also depends crucially on the notion of expansion in the range of options available to the child. And in work on artificial intelligence it has been found that the construction of programs for the generation and understanding of discourse is simplified if all possible sources of surface variation are specified in the system networks of the grammar.

Systemic choice has always been regarded by Halliday as meaningful choice: indeed, we have seen that he now regards the core of the linguistic system as itself being a set of options in meaning. This has again had an important effect on the applicability of systemic models. The creation of a text, literary or otherwise, is essentially a process of putting meanings into words, and this offers a way into stylistic analysis. Perhaps the most novel aspect of Halliday's theorizing about child language acquisition is the claim that learning language is 'learning how to mean', the progressive mastery of a semantic potential and of the means for translating meanings into forms. Workers in artificial intelligence have also commented favourably on the emphasis on meaning in systemic models, though we have seen that Davey's work suggests that it is not necessary to adopt a model in which the grammar is effectively a 'semantic syntax'.

Finally, it would seem that the functional basis of systemic grammars has been an important factor in their applicability. We have seen that Hallidayan grammars are functional in three related senses: they build in Malinowski's view that language is a mode of social action; they claim that the grammar is itself internally organised in terms of ideational, inter-personal and textual functional components; and they include, as fundamental categories, functional roles or microfunctions, such as Actor, Theme, and so on, which derive from the functional components. This functional orientation has proved insightful in stylistics, where literary effects can sometimes be shown to be localized in particular functional areas. Halliday's approach to language learning and teaching is also based on the claim that expansion of the learner's resources is essentially the development of a functional potential. The explicit labelling of micro-functions has been an asset in the construction of computer programs to simulate discourse production and understanding.

It is significant that all four of the properties discussed above are major areas of difference between systemic and transformational models. Trans-formational linguists have been largely concerned with sentences rather than with texts (though there has been some important work on anaphora). There has been little concern with text/context relations: transformationalist approaches to pragmatics have been concerned mainly with utterance-bound phenomena. Furthermore, transformational models have always been essentially syntagmatic in their orientation: certainly there is no such model which gives priority to paradigmatic relations. Transformational grammars are not primarily concerned with how the grammar is organised to convey meaning; neither are they functional grammars in any of the senses listed earlier.

Systemic grammars, then, build into their very foundations a number of properties which distinguish them quite sharply from transformational grammars, and form the basis of their remarkable applicability.

Epilogue: towards the future

There is ample evidence that interest in systemic linguistics is growing, both in Britain and overseas. The international Systemic Workshops which have been organized annually for the last decade attract an increasing number of participants, including many whose work has not so far been within the systemic framework, but who feel that the approach has much to offer for their own fields of interest. A considerable number of universities and other institutions of higher education throughout the world now include some systemic linguistics in their teaching and/or research activities.

At the time of writing this book, there is also a welcome flurry of publishing activity in systemic linguistics. Halliday's *Short Introduction to Functional Grammar* (Halliday, 1984b) will no doubt provide further insights into the functional basis of language. Berry is at present working on four books concerned with grammar and context, grammar and meaning, discourse cohesion and coherence, and argumentation in systemic linguistics (Berry, in preparation, a-d). Gregory, together with his student Karen Malcolm, is working on a 'communication linguistics' model based on Halliday's systemic functional grammar (for a preliminary sketch see Gregory, forthcoming). Two volumes of papers from the Ninth International Systemic Workshop are due to appear shortly (Greaves & Benson, in press a and b). A further collection of papers by systemic linguists is also expected soon (Halliday & Fawcett, forthcoming). A special issue of the *Nottingham Linguistic Circular* will be devoted to articles in the field.

What, then, are the directions which systemic linguistics may be expected to follow in the near future? It seems certain that there will be further developments in the analysis of discourse, and in the application of systemic models to stylistics and to work in artificial intelligence. A more penetrating analysis of the relationships between language and social context, developing the work of Hasan and Berry, seems likely. It is to be hoped that side by side with these activities there will be a radical reappraisal of the methodological bases of systemic linguistics, and a determined effort to make more rigorous the categories which are central to this fruitful approach to language.

Bibliography

ABERCROMBIE, D. (1964a) 'A phonetician's view of verse structure', *Linguistics*, no. 6, pp. 5-13. Reprinted in ABERCROMBIE (1965) pp. 6-25.

ABERCROMBIE, D. (1964b) 'Syllable quantity and enclitics in English', in ABERCROMBIE, D., FRY, D.B., MACCARTHY, P.A.D., SCOTT, N.C. & TRIM, J.L.M. (1964) *In Honour of Daniel Jones*, Longman, pp. 216-22. Reprinted in ABERCROMBIE (1965) pp. 26-34.

ABERCROMBIE, D. (1965) *Studies in Phonetics and Linguistics*, Oxford University Press.

ABERCROMBIE, D. (1967) *Elements of General Phonetics*, Edinburgh University Press.

AITKEN, A.J., BAILEY, R.W. & HAMILTON-SMITH, N. (1973) *The Computer and Literary Studies*, Edinburgh University Press.

ALBROW, K.H. (1968) *The Rhythm and Intonation of Spoken English*, Programme in Linguistics and English Teaching Paper 9, Longman.

ALBROW, K.H. (1972) *The English Writing System: Notes towards a Description*. Schools Council Programme in Linguistics and English Teaching Papers, series II, vol. 3, Longman for the Schools Council.

ANDERSON, J. (1969) 'A note on "rank" and "delicacy"', *Journal of Linguistics*, no. 5, pp. 129-35.

AUSTIN, J.L. (1962) *How to Do Things with Words*, Clarendon Press, Oxford.

BAZELL, C.E., CATFORD, J.C. & HALLIDAY, M.A.K. (1966) *In Memory of J.R. Firth*, Longman.

DE BEAUGRANDE, R. & DRESSLER, W. (1981) *Introduction to Text Linguistics*, Longman.

BERNSTEIN, B. (1971) *Class, Codes and Control 1: Theoretical Studies towards a Sociology of Language*, vol. IV of *Primary Socialization, Language and Education*, BERNSTEIN, B., ed., Routledge & Kegan Paul.

BERNSTEIN, B. ed., (1973) *Class, Codes and Control 2: Applied Studies towards a Sociology of Language*, vol. IV of *Primary Socialization, Language and Education*, BERNSTEIN, B., ed., Routledge & Kegan Paul.

BERRY, M. (1975) *Introduction to Systemic Linguistics: 1, Structures and Systems*, Batsford.

BERRY, M. (1977) *Introduction to Systemic Linguistics: 2, Levels and Links*, Batsford.

BERRY, M. (1979) 'A note on Sinclair and Coulthard's classes of acts including a comment on comments', *Nottingham Linguistic Circular*, no. 8, pp. 49-59.

BERRY, M. (1980) 'They're all out of step except our Johnny: a discussion of motivation (or the lack of it) in systemic linguistics', University of Nottingham: mimeo.

BERRY, M. (1981a) 'Polarity, ellipticity, elicitation and propositional development, their relevance to the well-formedness of an exchange', *Nottingham Linguistic Circular*, no. 10, pp. 36-63.

BERRY, M. (1981b) 'Systemic linguistics and discourse analysis: a multi-layered approach to exchange structure', in COULTHARD & MONTGOMERY (1981), pp. 120-45.

BERRY, M. (1982) 'Review of Halliday 1978', *Nottingham Linguistic Circular*, no. 11, pp. 64-94.

BERRY, M. (in preparation a) 'Grammar and Context'.

BERRY, M. (in preparation b) 'Meaning and Context'.

BERRY, M. (in preparation c) 'Coherence and Cohesion in English'. To be published in the series *Studies in Language and Linguistics*, LEECH, G.N. & SHORT, M.H., eds., Longman.

BERRY, M. (in preparation d) 'Argumentation in Systemic Linguistics'.

BERRY-ROGGHE, G.L.M. (1973) 'The computation of collocations and their relevance in lexical studies', in AITKEN *et al.* (1973) pp. 103-12.

BIRK, D. (1972) 'You never speak a dead language', in THORNTON, BIRK & HUDSON (1972) pp. 23-56.

BLOOMFIELD, L. (1933) *Language*, George Allen & Unwin.

BRAINE, M.D.S. (1963) 'The ontogeny of English phrase structure: the first phase', *Language*, no. 39, pp. 1-13.

BRAINE, M.D.S. (1971) 'The acquisition of language in infant and child', in REED, C.E., ed., *The Learning of Language*, Appleton Century Crofts, New York, pp. 7-95.

BRAZIL, D. (1975) *Discourse Intonation*, Discourse Analysis Monographs 1, English Language Research, University of Birmingham.

BRAZIL, D. (1978) *Discourse Intonation II*, Discourse Analysis Monographs 2, English Language Research, University of Birmingham.

BRAZIL, D.C. (1981) 'The place of intonation in a discourse model', in COULTHARD & MONTGOMERY (1981) pp. 146-57.

BRAZIL, D., COULTHARD, M. & JOHNS, C. (1980) *Discourse Intonation and Language Teaching*, Longman.

BRESNAN, J. (1978) 'A realistic transformational grammar', in HALLE, M., BRESNAN, J. & MILLER, G., eds., *Linguistic Theory and Psychological Reality*. MIT Press, Cambridge, Mass., pp. 1-59.

BROWN, G. & YULE, G. (1983) *Discourse Analysis*, Cambridge University Press.

BÜHLER, K. (1934) *Sprachtheorie*, Fischer, Jena.

BURTON, D. (1980) *Dialogue and Discourse*, Routledge & Kegan Paul.

BURTON, D. (1981) 'Analysing spoken discourse', in COULTHARD & MONTGOMERY (1981) pp. 61-81.

BURTON, D. (1982) 'Through glass darkly: through dark glasses', in CARTER (1982a) pp. 195-214.

BUTLER, C.S. (1979) 'Recent developments in systemic linguistics', *Language Teaching and Linguistics: Abstracts*, no. 12, pp. 71-89.

BUTLER, C.S. (1981) 'Review of Monaghan 1979', *Anglia*, no. 99, pp. 408-12.

BUTLER, C.S. (1982) *The Directive Function of the English Modals*, Ph. D. Thesis, University of Nottingham.

BUTLER, C.S. (forthcoming a) *Computers in Linguistics*, Blackwell, Oxford.

BUTLER, C.S. (forthcoming b) *Statistics in Linguistics*, Blackwell, Oxford.

BUTLER, C.S. (forthcoming c) 'Communicative function and semantics'. To appear in HALLIDAY & FAWCETT forthcoming.

BUTLER, C.S. (in press) 'Discourse systems and structures and their place within an overall systemic model'. To appear in GREAVES & BENSON in press a.

CARRELL, P.L. (1982) 'Cohesion is not coherence', *TESOL Quarterly*, no. 16, pp. 479-87.

CARTER, R., ed. (1982a) *Language and Literature: An Introductory Reader in Stylistics*, George Allen & Unwin.

CARTER, R. (1982b) 'Style and interpretation in Hemingway's "Cat in the Rain"', in CARTER (1982a) pp. 65-80.

CHAFE, W.L. (1970) *Meaning and the Structure of Language*, University of Chicago Press.

CHAO, Y.-R. (1934) 'The non-uniqueness of phonemic solutions of phonetic systems', *Academica Sinica*, Bulletin of the Institute of History and Philology no. 4, pp. 363-97. Reprinted in JOOS (1958) pp. 38-54.

CHIU, R. (1973) 'Measuring register characteristics', *IRAL* no. 11, pp. 51-68.

CHOMSKY, N. (1964) *Current Issues in Linguistic Theory*, Mouton, The Hague. Revised version of paper in FODOR, J.A. & KATZ, J.J., eds., *The Structure of Language: Readings in the Philosophy of Language,* Prentice Hall, Englewood Cliffs, New Jersey, pp. 50-118.

CHOMSKY, N. (1965) *Aspects of the Theory of Syntax*, MIT Press, Cambridge, Mass.

CHOMSKY, N. (1970) 'Remarks on nominalisation', in JACOBS, R.A. & ROSENBAUM, P., eds., *Readings in English Transformational Grammar*, Ginn, pp. 184-222.

CHOMSKY, N. & HALLE, M. (1968) *The Sound Pattern of English*, Harper & Row, New York.

COATES, J. & LEECH, G. (1980) 'The meanings of the modals in modern British and American English', *York Papers in Linguistics*, no. 8, pp.23-34.

COMRIE, B. (1981) *Language Universals and Linguistic Typology*, Blackwell, Oxford.

COOPER, R. (1980) 'Montague's syntax', in MORAVCSIK & WIRTH (1980) pp. 19-44.

COULTHARD, M. (1975) 'Discourse analysis in English – a short review of the literature', *Language Teaching and Linguistics: Abstracts*, no. 8, pp. 73-89.

COULTHARD, M. (1977) *An Introduction to Discourse Analysis*, Longman.

COULTHARD, R.M. & BRAZIL, D.C. (1979) *Exchange Structure*, Discourse Analysis Monographs 5, English Language Research, University of Birmingham.

COULTHARD M. & BRAZIL, D. (1981) 'Exchange structure', in COULTHARD & MONTGOMERY (1981) pp. 82-106.

COULTHARD, M. & MONTGOMERY, M. (1981) *Studies in Discourse Analysis*, Routledge & Kegan Paul.

COULTHARD, M., MONTGOMERY, M. & BRAZIL, D. (1981) 'Developing a description of spoken discourse', in COULTHARD & MONTGOMERY (1981) pp. 1-50.

CRUTTENDEN, A. (1969) 'Review of Halliday 1967a', *Journal of Linguistics*, no. 5, pp. 309-15.

CRYSTAL, D. (1969) *Prosodic Systems and Intonation in English*, Cambridge University Press.

DAHL, Ö. (1980) 'Some arguments for higher nodes in syntax: a reply to Hudson's "Constituency and dependency"', *Linguistics*, no. 18, pp. 485-88.

DAVEY, A. (1978) *Discourse Production: A Computer Model of Some Aspects of a Speaker,* Edinburgh University Press.

DAVIES, E. (1968) *Elements of English Clause Structure*, Programme in Linguistics and English Teaching Paper 10, Longman.

DAVIES, E.C. (1979) *On the Semantics of Syntax: Mood and Condition in English*, Croom Helm and Humanities Press, Atlantic Heights, New Jersey.

DIK, S.C. (1978) *Functional Grammar*, North Holland, Amsterdam.

DIK, S.C. (1980) 'Seventeen sentences: basic principles and application of functional grammar', in MORAVCSIK & WIRTH (1980) pp. 45-75.

DINNEEN, F.P. (1967) *An Introduction to General Linguistics*, Holt, Reinhart & Winston, New York.

DORE, J. (1977) 'Review of Halliday 1975a', *Language in Society*, no. 6, pp. 114-18.

DOUGHTY, P.S., PEARCE, J.J. & THORNTON, G.M. (1971) *Language in Use*, Schools Council Programme in Linguistics and English Teaching, Edward Arnold.

DOUGHTY, P.S., PEARCE, J.J. & THORNTON, G.M. (1972) *Exploring Language*, Edward Arnold.

DRESSLER, W. (1972) *Einführung in die Textlinguistik*, Niemeyer, Tübingen.

DRESSLER, W.U. (1978) 'Review of Halliday & Hasan 1976', *Language*, no. 54, pp. 676-78.

EDMONDSON, W. (1981) *Spoken Discourse: A Model for Analysis*, Longman.

ELLIS, J. & URE, J.N. (1969) 'Language varieties: register', in MEETHAM, A.R., ed., *Encyclopaedia of Linguistics, Information and Control*, Pergamon, Oxford.

EL-MENOUFY, A. (1969) *A Study of the Role of Intonation in the Grammar of English*, vol. 1: *Theory and Description*, vol. 2: *Texts*, Ph.D. thesis, University of London.

EL-RABBAT, A.H. (1978) *The Major Clause Types of Egyptian Colloquial Arabic: A Participant-Process Approach*, Ph. D. Thesis, University of London.

ENKVIST, N.E. (1978) 'Coherence, pseudo-coherence, and non-coherence', in ÖSTMAN, J.-O., ed., *Cohesion and Semantics*, Åbo Akademi Foundation, Åbo.

FAWCETT, R.P. (1973a) 'Systemic functional grammar in a cognitive model of language', University College London: mimeo.

FAWCETT, R.P. (1973b) 'Generating a sentence in systemic functional grammar', University College London: mimeo. Also in HALLIDAY & MARTIN (1981) pp. 146-83.

FAWCETT, R.P. (1974) 'Some proposals for systemic syntax, Part 1', *MALS Journal*, no. 1, pp. 1-15.

FAWCETT, R.P. (1975a) 'Summary of "Some issues concerning levels in systemic models of language"' paper read to Nottingham Linguistic Circle, December (1973), *Nottingham Linguistic Circular*, no. 4, pp. 24-37.

FAWCETT, R.P. (1975b) 'System networks, codes and knowledge of the universe: a cognitive perspective on the relationship between language and culture (paper presented to Burg Wartenstein Symposium No. 66: Semiotics of Culture and Language). Revised version to appear in FAWCETT, HALLIDAY, LAMB & MAKKAI (1984b) pp. 135-79.

FAWCETT, R.P. (1975c) 'Some proposals for systemic syntax, Part 2', *MALS Journal*, no. 2(1), pp. 43-68.

FAWCETT, R.P. (1976) 'Some proposals for systemic syntax, Part 3', *MALS Journal*, no. 2(2), pp. 35-68.

FAWCETT, R.P. (1980) *Cognitive Linguistics and Social Interaction: Towards an Integrated Model of a Systemic Functional Grammar and the other Components of a Communicating Mind*, Julius Groos Verlag, Heidelberg, and University of Exeter.

FAWCETT, R.P., HALLIDAY, M.A.K., LAMB, S.M. & MAKKAI, A., eds. (1984a) *The Semiotics of Culture and Language*, vol. 1; *Language as Social Semiotic*, Frances Pinter.

FAWCETT, R.P., HALLIDAY, M.A.K., LAMB, S.M. & MAKKAI, A., eds. (1984b) *The Semiotics of Culture and Language*, vol. 2, *Language and Other Semiotic Systems of Culture*, Frances Pinter.

FIRTH, J.R. (1935) 'The technique of semantics', *Trans. Phil. Soc.*, pp. 36-72. Reprinted in FIRTH (1957a) pp. 7-33.

FIRTH, J.R. (1948a) 'The semantics of linguistic science', *Lingua* no. 1, pp. 393-404. Reprinted in FIRTH (1957a) pp. 139-47.

FIRTH, J.R. (1948b) 'Sounds and prosodies', *Trans. Phil. Soc.*, pp. 127-52. Reprinted in FIRTH (1957a) pp. 121-38.

FIRTH, J.R. (1950) 'Personality and language in society', *Sociological Review*, no. xlii, pp. 37-52. Reprinted in FIRTH (1957a) pp. 177-89.

FIRTH, J.R. (1951a) 'Modes of meaning', in *The English Association: Essays and Studies*, John Murray, pp. 118-49. Reprinted in FIRTH (1957a) pp. 190-215.

FIRTH, J.R. (1951b) 'General linguistics and descriptive grammar', *Trans. Phil. Soc.*, pp. 69-87. Reprinted in FIRTH (1957a) pp. 216-30.

FIRTH, J.R. (1957a) *Papers in Linguistics 1934-1951*, Oxford University Press.

FIRTH, J.R. (1957b) 'Applications of general linguistics', *Trans. Phil. Soc.,* pp. 1-14. Reprinted in PALMER (1968) pp. 126-36.

FIRTH, J.R. (1957c) 'Ethnographic analysis and language with reference to Malinowski's views', in FIRTH, R.W., ed., *Man and Culture: An Evaluation of the Work of Bronislaw Malinowski*, Routledge & Kegan Paul, pp. 93-118. Reprinted in PALMER (1968), pp. 137-67.

FIRTH, J.R. (1957d) 'A synopsis of linguistic theory, 1930-55', in *Studies in Linguistic Analysis*, Special volume of the Philological Society, Blackwell, pp. 1-31. Reprinted in PALMER (1968) pp. 168-205.

GEFFROY, A., LAFON, P., SEIDEL, G. & TOURNIER, M. (1973) 'Lexicometric analysis of co-occurrences', in AITKEN *et al.* (1973) pp. 113-33.

GREAVES, W.S. & BENSON, J.D., eds., (in press a) *Systemic Perspectives on Discourse: Selected Theoretical Papers from the 9th International Systemic Workshop*, Ablex Publishing Corporation, Northwood, New Jersey.

GREAVES, W.S. & BENSON, J.D., eds., (in press b) *Systemic Perspectives on Discourse: Selected Applied Papers from the 9th International Systemic Workshop*, Ablex Publishing Corporation, Northwood, New Jersey.

GREENBERG, J. (1963) 'Some universals of grammar with particular reference to the order of meaningful elements', in GREENBERG, J., ed., *Universals of Language*, MIT Press, Cambridge, Mass., pp. 58-90.

GREGORY, M. (1967) 'Aspects of varieties differentiation', *Journal of Linguistics*, no. 3, pp. 177-98.

GREGORY, M. (1974) 'A theory for stylistics – exemplified: Donne's "Holy Sonnet XIV"', *Language and Style*, no. VII, pp. 108-18.

GREGORY, M. (1976) 'Review of Halliday 1973a', *Canadian Journal of Linguistics*, no. 21, pp. 196-99.

GREGORY, M. (1978) 'Marvell's "To his coy mistress": the poem as a linguistic and social event', *Poetics*, no. 7, pp. 351-62.

GREGORY, M. (1980a) 'Review of Monaghan 1969', *Canadian Journal of Linguistics*, no. 25, pp. 83-84.

GREGORY, M. (1980b) 'Review of Halliday 1978', *Applied Linguistics*, no. 1, pp. 74-81.

GREGORY, M. (forthcoming) 'Towards "Communication" Linguistics: a framework'. To appear in GREAVES & BENSON in press a.

GREGORY, M. & CARROLL, S. (1978) *Language and Situation: Language Varieties and their Social Contexts*, Routledge & Kegan Paul.

GRICE, H.P. (1975) 'Logic and conversation'. Harvard William Jones Lectures, 1967, in COLE, P. & MORGAN, J.L., eds., *Syntax and Semantics, vol. 3 (Speech Acts)*, Academic Press, pp. 41-58.

GRUBER, J. (1965) *Studies in Lexical Relations*, Doctoral Dissertation, Massachusetts Institute of Technology, Indiana University Linguistics Club, Bloomington.

HALLIDAY, M.A.K. (1956) 'Grammatical categories in Modern Chinese', *Trans. Phil. Soc.*, pp. 177-224. Reprinted in part in KRESS (1976) pp. 36-51.

HALLIDAY, M.A.K. (1959) *The Language of the Chinese 'Secret History of the Mongols'*, Publications of the Philological Society 17, Blackwell, Oxford.

HALLIDAY, M.A.K. (1961) 'Categories of the theory of grammar', *Word*, no. 17, pp. 241-92. Reprinted in part in KRESS (1976) pp. 52-72.

HALLIDAY, M.A.K. (1963a) 'The tones of English', *Archivum Linguisticum*, no. 15, pp. 1-28.

HALLIDAY, M.A.K. (1963b) 'Intonation and English grammar', *Trans. Phil. Soc.*, pp. 143-69.

HALLIDAY, M.A.K. (1963c) 'Class in relation to the axes of chain and choice in language', *Linguistics*, no. 2, pp. 5-15. Reprinted in part in KRESS (1976) pp. 84-87.

HALLIDAY, M.A.K. (1964a) 'Syntax and the consumer', in STUART (1964) pp. 11-24. Reprinted in part in HALLIDAY & MARTIN (1981) pp. 21-28.

HALLIDAY, M.A.K. (1964b) 'Descriptive linguistics in literary studies', in DUTHIE, A., ed., *English Studies Today: Third Series*. Edinburgh University Press, pp. 25-39. Reprinted in MCINTOSH & HALLIDAY (1966) pp. 56-69. Also reprinted in FREEMAN, D.C., ed., (1970) *Linguistics and Literary Style*, Holt, Rinehart & Winston, New York, pp. 57-72.

HALLIDAY, M.A.K. (1964c) 'The descriptive study of literary texts' in LUNT, H., ed., *Proceedings of the Ninth International Congress of Linguists*, Mouton, The Hague, pp. 302-307. Revised and reprinted in CHATMAN, S. & LEVIN, S.R., eds., (1967) *Essays on the Language of Literature*, Houghton Mifflin, Boston, pp. 217-23.

HALLIDAY, M.A.K. (1965) 'Types of structure', Working Paper for OSTI Programme in the Linguistic Properties of Scientific English. University College London: mimeo. Reprinted in HALLIDAY & MARTIN (1981) pp. 29-41.

HALLIDAY, M.A.K. (1966a) 'The concept of rank: a reply', *Journal of Linguistics*, no. 2, pp. 110-18.

HALLIDAY, M.A.K. (1966b) 'Some notes on "deep" grammar', *Journal of Linguistics*, no. 2, pp. 57-67. Reprinted in part in KRESS (1976) pp. 88-98.

HALLIDAY, M.A.K. (1966c) 'Lexis as a linguistic level', in BAZELL et al., pp. 148-62.

HALLIDAY, M.A.K. (1966d) 'Intonation systems in English', in MCINTOSH & HALLIDAY, pp. 111-33.

HALLIDAY, M.A.K. (1966e) 'General linguistics and its application to language teaching', in MCINTOSH & HALLIDAY (1966) pp. 1-41.

HALLIDAY, M.A.K. (1967a) *Intonation and Grammar in British English*, Janua Linguarum Series Practica 48, Mouton, The Hague.

HALLIDAY, M.A.K. (1967b) 'Notes on transitivity and theme in English, Part 1', *Journal of Linguistics*, no. 3, pp. 37-81.

HALLIDAY, M.A.K. (1967c) 'Notes on transitivity and theme in English, Part 2', *Journal of Linguistics*, no. 3, pp. 199-244.

HALLIDAY, M.A.K. (1967d) *Some Aspects of the Thematic Organization of the English Clause*, The RAND Corporation, Santa Monica (Memorandum RM-5224-PR). Reprinted in part in KRESS (1976) pp. 174-88.

HALLIDAY, M.A.K. (1967e) *Grammar, Society and the Noun*, H.K. Lewis (for University College London).

HALLIDAY, M.A.K. (1968) 'Notes on transitivity and theme in English, Part 3', *Journal of Linguistics*, no. 4, pp. 179-215.

HALLIDAY, M.A.K. (1969a) 'Options and functions in the English clause', *Brno Studies in English*, no. 8, pp. 81-8. Reprinted in HOUSEHOLDER, F.W., ed. (1972) *Syntactic Theory 1: Structuralist*, Penguin, (1972) pp. 248-57. Also reprinted in HALLIDAY & MARTIN (1981) pp. 138-45.

HALLIDAY, M.A.K. (1969b) 'Relevant models of language', *Educational Review*, no. 22, pp. 26-37. Reprinted in HALLIDAY (1973a) pp. 9-21.

HALLIDAY, M.A.K. (1970a) *A Course in Spoken English: Intonation*, Oxford University Press.

HALLIDAY, M.A.K. (1970b) 'Language structure and language function', in LYONS, J., ed., *New Horizons in Linguistics*, Penguin, pp. 140-65.

HALLIDAY, M.A.K. (1970c) 'Functional diversity in language, as seen from a consideration of modality and mood in English, *Foundations of Language*, no. 6, pp. 322-61. Reprinted in part in KRESS (1976) pp. 189-213.

HALLIDAY, M.A.K. (1971a) 'Language in a social perspective', *Educational Review*, no. 23, pp. 165-88. Reprinted in HALLIDAY (1973a) pp. 48-71.

HALLIDAY, M.A.K. (1971b) 'Linguistic function and literary style: an inquiry into the language of William Golding's *The Inheritors'*, in CHATMAN, S., ed., *Literary Style: A Symposium*, Oxford University Press, New York, pp. 330-65. Reprinted in HALLIDAY (1973a) pp. 103-43.

HALLIDAY, M.A.K. (1972) *Towards a Sociological Semantics*, Working Papers and Prepublications 14, Centro Internazionale di Semiotica e di Linguistica, University of Urbino, Urbino. Reprinted in HALLIDAY (1973a) pp. 72-102.

HALLIDAY, M.A.K. (1973a) *Explorations in the Functions of Language*, Edward Arnold.

HALLIDAY, M.A.K. (1973b) 'The functional basis of language' in BERNSTEIN (1973) pp. 343-66. Reprinted in HALLIDAY (1973a) pp. 22-47.

HALLIDAY, M.A.K. (1974) *Language and Social Man*, Schools Council Programme in Linguistics and English Teaching Papers series II, vol. 3. Longman for the Schools Council. Reprinted in slightly revised form in HALLIDAY (1978) pp. 8-35 and 211-35.

HALLIDAY, M.A.K. (1975a) *Learning How to Mean: Explorations in the Development of Language*, Edward Arnold.

HALLIDAY, M.A.K. (1975b) 'Language as social semiotic: towards a general sociolinguistic theory', in MAKKAI, A. & MAKKAI, V.B., eds. *The First LACUS Forum*. Hornbeam Press, Columbia, South Carolina, pp. 17-46. Revised and shortened version in HALLIDAY (1978) pp. 108-26.

HALLIDAY, M.A.K. (1975c) 'Sociological aspects of semantic change', in HEILMANN, L., ed., *Proceedings of the Eleventh International Congress of Linguists, Bologna 1972*, Il Mulino, Bologna, pp. 853-79. Slightly revised version in HALLIDAY (1978) pp. 60-92.

HALLIDAY, M.A.K. (1977) 'Text as semantic choice in social contexts', in VAN DIJK, T.A. & PETÖFI, J., eds., *Grammars and Descriptions*. de Gruyter, Berlin & New York, pp. 176-225. Shortened version in HALLIDAY (1978) pp. 128-51.

HALLIDAY, M.A.K. (1978) *Language as Social Semiotic: The Social Interpretation of Language and Meaning*, Edward Arnold.

HALLIDAY, M.A.K. (1979) 'Modes of meaning and modes of expression: types of grammatical structure and their determination by different semantic functions', in ALLERTON, D.J., CARNEY, E. & HOLDCROFT, D., eds., *Function and Context in Linguistic Analysis: Essays Offered to William Haas*, Cambridge University Press, pp. 57-79.

HALLIDAY, M.A.K. (1980a) 'Context of situation', *Sophia Linguistica*, no. 6, pp. 4-15.

HALLIDAY, M.A.K. (1980b) 'Functions of language', *Sophia Linguistica*, no. 6, pp. 31-42.

HALLIDAY, M.A.K. (1980c) 'Register variation', *Sophia Linguistica*, no. 6, pp. 60-74.

HALLIDAY, M.A.K. (1984a) 'Language as code and language as behaviour: a systemic-functional interpretation of the nature and ontogenesis of dialogue.' In FAWCETT *et al.* 1984a, pp. 3-35.

HALLIDAY, M.A.K. (1984b) *A Short Introduction to Functional Grammar*, Edward Arnold.

HALLIDAY, M.A.K. & FAWCETT, R.P., eds., (forthcoming) *Current Papers in Systemic Linguistics*, Batsford.

HALLIDAY, M.A.K. & HASAN, R. (1976) *Cohesion in English*, Longman.

HALLIDAY, M.A.K., & MARTIN, J.R., eds., (1981) *Readings in Systemic Linguistics*, Batsford.

HALLIDAY, M.A.K., MCINTOSH, A. & STREVENS, P. (1964) *The Linguistic Sciences and Language Teaching*, Longman.

HASAN, R. (1968) *Grammatical Cohesion in Spoken and Written English – Part One*, Programme in Linguistics and English Teaching Paper 7, Longman.

HASAN, R. (1973) 'Code, register and social dialect', in BERNSTEIN (1973) pp. 253-92.

HASAN, R. (1978) 'Text in the systemic-functional model', in DRESSLER, W.U., ed., *Current Trends in Textlinguistics*, du Gruyter, Berlin & New York, pp. 228-46.

HASAN, R. (1980a) 'The structure of a text', *Sophia Linguistica*, no. 6, pp. 16-30.

HASAN, R. (1980b) 'The identity of a text', *Sophia Linguistica*, no. 6, pp. 75-91.

HASKEL, P.I. (1971) 'Collocations as a measure of stylistic variety', in WISBEY, R.A., ed., *The Computer in Literary and Linguistic Research*, Cambridge University Press, pp. 159-68.

HAUGEN, E. (1958) 'Review of Firth 1957a', *Language*, no. 34. pp. 498-502.

HAWKINS, P.R. (1969) 'Social class, the nominal group and reference', *Language and Speech*, no. 12, pp. 125-35. Reprinted in BERNSTEIN (1973) pp. 81-92.

HAWKINS, P.R. (1977) *Social Class, the Nominal Group and Verbal Strategies*, vol. III in BERNSTEIN, B., ed., *Primary Socialization, Language and Education*, Routledge & Kegan Paul.

HERINGER, H.J. (1970) *Theorie der Deutschen Syntax*, Max Huber, Munich.

HUDDLESTON, R.D. (1965) 'Rank and depth', *Language*, no. 41, pp. 574-86. Reprinted in HALLIDAY & MARTIN (1981) pp. 42-53.

HUDDLESTON, R.D. (1966) 'Systemic features and their realization', University College London: mimeo. Reprinted in HALLIDAY & MARTIN (1981) pp. 58-73.

HUDDLESTON, R.D. (1977) 'Review of Berry 1975', *Language*, no. 53, pp. 190-92.

HUDDLESTON, R.D. (1978) 'Review of Halliday & Hasan 1976', *Lingua*, no. 45, pp. 333-54.

HUDDLESTON, R. & UREN, O. (1969) 'Declarative, interrogative and imperative in French', *Lingua*, no. 22, pp. 1-26. Reprinted in HALLIDAY & MARTIN (1981) pp.237-56.

HUDSON, R.A. (1964) *A Grammatical Study of Beja*, Ph. D. thesis, University of London.

HUDSON, R.A. (1967) 'Constituency in a systemic description of the English clause', *Lingua*, no. 18, pp. 225-50. Reprinted in HALLIDAY & MARTIN (1981) pp. 103-21.

HUDSON, R.A. (1971) *English Complex Sentences: An Introduction to Systemic Grammar*, North Holland, Amsterdam.

HUDSON, R.A. (1972a) 'Complex symbols dominating branching structures in Beja', *Folia Orientalia*, no. 14, pp. 37-51.

HUDSON, R.A. (1972b) 'An exercise in linguistic description', in THORNTON, BIRK & HUDSON (1972) pp. 57-101.

HUDSON, R.A. (1973a) 'Syllables, moras and accents in Beja', *Journal of Linguistics*, no. 9, pp. 53-63.

HUDSON, R.A. (1973b) 'An item-and-paradigm approach to Beja syntax and morphology', *Foundations of Language*, no. 9, pp. 504-48. Reprinted in HALLIDAY & MARTIN (1981) pp. 271-309.

HUDSON, R.A. (1974a) 'Systemic generative grammar', *Linguistics*, no. 139, pp. 5-42.

HUDSON, R.A. (1974b) 'A structural sketch of Beja', *African Language Studies*, no. 15, pp. 111-42.

HUDSON, R.A. (1975) 'The meaning of questions', *Language*, no. 51, pp. 1-31.

HUDSON, R.A. (1976) *Arguments for a Non-Transformational Grammar*, The University of Chicago Press, Chicago & London.

HUDSON, R.A. (1978) 'Daughter-dependency grammar and systemic grammar', *UEA Papers in Linguistics*, no. 6, pp. 1-14.

HUDSON, R.A. (1980a) 'Daughter-dependency grammar', in LIEB, H. -H., ed., *Oberflächensyntax und Semantik* (Symposium anlässlich der ersten Jahrestagung der Deutschen Gesellschaft für Sprachwissenschaft, Tübingen 28.2-2.3.1979), Max Niemeyer Verlag, Tübingen; pp. 32-50.

HUDSON, R.A. (1980b) 'Constituency and dependency', *Linguistics*, no. 18, pp. 179-98.

HUDSON, R.A. (1980c) 'A second attack on constituency: a reply to Dahl', *Linguistics*, no. 18, pp. 489-504.

HUDSON, R.A. (1981) 'Panlexicalism', *Journal of Literary Semantics*, no. X/2, pp. 67-78.

HUDSON, R.A. (1982) 'Word grammar', *Preprints of the Plenary Session Papers, XIIIth International Congress of Linguists, Tokyo 1982*, pp. 77-86.

HUDSON, R.A. (1984) *Word Grammar*, Blackwell, Oxford.

HYMES, D.H. (1971) *On Communicative Competence*, University of Pennsylvania Press, Philadelphia.

JACKENDOFF, R. (1972) *Semantic Interpretation in Generative Grammar*, MIT Press, Cambridge, Mass. & London.

JACKENDOFF, R. (1977) 'Constraints on phrase structure rules', in CULLICOVER, P.W., WASOW, T. & AKMAJIAN, A., eds., *Formal Syntax*. Academic Press, New York, San Francisco & London, pp. 249-83.

JONES, D. (1917) *An English Pronouncing Dictionary*, Dent. (14th edn. as *Everyman's English Pronouncing Dictionary*, Dent, 1977).

JONES, D. (1918) *An Outline of English Phonetics*, Teubner, Leipzig. (9th edn. Heffer, Cambridge 1960).

JONES, S. & SINCLAIR, J. MCH. (1974) 'English lexical collocations', *Cahiers de Lexicologie*, no. 24, pp. 15-61.

JOOS, M., ed. (1958) *Readings in Linguistics I*, American Council of Learned Societies, New York.

KARTUNNEN, L. & KAY, M. (1983)*Parsing in a Free Word Order Language*, Cambridge University Press.

KAY, M. (1979) 'Functional grammar', *Proceedings of the 5th Annual Meeting of the Berkeley Linguistic Society*, pp. 142-58.

KAY, M. (1983) *Parsing in Functional Unification Grammar*, Cambridge University Press.

KENNEDY, C. (1976) 'Systemic grammar and its use in literary analysis', *MALS Journal, New Series*, no. 1, pp. 17-38. Reprinted in CARTER(1982a) pp. 83-99.

KRESS, G., ed. (1976) *Halliday: System and Function in Language*, Oxford University Press.

LABOV, W. (1972) *Sociolinguistic Patterns*, University of Pennsylvania Press, Philadelphia.

LAMB, S.M. (1964) 'On alternation, transformation, realization and stratification, in STUART (1964) pp. 105-22.

LANGENDOEN, D.T. (1968) *The London School of Linguistics: A Study of the Linguistic Theories of B. Malinowski and J.R. Firth*, Research Monograph No. 46, MIT Press, Cambridge, Mass.

LANGENDOEN, D.T. (1971) 'Review of Palmer 1968', *Language*, no. 47, pp. 180-81.

LEECH, G.N. (1969) *Towards a Semantic Description of English*, Longman.

LEECH, G. (1981) *Semantics*, Penguin. 2nd edn.

LYONS, J. (1963) *Structural Semantics*, Blackwell, Oxford.

LYONS, J. (1966) 'Firth's theory of meaning', in BAZELL *et al.* pp. 288-302.

LYONS, J. (1968) *Introduction to Theoretical Linguistics*, Cambridge University Press.

LYONS, J. (1977) *Semantics*, vol. 1., Cambridge University Press.

MACKAY, D., THOMPSON, B. & SCHAUB, P. (1970) *Breakthrough to Literacy: Teacher's Manual. The Theory and Practice of Teaching Initial Reading and Writing*, Longman for the Schools Council.

MALINOWSKI, B. (1923) 'The problem of meaning in primitive languages', supplement to OGDEN, C.K. & RICHARDS, I.A. *The Meaning of Meaning*, Routledge & Kegan Paul.

MALINOWSKI, B. (1935) *Coral Gardens and Their Magic*, vol. 2, George Allen & Unwin.

MANN, W.C. (1982) *An Introduction to the Nigel Text Generation Grammar Computer Program*, USC/Information Sciences Institute, Technical Report.

MANN, W.C. (1983) 'Systemic encounters with computation', *Network,* no. 5, pp. 27-33.

MANN, W.C. & MATTHIESSEN, C.M.I.M. *Nigel: A Systemic Grammar for Text Generation*, USC/Information Sciences Institute, Technical Report RR-83-105, to appear in GREAVES & BENSON, in press a.

MARTIN, J.R. (1981a) 'How many speech acts?' *UEA Papers in Linguistics* nos. 14/15, pp. 52-77.

MARTIN, J.R. (1981b) 'Conjunction and continuity in Tagalog', in HALLIDAY & MARTIN (1981) pp. 310-36.

MARTIN, J.R. (forthcoming) 'The meaning of features in systemic linguistics', to appear in HALLIDAY & FAWCETT, forthcoming.

MATTHEWS, P.H. (1966) 'The concept of rank in Neo-Firthian linguistics', *Journal of Linguistics*, no. 2, pp. 101-09.

MCCORD, M.C. (1975) 'On the form of a systemic grammar', *Journal of Linguistics*, no. 11, pp. 195-212.

MCDONALD, D.D. (1980) *Natural Language Production as a Process of Decision-Making Under Constraints*, Ph.D. Thesis, Massachusetts Institute of Technology.

MCINTOSH, A. & HALLIDAY, M.A.K. (1966) *Patterns of Language: Papers in General, Descriptive and Applied Linguistics*, Longman.

MCKEOWN, K.R. (1982) *Generating Natural Language Text in Response to Questions about Database Structure*, Ph.D. Thesis, University of Pennsylvania.

MONAGHAN, J. (1979) *The Neo-Firthian Tradition and its Contribution to General Linguistics*, Max Niemeyer Verlag, Tübingen.

MONTGOMERY, M. (1976) 'Review of Halliday & Hasan 1976', *MALS Journal, New Series*, no. 1, pp. 59-61.

MORAVCSIK, E.A. (1980) 'Introduction: on syntactic approaches', in MORAVCSIK & WIRTH (1980) pp. 1-18.

MORAVCSIK, E.A. & WIRTH, J.R., eds. (1980) *Syntax and Semantics Vol. 13: Current Approaches to Syntax*, Academic Press, New York & London.

MORGAN, J.L. & SELLNER, M.B. (1980) 'Discourse and linguistic theory', in SPIRO, R.J., BRUCE, B.C. & BREWER, W.F., eds., *Theoretical Issues in Reading Comprehension*, Lawrence Erlbaum, New Jersey, pp. 165-200.

MUIR, J. (1972) *A Modern Approach to English Grammar: An Introduction to Systemic Grammar*, Batsford.

O'CONNOR, J.D. & ARNOLD, G.F. (1973) *Intonation of Colloquial English*, 2nd edn., Longman.

OWENS, J. (1978) *Aspects of Nubi Grammar*, Ph.D. Thesis, University of London.

PALMER, F.R. (1958) 'Linguistic hierarchy', *Lingua*, no. 7, pp. 225-41.

PALMER, F.R. (1964) '"Sequence" and "order"', *Monograph Series on Languages and Linguistics*, no. 17 , pp. 123-30.

PALMER, F.R. (1968) *Selected Papers of J.R. Firth, 1952-59*, Longman.

PALMER, F.R. (1979) *Modality and the English Modals*, Longman.

PARRET, H. (1974) *Discussing Language*, Mouton, The Hague.

PARTEE, B. (1975) 'Montague grammar and transformational grammar', *Linguistic Inquiry*, no. 6, pp. 203-300.

PIKE, K.L. (1959) 'Language as particle, wave and field', *The Texas Quarterly*, no. 2, pp. 37-54.

POSTAL, P. (1964) *Constituent Structure: A Study of Contemporary Models of Syntactic Description*, Mouton, The Hague.

QUIRK, R., GREENBAUM, S., LEECH, G. & SVARTVIK, J. (1972) *A Grammar of Contemporary English*, Longman.

ROBINS, R.H. (1970) 'General linguistics in Great Britain, 1930-1960', in KÜHLWEIN, W., ed., *Linguistics in Great Britain. II: Contemporary Linguistics*, Max Niemeyer Verlag, Tübingen, pp. 3 -24.

ROCHESTER, S. & MARTIN, J.R. (1979) *Crazy Talk: A Study of the Discourse of Schizophrenic Speakers*, Plenum, New York.

SAMPSON, G. (1980) *Schools of Linguistics*, Hutchinson.

SCHACHTER, P. (1978) 'Review of Hudson 1976', *Language*, no. 54, pp. 348-76.

SCHACHTER, P. (1980) 'Daughter-dependency grammar', in MORAVCSIK & WIRTH (1980) pp. 267-99.

SCOTT, F.S., BOWLEY, C.C., BROCKETT, C.S., BROWN, J.G. & GODDARD, P.R. (1968) *English Grammar: A Linguistic Study of its Classes and Structures*, Heinemann Educational Books.

SEARLE, J.R. (1969) *Speech Acts: An Essay in the Philosophy of Language*, Cambridge University Press.

SHIBATANI, M., ed., (1976a) *Syntax and Semantics, Vol. 6: The Grammar of Causative Constructions*, Academic Press, New York.

SHIBATANI, M. (1976b) 'The grammar of causative constructions: a conspectus', in SHIBATANI (1976a) pp. 1-40.

SHORT, M.H. (1976) 'Why we sympathise with Lennie', *MALS Journal, New Series*, no. 1, pp. 1-9.

SHORT, M.H. (1982) '"Prelude I" to a literary stylistics', in CARTER (1982a) pp. 55-62.

SINCLAIR, J. MCH. (1966a) 'Beginning the study of lexis', in BAZELL *et al.* (1966) pp. 410-30.

SINCLAIR, J. MCH. (1966b) 'Taking a poem to pieces', in FOWLER, R. ed., *Essays on Language and Style*, Routledge & Kegan Paul, pp. 68-81.

SINCLAIR, J. MCH. (1968) 'A technique of stylistic description', *Language and Style*, no. 1, pp. 215-42.

SINCLAIR, J. MCH. (1972) *A Course in Spoken English: Grammar*, Oxford University Press.

SINCLAIR, J. MCH. (1982) 'Lines about "Lines"', in CARTER (1982a) pp. 163-76.

SINCLAIR, J. MCH. & COULTHARD, R.M. (1975) *Towards an Analysis of Discourse: The English Used by Teachers and Pupils*, Oxford University Press.

SINCLAIR, J. MCH., JONES, S. & DALEY, R. (1970) *English Lexical Studies*, Report to OSTI on Project C/LP/08, Department of English, University of Birmingham.

SMITH, N. & WILSON, D. (1979) *Modern Linguistics: The Results of Chomsky's Revolution*, Penguin.

SOMMERSTEIN, A.H. (1977) *Modern Phonology*, Edward Arnold.

SPENCER, J. & GREGORY, M.J. (1964) 'An approach to the study of style', in SPENCER, J., ed., *Linguistics and Style*, Oxford University Press, pp. 57-105.

STOCKWELL, R.P. (1980) 'Summation and assessment of theories', in MORAVCSIK & WIRTH (1980) pp. 353-81.

STUART, C.I.J.M., ed. (1964) *Report of the Fifteenth Annual (First International) Round Table Meeting on Linguistics and Language Study*, Monograph Series in Languages and Linguistics 17, Georgetown University Press, Washington, D.C.

STUBBS, M. (1976) *Language, Schools and Classrooms*, Methuen.

STUBBS, M. (1979) 'Review of Coulthard & Brazil 1979', *Nottingham Linguistic Circular*, no. 8, pp. 124-28.

STUBBS, M. (1980) *Language and Literacy: The Sociolinguistics of Reading and Writing*, Routledge & Kegan Paul.

STUBBS, M. (1981) 'Motivating analyses of exchange structure', in COULTHARD & MONTGOMERY (1981) pp. 107-19.

STUBBS, M. (1983) *Discourse Analysis*, Blackwell, Oxford.

SWEET, H. (1877) *Handbook of Phonetics*, Clarendon Press, Oxford.

TALMY, L. (1976) 'Semantic causative types', in SHIBATANI (1976a) pp. 43-116.

TESNIÈRE, L. (1959) *Éléments de Syntaxe Structurale*, Klincksieck, Paris.

THORNTON, G. (1972) 'The individual and his development of a language', in THORNTON, BIRK & HUDSON (1972) pp. 1-22.

THORNTON, G., BIRK, D. & HUDSON, R.A. (1972) *Language at Work*, Schools Council Programme in Linguistics and English Teaching Papers series II, vol. 1. Longman for the Schools Council.

TURNER, G.J. (1973) 'Social class and children's language of control at age five and age seven', in BERNSTEIN (1973) pp. 135-201.

TURNER, G.J. & MOHAN, B.A. (1970) *A Linguistic Description and Computer Program for Children's Speech*, vol. II in BERNSTEIN, B., ed., *Primary Socialization, Language and Education*, Routledge and Kegan Paul.

TURNER, G. & PICKVANCE, R. (1971) 'Social class differences in the expression of uncertainty in five-year-old children', *Language and Speech*, no. 14, pp. 303-25. Reprinted in BERNSTEIN (1973) pp. 93-119.

ULLMANN, S. (1962) *Semantics*, Blackwell, Oxford, & Holt, Rinehart & Winston, New York.

URE, J.N. (1971) 'Lexical density and register differentiation', in PERREN, G.E. & TRIM, J.L.M., eds., *Applications of Linguistics: Selected Papers of the 2nd International Congress of Linguists, Cambridge 1969*, Cambridge University Press, pp. 443-52.

URE, J. & ELLIS, J. (1974) 'El registro en la lingüística descriptiva y en la sociologica lingüística', in URIBE-VILLEGAS, O., ed., *Sociolingüística Actual: Algunos de sus Problemas, Planteamientos y Soluciones*, Universidad Nacional Autónoma de México, Mexico, pp. 115-64. English version: 'Register in descriptive linguistics and linguistic sociology', in URIBE-VILLEGAS, O., ed., (1977) *Issues in Sociolinguistics*, Mouton, The Hague.

VACHEK, J. (1966) *The Linguistic School of Prague*, Indiana University Press, Bloomington.

VAN DIJK, T.A. (1972) *Some Aspects of Text Grammars*, Mouton, The Hague.

VAN DIJK, T.A. (1973) 'Text grammar and text logic', in PETÖFI, J. & RIESER, H., eds., *Studies in Text Grammars*, Reidel, Dordrecht.

VATER, H. (1975) 'Toward a generative dependency theory', *Lingua*, no. 36, pp. 121-45.

WELLS, R. (1947) 'Immediate constituents', *Language*, no. 23, pp. 81-111. Reprinted in JOOS, M. (1958) pp. 186-207.

WERNER, O. (1975) 'Chomskys Aspects-modell zu einer linearen Dependenz-grammatik', *Folia Linguistica*, no. 6, pp. 62-88.

WIDDOWSON, H.G. (1978) *Teaching Language as Communication*, Oxford University Press.

WINOGRAD, T. (1972) *Understanding Natural Language*, Edinburgh University Press.

WINOGRAD, T. (1983) *Language as a Cognitive Process. Vol. 1: Syntax*, Addison-Wesley Publishing Company, Reading, Mass.

WITTGENSTEIN, L. (1953) *Philosophical Investigations*, Blackwell, Oxford, & Macmillan, New York.

YOUNG, D. (1980) *The Structure of English Clauses*, Hutchinson.

Index

Passive: modulation 174, 176; voice 50-51, 53, 61, 107, 178, 223
Pearce, J.J. 203
Perception process 168, 200
Performance 3, 215, 218-19
Peripherality rule 116
Personal function in child language 72, 90, 225
Phenomenon (as functional role) 168
Phonematic unit 8-9
Phoneme 8, 28, 31, 138, 143
Phonetics 5, 59, 138, 143-4, 145, 202, 215, 223; early work by
     British linguists 1-2
Phonology ix, 5, 16, 28, 59, 69, 78, 102, 103, 104, 116, 197, 214,
     219, 220, 228
     prosodic *see* prosodic phonology
Phoric relationships 184, 195 *see also* anaphoric, cataphoric, endo-
     phoric *and* exophoric reference
Phrase structure rules 120, 158
Pickvance, R. 204-5
Pike, K.L. 4, 87
Pitch 8, 18, 140-48 *passim*; pitch sequence 146, 147
Plath, S. 200-01
Point of origin 40, 45, 82, 105
Polarity 85, 175-6; polarity information 155, 156-7
Polysystemic principle: criticism of 12; in Firth's work 8-9; in
     Hudson's work 105-6; in Scale and Category linguistics 14, 40;
     in systemic functional grammars 45
Positional control strategies 205
Postal, P. 29, 36, 38
Post-tonic 141
Pragmatic function in child language 73-4, 91
Prague School 4, 46, 84, 176-7, 178, 204
Predicate: semantic 124, 171; syntactic 118-19. 153
Predicator (P) 17-25 *passim*, 49-50, 52-3, 95-6, 99, 171, 196
Prepend 100; group 96, 100 *see also* prepositional group,
     prepositional phrase
Prepositional: group 23, 34, 96; phrase 34, 107, 123 *see also*
     prepend group
Pretonic (segment) 140, 141, 143-4
Probability, expression of 173-6, 205
Process (as functional role) 49-50, 52-3, 56, 160
Process type 164-71, 188, 224
Processer 168
Proclitic segment 145
Prominence 145
Propositional structure of an exchange 160-61
Prosodic: phonology 8-9, 12, 28, 137-8; type of structure 86-7, 174
Psycholinguistics 104, 209, 215, 219, 221
Psychological reality 83, 104, 125, 210, 221, 223

Qualifier 19, 26, 97, 99, 205, 207